Freedom and Equality

Freedom and Equality

Essays on Liberalism and Feminism

CLARE CHAMBERS

Great Clarendon Street, Oxford, OX2 6DP,
United Kingdom

Oxford University Press is a department of the University of Oxford.
It furthers the University's objective of excellence in research, scholarship,
and education by publishing worldwide. Oxford is a registered trade mark of
Oxford University Press in the UK and in certain other countries

© Clare Chambers 2024

The moral rights of the author have been asserted

All rights reserved. No part of this publication may be reproduced, stored in
a retrieval system, or transmitted, in any form or by any means, without the
prior permission in writing of Oxford University Press, or as expressly permitted
by law, by licence or under terms agreed with the appropriate reprographics
rights organization. Enquiries concerning reproduction outside the scope of the
above should be sent to the Rights Department, Oxford University Press, at the
address above

You must not circulate this work in any other form
and you must impose this same condition on any acquirer

Published in the United States of America by Oxford University Press
198 Madison Avenue, New York, NY 10016, United States of America

British Library Cataloguing in Publication Data
Data available

Library of Congress Control Number: 2023947799

ISBN 9780192897909

DOI: 10.1093/9780191919480.001.0001

Printed and bound in the UK by
Clays Ltd, Elcograf S.p.A.

Links to third party websites are provided by Oxford in good faith and
for information only. Oxford disclaims any responsibility for the materials
contained in any third party website referenced in this work.

Contents

Acknowledgements vii

    Introduction: A Feminist Liberalism   1

PART I   FEMINISM & LIBERALISM

1. Feminism   19
2. Feminism on Liberalism   43
3. Respect, Religion, and Feminism: Political Liberalism as Feminist Liberalism?   58

PART II   THE FAMILY

4. 'The Family as a Basic Institution': A Feminist Analysis of the Basic Structure as Subject   75
5. Liberalism, Feminism, and the Gendered Division of Labour   99
6. The Marriage-Free State   123

PART III   THE LIMITS OF LIBERALISM

7. Should the Liberal State Recognise Gender?   143
8. Reasonable Disagreement and the Neutralist Dilemma: Abortion and Circumcision in Matthew Kramer's *Liberalism with Excellence*   171

PART IV   EQUALITY OF OPPORTUNITY

9. Each Outcome Is Another Opportunity: Problems with the Moment of Equal Opportunity   203
10. Equality of Opportunity and Three Justifications for Women's Sport: Fair Competition, Anti-Sexism, and Identity   234

PART V CHOICE

11. Choice and Female Genital Cosmetic Surgery	265
12. Judging Women: 25 Years Further *Toward a Feminist Theory of the State*	279
13. Ideology and Normativity	301
References	321
Index	339

Acknowledgements

The chapters in this book were written over a span of nearly twenty years, meaning that I have acquired many debts along the way. Rather than attempt to collate all my thanks in one place I have given separate acknowledgments in each chapter.

Here I should like to record my hearty thanks to Peter Momtchiloff, Philosophy Editor at Oxford University Press, for his support of this volume. I first worked with Peter on my book *Against Marriage: An Egalitarian Defence of the Marriage-Free State* (OUP, 2017) and it has been a pleasure to work with him again now. I am also grateful to the anonymous referees commissioned by OUP for their insights and constructive suggestions. Ronja Griep and Sam Cole provided excellent research assistance. The Leverhulme Trust granted me a Major Research Fellowship which I held, with great appreciation, during the time I worked on putting this volume together and writing some of the new material. And I must record once again my deep gratitude for my partner Phil, and my children Harley and Caspar, for their ongoing support and love.

Several of the chapters in this book have been previously published elsewhere. They have been lightly edited for this volume. I am grateful for permission to reprint the following:

- Chapter 1: 'Feminism' was originally published in *The Oxford Handbook of Political Ideologies*, edited by Michael Freeden, Lyman Tower Sargent, and Marc Stears (Oxford University Press, 2013).
- Chapter 2: 'Feminism on Liberalism' was originally published in Ann Garry, Serene J. Khader and Alison Stone (eds), *The Routledge Companion to Feminist Philosophy* (Routledge, 2017).
- Chapter 3: 'Respect, Religion, and Feminism: Political Liberalism as Feminist Liberalism?' is newly extended for this volume: the original paper was published in *Journal of Applied Philosophy* (September 2020).
- Chapter 4: ' "The Family as a Basic Institution": A Feminist Analysis of the Basic Structure as Subject' was originally published in Ruth Abbey (ed.), *Feminist Interpretations of Rawls* (Penn State University Press, 2013). Reprinted with permission from The Pennsylvania State University Press © 2013.

Chapter 6: 'The Marriage-Free State' was originally published in *Proceedings of the Aristotelian Society* 113(2) (July 2013). Reprinted by courtesy of the Aristotelian Society © 2013.

Chapter 8: 'Reasonable Disagreement and the Neutralist Dilemma: Abortion and Circumcision in Matthew Kramer's *Liberalism with Excellence*' was originally published in *The American Journal of Jurisprudence* (2018).

Chapter 9: 'Each Outcome is Another Opportunity: Problems with the Moment of Equal Opportunity' was originally published in *Politics, Philosophy and Economics (PPE)* 8(4) (2009).

Chapter 11: 'Choice and Female Genital Cosmetic Surgery' was originally published in Sarah Creighton and Lih-Mei Liao, *Female Genital Cosmetic Surgery: Interdisciplinary Analysis & Solution* (Cambridge University Press, 2019).

Chapter 12: 'Judging Women: 25 Years Further *Toward a Feminist Theory of the State*' was originally published in *Feminist Philosophy Quarterly* 3(2) (2017).

Chapter 13: 'Ideology and Normativity' was originally published in *Aristotelian Society Supplementary Volume* 91(1) (2017). Reprinted by courtesy of the Aristotelian Society © 2017.

Introduction

A Feminist Liberalism

What is feminism? Consider the views of four prominent feminists:

> Feminism is just another word for equality. It means equality.
>
> Malala Yousafzai[1]
>
> Feminism is a deeply uncomfortable politics, because what we're having to do is say to men: "We don't need your approval."
>
> Julie Bindel[2]
>
> We should all be feminists.
>
> Chimamanda Ngozi Adiche[3]
>
> I'm a radical feminist, not the fun kind.
>
> Andrea Dworkin[4]

Almost every year since 2006 I have given a series of lectures on feminism to students at the University of Cambridge. In the first lecture I ask students to raise their hands if they would call themselves a feminist. In the early years of lecturing, only about half of the students would raise their hands. Nowadays, virtually everyone does. One year, a woman who did raise her hand was sat next to a man who didn't. She gasped, her eyes wide in shock, and turned to him aghast. "Why not?!" she asked, in a voice loud enough for the room to hear. "It just means equality!"

Another anecdote, this one from my own student days. I was a DPhil student at the University of Oxford and had the pleasure of taking a seminar series taught by two highly eminent political philosophers: David Miller and G. A. Cohen. This week, the topic was feminism. Cohen, one of the

---

[1] Malala Yousafzai, Interview at Open Forum Davos 2018, available at https://www.youtube.com/watch?v=wfxLLyM8iGI.

[2] Julie Bindel, *Feminism for Women: The Real Route to Liberation* (London: Constable, 2021).

[3] Chimamanda Ngozi Adiche, *We Should All Be Feminists* (London: Fourth Estate, 2014).

[4] Andrea Dworkin, 'Dworkin on Dworkin', in Diane Bell and Renate Klein (eds), *Radically Speaking: Feminism Reclaimed* (London: Zed Books, 1996).

discipline's most incisive thinkers and most principled egalitarians, was impatient. "Feminism", he said, "is intellectually uninteresting." That phrase I remember word-for-word. The explanation I paraphrase from memory. "Obviously there should be equality between women and men", Cohen continued. "Every egalitarian agrees that. So there's no philosophical question here. It's just about implementation."

Now, Cohen has always been one of my intellectual role models. As an undergraduate, reading his work and seeing him speak was a large part of the reason I wanted to do political philosophy. As a graduate student I was excited to be able to work with him more closely, and hoped to impress him. But I didn't feel I could let this one pass. "I think", I said to the room, "that the intellectual interest in feminism is this: if everyone agrees with equality between women and men in principle, why are we still so far from it? For example," I carried on, "if feminism is so uncontroversial, why I am I the only woman in this room?"

This collection of essays investigates the contours of feminist liberalism: a philosophical approach that is appealing but elusive. My aim is to show that feminist liberalism is both possible and necessary. It is possible because the two doctrines of feminism and liberalism are compatible, their fundamental values aligned. At its heart, feminism is just about equality, as Malala Yousafzai puts it; and it is also about freedom or women's liberation, as the radical feminist 'women's libbers' of the second wave put it. So a feminist liberalism is clearly possible. But is it necessary? In a way, Cohen was endorsing Chimamanda Ngozi Adiche's view: 'we', if we are egalitarians, should all agree on equality between women and men. But Cohen did not think that meant that we needed to be feminists, specifically—on his view, egalitarianism was enough on its own. But feminism *is* necessary, because liberalism has shown that it is simply not up to the task of securing gender equality and women's liberation. As Julie Bindel points out, feminism means telling men that we are not looking for their approval, and that means refusing the idea that feminism is easy to accommodate. It is not 'just' about anything. Feminism, as Andrea Dworkin points out, may not always be fun.

Liberalism is not necessary to feminism. There are varieties of feminism that are not defined by being liberal (which is not to say they are illiberal), including radical feminism, socialist feminism, post-structuralist feminism, and ecofeminism. These varieties of feminism are urgent and insightful, and I discuss them favourably in other works.[5] My argument, instead, is that *feminism*

---

[5] I discuss other varieties of feminism in Clare Chambers, *Sex, Culture, and Justice: The Limits of Choice* (University Park, PA: Penn State University Press, 2008); Clare Chambers, 'Judith Butler's Gender Trouble', in Jacob T. Levy (ed.), *Oxford Handbook of Classics in Contemporary Political Theory*

is necessary to *liberalism*: that liberalism without feminism cannot hope to achieve its aims or stay true to its deepest commitments.

Feminism may not be the only thing that liberalism requires. Liberal political philosophy has many omissions; another glaring one is race. Theorists such as Charles Mills, Tommie Shelby, and Serene Khader have shown that contemporary liberal political theory has ignored racial inequality in a way that exacerbates it.[6] Even in the liberal multiculturalism debates of 1990s, which grappled with the question of how liberal states could ensure equality in the context of cultural diversity, race and racism were not foregrounded—sometimes, they were barely acknowledged.

The topic of this volume, though, is the specific intersection between feminism and liberalism. I defend feminist liberalism. Its hallmark is a liberalism that prioritises equality and individual autonomy while offering a rigorous critique of using individuals' choices as the sole measure of justice. Liberalism *simpliciter* prioritises individual choice, a strategy that has played a crucial role in the liberal defence of freedom against authoritarianism and conformity. However, as feminism shows, relying on individual choice is insufficient to render an outcome just, because people often choose things that harm or disadvantage themselves. Often, these changes are made in response to social norms, including unjust, unequal, or harmful norms. It follows that relying on individual choice as a measure of justice actually leaves unjust social structures intact. Any defender of autonomy and equality must be prepared to criticise individuals' choices while prioritising individual choosers.

This nuanced perspective on choice means, as I argue in these essays, that feminist liberalism must go beyond political liberalism. Political liberalism is the form of liberalism defended by John Rawls in his work of the same name, and by many Rawlsians after him. It is characterised by a commitment to choice understood as what I call second-order autonomy. *First-order autonomy* refers to the amount of choice and control we have over the actions we take in our everyday lives. We have first-order autonomy to the extent that we actively choose how to act, deciding which rules and norms to follow and which to reject. *Second-order autonomy*, in contrast, applies to the choice we make about our way of life understood more broadly. We have second-order

---

(Oxford: Oxford University Press, 2017, online first); and Clare Chambers, *Intact: A Defence of the Unmodified Body* (London: Allen Lane, 2022).

[6] Charles Mills, *Black Rights/White Wrongs: The Critique of Racial Liberalism* (Oxford: Oxford University Press, 2017); Tommie Shelby, 'Race and Social Justice: Rawlsian Considerations', *Fordham Law Review* 72(5) (2004); Serene Khader, *Decolonizing Universalism: A Transnational Feminist Ethic* (Oxford: Oxford University Press, 2018).

autonomy to the extent that we have chosen the sort of life we lead, which may include past choices about our religious observance, our community membership, and the career or unpaid work we do.

First- and second-order autonomy can coincide, as when an individual makes a second-order autonomous choice to live a life of constant questioning and individuality. This combination of first- and second-order autonomy is advocated by comprehensive liberals such as John Stuart Mill. Political liberals like Rawls have no complaint with such lives, but they reject the idea that this level of autonomy is necessary for everyone. Instead, political liberals are willing to endorse lives with second-order autonomy but not first-order autonomy: lives in which people choose to live in a way that requires them to submit to others' rules. Thus political liberals defend restrictive lives with limited choices, if those who live them could in principle choose alternative ways of living. In practice, this means that political liberals defend religious, traditional, and shared ways of life that strongly shape their members' actions, as long as those ways of life exist in the context of a more diverse, liberal society that provides alternative options.

Political liberalism is perhaps the dominant form of academic liberalism, in part because it seems to offer an attractive solution to the problem of how to justify liberalism in the context of cultural diversity. Political liberals are able to argue that liberalism as a political doctrine, one that structures the political institutions of society, is compatible with ways of life and community values that are themselves not liberal. This is a useful strategy insofar as it widens the justificatory scope of liberalism and avoids awkward conflicts over highly controversial matters such as religious belief; whether women and men are or should be equal in any and every area of life, including the family; and whether autonomy precludes rule-following rules and traditions for their own sake.

However, *feminism* cannot avoid awkwardness—nor should it seek to. Feminists must take a stance on questions such as these, and their answers will not always align with the political liberal. Where equality conflicts with the sort of choice-based liberty favoured by political liberals, feminists must choose equality. A feminist liberalism cannot be a political liberalism. Or so I argue.

0.1 Freedom and Equality

The essays in this book all touch on three questions. *What does freedom require? What does equality require?* And *are they compatible?*

These three questions are important to various political ideologies and philosophical perspectives, because the values of freedom and equality are valued by so many. That there is some sense in which people are equal, or should be treated equally, is common to any doctrine that upholds the rule of law or even minimal human rights; that there is some value to liberty is virtually uncontested, even if some who value liberty for themselves seek to deny it to others. But in this volume I focus on the particular answers to those questions that have arisen from the doctrines of liberalism and feminism, and the productive philosophical enquiry that comes from their juxtaposition.

Both liberalism and feminism value freedom and equality *intrinsically* and *deeply*. Liberal political philosophy is in many respects the philosophy of what it is to be free, and what it is to be equal. There is strong disagreement on these questions within liberal theory, but there is also shared ground.

Liberal *freedom* is a property of individuals. Freedom is not amply secured if it is a property of groups or polities alone: individuals within any group must have the freedom to dissent. Freedom can be understood in minimal or maximal ways. It requires at the very least a measure of protection against coercion, paradigmatically by the state and other powerful persons. More extensive conceptions of freedom also call for the individual to have resources: these may be intellectual or mental capacities of choice, or the means to put desire into action. And most liberals prioritise individual choice as necessary for freedom.

Liberal *equality* is a commitment to equal status, translated into some measure of equality in the distribution of resources. For liberals, distributive equality should be situated somewhere between two extremes. Liberals defend more than a minimum of equal basic rights and equality of opportunity as non-discrimination—this minimum may be guaranteed by libertarians and conservatives. Yet liberals demand less than full equality of resources. Full equality of resources is rejected by liberals for ceding too little to liberty. People must be free to make choices that have the potential to undermine egalitarian distributions. And with that liberty comes some measure of responsibility and desert, which mitigate any claims to full equalising redistribution. Liberal egalitarians propose a variety of mechanisms for navigating between minimal and maximal redistribution.

Feminism is also committed to both liberty and equality as fundamental values. The equality that feminism centres is *gender equality* or *equality between women and men*, understood neither as merely formal equality of rights nor as identity or sameness between the sexes. Feminists want women and men to be equal, which does not mean that they must be identical either as individuals or viewed collectively. A vision of equality as sameness fails on multiple levels: typically, it takes the male as norm and requires women to adapt to male standards. Against that assumption, feminists insist that women can be equal on their own terms, in their own bodies, with their own experiences and plans of life. At the same time, they diagnose prevailing gender inequality. Feminist theory and activism recognises that inequality is both formal and informal; structural and societal; explicit and implicit.

Feminism also insists on the significance of liberty, as evident in the fact that many feminists saw their goal as *women's liberation*. Liberation means freeing women from oppression, subordination, restrictive roles, and violent suppression. Women must be liberated from the constraints imposed by what is variously described as gender inequality, male supremacy, patriarchy, or just plain sexism. These constraints are material, they are legal, they are social, and they are symbolic.

So, liberalism and feminism share a commitment to the values of freedom and equality. What then distinguishes them? One difference is in their analysis of how each value is thwarted in actually existing imperfect societies. What is it that prevents us, collectively and individually, from enjoying the freedom and equality to which we are entitled?

Liberals have typically placed the answer in the state, defending forms of government or legislative change that can enhance our freedom and equality. Thus liberals defend institutions such as democracy, the separation of powers, written constitutions, and bills of rights. They advocate legislation against discrimination, the creation of a welfare state and public services, and an economy that includes both market freedoms and redistributive taxation. Feminists observe that such instruments, even if necessary for liberation and equality, have not been sufficient. They note that freedom and equality are gendered and that liberal institutions have played out differently for men and for women. Women as a group systematically fare worse than men as a group, including in those times and places characterised by a shared commitment to liberalism. What this means, feminists point out, is that liberal theory and practice have not secured freedom and equality for women. What's more, many liberal theorists and regimes have neither noticed nor cared about the persistence of gender inequality. This deficiency must, then, be a deficiency in liberal theory.

In my own work I have tried to identify where liberalism goes wrong from a feminist perspective, and to consider whether liberalism should be abandoned in favour of feminism or can be productively merged with it. There has certainly always been liberalism that is not feminist, and feminism that is not liberal. But is there scope for a feminist liberalism that realises both doctrines adequately if not fully?

In my first book, *Sex, Culture, and Justice: The Limits of Choice*, I introduced the concept of a 'normative transformer'. A normative transformer is something that changes the normative character of an act or situation: it changes something from unjust to just, from wrong to right. Consent is one example of a normative transformer: many acts that are unjust or wrong if they are not consensual become just or morally acceptable if consent is present—at least according to liberalism. Thus consent turns rape into sex, theft into gift-giving, and violence into sport.

Liberals tend to use choice in just this way, too. In the context of body modification, for example, choice is what prevents surgery, tattoos, and medical treatment from being instances of criminal assault or bodily harm. In general, according to standard liberal theories, a disadvantage that might otherwise be unjust becomes compatible with egalitarian justice *if it is chosen*. For example, the gender pay gap, according to which women earn less than men, looks unjust—but if the gender pay gap is the result of women's choices (to work less, to choose less demanding or prestigious roles, to prioritise caregiving over career) then many liberals will deem the gender pay gap compatible with justice.

Similarly, if a religion treats women and men unequally, denying women access to religious rites, sacraments, or leadership roles, most liberals will condemn that religious inequality as unjust—unless women can be said to have *chosen* to remain in that religion, usually understood as requiring freedom of exit from it. Once minimal conditions are in place that allow religious observance to count as a choice, such as that the religion is not coercively imposed by the state, liberals tend to appeal to the value of choice as a normative transformer to say that religious gender inequality is unproblematic. In practice, this means that liberals condemn religious gender inequality as unjust when it occurs in societies that are structured around that religion, but defend religious gender inequality as just when it occurs in liberal societies. The result is an 'us v. them' dynamic which has overtones of colonial hypocrisy, as practices that are condemned when performed by 'others' in foreign countries are defended when performed by 'us' at home.

What's wrong with treating choice as a normative transformer? Doesn't a commitment to liberty also require allowing people to bear the consequences of their free choices? To an extent, yes. But what feminists are keenly aware of, and liberals tend to ignore, is that we do not make choices in a vacuum.

We choose within a context. All our choices are affected by social construction: by the need to fit in with, or respond to, the context we are in.

Our choices are socially constructed in two main ways. First, we can only choose from the options that are available to us. We cannot choose to become opera singers if our society does not have the cultural form of opera; we cannot choose to join the navy if our country does not maintain one. Moreover, the options presented to us by our society are often pre-sorted into those that are appropriate for us and those that are not. In the UK, opera is a cultural form that is particularly connected to the upper and middle classes. Many people with a working-class background do not experience opera as something that is appropriate for them to participate in, or watch, and so do not choose to do so—a choice that maintains class segregation. A career in the armed forces is also connected to class and sex, through the division between officers and rank-and-file and historical bans on women's service. Makeup, to take another example, is strongly gendered: women and girls grow up to understand that makeup is socially accepted or even expected for them; men and boys learn that, for them, it is odd or taboo. Unsurprisingly, then, many more women and girls choose to wear makeup than do men and boys. These choices may be free, in the liberal sense of not being coerced, and genuine, in the sense of being identified with. But they are socially constructed nonetheless.

The second way that our choices are socially constructed is through our preferences. Generally, we want to be accepted and praised by others. Sometimes we want to stand out as exemplars; more often, we want to fit in. Over time, as part of our inherently social natures, we take pleasure from doing precisely those things that are socially expected of us. Take fashion as an example. When fashions change, initially the new fashion may seem jarring or strange—we conform to meet the approval of others rather than ourselves. Before long, though, the new aesthetic becomes our own. Clothes we wore last season, last year, or last decade now look hopelessly unattractive. What we *want* to wear has shifted in response to social acceptability.

When a context is highly gendered, as all liberal societies are, it is not surprising that women and men make different choices. Certain choices are socially cast as appropriate for women and not for men; women and men consequently form different preferences.

Part of this gendered construction of choice is an incentive or a mechanism by which we all are vulnerable to making choices that harm us along some dimension. While this is something that all of us can do, regardless of our gender, once again we see gendered patterns in our behaviour. Men are liable to make choices that close down their emotional connection to others, particularly to other men; that limit their role in the family and in reciprocal relationships of care by focusing aggressively on career advancement or leisure pursuits; and that incur physical risks in the pursuit of masculinity such as heavy drinking, initiating aggression, or risking injury. Women are liable to make choices that harm them by making them financially worse off, limiting their earning potential by prioritising domestic life above career; or by conforming to feminine norms in a way that reflects women's lower social status; or by prioritising their physical appearance and conformity to standards of beauty or gender in a way that compromises their physical and mental health.

This is not a false consciousness argument. Choices such as these can be rational within a gendered system that rewards us for making them, or punishes us for doing otherwise. We might be fully, painfully aware of the injustice of gender norms, and yet correctly assess that we will be better off if we conform. The problem is not that people are making the wrong choices; the problem is that we are choosing within a context of injustice.

Both women and men face incentives to make choices that harm them in some way. But these gendered incentives do not balance out to create equality. The result is inequality since norms are gendered in a way that subordinates women. Conformity to norms of femininity is conformity to a role with lower social status: one in which even successful compliance brings a level of inferiority. And, of course, women are subordinated by things that they do not choose: a vulnerability to sexual violence, greater susceptibility to poverty, a gendered pay gap that cannot be reduced to choice.

But, someone might object, if women receive rewards for making gendered choices doesn't that in itself nullify any inequality? Women who are mothers might choose jobs that require fewer hours or less responsibility, receiving lower pay as a result—but don't they then receive various compensating benefits? More time with their children and for personal projects, less stress at work, social approval for being good mothers? If choosing this way is rational for women, doesn't it follow that it is compatible with liberal egalitarianism?

Things are not so simple. That a choice is rational from within circumstances of equality; that a decision to conform to a subordinated position can be more advantageous than a decision to resist: none of this is enough to exonerate the unequal social context that rationalises those choices. Liberals who care about freedom and equality—which is to say, all of them—must recognise that we choose *within* a social context. That means that it does not make sense to use our choices as a measure of the justice of that context.

0.2 The Essays to Come

The essays that follow chart a route through the choppy waters where feminism and liberalism meet. Some of the essays have been newly written for this book; those that have previously been published elsewhere have been edited and updated.

Part I, 'Feminism & Liberalism', launches us on our journey. It sets out definitions of both doctrines, and directly confronts their compatibility.

Chapter 1, 'Feminism', goes deeper into the question of what feminism is, viewed as a political ideology. While it is in some ways misleading to think of feminism as an ideology, rather than as a reaction against the dominant ideology of patriarchy, nevertheless some key themes can be identified. Feminism, I argue, stands *against* what I call 'the fetishism of choice' and 'the prison of biology'; it stands *for* three theses of feminism: 'the entrenchment of gender', 'the existence of patriarchy', and 'the need for change'. These three theses admit of a great deal of variety within feminist thought; nonetheless, they offer a coherent whole.

Chapter 2, 'Feminism on Liberalism', considers what liberalism is from the perspective of feminism. The chapter starts by considering the multiple feminist critiques of liberalism. It then moves to those who see the possibility of a productive partnership between the two, whether in philosophy or in activism. For some that partnership is forged by a liberal feminism or 'choice feminism' that centres women's choices, whatever they may be; others endorse a more critical feminist liberalism. It is this latter option, a feminist liberalism, that holds the most potential.

Chapter 3, 'Respect, Religion, and Feminism: Political liberalism as Feminist Liberalism?', considers whether political liberalism, specifically, can be used for feminist ends. There is significant disagreement among feminists and liberals about the compatibility between their two doctrines. Political liberalism is vulnerable to particular criticism from feminists, who argue that its restricted form of equality is insufficient. In contrast, Lori Watson and Christie Hartley argue that political liberalism can and must be feminist. This chapter raises three areas of disagreement with Watson and Hartley's incisive account of feminist political liberalism. First, I argue that an appeal to a comprehensive doctrine can be compatible with respecting others, if that appeal is to the value of equality. Second, I take issue with Watson and Hartley's defence of religious exemptions to equality law. Third, I argue that political liberalism can be compatible with feminism, but that it is not itself adequately feminist. The chapter concludes that political liberalism is not enough for feminists.

Part II turns to the foundational issue of the family. From the outset, feminists (and those adjacent to them) have argued that the family is a key site of oppression and inequality, such that any movement towards freedom and equality for women must start there. At the same time, liberals have traditionally defended the privacy of the family as a necessary part of a protected sphere of freedom. So the family has been a key site of contention in feminist/liberal dialogue.

Chapter 4, ' "The Family as a Basic Institution": A Feminist Analysis of the Basic Structure as Subject', engages with what has become known as the Rawls–Okin debate. The protagonists are John Rawls, widely credited with the late twentieth-century revival of liberalism as an academic political theory, and Susan Moller Okin, the preeminent liberal feminist in the same era. Rawls famously argued that justice was the first virtue of social institutions, but that it should apply only to those institutions that form part of the 'basic structure'. Was the family one of them? As Okin pointed out, Rawls' answer was both unclear and highly significant. Chapter 4 analyses their debate, points out where Okin's critique goes wrong and where it hits home, and shows that the issue of the family has serious consequences for Rawls's theory of justice as a whole. Once we consider the family, we see that the fundamental Rawlsian claim that justice applies distinctly to the basic structure of society is untenable.

Chapter 5, 'Liberalism, Feminism, and the Gendered Division of Labour', is new for this volume. Most feminists have argued that the gendered division of labour, according to which men specialise in career and paid employment while women specialise in unpaid domestic and care work, is a profound instance of gender injustice. Many liberals have argued that, even if the gendered division of labour creates and sustains inequality, it is essential to protect people's ability to *choose* the family structure that works best for them. On this issue, feminists and liberals seem to be in stalemate. Chapter 5 argues that the solution to the gendered division of labour is not to elevate paid employment above unpaid carework, as a liberal perspective tends to do. Instead, the solution starts with recognising that the gendered division of labour depends upon the systematic, enduring devaluation of care and domestic work and proceeds by *resisting* that devaluation. In this context, the injustice of the gendered division of labour cannot be solved by pushing mothers into paid employment. For the gendered division of labour truly to be undermined, *women must be valued for what they do*, including care and domestic work.

Chapter 6, 'The Marriage-Free State', is an overview of my 2017 book *Against Marriage: An Egalitarian Defence of the Marriage-Free State*. It sets out the case for abolishing state-recognised marriage and replacing it with piecemeal regulation of personal relationships. I start by analysing feminist objections to traditional marriage, and argue that the various feminist critiques can best be reconciled and answered by the abolition of state-recognised marriage. The chapter then considers the ideal form of state regulation of personal relationships. Contra other feminist proposals, equality and liberty are not best served by the creation of a new holistic status such as civil union, or by leaving regulation to private contracts. Instead, the state should develop piecemeal regulations that apply universally.

Part III, 'The Limits of Liberalism', considers what liberalism cannot do. The idea of liberalism's limits can be read in two ways: as a weakness, and as a boundary. Liberalism sets limits in the sense of boundaries when it forbids individuals or states from doing things. But liberalism also has limits in the sense of weaknesses when it is *unable* to intervene on some matter of injustice that demands redress. Both forms of limit apply particularly to political or neutralist liberalism.

Chapter 7, 'Should the Liberal State Recognise Gender?', considers the arguments I have made against the state recognition of marriage (in Chapter 6 and in *Against Marriage*) and applies them to the case of gender. I argue that a political liberal state cannot recognise gender since doing so would require it to define gender and enforce that definition, something that cannot be done without running counter to reasonable conceptions of the good. It follows that alternative methods to rectify the injustice of the gender binary must be sought. The chapter considers the difference between state recognition of gender and state recognition of sex, and argues for context-dependent solutions. This chapter is new to this volume.

Chapter 8, 'Reasonable Disagreement and the Neutralist Dilemma: Abortion and Circumcision in Matthew Kramer's *Liberalism with Excellence*', starts by investigating the idea of reasonable disagreement, a concept that is central to political liberal accounts of cooperation in the face of conflict. It then considers Matthew Kramer's argument that there is no neutral solution available to the disagreement over abortion. The chapter argues that Kramer's account has wider application, and identifies a neutralist dilemma. The neutralist dilemma applies when, of two policy options available to the state, one is unreasonable. It follows that the state should enact only the reasonable policy. However, in a neutralist dilemma the fact of reasonable disagreement due to the burdens of judgment means that it is not possible for the state to act at all, whether legislating or not, without deviating from neutrality. The chapter develops the concept of the neutralist dilemma and then applies it to another case discussed by Kramer: infant circumcision. The chapter argues that the debate over infant circumcision can be framed as a neutralist dilemma, but that the most plausible resolution of the dilemma results in an argument in favour of the legal prohibition of the practice. This is a surprising result, since most liberal states do not restrict circumcision and since prohibition of circumcision might initially appear to be non-neutral or even illiberal; however, it is consistent with the tenets of neutralist liberalism.

Part IV turns to the concept of equality of opportunity. This version of equality is regarded as the most basic and least controversial form of equality: no liberal will oppose it. Equality of opportunity thus has the potential to act as a beacon, guiding all liberals regardless of their differences. But, as the chapters in Part IV show, it is a complex concept with many different, conflicting forms.

Chapter 9, 'Each Outcome is Another Opportunity: Problems with the Moment of Equal Opportunity', considers those forms of equal opportunity that go beyond mere non-discrimination, and argues that each of them face a choice. They can employ what I call a 'Moment of Equal Opportunity', dividing a person's life around a key Moment at which opportunities are equalised and after which they are not. The problem with this option is that the injustice of unequal opportunities persists throughout life, meaning that equality of opportunity becomes an arbitrarily temporary state. But if a Moment of Equality of Opportunity is not used, and equality of opportunity is ensured throughout life, serious inefficiencies and bad decisions ensue. To put it simply, a theory of equality of opportunity is unjustified if it uses a Moment of Equal Opportunity, and unworkable if it does not.

Chapter 10, 'Equality of Opportunity and Three Justifications for Women's Sport: Fair Competition, Anti-sexism, and Identity', is new for this volume. There is currently a divisive public debate about whether trans women should be eligible to compete in women's sport, with prominent voices on both sides. Various sporting authorities have passed regulations that allow trans women to compete in women's competitions, including those that award titles, records, and scholarships. Several elite athletes have strongly criticised those rules, arguing that they are unfair to women who are not trans, and some sporting bodies have announced a return to sex-based categories. The debate is muddled, and it rests on a prior question that is often obscured: is women's sport justified at all? Any justification of women's sport must engage directly with questions of equality of opportunity, discrimination, and identity. This chapter identifies three possible justifications for women's sport: the fair competition argument, the anti-sexism argument, and the identity argument.

Each argument has merit. However, the arguments are in tension with each other at key points, and they have different implications for trans inclusion. Which argument should prevail depends on the social facts, the sporting context, and the sport itself. The chapter maps the argumentative terrain, showing where the key choices lie; it therefore aims to elucidate rather than end the public and philosophical debate. But it offers a general framework within which to think about dilemmas of discrimination, difference, and equality.

Part V returns to the issue of choice: its role in liberalism and the feminist critique.

Chapter 11, 'Choice and Female Genital Cosmetic Surgery', considers the role of choice as a normative transformer in relation to the practice of female genital cosmetic surgery. It is common, in law and practice, to distinguish between two sorts of female genital cutting. One is described as 'female genital mutilation' (FGM) and prohibited; the other is described as 'female genital cosmetic surgery' (FGCS) and permitted, even provided by the state in certain circumstances. The chapter argues that distinguishing between the two requires going beyond a simplistic contrast between choice and coercion. Both practices can be understood only within a cultural context that makes them available and marks them as appropriate. As with many other forms of cosmetic surgery, FGCS cannot be exonerated merely by an appeal to individual choice.

Chapter 12, 'Judging Women: 25 Years Further Toward a Feminist Theory of the State', engages with the work of landmark feminist Catharine MacKinnon to consider three ways of understanding the phrase 'judging women'. First, when is it acceptable or necessary to make judgments about what women do? The chapter argues that feminist analysis urges compassion and empathy for women, but also highlights the ways that choices are limited and shaped by patriarchy. Thus we cannot and should not avoid all judgment of women's—and men's—choices. Second, when can women engage in the act of judging? It is sometimes claimed that it is anti-feminist to engage in such judgment, and that feminists must above all else avoid being judgmental. The chapter rejects this idea and argues instead that feminism should insist on women's right to exercise judgment: women's voices matter. Third, how are we to judge who counts as a woman? The chapter shows that MacKinnon's work offers profound, sustained, rich analysis of these questions, but does not fully resolve them.

Chapter 13, 'Ideology and Normativity', investigates the possibility of what Sally Haslanger calls 'ideology critique' in the context of 'ideological oppression'. Like all oppression, ideological oppression involves unjust social practices. Its distinctive feature is that it is not recognised as oppression by its victims, or its perpetrators, or both—and this feature often applies to instances of sexist oppression. But ideological oppression causes problems for ideology critique, as Haslanger theorises it. Since ideological oppression is denied by those who suffer from it is it not possible to identify privileged epistemological standpoints in advance. The chapter argues that ideology critique cannot rely on epistemological considerations alone but must be based on a normative political theory.

PART I
FEMINISM & LIBERALISM

1
Feminism

Feminism is sometimes thought of as a political ideology.[1] But feminism is a refusal of that which is genuinely ideological: patriarchy. Patriarchy is so paradigmatically ideological, in the Marxist sense, that it is able to conceal its existence as such—and so is rarely discussed as an ideology except in connection with feminism.[2] Patriarchy is the ideology in which men constitute the dominant social group and masculinity is the dominant social practice. Under patriarchy this masculine perspective is presented as universal, and thus invisible as a perspective. Feminism's first priority has been to point out that patriarchy is an ideology, that its supposedly universal perspective is the perspective of a specific group that is unjustly dominant, and that it is so successful ideologically that it has become the default perspective of the subordinate group as well.

Staying for the moment with a Marxist conception of ideology, there are three senses in which feminism is an ideology and three in which it is not. Feminism *is* an ideology, firstly, because it presents a distinctive analysis of how things are: it interprets reality. Secondly, it emerges from the standpoint of a particular social group: it expresses the perspective of women as women. Thirdly, it has an inescapably reforming or revolutionary nature: it demands change.

Feminism is *not* an ideology in the Marxist sense, firstly, because its analysis of reality is not widely accepted: it is not mainstream. Secondly, it does not represent the standpoint of the powerful or dominant group: it is not hegemonic. Thirdly, feminism is inherently diverse, encompassing contrasting female perspectives and contrasting policy prescriptions: it is neither dogmatic nor pre-determined. Indeed, as bell hooks notes, "A central problem within feminist discourse has been our inability to either arrive at a consensus of opinion about what feminism is or accept definitions that could serve as points of unification."[3]

---

[1] This chapter was originally published in *The Oxford Handbook of Political Ideologies*, edited by Michael Freeden, Lyman Tower Sargent, and Marc Stears (Oxford University Press, 2013). I am grateful to the editors of that volume for their comments.

[2] I am grateful to Rebecca Flemming for observations on this point.

[3] bell hooks, 'Feminism: A Movement to End Sexist Oppression', in Sandra Kemp and Judith Squires (eds), *Feminisms* (Oxford: Oxford University Press, 1997), p. 22.

hooks' observation makes the task of writing this chapter particularly fraught: how to capture the nature of feminist ideology, while doing justice to its myriad histories and existences, in one short piece? This chapter is necessarily a simplification, and some feminist voices will be emphasised more than others. Later in this chapter I outline a set of criteria for feminism, which I call the three Theses of Feminism. These are designed to be compatible with feminist diversity. Nevertheless, they focus on some aspects of feminist ideology more than on others.

There are various ways of distinguishing between feminisms. One possible distinction is between academic and activist feminism, with some writers noting that feminism enjoys a predominance within the academy that it has lost in the active political arena.[4] Some academic feminism remains close to its activist roots.[5] But other academic feminists, particularly those associated with post-structural and psychoanalytical feminism, maintain an overtly theoretical approach, with work that can be inaccessible to those who are not already versed in the relevant terminology and discourse.[6] More accessible feminist works are read by more diverse audiences, and their success helps to energise new generations.[7]

Within academic feminism there has also been a shift in descriptions of the discipline, from 'women's studies' to 'gender studies'. The term 'women's studies' emphasised the distinctiveness of feminist thought, its significance for women, and its rejection of traditional disciplinary boundaries. As Michele Barrett notes, though, it has the disadvantage of leaving mainstream academic disciplines and departments "unchallenged and even denuded of feminist scholars".[8] A focus on women's studies also risks sidelining issues concerning men and masculinity, which feminists need to engage with since it is not only

---

[4] Sandra Kemp and Judith Squires (eds), *Feminisms* (Oxford: Oxford University Press, 1997).

[5] For example, the feminist legal scholar Catharine MacKinnon has always both written theory and engaged in political and legal practice on matters such as sexual harassment, war crimes against women, and pornography—the latter in a long-term collaboration with the non-academic feminist writer and activist Andrea Dworkin.

[6] For example, Martha Nussbaum writes of Judith Butler that "It is difficult to come to grips with Butler's ideas, because it is difficult to figure out what they are.... Her written style... is ponderous and obscure. It is dense with allusions to other theorists, drawn from a wide range of theoretical traditions" (Martha Nussbaum, 'The Professor of Parody', *The New Republic* 22(2) (1999), p. 38). And yet Butler's work has been incredibly influential and very widely read.

[7] For example, Natasha Walter, *Living Dolls: The Return of Sexism* (London: Virago, 2010); Cordelia Fine, *Delusions of Gender: The Real Science Behind Sex Differences* (London: Icon, 2010); Caroline Criado-Perez, *Invisible Women: Exposing Data Bias in a World Designed for Men* (London: Chatto & Windus, 2019); Chimamanda Ngozi Adichie, *We Should All Be Feminists* (London: Fourth Estate, 2014); Sarah Ahmed, *Living a Feminist Life* (Durham, NC: Duke University Press, 2017).

[8] Michelle Barrett, 'Words and Things: Materialism and Method in Contemporary Feminist Analysis', in Sandra Kemp and Judith Squires (eds), *Feminisms* (Oxford: Oxford University Press, 1997), p. 115.

women who are constructed and affected by patriarchy. Finally, the development of queer theory and transgender studies, areas of enquiry that have close connections with feminist thought, has put pressure on the idea that patriarchy, sexism, and gender can be adequately analysed under the label 'women's studies'. Thus many academic departments and centres of feminist thought have become self-defined centres of gender studies instead.

For example, the Department of Women's Studies at the University of California—Berkeley (founded as the Women's Studies Program in 1976) changed its name to the Department of Gender and Women's Studies in 2005.[9] Similarly the Yale University Women's Studies Program, started in 1979, has changed its name twice: to Women's and Gender Studies in 1998 and again to Women's, Gender, and Sexuality Studies in 2004—marking the increasing salience of sexuality and queer theory to feminist thought.[10] In Britain, too, centres of women's studies tend to pre-date centres of gender or gender studies.[11] While the names of some academic centres combine women's studies, feminism and gender studies,[12] thus emphasising their complementarity at the same time as their distinctiveness, the University of Cambridge Centre for Gender Studies states prominently on its website that "'Gender' is not a synonym for 'women' or 'feminism'."[13]

These trends reflect a general ambiguity within feminist thought broadly conceived about the specific relevance of *women* to feminism and to gender. Just as the move to gender studies de-emphasises women, so too some feminists have sought to question the nature and relevance of womanhood. As is explored later in this chapter, this contestation of the category 'woman' can come from various angles, including difference feminism, queer theory, post-structuralism, and transgender studies. Other feminists, such as those associated with the ethics of care, ecofeminism, and gender-critical feminism, argue for the protection of the category 'woman' and the value of womanhood. As Monique Wittig puts it, "For many of us [feminism] means someone who

---

[9] Department of Gender and Women's Studies, 'History', available at https://gws.berkeley.edu/about/history/.

[10] Yale University, 'Women's, Gender, and Sexuality Studies', available at https://wgss.yale.edu/about.

[11] For example, the University of York's Centre for Women's Studies was founded in 1984, whereas the LSE's Gender Institute and the Leeds University Centre for Interdisciplinary Gender Studies were founded in 1993 and 1997, respectively.

[12] As well as the UC-Berkeley and Yale examples already described, consider the Cornell University Feminist, Gender, and Sexuality Studies Program and the Harvard University Committee on Degrees in Studies of Women, Gender, and Sexuality.

[13] University of Cambridge Centre for Gender Studies, 'About the Centre', available at http://www.gender.cam.ac.uk/about/. One way of explaining this claim could be to say that a theory of gender informs the political practice of feminism. I am grateful to Juliet Mitchell, founder of the Cambridge Centre for Gender Studies, for this suggestion.

fights for women as a class *and for the disappearance of this class*. For many others it means someone who fights for woman and her defense – for the myth, then, and its reinforcement."[14]

And yet despite this ambiguity within feminism about the nature and status of womanhood there is a recognisable core, such that it can make sense to think of feminism as a political ideology. Feminism is inescapably political: it both analyses the political and engages in political struggle. The fundamentally political nature of feminism is perhaps easiest to see when considering feminism through traditional categories such as liberal feminism, Marxist and socialist feminism, and radical feminism, for these categories are distinguished by their analysis of political reality and their ideological approach to reform, and the labels of these approaches place feminists in recognisable places on a pre-existing political spectrum. But these traditional categories of feminism can seem rather dated and unappealing. As Sandra Kemp and Judith Squires argue, such taxonomies problematically imply "that feminist theory understand[s] itself as simple modification of the pre-existing canon" and have "at times worked to polarize perspectives and rigidify conflicts".[15] This chapter is thus not structured around such divisions, although I do indicate moments where there are differences between feminists along ideological lines.

The ideological nature of feminism is perhaps best seen in two parts: what feminism is *against*, and what feminism is *for*. The rest of this chapter considers these two parts. Feminism's critical aspect comes first so as to capture its rejection of patriarchy.

1.1 Against: The Fetishism of Choice and the Prison of Biology

Patriarchy structures social and political life everywhere, but here I focus on the forms of patriarchy and feminist resistance that are found in Western liberal capitalist societies. In those societies, feminist resistance to patriarchy must fend off two contrasting challenges: the fetishism of choice and the prison of biology. Neither biology nor liberalism is inevitably patriarchal (there are both feminist biologists and liberal feminists), but both have been

---

[14] Monique Wittig, 'One is Not Born a Woman', in Kemp and Squires (eds), *Feminisms*, p. 223. Emphasis added.
[15] Kemp and Squires (eds), *Feminisms*, p. 9.

appealed to in support of patriarchy. Patriarchal ideology insists both that women and men are ineluctably different, such that social inequality is premised upon biological difference (the prison of biology), and that any putative injustice of this inequality is mitigated by the liberal capitalist focus on individual choice (the fetishism of choice). In other words, gender inequality is inevitable yet unproblematic.

To expand this patriarchal story: women and men cannot be equal in the sense of identical, for they are constrained both physically and socially by their biology. Women and men are bound to lead different sorts of lives with different sorts of preferences, activities, positions in the family and workplace, and so on. These supposedly inevitable differences might look problematic from the perspective of liberalism, which prioritises equality but understands equality largely to mean sameness, until choice is brought in. For liberals of many varieties a situation can be unequal without being unjust, so long as those involved are able to make choices about their lives. If people have chosen things that disadvantage them or entrench difference, then the liberal is untroubled.[16] This liberal commitment to choice entrenches patriarchy if and when it is asserted that women generally do exercise free choice. Gender inequality thus becomes the result of some combination of natural difference and free choice, and disrupting it becomes both unnatural and unjust.

Against this patriarchal story feminism insists that women are neither imprisoned by biology nor liberated by individual choice. Gender inequality is entrenched, pervasive, and profound in its effects, but its domain is the social rather than the biological, and that which is created in the social arena can be disrupted there too.

1.1.1 The Fetishism of Choice

The ideal-typical liberal citizen is *in control*: of her career, of her consumer choices, of her family life, of her relationships, of her sex life, of her appearance, of her body. Members of Western liberal capitalist democracies are encouraged to take this ideal-type to heart and to see themselves as equal choosers. Feminism, particularly liberal feminism, does not reject the value of choice as an ideal. But feminism insists that we confront the ways in which we are constrained and unequal, disrupting the self-image of the liberal

---

[16] Clare Chambers, *Sex, Culture, and Justice: The Limits of Choice* (University Park, PA: Penn State University Press, 2008).

citizen. Feminism suggests that all women, even those who feel liberated and powerful, are affected by female social inferiority, and that all men, even those who feel disadvantaged, benefit from male privilege. This does not mean that women are victims and men are agents: feminism argues that all people, women and men, are constrained by socially constructed gender norms. To put it another way: feminism insists on the reality and ubiquity of sexist oppression, and demands an end to that oppression.[17]

The idea that liberal capitalism safeguards our freedom of choice is so entrenched that feminist insistence on the social constraints of gender inequality is anathema to many. Feminism confronts women and men with the idea that they are not in control. Their choices are shaped by the social construction of appropriate gendered behaviour. Their careers are shaped by pervasive sexism, ranging from straightforward discrimination and wage inequality to the more subtle but absolute clash between the norm of maternal care and the norm of the ideal worker.[18] Their sexual relationships take place within a socio-legal framework that refuses to guarantee women the sexual autonomy it sells.[19] While some women encountering feminist theory for the first time find it profound and motivating, others find its challenge to their self-image of unconstrained agency enraging. While some men recognise that gender norms both limit and privilege them, others react angrily to the idea that they are beneficiaries of injustice.[20] So someone encountering feminist ideas for the first time can feel as though it is *feminism* that constrains, unless and until she realises that feminism identifies these constraints precisely so as to urge their destruction.

To take an example, many feminists criticise the beauty norms to which women submit apparently willingly and even with pleasure.[21] In Western

---

[17] hooks, 'Feminism: A Movement to End Sexist Oppression'.

[18] Joan Williams, *Unbending Gender: Why Family and Work Conflict and What to Do About It* (Oxford: Oxford University Press, 2000).

[19] Women's sexual autonomy is sold both literally and figuratively. Figuratively, women are sold through advertising and other media the idea that they are and must be in control of their own sexuality, where 'being in control of' means 'using in order to succeed'. Literally, women's sexual autonomy is sold to others in prostitution, pornography, and traditional marriage.

[20] A classic example is Susan Brownmiller's claim that rape "is nothing more or less than a conscious process of intimidation by which *all* men keep *all* women in a state of fear" (Susan Brownmiller, *Against Our Will: Men, Women and Rape* (New York: Simon and Schuster, 1975), p. 15. Emphasis in the original). Men tend to react angrily to this statement, insisting that they have never raped nor do they desire to rape, thereby missing Brownmiller's point that women have no reliable way of distinguishing a rapist from a non-rapist and so rape places all men in a dominant position.

[21] See, for example, Sandra Lee Bartky, 'Foucault, Femininity and the Modernization of Patriarchal Power', in Diana Tietjens Meyers (ed.), *Feminist Social Thought: A Reader* (London: Routledge, 1997); Susan Bordo, *Unbearable Weight: Feminism, Western Culture, and the Body* (Berkeley and Los Angeles: University of California Press, 2003); Chambers, *Sex, Culture, and Justice*; Andrea Dworkin, *Woman*

societies women are assumed to take great pride in their appearance and to enjoy spending large amounts of time and money improving it. Having one's rough skin rubbed away, one's cuticles cut off and one's nails filed down is 'pampering'. Wearing extortionately expensive and excruciatingly uncomfortable high-heeled shoes is a luxurious indulgence. Spending money and energy on choosing, applying, removing, and re-applying hair products is justified "Because You're Worth It" (as L'Oreal would have it). At all levels women are supposed to enjoy submitting themselves to beauty rituals and judging themselves by prevailing standards, and many women do indeed adopt the cultural meaning of these practices as pleasurable and choice-worthy.

However, feminist analysis demonstrates that the beauty norms by which women are assessed are deeply problematic from the point of view of equality. Some beauty practices are damaging or risky in themselves, such as sun beds, high-heeled shoes, and cosmetic surgery. Some beauty standards, such as unwrinkled skin and non-grey hair, are unachievable beyond a certain age, leading to feelings of sadness or even shame. Some beauty standards increase the prevalence of psychological illness such as eating disorders. Other beauty practices are simply burdensome, effortful, and expensive. The sum of beauty practices to which women are subjected contributes to their inferior status in society for several reasons: it saps their finances and energy which could otherwise be devoted on other things, it imposes standards on women that are simply not imposed on men, and it makes the typical woman and girl at best dissatisfied with, and at worst ashamed of, her own body and in her own skin.[22]

The feminist conclusion is not that no woman actively chooses beauty practices, or that no woman enjoys participating in them. The conclusion is rather that it does not make sense to use a woman's choices as the sole measure of the justice of the context in which she is choosing. It is inevitable that women and men should find some enjoyment in conforming to cultural standards, should want to engage in behaviour that is culturally recognised as appropriate for them, and should take pleasure and pride in succeeding in the endeavours that are culturally mandated. What is at issue is whether those cultural standards are themselves compatible with equal status and genuine

---

Hating (New York: E. P. Dutton, 1974); Sheila Jeffreys, *Beauty and Misogyny: Harmful Cultural Practices in the West* (Hove: Routledge, 2005); Naomi Wolf, *The Beauty Myth* (London: Vintage, 1990).

[22] Chambers, *Sex, Culture, and Justice*; Clare Chambers, *Intact: A Defence of the Unmodified Body* (London: Allen Lane, 2022); Jeffreys, *Beauty and Misogyny*; Heather Widdows, *Perfect Me: Beauty as an Ethical Ideal* (Princeton, NJ: Princeton University Press, 2018).

autonomy. The choice to abide by a cultural standard does not in itself legitimate that standard.[23]

1.1.2 The Prison of Biology

Feminism thus resists the liberal idea that we are atomistic, autonomous individuals in need only of basic legal rights to protect our freedom of choice. Gender inequality is more salient than liberal theory allows. Yet it also resists the idea that gender inequality rests on biological inevitability. This idea has accompanied patriarchy for centuries, and though the details have shifted, its pervasiveness has not. Feminist historians of philosophy have pointed out that most 'great thinkers' of the philosophical canon have misogynist views, often premised on the notion of biological inferiority, and that the mainstream philosophical attitude of benign neglect of such views is incoherent.[24]

While the particular beliefs of philosophers such as Aristotle, Plato, Rousseau, Hegel, and Nietzsche as they concern the natural inferiority of women are seldom found convincing today, the same is not true of theories about the biological basis of gender inequality in general. Views about women's natural inability to think rationally, pursue careers, or participate in politics may seem ridiculous to contemporary sensibilities, but there has been a resurgence in 'natural' explanations for gender difference. Contemporary theses about the naturalness of gender difference include theories based on evolutionary psychology,[25] theories based on neuroscience,[26] theories based

---

[23] One might ask what would legitimate a cultural standard. The answer must surely be that the standard itself should be subject to scrutiny, not just the question of whether any individual will comply. When feminists have scrutinised standards of beauty they have come up with many alternative, more rational standards of appearance, such as the nineteenth-century Rational Dress Society and the multi-pocketed trousers and smocks worn in Charlotte Perkins Gilman, *Herland* (London: The Women's Press, 1979).

[24] Sandra Harding and Merrill B. Hintikka, *Discovering Reality: Feminist Perspectives on Epistemology, Metaphysics, Methodology, and Philosophy of Science* (New York: Springer, 2003); Carole Pateman, *The Sexual Contract* (Cambridge: Polity Press, 1988); Mary Lyndon Shanley and Carole Pateman, *Feminist Interpretations and Political Theory* (Cambridge: Polity Press, 1991); Linda Zerilli, 'Feminist Theory and the Canon of Political Thought', in John S. Dryzek, Bonnie Honig, and Anne Phillips (eds), *The Oxford Handbook of Political Theory* (Oxford: Oxford University Press, 2008).

[25] Helena Cronin, *The Ant and the Peacock: Altruism and Sexual Selection from Darwin to Today* (Cambridge: Cambridge University Press, 1991); Geoffrey Miller, *The Mating Mind: How Sexual Choice Shaped the Evolution of Human Nature* (London: William Heinemann, 2000); Randy Thornhill and Craig T. Palmer, *A Natural History of Rape: Biological Bases of Sexual Coercion* (Cambridge, MA: MIT Press, 2000).

[26] Simon Baron-Cohen, *The Essential Difference: Men, Women and the Extreme Male Brain* (London: Allen Lane, 2003); Louann Brizendine, *The Female Brain* (London: Bantam, 2007) and Louann Brizendine, *The Male Brain* (London: Bantam, 2010); Susan Pinker, *The Sexual Paradox: Men, Women, and the Real Gender Gap* (New York: Scribner, 2008).

on fetal exposure to testosterone, and others.[27] These theories purport to explain an astonishing variety of gendered behaviour as biologically hard-wired, ranging from map-reading ability, emotional sensitivity, attitude to pink, career choice, and rape.

There are a variety of feminist responses to such theories. In 1869 John Stuart Mill pointed out: "So true is it that unnatural generally means only uncustomary, and that everything which is usual appears natural.... I deny that any one knows, or can know, the nature of the two sexes, as long as they have only been seen in their present relation to one another."[28] In a similar if less speculative vein many contemporary feminist scientists have pointed out the dire inadequacy of the science behind these modern-day just-so stories.[29] Even a non-scientist can see the simple truth of Mill's observation that there is a great deal that is social. Moreover, normativity is inescapably social: regardless of what is, we can always ask what ought to be or what follows from what is.

1.2 For: The Three Theses of Feminism

In the remainder of this chapter I present three theses with which feminism steers a path between the fetishism of choice and the prison of biology. The three theses of feminism can be found in all forms of feminism, though they are interpreted in different ways by different feminists. Moreover, feminists differ in the weight they give to each thesis, and the theses do not exhaust feminist concerns. But they provide a way to identify and analyse feminist thinking. The theses are deliberately vague, so as to ensure their compatibility with the wide range of feminist thought.

The three theses of feminism are:

1. *The Entrenchment of Gender.* Gender is a significant and enduring social cleavage.

---

[27] Fine, *Delusions of Gender.*
[28] John Stuart Mill, 'The Subjection of Women', in *On Liberty and the Subjection of Women* (Ware: Wordsworth, 1996 [1868]), pp. 128–36.
[29] Deborah Cameron, *The Myth of Mars and Venus: Do Men and Women Really Speak Different Languages?* (Oxford: Oxford University Press, 2007); John Dupré, *Human Nature and the Limits of Science* (Oxford: Oxford University Press, 2001); Anne Fausto-Sterling, *Myths of Gender: Biological Theories About Women and Men* (New York: Basic Books, 1985) and *Sexing the Body* (New York: Basic Books, 2000); Fine, *Delusions of Gender*; Hilary Rose and Steven P. R. Rose, *Alas Poor Darwin: Arguments Against Evolutionary Psychology* (London: Vintage, 2001); Cheryl Brown Travis (ed.), *Evolution, Gender, and Rape* (Cambridge, MA: MIT Press, 2003).

2. *The Existence of Patriarchy*. The social cleavage of gender is not normatively neutral: it is profoundly unequal, with women the disadvantaged and men the advantaged group.
3. *The Need for Change*. The fact of entrenched patriarchal gender division is normatively wrong, and political action is needed to counteract it.

The first and second theses are different in kind from the third. The first two theses are claims about what society *is* like, whereas the third thesis is a claim about what society *should* be like.[30] To put it another way: the assertion of the Need for Change is in part the demand that the Existence of Patriarchy should ultimately become false—a change which, for some feminists, also requires the end of the Entrenchment of Gender. So, when discussing the first two theses it is important to note that feminists believe that they are in fact true, not that they ought to remain true.

1.2.1 The Entrenchment of Gender

For all feminists there is something special about gender difference. Most basically, it exists. More substantively, it is significant. Indeed, feminism insists that gender is more significant than at least some other cleavages at least some of the time; to put it another way, gender has explanatory power. More controversially, many feminists argue that gender is one of the most significant social cleavages.

The claim that gender difference exists can take many forms within feminism and can also be endorsed by non-feminists. But what is gender? It is commonplace to note that there is, speaking generally, a biological difference between male and female. This difference inheres in the physical shapes of our bodies: in the complementary yet by no means straightforwardly coherent dualities of vulva/penis, uterus/testes, XX/XY chromosomes, less/more bodily hair, different proportions of estrogen and testosterone, and so on. It inheres in the functions of those bodies: women and not men (again, generally rather than universally) can gestate and lactate, men and not women have certain forms of physical strength. And it inheres in the different behaviours and attitudes that are associated with and expected of women and men, with respect to the priority and urgency given to things such as nurturing,

---

[30] By 'society' I mean whichever society the feminist thought under consideration is criticising—which, in practice, means all actually existing societies.

competition, beauty, romance, sexual stimulation, violence, relationships, family, money, and power.

The biological and sociological reality of such dichotomies cannot reasonably be disputed. The Entrenchment of Gender becomes a feminist thesis because feminists *analyse* and *question* gender difference. Feminists point out that gender has crucial significance and wide-ranging consequences. At the same time they insist on its complexity and need for analysis, undermining the idea that gender difference is inevitable, immutable, and desirable. In particular, feminists dispute any idea that gender difference is desirable *because* it is natural: they dispute the Prison of Biology.

One paradigmatic feminist method for problematising gender difference while maintaining the Entrenchment of Gender is the sex/gender distinction. According to this distinction, patriarchal discourse blurs two discrete phenomena. There is *sex*, which is the natural (and hence assumed inevitable and unproblematic) biological distinction between male and female humans, and there is *gender*, which is the social (and hence considered mutable and open to problematisation) categorisation of people into masculine and feminine. In insisting that sex and gender are distinct, feminists call attention to the fact that much of what is often attributed to biology should more properly be attributed to culture.

The idea of the sex/gender distinction is at once basic to feminism and problematic within it. There are many opportunities for contention. For some feminists the liberatory potential of distinguishing sex from gender lies in the claim that very little is, in fact, sex; that most of the differences we observe between men and women, differences which are often attributed to biology, result instead from culture. This claim can take a number of forms. Mill argues that "what is now called the nature of women is an eminently artificial thing – the result of forced repression in some directions, unnatural stimulation in others."[31] Simone de Beauvoir writes that "one is not born, but rather becomes, a woman."[32] Germaine Greer begins *The Female Eunuch* with a sustained argument for the indeterminacy of biology.[33] Typically, as in these examples, feminists have focused their claims on women, but the same arguments apply equally to men: a boy must learn masculinity in just the same way as a girl learns femininity. Such claims are liberating because they suggest that we are not imprisoned by our biology; that we can be male and female

---

[31] Mill, 'The Subjection of Women', p. 136.
[32] Simone de Beauvoir, *The Second Sex* (New York: Bantam, 1952), p. 249.
[33] Germaine Greer, *The Female Eunuch* (London: Flamingo, 1991).

without being masculine and feminine. It is this insight, basic and yet profound, which in many ways forms the *core* of feminist ideology.

However, there are a number of challenges to the sex/gender distinction even from within feminism. Feminists have challenged the idea that sex and gender are distinct, as well as the idea that their distinctiveness is necessary for, or even conducive to, liberation. Some feminists insist that the sex/gender distinction helps the project of liberation only on problematic assumptions. First, one must assume that socially motivated and maintained behaviour is more malleable than biologically motivated and maintained behaviour, and this is by no means obvious.[34] Second, one must assume not only that biology and culture are different phenomena, but also that they do not interact: that there is no such thing as a socially affected biology or a biologically grounded sociality. But this assumption is unwarranted.

Take the example of parenthood, and the differences between motherhood and fatherhood. Using the feminist sex/gender distinction in a traditional, unproblematised way we might say: there is biological mothering and there is cultural mothering. People of sex female are different from people of sex male, in that the former and not the latter are capable of gestating, birthing, and breastfeeding a child. But this sex difference does not in itself necessitate or legitimate the cultural, gendered difference that results when women are given significantly longer parental leave than men, are more likely to be full-time parents than are men, and are consequently less likely to be successful in the workplace (where success is measured by conventional (=patriarchal) indicators such as money and prestige). There is therefore no reason why mothers and fathers should not play equal roles as parents, where equal means identical, in all areas aside from those very few biologically mandated areas of gestation, birth, and breastfeeding.

This feminist use of the sex/gender distinction has been dominant in liberal feminism, and feminist arguments such as these have played a key role in a great many of the landmark victories of the struggle for women's liberation: female suffrage, sex discrimination legislation, demands for equality within the family. But this approach has several flaws. It may be too optimistic, insofar as it suggests that cultural change is easier than biological change, and yet there is surely nothing easy in changing entrenched patterns of male and female parenting and employment.[35] It may be dystopian, insofar as it suggests that even biological sex differences would be better obliterated for they stand in the way of equality-as-identity. And this yoking of equality to

---

[34] Chambers, *Sex, Culture, and Justice*.   [35] Williams, *Unbending Gender*.

identity implies that women must be like men in order to be valued.[36] Would it be better still for women's equality if they did not gestate their children?[37] Is breastfeeding anti-feminist?[38] Is a woman who returns to work five days after giving birth[39]—just like most men return to work only days after becoming fathers—better than one who stays at home? While some feminists have answered 'yes' to these questions others would vehemently disagree, fearing that the value of womanhood can be all too easily erased.

So a feminist insistence on the Entrenchment of Gender need not rely on a traditional understanding of the sex/gender distinction. For some feminists the social construction of differences between men and women burrows beneath what is usually thought of as gender to reach even the biological category of sex.[40] Cultural practices such as cosmetic surgery, high heels, and corsets literally shape our bodies, as do rules of behaviour such as the requirement that women should keep their legs closed when seated, be or appear shorter than men (even while wearing high heels),[41] or engage in physical activities only with restricted deportment.[42] And even parts of our bodies not yet *physically* shaped by social, gendered requirements are nevertheless imbued with gendered *significance* only by contingent social practices. It is biology not culture that dictates that human fertilisation involves sperm and egg. But it is culture not biology that portrays that process as one in which active sperm compete among themselves to conquer a passive egg, a standard portrayal that ignores the agency of the female reproductive system in sorting

---

[36] For feminists who reject the idea that equality must be premised upon sameness, see Nancy Fraser, *Justice Interruptus: Critical Reflections on the "Postsocialist" Condition* (London: Routledge, 1997) and Catharine A. MacKinnon, *Are Women Human? And Other International Dialogues* (Cambridge, MA: Harvard University Press, 2006).

[37] Shulamith Firestone, *The Dialectic of Sex: The Case for Feminist Revolution* (London: The Women's Press, 1979); Sophie Lewis, *Full Surrogacy Now: Feminism Against Family* (London: Verso, 2019).

[38] Hanna Rosin, 'The Case Against Breast-Feeding', *The Atlantic* (April 2009), available at https://www.theatlantic.com/magazine/archive/2009/04/the-case-against-breast-feeding/307311/.

[39] As Rachida Dati, French Justice Minister, did in 2009. See 'Just Five Days Off', *The Guardian* (9 January 2009), available at http://www.guardian.co.uk/lifeandstyle/2009/jan/09/women-maternitypaternityrights?INTCMP=ILCNETTXT3487.

[40] Fausto-Sterling, *Myths of Gender* and *Sexing the Body*; Greer, *The Female Eunuch*; Catharine A. MacKinnon, *Toward A Feminist Theory of the State* (Cambridge, MA: Harvard University Press, 1989).

[41] See, for example, the debate about how Tom Cruise managed to appear taller than Cameron Diaz at the premier of *Knight and Day*: 'Tom Cruise & Cameron Diaz in London: How Is He So Tall? (PHOTOS)', *Huffpost* (22 July 2010), available at http://www.huffingtonpost.com/2010/07/22/tom-cruise-cameron-diaz-i_n_656203.htm.

[42] Pierre Bourdieu, *Masculine Domination* (Cambridge: Polity Press, 2001); Greer, *The Female*; Iris Marion Young, *On Female Body Experience: "Throwing Like a Girl" and Other Essays* (New York; Oxford: Oxford University Press, 2005).

and selecting sperm.[43] As Catharine MacKinnon writes, "Distinctions of body or mind or behavior are pointed to as cause rather than effect, with no realisation that they are so deeply effect rather than cause that pointing to them at all is an effect. Inequality comes first, difference comes after."[44]

Another feminist controversy around the Entrenchment of Gender comes to light when considering queer theory. The core of queer theory is a critique of heteronormativity, a critique which has clear affinities with feminism. But beyond this core there are complexities and controversies, with some feminists arguing that queer theory is not feminist.[45]

Some queer theorists argue that gender is entrenched but that its entrenchment is an illusion of patriarchy that must be dispelled. For example, Judith Butler's famous claim that gender is 'performative' can be read as a claim about the essential non-essentiality of gender.[46] If we view gender in this way, as a category without stable roots in physical sex difference, then the entrenchment of gender becomes crucial to the project of patriarchy, and uprooting it becomes crucial to the project of feminism. On this analysis gender is entrenched as a social construct precisely because it lacks a solid grounding in biology: if femaleness does not require femininity then femininity's compulsion must be located elsewhere. Resistance becomes possible, located in alternative performances or in acts that make clear that gender is performed and not natural.

On the other hand, there can be a temptation for the gay rights movement to insist on the biological or at least unchosen nature of sexuality. There is great political mileage in the idea of immutable biological sexuality, for if sexuality is natural then homosexuality cannot be unnatural; if people do not choose to be lesbian or gay then they cannot be asked to choose *not* to be lesbian or gay. Indeed, public support for gay rights is correlated with the belief that homosexuality is the result of biology or genes and is thus uncontrollable.[47] Such rhetoric has doubtless been vital to much political action against homophobia, and coheres with most people's interpretations of their own sexuality, whether they are gay or straight. But it is a form of analysis that

---

[43] Catherine Blackledge, *The Story of V: Opening Pandora's Box* (London: Orion Books, 2003).
[44] MacKinnon, *Toward A Feminist Theory of the State*, p. 219.
[45] Sheila Jeffreys, *Unpacking Queer Politics* (Cambridge: Polity Press, 2003).
[46] Judith Butler, *Gender Trouble* (Cambridge: Polity Press, 1999) and 'Performativity's Social Magic', in Richard Shusterman (ed.), *Bourdieu: A Critical Reader* (Oxford: Blackwell, 1999). See also Clare Chambers, 'Judith Butler's Gender Trouble', in Jacob T. Levy (ed.), *Oxford Handbook of Classics in Contemporary Political Theory* (Oxford: Oxford University Press, 2017, online first).
[47] Donald P. Haider-Markel and Mark R. Joslyn, 'Beliefs About the Origins of Homosexuality and Support For Gay Rights: An Empirical Test of Attribution Theory', *Public Opinion Quarterly* 72(2) (2009).

does not sit easily with feminist concerns about biological essentialism. Radical lesbian feminists insist that it is possible to choose to be lesbian that living with and for other women can be both a personal choice and a political imperative.[48]

Disagreements come to a head with the issue of trans identity and politics. The term 'trans', sometimes rendered with an asterisk as 'trans*' has come to indicate the variety of ways that people understand, reconfigure, inhabit, or reject gender identity. It is intended to cover a variety of positions including people who identify as 'transsexual' (a term now fallen out of favour for many trans people), as trans women or trans men, as non-binary, as genderqueer, and many others. As Jack Halberstam puts it, "trans*" is intended "to open the term up to unfolding categories of being organized around but not confined to forms of gender variance".[49] Trans people might wish to take on the mainstream gendered practices of their preferred, chosen, or self-identified gender, disrupting the association between sex and gender but not gendered norms as such, or they might wish to unsettle the gender binary by eschewing gendered practices or creatively disrupting gender norms.

Trans identity and transgender studies can be seen as either complementary or opposed to feminism. The two are complementary insofar as trans people call into question the rigidity of gender difference and assert the importance of undermining the gender binary, a stance sometimes known as transfeminism.[50] But some feminists argue that certain forms of trans theory undermine feminism by entrenching the gender binary, as when some trans people use the concept of being *born in the wrong body*, an idea that implies a biological truth of gender into which each person naturally belongs.[51] The

---

[48] Radicalesbians, 'The Woman-Identified Woman', in Shane Phelan and Mark Blasius (eds), *We Are Everywhere: A Historical Sourcebook of Gay and Lesbian Politics* (London: Routledge, 1997); Charlotte Bunch, 'Lesbians in Revolt', in Phelan and Blasius (eds), *We Are Everywhere*.
[49] Jack Halberstam, *Trans*: A Quick and Quirky Account of Gender Variability* (Berkeley, CA: University of California Press, 2018), p. 4.
[50] Kate Bornstein, *Gender Outlaw: On Men, Women and the Rest of Us* (New York: Vintage, 1995); Patrick Califia, *Sex Changes: Transgender Politics* (San Francisco, CA: Cleis Press, 1997); Leslie Feinberg, *Trans Liberation: Beyond Pink or Blue* (Boston, MA: Beacon, 1998); Cressida J. Heyes, 'Feminist Solidarity after Queer Theory: The Case of Transgender', *Signs* 28(4) (2003); Stephen Whittle, 'Where Did We Go Wrong? Feminism and Trans Theory – Two Teams on the Same Side?', in Susan Stryker and Stephen Whittle (eds), *The Transgender Studies Reader* (New York: Routledge, 2006); Finn Mackay, *Female Masculinities and the Gender Wars: The Politics of Sex* (London: Bloomsbury, 2021); Shon Faye, *The Transgender Issue: An Argument for Justice* (London: Allen Lane, 2021).
[51] Feminist critiques of trans theory include Kathleen Stock, *Material Girls: Why Reality Matters for Feminism* (London: Fleet, 2021); Holly Lawford-Smith, *Gender-Critical Feminism* (Oxford: Oxford University Press, 2022); Julie Bindel, *Feminism for Women: The Real Route to Liberation* (London: Little Brown, 2021); Helen Joyce, *Trans: When Ideology Meets Reality* (London: Oneworld, 2021). For discussion of *born in the wrong body* discourse, see Chambers, *Intact*, pp. 268–79.

diversity of both feminist theory and trans theory means that there are multiple opportunities for conflict as well as compatibility.

The tensions that arise within feminism when considering the implications of queer and trans theory reflect a general ambiguity within feminism. It has been, and remains, crucial to feminism to insist on both the importance of embodied experience and the irreducibility of women to their bodies. So much feminist work rails against the traditional dualist claim that the mind is distinct from and superior to the body, along with the idea that reason is distinct from and superior to emotion. Feminists argue that bodily experience is crucial to both subjectivity and politics.[52] At the same time feminists reject the patriarchal reduction of women to their bodies. Feminists insist that bodily experience is crucial to both women and men, and that there should not be a hierarchy between the physical or emotional and the mental or rational. These phenomena are inextricably interwoven, inevitably social, and inescapably political. The role of the body is thus extremely complex within feminism.[53]

While all feminists assert the thesis of the Entrenchment of Gender, feminists differ in their views about the categories of 'women' and 'men' which it creates. All feminists agree there is *something* that women have in common by virtue of being women, but there is controversy about what this is, about how much women share in terms of experience or observable characteristics, and about the salience of gender as opposed to other social cleavages such as race, class, sexuality, and culture. Feminists such as bell hooks and Audre Lorde argue that much second-wave feminism is unthinkingly focused on the experience of a sub-category of women: those who are middle-class and white.[54] For example, Lorde writes of the merits of Mary Daly's *Gyn/Ecology* but critiques Daly's lack of engagement with African culture and the work of black feminists. "To imply", Lorde writes, "that all women suffer the same oppression simply because we are women is to lose sight of the varied tools of patriarchy."[55] For hooks, classic feminist tracts such as Betty Friedan's *The Feminine Mystique* claim to speak for all women, identifying the "problem that has no name" of housewives' experience of alienation and isolation and asserting that liberation for women lies in accessing the workplace and the public sphere.[56] But hooks points out that the problems faced by housewives

---

[52] Rose Weitz (ed.), *The Politics of Women's Bodies: Sexuality, Appearance, and Behavior* (Oxford: Oxford University Press, 2003); Young, *On Female Body Experience*.
[53] Chambers, *Intact*.
[54] bell hooks, *Ain't I a Woman: Black Women and Feminism* (London: Pluto Press, 1983); Audre Lorde, 'An Open Letter to Mary Daly', in *Your Silence Will Not Protect You* (London: Silver Press, 2017).
[55] Lorde, 'An Open Letter to Mary Daly', p. 40.
[56] Betty Friedan, *The Feminine Mystique* (Harmondsworth: Penguin, 1983), title of chapter 1.

are problems of women who are economically privileged enough to be able to afford not to work outside the home, a privilege which, in the twentieth-century USA of Friedan's writing, was a privilege mainly reserved for white women.

In general, hooks argues that black women are often ignored by both the feminist and the black liberation movements. Those movements use terms such as 'women' and 'black people' without acknowledging that what is really meant by such terms is 'white women' and 'black men', so that black women become invisible.[57] For example, when some women in the suffrage movement argued that 'women' should have the vote before 'blacks', what was really meant was that *white* women should have the vote before black *men*. Black women disappear from this picture. On hooks' analysis black women's experience of gender is not like white women's experience of it: there is an intersectionality between categories that requires its own theorising and activism.

While it is undoubtedly true that different women have different experiences and locations in the various dimensions of relative privilege, it does not follow that feminism does not make sense as a unifying movement. Women are differently placed in their abilities to compensate for the disadvantages of being a woman in patriarchy, and vulnerable to different aspects of a hierarchical society. But all women face the task of negotiating their identity as the dominated sex in a society that places great weight on the maintenance of gender difference.

A feminist insistence on the entrenchment of gender need not undermine the salience of other social cleavages; indeed, it may be that gender inequality is interwoven with other inequalities such as those pertaining to race and class. For example, Andrea Dworkin argues that the logic of gender inequality and the logic of racism are highly complementary.[58]

Another significant aspect of differences between women is culture. Multiculturalism has many similarities with feminism. Both argue that group identities matter: whereas liberalism tends to focus only on the individual, both feminism and multiculturalism point out that inequality can be based on other group identities (gender and culture). Both feminists and multiculturalists argue, as a result, that we should focus on marginalised groups, and criticise prevailing political structures for failing to secure equality for all. Indeed, both feminists and multiculturalists claim that existing political

---

[57] hooks, *Ain't I a Woman*; Elizabeth V. Spelman, *Inessential Woman: Problems of Exclusion in Feminist Thought* (London: The Women's Press, 1990); Kimberlé Crenshaw, *On Intersectionality: Essential Writings* (New York: The New Press, 2023).

[58] Andrea Dworkin, *Scapegoat: The Jews, Israel and Women's Liberation* (London: Virago, 2000).

structures or philosophical approaches cannot provide equality for all without significant change. And both feminists and multiculturalists are suspicious of 'universal' claims that actually reflect the standpoint of dominant groups, and insist that justice must take account of differences between people. As a result a significant number of feminist multiculturalists defend both the claims of culture and the claims of women.[59]

However, some feminists argue that multiculturalism is problematic for feminism—or, in the words of Susan Moller Okin, that multiculturalism is "bad for women".[60] According to Okin, most cultures are patriarchal; and, in multicultural societies, the minority cultures are often more patriarchal than the dominant (liberal) culture. For Okin, then, women and feminism are best served by a strong commitment to liberal universalism, and a focus on the rights of women as individuals.

1.2.2 The Existence of Patriarchy

Feminists add to the Entrenchment of Gender the thesis of the Existence of Patriarchy: gender *difference* means gender *inequality*.[61] Women suffer from gender difference, and men benefit. Feminists need not claim that patriarchy is an inevitable consequence of gender difference, but they do claim that it accompanies actually existing difference in actually existing societies. The Existence of Patriarchy is thus an empirical claim about the position of women and men in society. Feminists employ a variety of methods to establish the Existence of Patriarchy, some of which are familiar to non-feminist social theorists. Other methods, such as consciousness-raising, are specifically feminist.[62]

---

[59] Ayelet Shachar, *Multicultural Jurisdictions: Cultural Differences and Women's Rights* (Cambridge: Cambridge University Press, 2001); Iris Marion Young, *Justice and the Politics of Difference* (Princeton, NJ: Princeton University Press, 1990).

[60] Susan Moller Okin, 'Is Multiculturalism Bad for Women?', in Susan Moller Okin, Joshua Cohen, Matthew Howard, and Martha Nussbaum (eds), *Is Multiculturalism Bad for Women?* (Princeton, NJ: Princeton University Press, 1999).

[61] I use the term 'patriarchy' to refer to a society characterised by inequality between women and men, with men as the advantaged and women the disadvantaged. This definition does *not* entail claims such as: men are in positions of power, political or otherwise; men actively choose and maintain inequality while women are passive victims; there is a male conspiracy; men like inequality and women dislike it; all men are better off than all women. Some of these claims may be true of any particular patriarchal society, but none of them are necessary, individually or jointly.

[62] Catharine MacKinnon describes consciousness-raising as "feminism's method" (MacKinnon, *Toward A Feminist Theory of the State*, p. 83). For further discussion of consciousness-raising, see Chambers, *Sex, Culture, and Justice*, pp. 58–63 and Clare Chambers and Phil Parvin, 'What Kind of Dialogue Do We Need? Gender, Deliberation and Comprehensive Values', in Jude Browne (ed.), *Dialogue, Politics and Gender* (2013).

As with each of the three feminist theses, the Existence of Patriarchy is developed in different ways within feminism. The simplest conception of a patriarchal society, and the one associated with liberal feminism, is one in which there are clear, measurable inequalities: unequal legal rights, sex discrimination, unequal pay, unequal representation in the job market and in positions of power.

Unequal legal rights have been the lot of women in most societies, and those societies which are now broadly equal in this respect have become so only recently.[63] Fights for women's rights to vote, to hold property, to have custody of their children, to be educated, to be employed, to be considered as legal persons, to have bodily integrity, and to retain these rights even if married or mothers, have been crucial and arduous feminist struggles. Unequal representation and unequal pay are, for most feminists, both symptoms and causes of patriarchy. Because women are relatively powerless they are unable to access powerful positions and command high (or just equal) salaries. Because women tend to be paid less than men their interests and careers tend to be subordinated to those of men. And because women lack power, in politics and in business, it is difficult for them to change these facts.

Liberal feminists face an enormous challenge when asserting the Existence of Patriarchy: the Fetishism of Choice discussed above. Choice is a key liberal value: for a liberal, one respects individuals by respecting their choices. And so liberals are always vulnerable to the charge that a putative unjust inequality is actually a chosen, and therefore just, inequality. Within liberalism choice is what I call a *normative transformer*: something that, by its mere presence, transforms an unjust (because unequal) situation into a just one. For example, it might be said of a woman who becomes economically dependent on her husband by leaving paid employment in favour of domestic work that the subsequent inequality between husband and wife is unproblematic because it results from a choice.

Liberal feminists must adopt one of the following strategies in response. On the one hand, a liberal feminist might bite the bullet, arguing that any woman who chooses an unequal position for herself is therefore not oppressed. A lot then hangs on the concept of choice. If choice is defined as the mere absence of coercion liberal feminism becomes a very weak ideology, indistinguishable from liberalism that is not specifically feminist. The Entrenchment of Gender hardly matters to such a position.

---

[63] For example, the vote was not extended to all women until 1928 in the UK and 1920 in the USA. Britain has had only one female prime minister out of 53, and there has never been a female president of the USA.

On the other hand, the liberal feminist might dispute the extent to which women really do choose things that make themselves unequal. She might argue that much of our action is socially mandated, that many of our preferences are socially constructed, and that even if we choose certain activities (such as mothering) we do not choose that those activities should bring with them decreased status and resources.[64] Indeed, it is a hallmark of most feminist thought to recognise the pervasiveness of social construction, for this recognition makes sense of the otherwise puzzling entrenchment of gender difference despite legal change. As a result many feminists move away from liberal theory's relative disregard for the cultural conditions of choice and towards radical analysis and critique of social construction.

Analysis and critical perspectives on social construction that can be useful to feminism can come from social theorists who do not themselves explore gender,[65] from social theorists who sometimes consider gender,[66] and from theorists who are explicitly feminist.[67] Jane Flax argues that this recognition of social construction invites an affinity between feminism and postmodernism.[68] And yet, as Flax also notes, the relationship between feminism and postmodern theory is a tense one. Feminists emphasise the existence of patriarchal social construction and the insufficiency of free choice, but feminism is also a movement that is based on listening to the experiences of women and valuing their choices. Feminists are thus uneasy with a position that implies that women are acting wrongly.

The tension between valuing women's choices and recognising social construction is lessened by the feminist thesis of the Existence of Patriarchy, and the feminist commitment to consciousness-raising. The Existence of Patriarchy reminds us that women (and men) are choosing and acting within a patriarchal context. It therefore follows that both our options and our preferences are shaped by this context. We *can* only act within the options that are available to us. And we *want* to act in ways that situate us happily within a social context, as deserving of social approval. Moreover, it is rational for us to make choices that are compatible with the options open to us and the expectations placed on us, for such choices enable us to succeed within our social context. Choices made from within constraints are not necessarily poor choices.

---

[64] Chambers, *Sex, Culture, and Justice*.
[65] Michel Foucault, *Discipline and Punish: The Birth of the Prison* (Harmondsworth: Penguin, 1991).
[66] Bourdieu, *Masculine Domination*. [67] Greer, *The Female Eunuch*.
[68] Jane Flax, 'Postmodernism and Gender Relations in Feminist Theory', in Kemp and Squires (eds), *Feminisms*, p. 173.

The feminist method of consciousness-raising also enables feminists to highlight the constraints on women's action at the same time as valuing women's experiences.[69] Consciousness-raising is the process by which group reflection on the everyday lives of their members highlights and makes explicit commonalities of experience and broader political phenomena. If women's experiences are profoundly shaped by patriarchy, then introspection on and discussion of those experiences goes beyond the individual and provides insight into the structures of patriarchy.[70]

1.2.3 The Need for Change

All feminists are committed to the Need for Change. One cannot be a feminist without believing that the gender inequality highlighted by the first two theses is unjust and must be abolished. Feminism is thus inherently a reforming or revolutionary movement. But this commitment to change also leaves feminism particularly vulnerable to internal disputes. Feminists want to change aspects of current society and to label existing social arrangements as unjust. Moreover, feminists locate many of the injustices of patriarchy within personal life: in our intimate relationships with our families, in our sexual behaviour, in our appearance. It is unsurprising that women as well as men can feel threatened by the challenges of feminism.

It is thus crucial to feminism as an ideology to articulate the Need for Change clearly and persuasively. Some areas for reform are uncontroversial both within and without feminism—for example, most citizens in liberal democracies will agree that there should be legal equality between the sexes. Other reforms are uncontroversial within feminism but face challenges in the mainstream, such as the idea that equality in the workplace requires more than simple legal anti-discrimination measures as these have proved consistent with a persistent gender pay gap. Still more reforms are controversial even within feminism, with ongoing debates about what feminism implies for such things as pornography, sex work, and gender identity.

One way of making sense of the panoply of feminist reforms is to think in terms of reforming each of the first two Theses of Feminism. Some feminists want to change the Entrenchment of Gender, arguing that gender categories

---

[69] Men's actions are also constrained by patriarchy, and there were consciousness-raising groups for men, but feminism has focused on women's experiences.
[70] Chambers, *Sex, Culture, and Justice*; Chambers and Parvin, 'What Kind of Dialogue Do We Need?'.

themselves must be transcended. One approach to transcendence, known as genderqueer, builds on aspects of trans* and queer theory to develop a vision of a society that is not built on the gender binary of male v. female.[71] Some trans theorists, such as Kate Bornstein, also advocate the demolition of gender as a system of classification.[72] Butler develops a theory that is based both on unsettling the gender binary through parodies such as drag and on developing a transformative politics.[73] Nancy Fraser argues, from a socialist/postcolonial perspective, for a transformative reconfiguration of group identities such as gender.[74] Liberal feminist Okin urges her readers to "put our best efforts into promoting the elimination of gender".[75] These and other feminists who advocate changes to the Entrenchment of Gender do so because they argue that such changes will also have implications for patriarchy. So Okin argues that eliminating gender will facilitate equality within the family and lead to a "humanist justice", and Fraser argues that transformation is needed to overcome the twin injustices of recognition and redistribution that women and other "bivalent groups" suffer.[76]

Radical feminism is an excellent example of a feminist analysis of patriarchy that sees gender difference and gender inequality as deeply entangled.[77] For radical feminists patriarchy is a system and ideology based on male domination and female submission. That is to say, patriarchal gender norms cast the male as dominant and the female as submissive, an elucidation of gender difference that is inherently unequal. Radical feminists argue that patriarchy upholds this form of gender difference in all areas of life: in family life, in the workplace, in public political life. But its logic can most clearly be seen in patriarchal understandings of sex, and in the sexual practices and industries that are so central to Western societies: prostitution, pornography, rape, and child abuse. All feminists see ending sexual violence as a priority, but radical feminists insist that this is not a goal that can be achieved merely by legal remedies that do not disrupt the underlying gender system. For example, rape tends to have very low prosecution rates, such that laws against rape do not act as an effective deterrent or punishment.[78] Sexual violence is not an

---

[71] Joan Nestle, Clare Howell, and Riki Anne Wilchins (eds), *GenderQueer: Voices from Beyond the Sexual Binary* (Boston, MA: Alyson Books, 2002).
[72] Bornstein, *Gender Outlaw*.   [73] Butler, *Gender Trouble*.
[74] Fraser, *Justice Interruptus*.
[75] Susan Moller Okin, *Justice, Gender, and the Family* (New York: Basic Books, 1989), p. 184.
[76] Okin, *Justice, Gender, and the Family*, p. 184; Fraser, *Justice Interruptus*, pp. 16ff.
[77] Radical feminists include Catharine MacKinnon, Andrea Dworkin, Sheila Jeffreys, Shulamith Firestone, Mary Daly, and Robin Morgan, to name but a few.
[78] Sue Lees, *Carnal Knowledge: Rape on Trial* (London: The Women's Press, 2002).

aberration but part and parcel of a system that treats women as sexual objects to be bought and sold to meet men's desires and maintain their position of dominance.

Other feminisms (or other aspects of feminism) focus on the need to change the patriarchal associations of gender difference, rather than that difference itself. So difference feminists argue that gender equality can be compatible with gender difference, even if current patriarchal structures prevent this. Such feminists argue that justice requires that feminine roles are properly valued and rewarded, and that the women who take them on are afforded the status traditionally reserved for male activities. It is not enough, then, to be content with the status quo: extensive political and social change is required.

The most prominent idea of difference feminism is the ethics of care.[79] The thesis of the ethics of care is that there are two different ways of thinking about morality, one based on justice (impersonal, abstract, impartial rules of entitlement) and one based on care (relational, particular, nuanced duties and obligations). Proponents of the ethics of care claim that these modes of moral thinking are gendered, with women associated with care and men associated with justice. Equality for such feminists requires not the elimination of difference but a revaluing of women's distinctiveness: care-based thinking needs to be recognised as a distinct and valuable method of being and acting in the world, not dismissed as a facet of unreason. Associated with this valuing of traditionally female thinking is the valuing of traditionally female activities, such as caring work.

Difference feminists are indeed feminists because they recognise that inequality attaches to women's identification with distinct activities such as care, even if they argue for the preservation of these activities or their femininity. In other words, difference feminists envisage a world in which difference is compatible with inequality, but they argue that such a world is not our world.

Another way of asking what is required by the Need For Change is to ask how and why patriarchy accompanies gender. For some feminists the answer lies beyond either patriarchy or gender: other social phenomena account for the inequality between men and women. Thus Marxist and socialist feminists situate gender inequality within the broader ambit of economic and class

---

[79] Carol Gilligan, *In a Different Voice* (Cambridge, MA: Harvard University Press, 1982); Virginia Held, *The Ethics of Care* (Oxford: Oxford University Press, 2005).

inequality that are endemic to capitalism.[80] More recently, feminists have begun to analyse the gendered implications and effects of the global system of politics and of globalisation. They point out that women are adversely and specifically affected by many aspects of globalisation, and that existing transnational structures for implementing global justice and human rights can ignore the position of women.[81] Such work opens up an ever-expanding arena in which change must occur.

1.3 Conclusion

This chapter has touched on just a small sample of feminist thinking. But it aims to capture the challenges facing feminism in the current context. In Western liberal orthodoxy, patriarchy rarely publicly presents women as inferior; instead it presents women as differently choosing. The fact that this re-presentation does nothing to shift women's material position in society: their disproportionate vulnerability to economic disadvantage, to sexual violence, to clashes between career and family, to under-representation in formal power structures, is somehow obscured. Feminists expose gender inequality and demand its abolition.

Freedom and Equality: Essays on Liberalism and Feminism. Clare Chambers, Oxford University Press.
© Clare Chambers 2024. DOI: 10.1093/9780191919480.003.0002

---

[80] Angela Yvonne Davis, *Women, Race and Class* (New York: Vintage Press, 1983); Christine Delphy, *Close to Home: A Materialist Analysis of Women's Oppression* (Amherst, MA: University of Massachusetts Press, 1984).
[81] Alison Jaggar, 'Global Gender Justice Edition', *Philosophical Topics* 37 (2009); Sheila Jeffreys, *The Industrial Vagina: The Political Economy of the Global Sex Trade* (London: Routledge, 2008); MacKinnon, *Are Women Human?*

2
Feminism on Liberalism

For some feminists, liberalism is little more than patriarchy in disguise; for others, it is the framework for securing justice.[1] Feminism, like all other positions in political philosophy, is a range of views rather than a single determinate viewpoint. One aspect of this range is that feminism includes both academics and activists, for whom the term 'liberalism' can signify rather different things; after all, liberalism is not one single thing either.

In this chapter, I start by considering feminist criticisms of liberalism. I discuss two aspects of feminist critique: first, academic feminist critiques of non-feminist liberal philosophy; second, activist feminist critiques of what is variously called 'choice feminism', 'third-wave feminism', or simply 'liberal feminism'.

I then move to those feminists who endorse liberalism and argue that a suitably modified liberalism offers the best path to gender equality. This position, 'feminist liberalism', is mostly found in contemporary Anglo-American political philosophy. Feminist liberals understand liberalism as a commitment to substantive, demanding principles of justice based on freedom and equality. Included in this section are those feminist approaches that combine radical feminism's insights about the limitations of individual choice with feminist liberalism's commitment to autonomy, equality, and justice.

2.1 Feminist Critiques of Liberalism

To get a handle on feminist critiques of liberalism we first need an account of what liberalism is. Paradigmatic twentieth-century liberal John Rawls defines liberal accounts of justice as having "three main elements: a list of equal basic rights and liberties, a priority for these freedoms, and an assurance that all members of society have adequate all-purpose means to make use of these

---

[1] This chapter was originally published in Ann Garry, Serene J. Khader, and Alison Stone (eds), *The Routledge Companion to Feminist Philosophy* (Routledge, 2017). I am grateful to the editors of that volume for their comments.

rights and liberties".[2] A simplified version of Rawls' account would describe contemporary liberalism as combining two key values: freedom and equality. Liberals want individuals to have a significant and protected domain of freedom, they believe that individuals are equally eligible for this freedom, and they believe that this freedom requires a certain amount of, and possibly equal, economic resources.

Beyond these basic liberal premises there is much variation. For example, some but not all liberals base their understanding of justice and obligation on a contractarian view of relationships between individuals, and between individuals and the state. Liberals also differ in how they understand freedom—is it constituted by the mere absence of coercion, or does it require the presence of rationality? All liberals utilise some sort of distinction between the public or political sphere, considered to be the appropriate place for politics and power, and the private or non-political sphere, considered to be the appropriate place for non-interference. Once again, there is significant variation in the detail.

A detailed, critical account of liberalism is offered by radical feminist Catharine MacKinnon in her landmark work *Toward a Feminist Theory of the State*. MacKinnon identifies five aspects of liberal theory: individualism, naturalism, voluntarism, idealism, and moralism.[3] For MacKinnon, each of these is problematic and must be rejected. Feminism, she argues, must necessarily be radical rather than liberal.

Individualism means that liberalism sees people as individuals first and foremost, and assesses the political position of each individual separately. John Stuart Mill, for example, devotes much of his *On Liberty* to defending the rights and interests of the individual and the need for individuality in living; Rawls criticises utilitarian theory for failing to respect the separateness of persons.[4] Radical feminism, in contrast, sees people as necessarily socially constructed and analyses their freedom and equality as a structural aspect of the social group to which they belong.[5]

Naturalism means that liberalism assumes that there is such a thing as human nature. For classical liberals, accounts of human nature are often

---

[2] John Rawls, *Lectures on the History of Political Philosophy* (Cambridge, MA: Harvard University Press, 2007), p. 12.

[3] Catharine A. MacKinnon, *Toward a Feminist Theory of the State* (Cambridge, MA: Harvard University Press, 1989), p. 45.

[4] John Stuart Mill, 'On Liberty', in *Utilitarianism, On Liberty, Considerations on Representative Government* (London: Everyman 1993 [1859]); John Rawls, *A Theory of Justice* (Oxford: Oxford University Press, 1971).

[5] MacKinnon, *Toward a Feminist Theory of the State*; see also Alison Jaggar, *Feminist Politics and Human Nature* (Totowa, NJ: Rowman and Allanheld, 1983).

substantive and gendered. For example, John Locke connects political power and freedom to a rationality that is denied to women,[6] and Immanuel Kant "constructs women as unfree subjects".[7] Some later liberals reject crude versions of essentialist gender roles: Mill argues at length that most differences between men and women are wrongly attributed to nature rather than culture.[8] Nonetheless, liberals generally assume that there is some biological truth to sex difference, and may employ a sex/gender distinction to separate biological from cultural roles. So, liberals might critically assess masculinity and femininity, but they tend to retain faith in male and female as natural, biological categories. For MacKinnon, feminism shows that even biological sex difference is social, since it is a social act to identify particular biological features as politically relevant and to create social hierarchy around them.[9]

Voluntarism occurs when liberalism conceptualises people as autonomous, choosing, intentional individuals. According to voluntarism people have freedom before and unless they are constrained by others. This way of thinking about freedom is often referred to as negative liberty, and is a central tenet of much liberal thought. Negative liberty means the absence of coercion, understood as intentional interference by other humans.[10] Liberals focus on minimising coercion: a person is free just so long as there is no other human being deliberately interfering in her actions, and the way to maximise liberty is to minimise wrongful interference.[11] MacKinnon argues that feminists reject voluntarism in favour of "a complex political determinism".[12] Our actions and our identities are socially constructed: they respond to the social conditions in which we find ourselves. But our actions also act as conditions for other people: we both respond to, and create, the social conditions in which we must all live. MacKinnon recognises and praises Mill's recognition that liberty is restricted by private oppression and social norms as well as formal coercive law, but for her his fundamentally voluntaristic instinct remains problematic.[13]

---

[6] Nancy J. Hirschmann, *Gender, Class, and Freedom in Modern Political Theory* (Princeton, NJ: Princeton University Press, 2008), p. 48.
[7] Hirschmann, *Gender, Class, and Freedom*, p. 62.
[8] John Stuart Mill, 'The Subjection of Women', in *On Liberty and the Subjection of Women* (Ware: Wordsworth, 1996 [1868]).
[9] MacKinnon, *Toward a Feminist Theory of the State*.
[10] Friedrich von Hayek, *The Constitution of Liberty* (London: Routledge and Kegan Paul, 1960); Isaiah Berlin, 'Two Concepts of Liberty', in *Four Essays on Liberty* (Oxford: Oxford University Press, 1969).
[11] Mill, 'On Liberty'.   [12] MacKinnon, *Toward a Feminist Theory of the State*, p. 46.
[13] MacKinnon, *Toward a Feminist Theory of the State*, p. 41.

Idealism means that liberalism tends to "treat thinking as a sphere unto itself and as the prime mover of social life".[14] Rationality, on this view, exists independently of action and of social context. This tendency can be seen in the core tenets of Enlightenment liberalism, in contemporary liberal theories that focus on idealised accounts of justice, and indeed in landmark early feminists such as Mary Wollstonecraft and Mill.[15] Radical feminism requires the rejection of idealism in favour of an account that sees consciousness as inseparable from the social conditions in which it is situated, and sees consciousness-raising as the method by which change can be effected.[16]

Finally, *moralism* means that liberalism proceeds in terms of principles of behaviour that are right or wrong in themselves, viewed in the abstract. Contemporary liberal theory provides many examples of this approach, with Rawls' principles of justice being the most prominent.[17] Rawls also distinguishes political and comprehensive liberalism. Comprehensive liberalism is a controversial commitment to autonomy and equality as essential parts of a good or valuable life, but Rawls argues that political liberalism is neutral between conceptions of the good and thus acceptable to all reasonable people.[18] Many feminists find political liberalism appealing as it offers a way of protecting equality while respecting diversity,[19] but others criticise it for failing to protect women adequately from cultural oppression.[20] A more general problem with moralism is that claims to neutrality and objectivity often conceal partiality and bias, specifically the bias of the dominant group.[21] Radical feminism proceeds in terms of an analysis of power and powerlessness, and aims for a redistribution of power as a precondition of a theory of justice.

A recurring theme in MacKinnon's account of liberal theory is thus liberalism's failure to understand the existence and significance of *power*. A number of contemporary feminists take up that theme, often using the work of

---

[14] MacKinnon, *Toward a Feminist Theory of the State*, p. 46.
[15] Mary Wollstonecraft, 'A Vindication of the Rights of Woman', in Janet Todd (ed.), *A Vindication of the Rights of Woman and A Vindication of the Rights of Man* (Oxford: Oxford University Press, 2003 [1792]); Mill, 'On Liberty'; Mill, 'The Subjection of Women'.
[16] MacKinnon, *Toward a Feminist Theory of the State*.   [17] Rawls, *A Theory of Justice*.
[18] John Rawls, *Political Liberalism* (New York, NY: Columbia University Press, 1993).
[19] Martha C. Nussbaum, 'A Plea for Difficulty', in Susan Moller Okin, Joshua Cohen, Matthew Howard, and Martha Nussbaum (eds), *Is Multiculturalism Bad for Women?* (Princeton, NJ: Princeton University Press, 1999); Christie Hartley and Lori Watson, 'Is a Feminist Political Liberalism Possible?', *Journal of Ethics and Social Philosophy* 5(1) (2010).
[20] Susan Moller Okin, 'Is Multiculturalism Bad for Women?', in Susan Moller Okin et al. (eds), *Is Multiculturalism Bad for Women?*; Clare Chambers, *Sex, Culture, and Justice: The Limits of Choice* (University Park, PA: Penn State University Press, 2008).
[21] MacKinnon, *Toward a Feminist Theory of the State*; see also Iris Marion Young, *Justice and the Politics of Difference* (Princeton, NJ: Princeton University Press, 1990).

non-liberal theories of power such as those of Michel Foucault to explore the ways that power exists in all social interactions, and is thus both the cause and the effect of gender hierarchy.[22]

A failure to recognise the significance of power is one of the five feminist critiques of liberalism identified by Ruth Abbey. The others are: a critique of *contract thinking*, a critique of the *public–private distinction*, a critique of the *gendered* nature of liberalism as a tradition, and the significance of *care*.[23]

Feminism's critique of liberal *contract theory* is most significantly stated in Carole Pateman's classic text *The Sexual Contract*.[24] Pateman argues that liberalism bases its ideas of freedom and equality on contract thinking, most prominently in social contract theory. Social contract theory is the approach exemplified by philosophers such as Thomas Hobbes, Locke, and Jean-Jacques Rousseau, who justify political obligation (the obligation we have to obey the law) by reference to some sort of contractual agreement between people, or between citizens and the state.[25] This contract may be explicit or tacit, actual or hypothetical. Social contract theorists argue that contract is a mechanism for preserving equality and freedom while justifying authority and constraint, solving the puzzle of how a liberal state could ever be legitimate. But Pateman asks how a social contract, supposedly based on free consent between equals, can justify the existing social order in which men and women are unequal. She concludes that women are excluded from the social contract both implicitly and explicitly. Instead of a social contract women are the subjects of a sexual contract, one that subordinates them to men in marriage and private life. Liberals continue to use contract thinking as a mechanism for securing freedom in areas such as economics, employment, and marriage. But, for Pateman, the sexual contract shows that contract thinking does not always secure freedom. If the parties are unequal, contract entrenches inequality.

Pateman's account leads to the feminist criticism of liberalism's *public–private distinction*. This distinction takes different forms in different versions of liberalism. In some versions of liberalism the public–private distinction separates a public sphere of government, law, economics, and civil society

---

[22] Judith Butler, *Gender Trouble* (Cambridge: Polity Press, 1999); Lois McNay, *Foucault and Feminism* (Cambridge: Polity Press, 1992); Caroline Ramazonoğlu, *Up Against Foucault: Explorations of Some Tensions Between Foucault and Feminism* (London: Routledge, 1993).
[23] Ruth Abbey, *The Return of Feminist Liberalism* (Durham: Acumen, 2011).
[24] Carole Pateman, *The Sexual Contract* (Cambridge: Polity Press, 1988).
[25] Thomas Hobbes, *Leviathan*, ed. Edwin Curley (Indianapolis, IN: Hackett, 1994 [1651]); John Locke, 'Second Treatise of Government', in *Two Treatises of Government*, ed. Peter Laslett (Cambridge: Cambridge University Press, 1994 [1689]); Jean-Jacques Rousseau, 'On the Social Contract', in *The Basic Political Writings*, ed. and trans. Donald A. Cress (Indianapolis, IN: Hackett, 1987 [1762]).

from a private sphere of family and intimate relationships. The public sphere, on this account, is the proper concern of politics and also of men, whereas the private sphere lies outside the purview of justice and is the proper location for women.[26] More recent versions of this idea include the Rawlsian notion that justice should apply only to the basic structure of society.[27] In other versions of liberalism the distinction concerns the appropriate scope of interference from others: interference may be legitimate in the public sphere but not in the private sphere. For Hayek the private sphere is an area of state non-interference, a necessary protection from coercion;[28] for Mill the public–private distinction is best understood as the distinction between other-regarding and self-regarding actions and should not be understood as corresponding to the distinction between public life and family life.[29] But many feminists point out that the public–private distinction, in whatever form, generally serves to exclude women's lives and activities from consideration as matters of politics, as relevant for justice, as areas of freedom or unfreedom, power and subordination, when in fact they are all of these things.[30] 'The personal is political' is a feminist slogan that insists that the distinction is untenable.

Much liberal theory pays no special attention to sex. Feminists argue that liberalism is a *gendered tradition*, sometimes explicitly and sometimes not. Susan Moller Okin identifies what she calls "false gender neutrality" in philosophers of all kinds, from Aristotle to the present day. Even if they abandon the use of "man" and "he" as generics in favour of gender-neutral terms, liberals and other non-feminists err by "ignoring the irreducible biological differences between the sexes, and/or by ignoring their different assigned social roles and consequent power differentials, and the ideologies that have supported them".[31] A prominent example of false gender neutrality is the 14th Amendment to the US Constitution (1868) which declares "No state shall...deny to any person within its jurisdiction the equal protection of the

---

[26] Jean Bethke Elshtain, *Public Man, Private Woman* (Princeton, NJ: Princeton University Press, 1981).

[27] Rawls, *A Theory of Justice*; Susan Moller Okin, *Justice, Gender, and the Family* (New York, NY: Basic Books, 1989); Abbey, *The Return of Feminist Liberalism*; Clare Chambers, '"The Family as a Basic Institution": A Feminist Analysis of the Basic Structure as Subject', Chapter 4 in this volume.

[28] von Hayek, *The Constitution of Liberty*. [29] Mill, 'On Liberty'.

[30] Arlie Russell Hochschild and Anne Machung, *The Second Shift: Working Parents and the Revolution at Home* (London: Piatkus, 1990); Okin, *Justice, Gender, and the Family*; Martha Albertson Fineman, *The Neutered Mother, The Sexual Family, and Other Twentieth Century Tragedies* (New York: Routledge, 1995); Claudia Card, 'Against Marriage and Motherhood', *Hypatia* 11(3) (1996); Eva Feder Kittay, *Love's Labor: Essays on Women, Equality, and Dependency* (New York: Routledge, 1999); Joan Williams, *Unbending Gender: Why Family and Work Conflict and What to Do About It* (Oxford: Oxford University Press, 2000).

[31] Okin, *Justice, Gender, and the Family*, p. 11.

laws" but goes on to guarantee the vote only to "male citizens". It seems that, at the time of writing, the only 'persons' were men. As MacKinnon puts it:

> Men's physiology defines most sports, their health needs largely define insurance coverage, their socially designed biographies defined workplace expectations and successful career patterns, their perspectives and concerns define quality in scholarship, their experiences and obsessions define merit, their military service defines citizenship, their presence defines family, their inability to get along with each other – their wars and rulerships – defines history, their image defines god, and their genitals define sex. These are the standards that are presented as gender neutral.[32]

Finally, a strand of feminist philosophy known as the *ethics of care* criticises liberalism for focusing on justice and abstract reasoning at the expense of care and relationships. Many feminists argue that liberalism fetishises abstract principles of impartial justice between isolated independent individuals.[33] This fetish is problematic for several reasons. First, it is based on distortion: all human beings are dependent on others. No human being reaches adulthood without extensive care from parents or guardians, and we all need care throughout our lives when ill or frail. Moreover, the sort of care that is required for human flourishing and even basic well-being goes beyond the provision of basic survival needs: we are fundamentally social beings who cannot do well without intimate, reciprocal relationships. It follows, according to advocates of the ethics of care, that a liberal approach to morality and justice that relies on abstract principles of impartial rights and obligations misses the most salient and valuable forms of human interaction and normative thinking.

The criticisms of liberalism discussed so far come from academic feminism. Contemporary radical feminist activists extend this critique to include what they sometimes call 'liberal feminism'. In the activist context, and sometimes elsewhere, 'liberal feminism' refers to a version of feminism that prioritises the individual above the social, and choice above construction. Liberal feminism of this kind is mostly located in popular culture and media, associated with terms like 'girl power', 'choice feminism', and 'third wave feminism'.

---

[32] MacKinnon, *Toward a Feminist Theory of the State*, p. 229.

[33] Carol Gilligan, *In a Different Voice* (Cambridge, MA: Harvard University Press, 1982); Jaggar, *Feminist Politics and Human Nature*; Kittay, *Love's Labor*; Joan C. Tronto, *Moral Boundaries: A Political Argument for an Ethic of Care* (London: Routledge, 1993); Virginia Held, *The Ethics of Care* (Oxford: Oxford University Press, 2005); Jennifer Nedelsky, *Law's Relations: A Relational Theory of Self, Autonomy, and Law* (Oxford: Oxford University Press, 2012).

It involves the claim that feminism means allowing individual women to make their own choices free from judgment, even if those choices involve participating in activities that other feminists criticise, such as pornography, prostitution, or cosmetic surgery.[34]

Radical feminists criticise this focus on choice. Miranda Kiraly and Meagan Tyler argue:

> Individualism lies at the heart of liberal feminism, championing the benefits of 'choice' and the possibility that freedom is within reach...Liberal feminism has helped recast women's liberation as an individual and private struggle, rather than one which acknowledges the systemic shortcomings of existing systems of power and privilege that continue to hold women back, as a class.[35]

For radical feminists, gender inequality is explained by structural patterns of male dominance, particularly centred around sex. Women are a sex class, subordinated by virtue of their sex and by the eroticisation of male dominance and female submission. Practices such as pornography, prostitution, BDSM, and beauty practices are thus not neutral *choices* but structural *requirements*, part and parcel of women's subordination.

2.2 Feminist Liberalism

In this section, I discuss those feminists who recognise and even endorse the strong critiques of liberalism just described, yet who still think that liberalism

---

[34] Naomi Wolf, *Fire with Fire: The New Female Power and How It Will Change the 21st Century* (London: Chatto and Windus, 1993); Rebecca Walker (ed.), *To Be Real: Telling the Truth and Changing the Face of Feminism* (New York: Anchor, 1995); Natasha Walter, *The New Feminism* (London: Little, Brown and Company, 1998); Jennifer Baumgardner and Amy Richards, *Manifesta: Young Women, Feminism and the Future* (New York, NY: Farrar, Straus, and Giroux, 2000); Claire R. Snyder-Hall, 'Third Wave Feminism and the Defense of "Choice"', *Perspectives on Politics* 8(1) (2010); for discussion, see Ariel Levy, *Female Chauvinist Pigs: Women and the Rise of Raunch Culture* (New York, NY: Free Press, 2006); Claire R. Snyder, 'What is Third-Wave Feminism? A New Directions Essay', *Signs* 34(1) (2008); Michaele L. Ferguson, 'Choice Feminism and the Fear of Politics', *Perspectives on Politics* 8(1) (2010); Nancy J. Hirschmann, 'Choosing Betrayal', *Perspectives on Politics* 8(1) (2010); Jennet Kirkpatrick, 'Selling Out? Solidarity and Choice in the American Feminist Movement', *Perspectives on Politics* 8(1) (2010).

[35] Miranda Kiraly and Meagan Tyler, *Freedom Fallacy: The Limits of Liberal Feminism* (Ballarat, Victoria: Connor Court, 2015), p. xi; see also Sheila Jeffreys, *The Idea of Prostitution* (Melbourne: Spinifex Press, 1997) and *Beauty and Misogyny: Harmful Cultural Practices in the West* (Hove: Routledge, 2005); Catharine A. MacKinnon, '"The Case" Responds', *American Political Science Review* 95(3) (2001).

is the best path towards women's equality. The feminists discussed in this section do not endorse the simplistic choice-based liberal feminism that has just been outlined. I refer to them as 'feminist liberals' to distinguish them from that approach. This section also discusses how feminist liberals respond to some of the critiques of liberalism raised in Section 2.1.

For feminist liberals writing within contemporary political philosophy, 'liberalism' signals the strongly egalitarian school of thought that is exemplified, in its non-feminist form, by the work of theorists such as Rawls and Ronald Dworkin.[36] Feminist liberalism focuses on the implications of that work for women, and on the question of whether the extremely demanding egalitarianism of this sort of liberalism is, or can be, enough to satisfy the feminist demand for gender equality. For feminist liberals, a version of contemporary liberal egalitarianism is the correct approach, perhaps after modification in response to the criticisms described in Section 2.1.

Martha Nussbaum is a feminist liberal who argues that three liberal insights are crucial to women. These are that all humans are "of equal dignity and worth", that "the primary source of this worth is a power of moral choice within them", and that "the moral equality of persons gives them a fair claim to certain types of treatment at the hands of society and politics".[37] Nussbaum endorses some of the feminist critiques of liberalism that have been discussed so far: she rejects the *public–private distinction* in favour of paying close attention to inequality within families and relationships; she rejects simple *voluntarism* and *idealism* in favour of recognising the social construction of choices, emotions and desires—although choice retains a prominent role in her account.[38] In these respects, then, Nussbaum endorses the general feminist critique of liberalism. But she argues that liberalism should not be abandoned. On the contrary, she argues that the liberal values of *individualism* and *moralism* both require liberalism to become more feminist, and provide reasons for feminism to be liberal.

For Nussbaum, the individualism of liberalism is not a problematic egoism or a denial of the significance of groups. Instead, "It just asks us to concern ourselves with the distribution of resources and opportunities in a certain way, namely, with concern to see how well *each and every one of them* is doing, seeing each and every one as an end, worthy of concern."[39] This concern is

---

[36] Rawls, *A Theory of Justice*; Ronald Dworkin, *Sovereign Virtue: The Theory and Practice of Equality* (Cambridge, MA: Harvard University Press, 2000).
[37] Martha C. Nussbaum, *Sex and Social Justice* (Oxford: Oxford University Press, 1999), p. 57.
[38] See Chambers, *Sex, Culture, and Justice* for discussion.
[39] Nussbaum, *Sex and Social Justice*, p. 63.

vital for feminism, Nussbaum argues, since "women have too rarely been treated as ends in themselves, and too frequently been treated as means to the ends of others... where women and the family are concerned, liberal political thought has not been nearly individualist enough."[40] In making this claim, Nussbaum endorses the feminist critique of the liberal *public–private distinction*. It is necessary to apply liberal principles within the family, and to the care work that is an essential part of human life, because both care and family have been a source of gender injustice. Liberals have largely failed to take that into account.[41] But Nussbaum believes that liberalism is up to the challenge: its commitment to individualism provides the conceptual tools and the conceptual necessity to do so, particularly if complemented by a focus on capabilities.[42]

Nussbaum also sees *moralism* and one version of *idealism* as strengths rather than weaknesses of liberalism. Moralism, recall, is the idea that there can be abstract principles of right and wrong or, as contemporary liberals would put it, principles of justice. Idealism is the related idea that reason is at least some of the way to get there. While it is true that reason and justice are historically associated with men, and tradition and emotion are associated with women, Nussbaum argues that reason and justice actually serve women's interests. As she puts it, "wherever you most mistrust habit, there you have the most need for reason. Women have lots of grounds to mistrust most habits people have had through the centuries, just as poor people have had reasons to distrust the moral emotions of kings. This means that women have an especially great need for reason."[43]

In a similar vein, Jean Hampton argues that *contractarianism* can actually help the feminist concern to secure justice in all relationships, including intimate ones.[44] Hampton's idea is that relationships can be subjected to a "contractarian test" that asks:

> Given the fact that we are in this relationship, could both of us reasonably accept the distribution of costs and benefits (that is, the costs and benefits that are not themselves side effects of any affective or duty-based tie between

---

[40] Nussbaum, *Sex and Social Justice*, p. 63.
[41] Martha C. Nussbaum, 'The Future of Feminist Liberalism', in Amy R. Baehr (ed.), *Varieties of Feminist Liberalism* (Oxford: Rowman & Littlefield, 2004).
[42] Nussbaum, *Sex and Social Justice* and 'The Future of Feminist Liberalism'.
[43] Nussbaum, *Sex and Social Justice*, p. 79; see also Anthony Simon Laden, 'Radical Liberals, Reasonable Feminists: Reason, Power, and Objectivity in MacKinnon and Rawls', in Abbey (ed.), *Feminist Responses to John Rawls*.
[44] Jean Hampton, 'Feminist Contractarianism', in Baehr (ed.), *Varieties of Feminist Liberalism*, p. 172; for discussion, see Janice Richardson, 'Jean Hampton's Reworking of Rawls: Is "Feminist Contractarianism" Useful for Feminism?', in Abbey (ed.), *Feminist Responses to John Rawls*.

us) if it were the subject of an informed, unforced agreement in which we think of ourselves as motivated solely by self-interest?[45]

For Hampton, this test enables us to take full account of a person's human worth and legitimate interests, and avoids making women into martyrs to others as the ethics of care threatens to do.

More specifically, various feminists find the work of paradigmatic contemporary liberal Rawls useful for feminism. Prominent among them is Okin, who criticises Rawls for failing adequately to take gender inequality to account in his actual writing, while at the same time praising his theory for having the potential to be profoundly feminist. Okin joins the chorus of feminists who have no time for liberalism's *public–private distinction*: justice must apply to the family, she argues, since the personal is political in four different ways. First, the private sphere is a sphere of power: "what happens in domestic and personal life is not immune from the dynamics of power, which has typically been seen as the distinguishing feature of the political."[46] Second, the private sphere is a political creation: it is law that defines what counts as a family or a marriage or a legitimate sexual relationship. Third, the private sphere creates psychological conditions that govern public life: it is an important school of justice and injustice (see also Mill 1868). Fourth, the gendered division of labour within the family affects women everywhere: it creates barriers in public life, as women are not represented in positions of power or when their words are not taken seriously in the workplace, in civil society, or in personal relationships.

Justice must apply within the family, then, and Okin is highly critical of Rawls' *A Theory of Justice* for considering only heads of households and for failing adequately to consider whether sex should be concealed behind the veil of ignorance.[47] "On the other hand", she argues, "the feminist *potential* of Rawls's method of thinking and his conclusions is considerable. The original position, with the veil of ignorance hiding from its participants their sex as well as their other particular characteristics, talents, circumstances, and aims, is a powerful concept for challenging the gender structure."[48] Justice, including as Rawls conceives it, is incompatible with gender difference and requires significant changes to all aspects of society. In his later work, Rawls directly addresses Okin's critique and concludes "I should like to think that Okin is

---

[45] Hampton, 'Feminist Contractarianism', p. 173.
[46] Okin, *Justice, Gender, and the Family*, p. 128.
[47] Okin, *Justice, Gender, and the Family*; Rawls, *A Theory of Justice*.
[48] Okin, *Justice, Gender, and the Family*, p. 109.

right."[49] Moreover, whereas Okin sees feminist potential mainly in Rawls' earlier work, other feminists argue that his later political liberalism best meets women's interests.[50]

Some feminist liberals argue that liberalism can—and should—take proper account of *care*. Eva Kittay argues that care and caring relationships count as primary goods in the Rawlsian sense, even though Rawls himself fails to recognise this, so that care is a crucial part of liberal justice.[51] Jennifer Nedelsky develops an account of relational autonomy that, she argues, speaks to both feminist and liberal concerns.[52] And Elizabeth Anderson develops a version of democratic equality that is both fundamentally relational and appeals to liberal egalitarianism.[53]

Finally, a number of contemporary feminists argue that it is possible to develop feminist approaches that combine a deep understanding of *power* of the sort that is found in radical feminism, critical theory, or post-modern/post-structural theory with a commitment to liberal values such as autonomy, equality, democracy, and universalism. For Nancy Hirschmann, feminism requires both a detailed understanding of the processes of social construction and a liberal-like commitment to freedom as a fundamentally important political value.[54] The problem with liberalism, Hirschmann argues, is that its conception of freedom is inadequate. What is needed is a "feminist freedom" with a "*political* analysis of patriarchal power"[55] and an understanding of how the very subject of freedom is shaped. Marilyn Friedman argues that the liberal conception of autonomy is vital for women, and that understanding it requires deep analysis of the limiting conditions of systematic injustice, subordination, and oppression;[56] oppression is also the focus of the work of feminist liberal Ann Cudd.[57]

---

[49] John Rawls, *Justice as Fairness: A Restatement* (Cambridge, MA: Harvard University Press, 2001), p. 176; for discussion, see Amy R. Baehr, 'Toward a New Feminist Liberalism: Okin, Rawls, and Habermas', *Hypatia* 11(1) (1996); Abbey, *The Return of Feminist Liberalism*; Chambers, '"The Family as a Basic Institution"'.

[50] Drucilla Cornell, *The Imaginary Domain: Abortion, Pornography, and Sexual Harrassment* (London: Routledge, 1995); Nussbaum, 'A Plea for Difficulty'; S. A. Lloyd, 'Toward a Liberal Theory of Sexual Equality', in Baehr (ed.), *Varieties of Feminist Liberalism*; Hartley and Watson, 'Is Feminist Political Liberalism Possible?'; Elizabeth Brake, *Minimizing Marriage: Marriage, Morality, and the Law* (Oxford: Oxford University Press, 2012); Amy R. Baehr, 'Liberal Feminism: Comprehensive and Political', in Abbey (ed.), *Feminist Responses to John Rawls*; Laden, 'Radical Liberals, Reasonable Feminists'.

[51] Kittay, *Love's Labor*; see also Brake, *Minimizing Marriage*.   [52] Nedelsky, *Law's Relations*.

[53] Elizabeth Anderson, 'What Is the Point of Equality?', *Ethics* 109(2) (1999).

[54] Nancy J. Hirschmann, *The Subject of Liberty: Toward a Feminist Theory of Freedom* (Princeton, NJ: Princeton University Press, 2003).

[55] Hirschmann, *The Subject of Liberty*, p. 217.

[56] Marilyn Friedman, *Autonomy, Gender, Politics* (Oxford: Oxford University Press, 2003).

[57] Anne E. Cudd, *Analyzing Oppression* (Oxford: Oxford University Press, 2006).

Seyla Benhabib argues that there is a "powerful kernel of truth" in many feminist criticisms of liberalism. Nonetheless, she argues in favour of what she calls a "post-Enlightenment defence of universalism", one which is "interactive not legislative, cognisant of gender difference not gender-blind, contextually sensitive and not situation indifferent".[58] In later work, Benhabib develops "discourse ethics", a version of deliberative democracy that draws on both liberal principles of freedom and equality and feminist/postmodern theories of power.[59]

Nancy Fraser argues in favour of a feminism that combines both an awareness of inequalities of power and recognition with a commitment to egalitarian redistribution.[60] Fraser identifies redistribution and recognition as "two analytically distinct paradigms of justice",[61] the former allied with liberalism and the latter with communitarianism and postmodernism. But women, she argues, face both distributive and recognitional injustice, requiring "socialism in the economy plus deconstruction in the culture".[62] Realising this sort of justice requires the sort of universal standpoint that liberals advocate: "all people [must] be weaned from their attachment to current cultural constructions of their interests and identities".[63]

Finally, in my own work I argue that the liberal reliance on choice is deeply problematic since it makes it difficult for liberalism to explain or criticise what is going on when people make choices that harm them.[64] For liberals, choices that harm only the choosing individual are normatively unproblematic; and yet social norms mean that many such choices are gendered. That is, women are strongly encouraged to choose or accept many harmful practices ranging from gendered appearance norms and sexual objectification to the gendered division of labour and explicit political and legal inequality. Liberals tend to argue that these inequalities are unproblematic if they are chosen, as in this example from Brian Barry:

Suppose...that women were as highly qualified as men but disproportionately chose to devote their lives to activities incompatible with reaching the

---

[58] Seyla Benhabib, *Situating the Self: Gender, Community and Postmodernism in Contemporary Ethics* (Cambridge: Polity Press, 1992), p. 3.
[59] Seyla Benhabib, *The Claims of Culture: Equality and Diversity in the Global Era* (Princeton, NJ: Princeton University Press, 2002); see also Seyla Benhabib, Judith Butler, Drucilla Cornell, and Nancy Fraser, *Feminist Contentions* (London: Routledge, 1995).
[60] Nancy Fraser, *Justice Interruptus: Critical Reflections on the "Postsocialist" Condition* (London: Routledge, 1997) and *Fortunes of Feminism: From State-Managed Capitalism to Neoliberal Crisis* (London: Verso, 2013).
[61] Fraser, *Justice Interruptus*, p. 13.
[62] Fraser, *Justice Interruptus*, p. 31.
[63] Fraser, *Justice Interruptus*, p. 31.
[64] Chambers, *Sex, Culture, and Justice*.

top of a large corporation. An egalitarian liberal could not then complain of injustice if, as a result, women were underrepresented in 'top corporate jobs.'[65]

In this example, Barry is using choice as what I call a 'normative transformer', something that transforms an inequality from unjust to just by its mere presence. This is a common move in liberalism just as it was in liberal or choice feminism. But it is deeply problematic to consider choice as a normative transformer.

The reason that choice is problematic is that we choose in a context of social construction. There are two main aspects of social construction: the construction of options and the construction of preferences. The social construction of options means that our social context affects which options are available to us and which options are cast as appropriate for us. The choice to be a rocket scientist, for example, is only available in a society that contains rocket science; and it will only be available to women if it is not set up as a role for men. The social construction of preferences means that we often want precisely those things that our society presents as appropriate for us. Extensive gendered socialisation means that women are more likely to want careers, activities, and products that are gendered as female and men are more likely to want things that are gendered as male.

But if our options and our preferences are socially constructed, it does not make sense to use those choices to legitimate the social context on which they depend. We choose things because our society makes those things available to us and, in large part, because it casts them as appropriate for us. Women are more likely than men are to choose family over career because gendered societies construct working life around the assumption that someone else will be looking after children, and social norms dictate that that person should almost always be a woman.

Liberal values still have a place, though. If social construction is not to lead to relativism (a situation in which we may as well rely on choice since we have no standards of judgment) then we need normative standards and a commitment to at least some universal values. Liberalism offers both. It offers the twin values of freedom and equality, so crucial to women's liberation, and it offers a variety of philosophical mechanisms for theorising those values as universal, crucial to ensuring that liberation is not the preserve of the privileged. What we need is an uncompromisingly feminist liberalism that takes social construction seriously.

---

[65] Brian Barry, *Culture and Equality: An Egalitarian Critique of Multiculturalism* (Cambridge: Polity Press, 2001), p. 95.

2.3 Conclusion

It is possible, then, to combine feminist and liberal insights, and many contemporary feminist liberals do just that. But why should feminists want to be liberals? As MacKinnon points out, liberalism has "yet to face either the facts or implications of women's material inequality as a group, has not controlled male violence societywide, and has not equalised the status of women relative to men.... if liberalism 'inherently' can meet feminism's challenges, having had the chance for some time, why hasn't it?"[66] Some feminists thus abandon the language and traditions of liberalism, arguing for, as MacKinnon puts it in the title of one of her books, *Feminism Unmodified*.

For other feminists, the language and "radical vision" of liberalism still resonate.[67] Liberalism has certainly failed fully to realise its commitments to universal freedom and equality, both philosophically and politically, but few if any liberals claim that the project is complete. The political and philosophical dominance of liberalism makes constructive engagement with it essential. Feminists cannot ignore liberalism, and liberalism certainly cannot ignore feminism. The question is how to realise both liberal and feminist commitments to genuine equality and liberation for all.

Freedom and Equality: Essays on Liberalism and Feminism. Clare Chambers, Oxford University Press.
© Clare Chambers 2024. DOI: 10.1093/9780191919480.003.0003

---

[66] MacKinnon, '"The Case" Responds', p. 709. [67] Nussbaum, *Sex and Social Justice*, p. 79.

3

Respect, Religion, and Feminism

Political Liberalism as Feminist Liberalism?

Consider three women:

REBECCA is a Jewish woman who rejects the practice of neonatal circumcision. Rebecca sees circumcision as a violation of bodily integrity, and considers it a gender injustice that boys are denied the legal protections from genital cutting given to girls.

NAOMI is a Catholic woman who is deeply committed to her faith: so much so that she wishes to become a priest. Since the Catholic Church does not ordain women she converts to Anglicanism and becomes a vicar in the Church of England.

IQRA is a Muslim woman who reads the work of Islamic feminists and admires those activists who protest sex segregation in mosques. However, out of respect for the traditions and members of her local mosque, she complies with sex segregated worship there.

Each of these women face conflicts between their religious faith, their feminist or gender analysis, and their personal freedom. Each of them chooses to resolve the conflict in her own way. Rebecca chooses to remain within her religion but rejects and reinterprets a significant tenet of it. She exercises first-order autonomy, choosing to conform only to rules and practices that she personally endorses. Naomi cannot exercise first-order autonomy in this way, since she cannot choose to defy the Catholic Church by being ordained within it. Instead, she exercises her second-order autonomy and decides to leave her religion. Only then can she pursue her first-order desire to become a priest—albeit at the serious cost of aspects of Catholic rite and faith that she endorses. Iqra chooses to remain within her religion and to submit to its local practices. In that respect she exercises both first- and second-order autonomy. However, she would strongly prefer a situation in which her local mosque changed its practices of sex segregation.

All three women exercise their choice. None are forced to stay in their religion. None are forced to submit to a coercive rule by doing something they oppose—although Naomi is forcibly *prevented* from doing something she deeply longs to do. In one sense, then, they are all operating freely as liberal citizens. Certainly, they are all in situations that most political liberals would regard as compatible with justice. But, from a feminist perspective, each is in a situation of injustice. If Rebecca's feminist analysis is correct, then the persistence of circumcision as an accepted or required practice is a persistent injustice to boys. From Naomi's point of view, her exclusion from the Catholic priesthood is straightforward sex discrimination that would be illegal in most other contexts. And from Iqra's perspective, her mosque maintains practices that are sexist and lacking in adequate Quranic justification. And so each is in a situation that suggests a clash between feminist and political liberal accounts of justice.

There is significant disagreement among feminists and liberals about the compatibility between their two doctrines.[1] Political liberalism has come under particular criticism from feminists, who argue that its restricted form of equality is insufficient. In contrast, Lori Watson and Christie Hartley argue that political liberalism can and must be feminist. This chapter raises three areas of disagreement with Watson and Hartley's incisive account of feminist political liberalism. First, I argue that an appeal to a comprehensive doctrine can be compatible with respecting others, if that appeal is to the value of equality. Second, I take issue with Watson and Hartley's defence of religious exemptions to equality law. Third, I argue that political liberalism can be compatible with feminism but that it is not itself adequately feminist. The chapter concludes that political liberalism is not enough for feminists.

Watson and Hartley's *Equal Citizenship and Public Reason: A Feminist Political Liberalism* is a much-needed intervention in the scholarship surrounding political liberalism. It is scholarly, progressive, and insightful. I agree with much of their analysis, and I learned a lot from it too. *Equal Citizenship and Public Reason* is a work of great significance and ambition. It should feature on all reading lists on political liberalism and feminist liberalism, and is worthy of very serious engagement.

Part I of the book engages in what might be thought of as traditional scholarship in public reason. Watson and Hartley explain and explore the meaning of

---

[1] A version of this chapter was originally published in *Journal of Applied Philosophy* (September 2020). I am very grateful to Lori Watson, Christie Hartley, Paul Billingham, and an anonymous referee for comments on earlier versions of that paper.

public reason liberalism, setting out its demands and implications. Their focus here is to develop a coherent account of the doctrine and to intervene in various areas of controversy and ambiguity in the work of John Rawls and his followers. Part I will be of great interest and use to scholars of public reason—regardless of their feminist commitment (or lack thereof). It is an admirable engagement with Rawlsian doctrine.

In Part II, Watson and Hartley turn to the argument that I find the most interesting and important, and that I focus on here. That is, they want to demonstrate that political liberalism is a *feminist* endeavour. Since many philosophers, including myself, have seen political liberalism's main limitation as that it is insufficiently feminist, this argument is of profound significance. If political liberalism is truly feminist, many criticisms of the doctrine drop away.

In this chapter, I focus on areas of doubt and disagreement. I actually agree with the authors on a great many areas of substantive policy and theory, such as their critique of prostitution and their defence of caring work as socially necessary work. We all share a fundamental commitment to feminism: though I cannot speak for Watson and Hartley I expect that, if forced to choose between feminism and political liberalism, they would choose feminism. (I certainly would.) In personal conversation, and in academic discussion in seminars and conferences, we agree far more often than we disagree.

These authors are my natural allies, and I look to them for guidance on many areas of political philosophy. My sense is that, in the vast majority of cases, the authors and I want the same things for society. So why do we have such different ideas about how to get there? In these comments I press some of the concerns I still have about political liberalism as a route to the shared goal of gender equality.

3.1 Respect and Public Reason

First, I want to put some pressure on the idea that the role of equality should be limited in political liberalism. For political liberals, the fundamental moral equality of citizens is a premise that underpins the theory, but it should be interpreted as requiring citizens to be treated equally only in the political context. Political liberalism leaves space for commitments to and practices of inequality within citizens' conceptions of the good.

To be clear: I agree with Watson and Hartley that political liberalism does entail limiting the role of equality. So this is not a doctrinal disagreement.

Instead, in my view the fact that political liberalism does limit the role of equality is a major problem with political liberalism; indeed, it is a reason to reject political liberalism in favour of comprehensive liberalism or some other form of egalitarianism, such as feminism.

In thinking about the demands of public reason, Watson and Hartley invite us to "consider whether it is compatible with showing proper respect for fellow citizens to appeal to one's comprehensive doctrine within public reasoning. We think it is not."[2] Certainly, public reason does preclude appeals to comprehensive doctrines, but is it correct to state that this restriction is necessary for *respect*? I want to put pressure on this claim in two ways.

First, whether an appeal to one's comprehensive doctrine is compatible with respecting others depends a great deal on what one's comprehensive doctrine is. Clearly, appeals to some comprehensive doctrines are straightforwardly incompatible with respect for others. For example, if we were discussing as citizens whether to pass or retain laws that make sex discrimination illegal it would not compatible with respect to argue in the following way: "There should not be laws against sex discrimination, because (according to my comprehensive doctrine) women are made inferior by God. It is their divinely given position to be below men, and so it is right that it should be legal to discriminate against them."

On the other hand, I suggest that it is perfectly compatible with respect for one's fellow citizens to argue in the opposite way. It is compatible with respect to say "There should be laws against sex discrimination, because women are morally equal to men (in a way that extends beyond the political recognition of their equal citizenship). Women are of *equal moral worth* to men and must be treated as such in all contexts."

It would even be compatible with respect for one's fellow citizens, or so I suggest, to say "There should be laws against sex discrimination because God has created women and men as equals." This claim is not a claim that is compatible with public reason. It is not a claim that political liberals could allow to be made in a public reason context. But it is a claim that is compatible with *respect*, for the simple reason that the principle being argued for—equality—is a principle that entails respect for everyone. A comprehensive statement of equality is precisely a demand for equal respect of all one's fellow citizens. It is compatible with respect because it is a demand for respect.

---

[2] Lori Watson and Christie Hartley, *Equal Citizenship and Public Reason: A Feminist Political Liberalism* (Oxford: Oxford University Press, 2018), p. 80.

Watson and Hartley may respond at this point to say that I have wrongly understood the concept of respect that they are appealing to. The sort of respect that we owe to fellow citizens in the pursuit of public reason, they may say, is not respect for their equal moral status as humans but rather respect for the fact that they hold different views from us. This sort of respect is necessary because political liberalism is concerned with the legitimate uses of state coercion. If the state is to force compliance with its laws, it is a requirement of respect for its citizens that it provides justifications for those laws that do not conflict with its citizens' own conceptions of the good. The point then is not whether our conceptions of the good are internally committed to respect; the point is that, by expecting others to be moved by our comprehensive doctrines and conceptions of the good, we are failing to respect theirs.

Certainly, there is a difference between respect for a person and respect for their opinions or beliefs. In my view, respecting others does not mean refraining from engaging with them on matters about which they disagree. On the contrary, I think that respect for others survives an attempt—or at least, a respectful attempt(!)—to persuade others to change their minds. We could go further, and say that an attempt to persuade another person shows that we have respect for them as reasoning beings.

There is an important difference between relying on a comprehensive doctrine to justify a policy that has already been implemented, and using arguments from one's comprehensive doctrine in a process of ongoing debate. If a policy has already been implemented and the only justification offered for it is one that relies on a comprehensive doctrine, respect for fellow citizens has not adequately been shown—on this I agree with the political liberal position. State coercion cannot be justified merely by recourse to a particular conception of the good.

But Watson and Hartley argue that respect goes further than the need to provide public reasons to justify actually existing state coercion: they argue that it is not compatible with respect "to appeal to one's comprehensive doctrine within public reasoning".[3] It does not seem right to suggest that respect is incompatible with offering a controversial argument in favour of proposed policy in the context of public debate. The Rawlsian idea, quoted by Watson and Hartley, of "argument addressed to others"[4] captures this point, because it emphasises two things. First, reasons put forward are *arguments*: they are positions that are meant to persuade and which, as such, are positions not

---

[3] Watson and Hartley, *Equal Citizenship and Public Reason*, p. 80.
[4] Watson and Hartley, *Equal Citizenship and Public Reason*, p. 80.

already held by the listeners. Second, these arguments are 'addressed to others': they are attempts to affect others and make them change their minds. It therefore is neither surprising nor problematic that some reasons put forward in the process of debate will be "reasons (grounded in comprehensive doctrines) that other citizens reasonably reject".[5] The point of debate is to offer reasons and arguments that one's interlocutor does not necessarily agree with, and to see if minds can be changed.

Respect is being treated as if you matter. An appeal to equality, even as a comprehensive value, affirms that everyone matters. It may not be enough to convince those who disagree, but it does not disrespect people to treat them equally.

3.2 Equality and Religious Exemptions

I turn now to a specific case discussed by Watson and Hartley, and by myself in my own work. This is the case of religious exemptions from sex discrimination law. The example that they and I focus on is the exemption granted in both our countries (the UK and the USA) to the Catholic Church, enabling it to ordain only men as priests. This is the exemption that affects Naomi, prompting her to convert to Anglicanism. In my own work, in particular *Sex, Culture, and Justice*[6] but also in *Against Marriage*[7] I argue that such exemptions should not be granted by a liberal egalitarian state. Watson and Hartley argue that exemptions can be justified by political liberalism and thus, since they endorse political liberalism, that exemptions like these are justified in general.

Watson and Hartley's defence proceeds as follows. First, they concede that there may be circumstances in which a religion's hold over "the background culture of society" is so absolute that Church discrimination against women threatens "women's position as free and equal citizens in society".[8] In such cases, they grant, religious exemptions from equality law may be unjustified. I agree. But this is a very strange case. If a sexist religion's hold over society is so absolute, it is unlikely that the society would have anti-discrimination law in

---

[5] Watson and Hartley, *Equal Citizenship and Public Reason*, p. 81.
[6] Clare Chambers, *Sex, Culture, and Justice: The Limits of Choice* (University Park, PA: Penn State University Press, 2008).
[7] Clare Chambers, *Against Marriage: An Egalitarian Defence of the Marriage-Free State* (Oxford: Oxford University Press, 2017).
[8] Watson and Hartley, *Equal Citizenship and Public Reason*, p. 123.

the first place. Put simply, such a society would not be a liberal society. It would not be one with the necessary public political culture to sustain liberal egalitarian justice.

The relevant case, then, is one in which equality between the sexes is recognised sufficiently for there to be a operational and generally supported regime of equality law, but in which there exist religions that do not endorse that regime as it applies to them. To put it in Rawlsian terms, the case of religious exemptions only applies to a well-ordered society, one in which the principles of justice apply, people generally understand what justice requires, and people are motivated by justice. In this paradigmatic case, Watson and Hartley argue, "a number of factors must be taken into account, which most likely support permitting a religious exemption for sex discrimination in employment."[9]

Their reasons for this position fall into two categories. First is a set of arguments that amount to the claim that religious sex discrimination isn't that bad, all things considered. So Watson and Hartley argue that religious discrimination "is not benign" but "its [e]ffect is blunted in the background culture by various other views."[10]

I am not so sure this is true. I think the effect of legally mandated discrimination against women by one of the major world faiths, one that lays claim to its own state, its own set of laws, and to the keys to eternal salvation or damnation, is pretty significant. Empirically, I think it fair to say that the Catholic Church has an immense impact on the lives of women and girls around the world.

But even if I am wrong, an argument that says 'discrimination isn't that bad really' goes wrong in confusing the *severity* of a wrong from the *wrongness* of a wrong. A first world problem is still a problem. A blunted injustice is still an injustice. A little bit of unjust discrimination is still unjust discrimination.

Moreover, there is an enormous significance, both practical and symbolic, to religious exemptions from equality law. Legal exemptions show that the state deems discrimination against women to be acceptable (or not that bad really). And that is, itself, very bad indeed. Moreover, political liberalism rests on the idea that there is a special sort of badness attached to state or basic structure inequality. So even if Catholic discrimination were not a great problem, *state endorsement* of Catholic discrimination remains a serious injustice. To put it another way: even if the severity of religious discrimination is lessened by the presence of competing cultural forces, it is worsened by being sanctioned by the state in the form of a legal exemption from anti-discrimination law.

---

[9] Watson and Hartley, *Equal Citizenship and Public Reason*, p. 123.
[10] Watson and Hartley, *Equal Citizenship and Public Reason*, p. 124.

This is actually an argument that Watson and Hartley make themselves in relation to polygamous marriage. They argue that the state should not recognise traditional forms of polygamy, in which there is a central spouse with more power than the various peripheral spouses, because doing so would involve the state in enforcing inequality. In their words, "there is a strong public reason argument for prohibiting this form of polygamy.... If there was a legal form of marriage in which one individual could be a center spouse with more power within each of his or her marital relationships and fewer obligations to each spouse, then the state will have to enforce different and unequal rights and entitlements among spouses. The state will be an instrument of inequality."[11] Watson and Hartley do not think that the state should be an instrument of inequality, and I agree. But of course this is precisely the situation in which a state allows religious exemptions from equality law. Someone who seeks legal remedy for religious sex discrimination will find their case unsupported by the law. The state will then be an instrument of inequality.

In any case, Watson and Hartley still need to show that religious exemptions are justified. They need to claim not only that exemptions are not too bad; they must also provide a second set of arguments that show why they are good, and thus why the exemption is justified while the legislative framework that generally forbids discrimination should remain intact. Typically religious exemptions are justified along a number of lines that appeal to liberal values. Key amongst these is the claim that religions should be understood as private associations, not as part of the public institutions that are essential to equal citizenship (in Rawlsian terms, not as part of the basic structure). That difference is supposed to justify excluding their discrimination from the non-negotiable equality of citizenship in public reason liberalism. Next it can be argued that liberals must protect individual freedom of conscience and freedom of association, and that these values justify allowing sex discrimination by religions.

The problem for any advocate of religious exemptions is explaining why religions are distinct. Liberal states and political liberal doctrine do not generally take the considerations of freedom of conscience and association as being adequate to excuse sex discrimination in the employment contexts of other private associations. On the contrary, sex discrimination law exists precisely to prevent private employers from discriminatory hiring practices, even where discrimination would further the freedom of conscience and freedom of association of those employers.

---

[11] Watson and Hartley, *Equal Citizenship and Public Reason*, p. 242.

In fact, it seems easier to justify sex discrimination in non-religious employment than it is within a religion. This is because employees who object to being discriminated against in a secular employment context can simply find another job. Assuming economic conditions such that comparable jobs are available in other companies, the discriminated-against employee will not be seriously disadvantaged by moving to alternative employment. But religious believers who object to being discriminated against will not find adequate recompense in switching faiths. What they want is to be treated equally in their own faith. The inadequacy of the option of changing faiths applies to all believers, but it applies particularly strongly to those, such as Naomi, who are so committed to their original faith that they seek ordination within it.

I make this argument in *Sex, Culture, and Justice*, where I also note that religions are not really like free associations since they deliberately include children and the adults they become, aiming to instruct children in faith and keep them there. Watson and Hartley acknowledge my position, but they think it 'overblown' when applied to adult women who have grown up inside the church. This is because, on their analysis, "under liberal conditions it seems unlikely that too many adult women feel trapped in their religion."[12] Whether this is true or not is an empirical matter on which I do not have data. However, this objection misses my main concern. The problem with religious exemptions from equality law is not that women may be trapped in their religion, unable to exit; it is that religious women may not *want* to leave their religion, but will find that exit is the only remedy for the discrimination they suffer. They must either leave, like Naomi, or comply, like Iqra.

A woman who wants to become a Catholic priest, or who wants her Church to ordain such priests, does not want to leave the Church. She wants to be recognised as a member of full and equal standing by the Church in which she may well have been raised and to which she remains deeply committed. She wants to be considered as an equal within that Church. Her freedom of conscience and freedom of association depends on it.

Again, the employment case is instructive here. An employee who suffers sex discrimination at work is not wronged (only) because she is trapped in her job; she is wronged because she wants to keep her job and not have to suffer discrimination to do so. Similarly, the significance of religions not confining themselves to free associations of adults is not (only) that adults are trapped within them; it is that adults did not give informed consent to being

---

[12] Watson and Hartley, *Equal Citizenship and Public Reason*, p. 125.

socialised and indoctrinated into a faith that denies their equality. This is a fundamental violation of liberal equality and liberal freedom.

Indeed, thinking of religious exemptions from equality law as necessary protections of freedom is already to hold a highly partial, inegalitarian view of whose freedoms count. Some religious exemptions do straightforwardly give more freedom to religious believers. Exempting Sikhs from laws forbidding the carrying of knives so they can carry a *kirpan* is like this. But exemptions from equality law involve allowing a religion to discriminate between its own members. We cannot therefore say that an exemption straightforwardly benefits or enhances the freedom of members of the religion, since some members of the religion are those being discriminated *against*, and their freedom of religion is thereby curtailed.

As I argue in *Against Marriage*, when the Catholic Church seeks to employ only male priests it wishes to enjoy a benefit that other employers do not have, namely freedom from the constraints of equality legislation, while at the same time imposing a burden on Catholic women that is not imposed on women outside the Church or on men at all, be they insiders or outsiders, namely exclusion from employment on grounds of sex. It also wishes to deny a freedom to Catholic women that Catholic men have, namely the ability to seek and be granted ordination. We cannot therefore speak of religious exemptions from equality legislation as being in the interests of that religion's members, or as securing freedom of religion, unless we clarify that we mean 'the interests and freedom of the religion's leadership and dominant group'.

Standard defences of religious exemptions often gloss over this fact and write as if the only interests at stake are those of outsiders, who are potentially harmed by being subject to a non-universal law, and insiders, who are benefitted from the exemption. But equality legislation *benefits* religious insiders who would otherwise be discriminated against, often religious women, and it is the exemption that harms them. They are harmed because they are not treated equally with respect to whatever matter is at hand: access to a religious marriage or divorce, employment as a priest, and so on. But they are also harmed by the denial of their religious freedom, since the exemption prevents them from practising their religion unless they fit in with the discriminatory practice.[13]

Similarly, Iqra's mosque practises sex segregation and is permitted to do so under UK Equality law, which grants extensive scope for religions to discriminate on grounds of sex and other protected characteristics in the course of

---

[13] These two paragraphs are edited extracts from *Against Marriage*, pp. 179–80.

their worship. But sex segregation does not benefit Muslim women and men equally, because traditional forms of segregation allow men to worship alongside the Imam in the main prayer hall, while women are placed behind screens or must use back rooms and entrances.

Watson and Hartley claim "a religious institution is a private association, composed of individuals who affirm, roughly, the same doctrine".[14] But the devil is in the details. Co-religionists share "roughly" the same doctrine. Who gets to decide which parts of the doctrine count and which do not? Usually, the men.

3.3 A Feminist Political Liberalism

Turn now to the central claim of Watson and Hartley's book: that their approach is a feminist political liberalism. Their claim is that political liberalism not only *can* be feminist, in the sense that it can allow for feminist conceptions of the good (a claim which they note is also made by Amy Baehr and S. A. Lloyd and with which I agree, as the example of Rebecca shows) but that it *must* be feminist.

In other words, Watson and Hartley argue that political liberalism rules out social arrangements that undermine women's equality. However, its route for ruling out unequal social arrangements is not a comprehensive commitment to the value of equality, for that would result in a feminist comprehensive liberalism. Instead, they argue that political liberalism is feminist via a commitment to the value of reciprocity.

Reciprocity, so they argue, "requires the elimination of social positions (created by norms, expectations, etc.) that compromise persons' ability to be viewed as free and equal citizens and have standing as equal citizens". This is not the same as full comprehensive feminist equality, because "The criterion of reciprocity does not require the elimination of gender altogether... It does not even require the elimination of all possible hierarchical notions of gender or social identities."[15]

The question then becomes twofold. First, is this reciprocity-based justification of gender equality sufficiently different from an equality-based justification of gender equality? Second, is this reciprocity-based justification of

---

[14] Watson and Hartley, *Equal Citizenship and Public Reason*, p. 125.
[15] Watson and Hartley, *Equal Citizenship and Public Reason*, p. 151.

gender equality adequate to be called feminist, in the sense that makes political liberalism *necessarily* feminist and not just *possibly* feminist?

My suspicion is that the answers to these two questions will pull apart from each other in a way that undermines Watson and Hartley's thesis. That is, if political liberalism truly is to be necessarily feminist then it will not be sufficiently distinct from a liberalism based on the comprehensive value of equality; alternatively, insofar as a reciprocity-based justification is distinct from a comprehensive equality-based justification, the gender equality that results will be too weak to meet the criterion of being fully and necessarily feminist.

No feminist critic of political liberalism doubts that it is committed to the formal equality of women and men. What they doubt is that liberalism, and certainly the political varieties of it, is adequate to the task of securing *full* equality. As Catharine MacKinnon asks, "If liberalism 'inherently' can meet feminism's challenges, having had the chance for some time, why hasn't it?"[16] For example, Watson and Hartley themselves argue that political liberalism is compatible with legalised sex discrimination, as I have just discussed. One only has to be a feminist who thinks that a society with legal sex discrimination is not an equal or feminist society in order to reject Watson and Hartley's claim that political liberalism is necessarily feminist.

In general, Watson and Hartley claim that "most comprehensive doctrines in modern democratic states are compatible" with their form of political liberalism.[17] Even if we grant that claim for the sake of argument, they must surely acknowledge that most comprehensive doctrines in modern democratic societies are not feminist. Moreover, many are not compatible with feminism.

Watson and Hartley argue that "We do not see why believing, for example, that God requires a kind of gender hierarchy in the church and home necessarily prevents individuals from also recognizing that persons regardless of sex are equal citizens and have certain entitlements and responsibilities."[18] The connection between believing in God-given hierarchy in the home and God-given hierarchy in politics may not be necessary, granted, although historical and current experience suggests that a connection is likely. How many Evangelical Christians in the USA would vote for a female president? Eighty-one per cent of them voted for a man who advocates grabbing women "by the

---

[16] Catharine A. MacKinnon, '"The Case" Responds', *American Political Science Review* 95(3) (2001), p. 709.
[17] Watson and Hartley, *Equal Citizenship and Public Reason*, p. 160.
[18] Watson and Hartley, *Equal Citizenship and Public Reason*, p. 161.

pussy";[19] polls showed that 48 per cent of white Evangelicals thought that Brett Kavanaugh should be confirmed even if Christine Blasey Ford's allegations that he sexually assaulted her were true.[20] One objection to political liberalism, and an objection that I press in my own work, is that it is naïve to think that formal equality and freedom of choice can survive independently, untouched by social conditions and wider social norms.

But even if I am wrong, and Watson and Hartley are right, so that it is not only possible but also generally the case that the recognition of women's equal citizenship can survive a belief in God-given male superiority, *feminism* is not compatible with a belief in God-given male superiority, even one that operates 'only' in the home and church. Iqra complies with her mosque's practices, but she does not believe them to be compatible with feminism.

The next question is what to do about it. I fully admit that it is not easy to work out what can be done about social and religious beliefs in sex hierarchy, and it is not easy to work out what sorts of state action are best. But a commitment to feminism must surely be a commitment to doing something about sex hierarchy, wherever it occurs; whereas a commitment to political liberalism is precisely a commitment to the state doing nothing about it in many cases. Feminism wants more than political liberalism delivers.

At the heart of the disagreement between Watson and Hartley and myself, I think, is not what political liberalism entails for gender equality. We may have some disagreements about particular cases, but in general we agree that political liberalism's implications for equality have limits. Instead, we disagree about whether the gender equality political liberalism secures is adequate for feminism.

Watson and Hartley note Susan Moller Okin's concern that political liberalism is inadequate for feminist purposes since it "is likely to leave unaddressed many of the obstacles to substantive equality women face."[21] Watson and Hartley state that their view "effectively responds to this worry" and that it "does not entail that comprehensive doctrines that contain some sexist elements (according to some) will necessarily be unreasonable".[22] In other words,

---

[19] Ed Stetzer and Andrew MacDonald, 'Why Evangelicals Voted Trump: Debunking the 81%', *Christianity Today* (18 October 2018), available at https://www.christianitytoday.com/ct/2018/october/why-evangelicals-trump-vote-81-percent-2016-election.html.

[20] Tara Isabella Burton, 'Poll: 48% of White Evangelicals Would Support Kavanaugh Even if the Allegations Against Him Were True', *Vox* (27 September 2018), available at https://www.vox.com/policy-and-politics/2018/9/27/17910016/brett-kavanaugh-christine-blasey-ford-white-evangelicals-poll-support.

[21] Watson and Hartley, *Equal Citizenship and Public Reason*, p. 158.

[22] Watson and Hartley, *Equal Citizenship and Public Reason*, p. 158.

they think it can be reasonable for a comprehensive doctrine to "contain some sexist elements". They do argue that political liberalism "can curtail the power of comprehensive doctrines to perpetuate the subordination of women" but only "with respect to the dimensions of social life central to equal citizenship".[23]

The broader question, then, is which dimensions of social life are central to equal citizenship, and which are not. Watson and Hartley argue that political liberalism can go further than is often thought in securing equality on issues such as marriage and the gendered division of labour. But the hallmark of political liberalism is that it does not go all the way towards securing equality, including gender equality. The egalitarian frontier of political liberalism is the barrier over which it cannot cross; but feminism can.

The point is that the sort of equality Watson and Hartley deem adequate for equal citizenship is not adequate to secure women's equality more generally, for the reasons they themselves give. As they conclude, "This is as much as any liberal view can do."[24] It may be as much as any political liberal view can do, but it is not clearly as much as any comprehensive liberal view can do. And it is certainly not as much as any feminist view can do.

I agree with Watson and Hartley that there are limits to what political liberalism can do to bring about gender equality. My conclusion is that political liberalism is not fully—not even adequately—feminist. Political liberalism is inadequate to forms of feminism that are not themselves politically liberal.

I applaud the aim of pressing the feminist potential of political liberalism. Political liberalism is a dominant form of liberalism, and anything which can push it and its adherents towards gender equality is to be welcomed. But political liberalism draws its distinctiveness from the limits of its commitments to equality (and autonomy, though I have not much explored that aspect in these remarks). There are, and must be, measures to promote equality that political liberals cannot take and in some sense think it would be *wrong* to take. In that reticence remains a feminist critique.

Freedom and Equality: Essays on Liberalism and Feminism. Clare Chambers, Oxford University Press.
© Clare Chambers 2024. DOI: 10.1093/9780191919480.003.0004

---

[23] Watson and Hartley, *Equal Citizenship and Public Reason*, p. 158.
[24] Watson and Hartley, *Equal Citizenship and Public Reason*, p. 158.

PART II
THE FAMILY

4
'The Family as a Basic Institution'

A Feminist Analysis of the Basic Structure as Subject

In Section 50 of *Justice as Fairness: A Restatement*, titled 'The Family as a Basic Institution' (hereafter FBI), John Rawls replies to Susan Moller Okin's feminist critique of *A Theory of Justice*.[1] Rawls states:

> If we say the gender system includes whatever social arrangements adversely affect the equal basic liberties and opportunities of women, as well of those of their children as future citizens, then surely that system is subject to critique by the principles of justice.[2]

The question of *how* Rawlsian justice might secure gender equality has been discussed by many feminists, most notably by Okin.[3] However, as I argue in this chapter, the Rawls–Okin debate raises more questions than it answers. Okin criticises Rawls for failing to apply his theory adequately to the family: she criticises not Rawls' approach in general, but his attitude to the family in particular. Okin argues that a consistent application of Rawlsian theory *would* secure gender justice, but that Rawls is remiss in refusing such consistency. In fact, as I show, Rawls' remarks on the family reveal a more fundamental problem with Rawlsian theory than Okin allows. It is not that

---

[1] This chapter was originally published in Ruth Abbey (ed.), *Feminist Interpretations of Rawls* (Penn State University Press, 2013). I thank Ruth Abbey, Chris Brooke, Andy Mason, Miriam Ronzoni, Peter Stone, and Andrew Williams for written comments on earlier versions of that chapter.

[2] John Rawls, *Justice as Fairness: A Restatement* (Cambridge, MA: Harvard University Press, 2001), pp. 167–8.

[3] For Okin's discussion of Rawls, see Susan Moller Okin, *Justice, Gender, and the Family* (New York, NY: Basic Books, 1989); Susan Moller Okin, 'Justice and Gender: An Unfinished Debate', *Fordham Law Review* 72(5) (2004), and Susan Moller Okin, '"Forty Acres and a Mule" for Women: Rawls and Feminism', *Politics, Philosophy and Economics* 4(2) (2005). For other feminist discussions of Rawls, see Ruth Abbey, 'Back Towards a Comprehensive Liberalism? Justice as Fairness, Gender, and Families', *Political Theory* 35(5) (2007); Ruth Abbey, *The Return of Feminist Liberalism* (Durham: Acumen, 2011); Amy R. Baehr, 'Toward a New Feminist Liberalism: Okin, Rawls, and Habermas', *Hypatia* 11(1) (1996); Corey Brettschneider, 'The Politics of the Personal: A Liberal Approach', *American Political Science Review* 101(1) (2007); S. A. Lloyd, 'Situating a Feminist Criticism of John Rawls's Political Liberalism', *Loyola of Los Angeles Law Review* 28(4) (1995); Martha C. Nussbaum, 'The Future of Feminist Liberalism', in Amy R. Baehr (ed.), *Varieties of Feminist Liberalism* (Oxford: Rowman & Littlefield, 2004); Stephen de Wijze, 'The Family and Political Justice – The Case for Political Liberalisms', *The Journal of Ethics* 4(3) (2000).

Rawls fails to apply his theory correctly to the family, but rather that the specific case of the family illustrates deep-seated difficulties with Rawlsian justice as a whole.

The problem, to give an outline, is that Rawls' ambiguous remarks on the family are comprehensible only at the expense of his fundamental claim that there is something distinctive about the application of justice to the basic structure. Okin criticises Rawls for failing to make good on the fact that the family is part of the basic structure. If he did make good, Okin claims, he would see that the principles of justice must apply to the family in a much more extensive way than he actually allows. As I show, however, the family is one illustration of the fact that how the principles of justice apply to an institution does *not* depend on whether that institution is part of the basic structure. This is a problem for Rawls because the distinctiveness of the basic structure is a crucial part of the political liberalism which, by the end of his work, has become essential to the Rawlsian project.[4]

In this chapter, I first outline Okin's critique of Rawls in more detail, and provide a valid formalisation of her argument against Rawls. I then examine the main premises of her argument and look for evidence to support Okin's interpretation of Rawls. I conclude that Okin's interpretation is flawed but nonetheless highlights problems with Rawls' claim that the basic structure is the subject of justice. I then consider and reject the argument that Rawls' theory is consistent according to what I call the 'whole structure view': that the principles of justice apply to the basic structure *considered as a whole*. Finally, I consider G. A. Cohen's argument that the basic structure distinction is problematic. I agree with Cohen's criticism of the distinction, but suggest that Cohen is wrong in situating the problem with the issue of coercion. I conclude that Rawls' position on justice in the family is at odds with his claim that the basic structure is uniquely the subject of justice.

4.1 Okin's Critique

In *Justice, Gender, and the Family*, Okin argues that Rawlsian justice has the potential to secure gender equality, but that Rawls fails to bring out this

---

[4] There is some controversy as to whether Rawls' introduction of political liberalism in the book of the same name represents a change to, or merely a clarification of, his views in *A Theory of Justice*. I do not attempt to settle that question here. My focus is on the complete picture of Rawlsian justice we have at the end of his writing career, according to which Rawls advocates political liberalism, the political character of which depends in part on the idea that justice applies in a distinctive or unique way to the institutions of the basic structure.

potential.[5] Okin argues that Rawls fails to note three consequences of his stipulation that sex is one of the unknown characteristics behind the veil of ignorance. First, that stipulation seriously undermines Rawls' claim that the parties in the original position are heads of households, since that implies that they are male and thus perpetuates patriarchal divisions of labour. Second, if sex were behind the veil of ignorance then those in the original position would be greatly concerned about matters that Rawls does not discuss, such as "many aspects of social gendering and sex discrimination as well as matters affected by biological sex differences".[6] Third, if sex were unknown then "families would certainly have to be taken seriously as part of the basic structure of society".[7]

Okin is right to press the first two problems, and I do not discuss them further here.[8] It is the third problem that is the focus of this chapter: that the family needs special consideration *because it is part of the basic structure*. Okin argues that *Political Liberalism* makes the problem worse, because in it and later works Rawls denies that the principles of justice apply to the family. Three passages from Okin illustrate her critique:

> Though he lists 'the nature of the family' as part of the basic structure, in *Political Liberalism* he also explicitly places families on the non-political side of the public-private divide.... Rawls also asserts that the family is like other 'voluntary institutions', such as churches and universities, firms and labor unions, and thus is not itself subject to the principles of justice or expected to run democratically. But this notion is simply *implausible*.... The notion that families are not distinct from other voluntary institutions is also completely inconsistent with the crucial place that supposedly *just* families play in Rawls's theory of early moral development.[9]

> If the family, unlike the other voluntary associations, is both *part of the basic structure of society and the place where a sense of justice is first developed in the young*, then does it not need to be *internally just*?[10]

> Only by allowing that his principles of justice apply directly to the internal life of families – which Rawls clearly resists –... could one revise the theory

---

[5] Okin, *Justice, Gender, and the Family*.
[6] Okin, '"Forty Acres and a Mule" for Women', pp. 237–8.
[7] Okin, '"Forty Acres and a Mule" for Women', p. 238.
[8] For detailed discussion of the second problem, see Clare Chambers, *Sex, Culture, and Justice: The Limits of Choice* (University Park, PA: Penn State University Press, 2008).
[9] Okin, '"Forty Acres and a Mule" for Women', p. 241. Emphasis in the original.
[10] Okin, '"Forty Acres and a Mule" for Women', pp. 245–6. Emphasis in the original.

so that it both includes women and has an effective *and consistent* account of moral development.[11]

Thus Okin argues that Rawls fails to make good on the implications of his theory: that, as part of the basic structure, the principles of justice should apply internally to the family. Indeed he explicitly denies that they should do so, drawing an "implausible" analogy between the family and voluntary associations. The result is that Rawls' theory "contains an internal paradox".[12]

The idea that the family should be "internally just", together with Rawls' formulation that discusses whether principles of justice should apply "to the internal life" of the family, is not fully specified. I discuss this terminology in detail later in the chapter. For now the family will be considered internally just if, considered in isolation, activities and distributions within it conform to the principles of justice. So, family members must enjoy equal basic liberties and equal opportunities with respect to family concerns, and any inequalities within the family must benefit the worst-off members.

The final phrase of this sentence is deliberately ambiguous: if the family is to be internally just, should inequalities benefit the worst-off members *of the family* or the worst-off members *of society*? Okin certainly claims at least the latter: Rawls is wrong, she argues, to consider heads of households as the units of distribution for the difference principle, and so we must look inside the family to consider the distributive shares of individual members when assessing whether a society conforms to the difference principle. This understanding of the family being internally just is one that I think Rawls both should and could accept. However, Okin also defends the former interpretation: that there should be a separate difference principle governing inequalities within the family, viewed in isolation from society as a whole.[13] I discuss and criticise this interpretation later in the chapter.

A valid formalisation of Okin's argument has the following form:

1. The family is part of the basic structure.
2. Rawls' theory entails that the principles of justice should apply internally to institutions that are part of the basic structure (but not to others).

---

[11] Okin, 'Justice and Gender: An Unfinished Debate', pp. 1538–9. Emphasis added.
[12] Okin, *Justice, Gender, and the Family*, p. 108.
[13] "I can see no good reason…to apply the difference principle to the property-holdings of a legislative body.…On the other hand, neither can I see any good reason…why the difference principle should not be applied within families" (Okin, 'Justice and Gender: An Unfinished Debate', p. 1564).

3. Therefore: for Rawls, the principles of justice should apply internally to the family.
4. Rawls states that the principles of justice should not apply internally to the family.
5. Therefore: Rawls' position on the family is inconsistent

This argument is valid, but it is not sound, and the problem is with Premise 2. Rawls does consistently affirm Premise 4. For example, he states "We wouldn't want political principles of justice – including principles of distributive justice – to apply directly to the internal life of the family."[14] Premise 1 is also repeatedly affirmed by Rawls; I discuss some ambiguities of the Premise below but conclude that they do not undermine Okin's critique. As for Premise 2, however, Rawls does state the claim in brackets but does not affirm the premise as a whole, and his theory does not entail that he should affirm it. Instead, Rawls argues that the principles should apply *directly* to basic structure institutions, and this locution does not carry the same implications as the idea of *internal* application.

I expand and reference these claims in the next sections, and show why Okin's argument that the principles of justice should apply internally to the family rests on a misunderstanding of Rawls. It is not new to say that Okin's interpretation of Rawls is problematic.[15] But my claim is that Okin's critique of Rawls nevertheless highlights very deep problems for Rawls' theory: problems that extend beyond family justice. As I show, the reason that Okin's interpretation is wrong is that Rawls cannot (indeed, does not) support his central claim that the principles of justice apply directly to the basic structure but not other institutions. Principles of justice do apply directly to some institutions but not others, but the difference is not explained by the basic structure/non-basic structure distinction. Okin is wrong about what Rawls claims for his own theory, then, but Rawls' theory is left extremely muddled. To put it another way, while the argument is invalid it remains possible that both conclusions (3 and 5) are true.

---

[14] John Rawls, 'The Idea of Public Reason Revisited', in *The Law of Peoples with "The Idea of Public Reason Revisited"* (Cambridge, MA: Harvard University Press, 1999), p. 159; see also Rawls, *Justice as Fairness: A Restatement*, pp. 163, 165.
[15] For other claims that Okin's criticism of Rawls is problematic, see Lloyd, 'Situating a Feminist Criticism of John Rawls's Political Liberalism'; Baehr, 'Toward a New Feminist Liberalism'; Nussbaum, 'The Future of Feminist Liberalism'; de Wijze, 'The Family and Political Justice'; and the discussion in Abbey, *The Return of Feminist Liberalism*.

4.2 Okin's Argument in More Detail

First, consider the grounds for Okin's critique. One passage from FBI provides some support for Okin's interpretation of Rawls. The numerical insertions indicate support for the relevant premises of the formalisation of Okin just given.

> [1] [T]he family is part of the basic structure, the reason being that one of its essential roles is to establish the orderly production and reproduction of society and of its culture from one generation to the next.... [T]he primary subject of justice is the basic structure of society understood as the arrangement of society's main institutions into a unified system of social cooperation over time. [2] The principles of political justice are to apply directly to this structure, but they are not to apply directly to the internal life of the many associations within it, [4] the family among them.[16]

Insofar as this short excerpt supports Okin's argument,[17] then it reveals Rawls making what seem straightforwardly contradictory statements within the space of two short pages. For Rawls claims that the family is part of the basic structure, and that the principles of justice should apply directly to the basic structure, but that they should not apply directly to the family.

The extent of this apparent contradiction gives pause for thought. Rawls is a serious, enormously important political philosopher, and it seems incredible that his view could be quite so muddled. A charitable reader should attempt to reconstruct his view so as to make at least some sort of sense.

How, then, might we reconcile Rawls' apparent contradiction? I do not attempt any reinterpretation of Premise 4: wherever he makes remarks on the subject Rawls does indeed state that the principles of justice should not apply internally to the family. Instead, I highlight ambiguities that modify Premises 1 and 2.

4.2.1 Premise 1: The Family Is Part of the Basic Structure

There are many places in which Rawls is unambiguous that the family is part of the basic structure. As well as in the excerpt from FBI quoted above, we find this claim made right from the start of *A Theory of Justice*:

---

[16] Rawls, *Justice as Fairness: A Restatement*, pp. 162–3.
[17] This excerpt is very similar to material in Rawls, 'The Idea of Public Reason Revisited'.

> For us the primary subject of justice is the basic structure of society, or more exactly, the way in which the major social institutions distribute fundamental rights and duties and determine the division of advantages from social cooperation.... Thus the legal protection of freedom of thought and liberty of conscience, competitive markets, private property in the means of production, and the monogamous family are examples of major social institutions.[18]

The family is part of the basic structure, then, because the basic structure is comprised of the major social institutions, and the family is an example of a major social institution.

Perhaps, however, there are two ways that one thing can be part of another. Imagine that you and I stand on a driveway and I draw a chalk circle around us. We are each 'part of' the circle in the sense that we stand within it and are encompassed by its boundaries. But we are not 'part of' the circle in the sense that you and I are not particles of the chalk that comprises the circle.

Some distinction of this sort may be going on in Rawls. Rawls characterises churches and universities as associations that are "within" the basic structure, and this category of being "within" seems distinct from the category of actually comprising the basic structure:

> Since justice as fairness starts with the special case of the basic structure, its principles regulate this structure and do not apply directly to or regulate internally institutions and associations *within* society.[19]

> The first principles of justice as fairness are plainly not suitable for a general theory.... The most we can say is this: because churches and universities are *within* the basic structure, they must adjust to the requirements that this structure imposes in order to establish background justice.[20]

Although churches and universities are "within" the basic structure they do not themselves comprise the basic structure: Rawls talks about the structure imposing requirements on them, and it could not do this if the two were equivalent. This passage, then, suggests a hierarchy between institutions that *comprise*, that *are*, the basic structure, and associations *within* the basic

---

[18] John Rawls, *A Theory of Justice* (Oxford: Oxford University Press, 1973), p. 7.
[19] Rawls, *Justice as Fairness: A Restatement*, p. 10. Emphasis added.
[20] John Rawls, *Political Liberalism* (New York, NY: Columbia University Press, 1993), p. 261. Emphasis added.

structure.[21] Churches and universities stand within the circle of the basic structure but they are not themselves made of chalk.[22]

This distinction would solve the contradiction about the family if Rawls' statement "the family is part of the basic structure"[23] meant "the family is within the basic structure" *not* "the family comprises the basic structure". Such an interpretation would make sense of his otherwise puzzling claim that "The principles of political justice are to apply directly to this [basic] structure, but they are not to apply directly to the internal life of the many associations within it, the family among them."[24] On this interpretation there would be no inconsistency in Rawls, and Okin's critique would be wrong. For when she says that the principles of justice should apply internally to the family because the family is part of the basic structure, she means that they should so apply because the family *comprises* the basic structure. But the family would not (on the hypothesis currently under consideration) comprise the basic structure, and so there would be no reason why the principles of justice should apply directly to it.

There are several problems with this solution, however. Firstly, it is not the usual interpretation of Rawls. Of course, this in itself is not conclusive: the usual interpretation could be wrong. But one might think that Rawls would have attempted to correct the usual interpretation if it were indeed wrong. Not only did he not correct it, but the words he uses naturally invite the usual interpretation. The phrase "the family is part of the basic structure" suggests more strongly that the family *comprises* the basic structure than that it is merely an association *within* the basic structure. After all, if churches and universities are associations 'within' the basic structure it seems that all associations are similarly placed. Being 'within' the basic structure looks like

---

[21] Andrew Williams also distinguishes between something being 'within' and 'comprising' the basic structure in Andrew Williams, 'Incentives, Inequality, and Publicity', *Philosophy and Public Affairs* 27(3) (1998), p. 229.

[22] Discussion with Chris Brooke, Thom Brooks, Daniel Butt, Jon Quong, Ben Saunders, and Andrew Williams (to whom I am very grateful) reveals that there is significant controversy as to whether churches and universities are part of the basic structure. Additional textual support for my claim that Rawls excludes them can be found in *Justice as Fairness: A Restatement*, where Rawls writes: "The principles of justice to be followed directly by associations and institutions within the basic structure we may call principles of local justice. Altogether then we have three levels of justice, moving from inside outwards: first, local justice (principles applying directly to institutions and associations); second, domestic justice (principles applying to the basic structure of society); and finally, global justice (principles applying to international law)" (Rawls, *Justice as Fairness: A Restatement*, pp. 11–12). Further support for the idea that churches and universities are associations and institutions within the basic structure, not part of that structure, is found in Samuel Freeman, *Rawls* (London: Routledge, 2007), p. 101.

[23] Rawls, *Justice as Fairness: A Restatement*, p. 162.

[24] Rawls, *Justice as Fairness: A Restatement*, p. 163; see also Rawls, *Justice as Fairness: A Restatement*, p. 10.

simply being 'within' society. There is no need to single out the family with statements like "the family is part of the basic structure" if all that is meant is "the family is an association within the basic structure, like every other association that exists within a society". Moreover, elsewhere Rawls refers to the family as an "institution of the basic structure",[25] a phrasing which once again suggests the family comprises the basic structure.

There are also good reasons within Rawls' theory to think that the family is part of the basic structure in the sense of *comprising* it, reasons which Okin rightly highlights. Rawls argues that the family does have a special place within society: it is a basic institution in that it plays an essential role in reproducing society and ensuring that citizens have the sense of justice that is necessary for society to be well-ordered. The family is different from churches and universities because of these extra features.[26] Indeed, Rawls makes these claims as an explanation of the claim that the family is part of the basic structure.[27]

There thus remains an apparent contradiction between Rawls' claim that "the family is part of the basic structure" to which principles of justice are to "apply directly", and the claim that the principles of justice "are not to apply directly to the internal life of the many associations within it, the family among them". This contradiction cannot be removed by modifying Premise 1: the family *is* a central part of the basic structure, and if there is a distinction between institutions that comprise the basic structure and those that are merely within it, the family belongs in the former category.

I turn now to Premise 2 of the formalised version of Okin's critique.

4.2.2 Premise 2: Rawls' Theory Entails that the Principles of Justice Should Apply Internally to Basic Structure Institutions (But Not Others)

Rawls certainly states that the principles of justice should not apply to the internal life of non-basic structure institutions: he affirms the bracketed part of Premise 2. In the *Restatement* he writes: "Since justice as fairness starts with the special case of the basic structure, its principles regulate this structure and do not apply directly to or regulate internally institutions and associations within society."[28]

---

[25] Rawls, 'The Idea of Public Reason Revisited', p. 163.
[26] Freeman, *Rawls*, pp. 101–2.
[27] Rawls, *Justice as Fairness: A Restatement*, p. 162.
[28] Rawls, *Justice as Fairness: A Restatement*, p. 10.

Notice, though, that in this formulation there are two things that the principles of justice do *not* do to non-basic institutions: they neither "apply directly" to nor "regulate internally" such institutions. This ambiguity is essential. The natural implication of many of Rawls' statements is that the principles of justice *do* "apply directly to" and "regulate internally" the institutions of the basic structure. However, while Rawls makes many references to the principles applying *directly* to the basic structure, he makes no reference that I can find to the principles regulating basic structure institutions *internally*. Whenever he explains how the principles of justice differ with regard to the basic and non-basic institutions he uses the idea of internal application only to describe what does *not* happen for institutions that are *not* part of the basic structure. The excerpt from FBI quoted earlier repeats this formulation: "The principles of political justice *are to apply directly* to this [basic] structure, but they are *not to apply directly to the internal life* of the many associations within it."[29]

If there is a difference between the principles applying "directly" and applying "internally" that is to rescue Rawls from Okin's critique of inconsistency then it must be the case that the principles of justice do not apply "directly to the internal life" of *any* institutions, whether part of the basic structure or not. Since we are told explicitly both that the family is part of the basic structure and that the principles do not apply directly to its internal life, it must be that the principles of justice simply do not apply to the internal life of basic structure institutions.[30]

Moreover, as we have seen, Rawls explains that the principles do not apply to the internal life of non-basic structure institutions such as churches and universities. So Rawls introduces a red herring in the many passages where he discusses the basic structure/non-basic structure distinction alongside the lack of internal application of the principles: the two concepts cannot be related if he is to remain consistent. The principles of justice do not apply to the internal life of *any* institutions. However, the analysis cannot stop here. To repeat, a central aspect of Rawls' theory is the idea that justice applies in a

---

[29] Rawls, *Justice as Fairness: A Restatement*, p. 163. Emphasis added.

[30] S. A. Lloyd makes this point: "The fact that an institution belongs to the basic structure does not imply that it is to be *internally* ordered by Rawls's two principles of justice.... For instance, a supreme court is an institution of the basic structure, but it is not supposed to decide individual cases affecting the wealth of the litigants according to the difference principle" (Lloyd, *Situating a Feminist Criticism of John Rawls's Political Liberalism*, pp. 1326–7). Emphasis in the original. As I show later, the fact that a supreme court should not act in this way is explained by the fact that the difference principle should not be applied in this way; other principles (such as the equal opportunity principle) do apply to the internal life of a supreme court, but not because it is an institution of the basic structure.

special way to the basic structure. There must therefore be something that the principles *do* do to the family "as part of the basic structure". The alternative to the idea of internal application that we find in Rawls is the idea of "direct" application.

There are several passages that both (i) support the Rawls-rescuing idea that there is a crucial difference between direct application and internal application and (ii) demonstrate how Rawls introduces the red herring of discussing claim (i) alongside references to the basic structure. For example, in FBI he writes:

> political principles do not apply directly to [the family's] internal life but they do impose essential constraints on the family as an institution and guarantee the basic rights and liberties and fair opportunities of all its members. This they do... by specifying the basic claims of equal citizens who are members of families. The family as part of the basic structure cannot violate these freedoms. Since wives are equally citizens with their husbands, they have all the same basic rights and liberties and fair opportunities as their husbands.[31]

So, the principles of justice do apply to the family in the sense that the family may not violate the freedom and equality of its members *as citizens*. Husbands cannot prevent their wives from voting, for example—one of the equal basic liberties that all citizens enjoy—and wifehood cannot be a status that legally removes one's right to vote. However, this requirement of justice does not apply to the "internal life" of the family. Wives are not required to have a vote inside the family on matters of domestic life.

May we say that we have found the way that the principles of justice apply "directly" to the family? Remember, in order to support Rawls' basic/non-basic structure distinction we are looking for a way that the principles do apply to the basic structure but not to other institutions (such as churches and universities). This idea, that the principles apply directly by imposing "essential constraints" on basic institutions, is supported by Rawls' just-quoted claim that the family **"as part of the basic structure"** may not violate the "basic rights and liberties and fair opportunities of its members". But there is a problem: the phrase in bold is unnecessary, since no associations, whether part of the basic structure or not, may violate the equal basic liberties of their members as citizens. A husband may not remove his wife's legal right to vote,

---

[31] Rawls, *Justice as Fairness: A Restatement*, p. 164.

but then nor may a church remove that right from its members, nor a university from its employees and students. It is not because the family is part of the basic structure that it cannot interfere with the rights of citizens. As Rawls himself puts it:

> Even if the basic structure alone is the primary subject of justice, principles of justice still put essential restrictions on the family *and all other associations*. The adult members of families and other associations are equal citizens first: that is their basic position. *No institution or association in which they are involved can violate their rights as citizens.*[32]

So, imposing "essential constraints" or "essential restrictions" *cannot* be the thing that the principles of justice do uniquely to the basic structure, and cannot be what is meant by the principles applying "directly".

This and similar passages undermine the idea that whether the principles of justice apply to an institution depends on whether that institution is part of the basic structure. There seems to be no difference between the way the principles of justice apply to the family "as part of the basic structure" and the way they apply to it simply as an association like any other. If it is correct to say that the requirement not to violate people's rights and liberties *as citizens* means that the principles of justice apply "directly" to the family, then it would also be true to say that the principles apply directly to institutions that are merely within, and do not comprise, the basic structure. To put the point another way: Rawls does not explain in what special, additional ways the principles of justice apply to the family *as a basic institution*.

4.3 The Basic Structure as Subject

This problem is of wider application. A fundamental aspect of Rawls' theory is the idea that the principles of justice apply differently to the basic structure than to non-basic structure institutions. Consider, for example, his remarks in the *Restatement*:

> One main feature of justice as fairness is that it takes the basic structure as the primary subject of political justice.... One should not assume in advance

---

[32] Rawls, *Justice as Fairness: A Restatement*, p. 166. Emphasis added. Abbey refers to passages such as these as a "totalizing" view in Abbey, 'Back Towards a Comprehensive Liberalism?', pp. 17–18.

that principles that are reasonable and just for the basic structure are also reasonable and just for institutions, associations, and social practices generally.[33]

The distinctiveness of the basic structure is a "main feature of justice as fairness" because it is that distinction that preserves the *political* (i.e. non-comprehensive) nature of Rawls' liberalism. By limiting justice to the basic structure Rawls is able to put forward a political conception of justice that stands apart from any comprehensive conception of the good (such as a religion): it neither relies on a conception of the good for its support nor imposes standards that adherents of a reasonable conception of the good could not accept. Without the basic structure distinction Rawlsian liberalism loses this distinctive feature.[34] Moreover, G. A. Cohen argues that the focus on the basic structure is crucial for Rawls to retain his limited and distinctively liberal egalitarianism: without it, Cohen argues, Rawls becomes a "radical egalitarian socialist".[35]

The mechanism for the supposedly freedom-enhancing *politically* liberal distinction between the basic structure and all else is via a difference in the way that justice applies to the basic structure and the way it applies elsewhere: Rawls describes an "institutional division of labor between the basic structure and the rules applying directly to individuals and associations and to be followed by them in particular transactions".[36] Rawls emphasises that this is not to say that justice does not apply at all to institutions that are not part of the basic structure: "there is no such thing" as "a space exempt from justice".[37] Rawls is not, therefore, employing a traditional public–private distinction. But there are certainly supposed to be differences between the application of justice in the basic structure and elsewhere.

---

[33] Rawls, *Justice as Fairness: A Restatement*, pp. 10–11.
[34] Of course, Rawls introduced the idea of the basic structure in *A Theory of Justice* before making the distinction between political and comprehensive liberalism in *Political Liberalism*, and so it is not clear whether he had that distinction in mind when writing about the basic structure. Opinions differ as to whether *Political Liberalism* is a modification or clarification of *A Theory of Justice*. Nonetheless, once the distinction between political and comprehensive liberalism has been constructed it is crucially underpinned by the distinctiveness of the basic structure. It is worth noting that I find comprehensive liberalism more convincing than political liberalism. The fact that Rawlsian liberalism has difficulties maintaining its political credentials is, in my view, problematic for Rawls' own purposes, not because comprehensive liberalism is implausible.
[35] G. A. Cohen, *Rescuing Justice and Equality* (Cambridge, MA: Harvard University Press, 2008), p. 129 n. 27.
[36] Rawls, *Political Liberalism*, pp. 268–9.
[37] Rawls, 'The Idea of Public Reason Revisited', p. 161.

Rawls does provide an account of what it means to say that the principles of justice do *not* apply internally to the family, but it is not enormously helpful. He states:

> We wouldn't want political principles of justice to apply directly to the internal life of the family. It is hardly sensible that as parents we be required to treat our children in accordance with political principles. Here those principles are out of place. Certainly parents should follow some conception of justice (or fairness) and due respect in regard to each of their children, but, within certain limits, this is not for political principles to prescribe.[38]

There are various problems with this passage. First, Rawls appeals to the intuition that we would not want political principles to apply to the relationships between parents and children. But this intuition is not explained by the basic structure/internal life distinction, since in no area of society are children accorded equal basic liberties. Parents should not treat their children according to political principles because children should not be treated according to such principles, not because such treatment occurs 'inside' the family.

A more pertinent question, then, is whether adult members of a family should relate to one another according to the political principles of justice. Rawls discusses this question in only one place: 'The Idea of Public Reason Revisited' (IPRR), where he states:

> the government would appear to have no interest in the particular form of family life, or of relations among the sexes, except insofar as that form or those relations in some way affect the orderly reproduction of society over time.... Of course, there may be other political values in the light of which such a specification would pass muster: for example, if monogamy were necessary for the equality of women, or same-sex marriages destructive to the raising and educating of children.[39]

These remarks have the potential for fairly radical feminist interpretation, particularly given Rawls' aside in FBI that "I should like to think that Okin is right."[40] After all, Okin claims that the family's role as a school of justice

---

[38] Rawls, *Justice as Fairness: A Restatement*, p. 165.
[39] Rawls, 'The Idea of Public Reason Revisited', p. 147.
[40] Rawls, *Justice as Fairness: A Restatement*, p. 167.

requires an equal division of labour between women and men, and if Rawls accepts that the "equality of women" is a political value that appropriately constrains the family then the potential for feminist reform of the family might be considerable.

This 'Eureka!' moment is short-lived, however. For once again, Rawls introduces caveats that both limit the egalitarian potential of his theory and further undermine the distinctiveness of the basic structure. IPRR continues:

> Some want a society in which division of labor by gender is reduced to a minimum. But for political liberalism, this cannot mean that such division is forbidden. One cannot propose that equal division of labor in the family be simply mandated, or its absence in some way penalised at law for those who do not adopt it. This is ruled out because the division of labor in question is connected with basic liberties, including the freedom of religion. Thus, to try to minimize gendered division of labor means, in political liberalism, to try to reach a social condition in which the remaining division of labor is voluntary. This allows in principle that considerable division of labor may persist. It is only involuntary division of labor that is to be reduced to zero.[41]

There is a great deal of literature criticising the concept of voluntariness as it applies to gender inequality, and I cannot discuss the matter further here.[42] The key point for our purposes is that Rawls' remarks just quoted could apply equally to non-basic structure institutions, such as churches. Much of the literature concerning political liberalism and Rawlsian multiculturalism centres on Rawls' claim that while cultures and religions must refrain from the involuntary imposition of inequality there can be no political critique of, or coercive intervention in, *voluntary* inequality.[43] So once again there is no uniqueness in the application of the principles of justice to the basic structure.

4.4 The Whole Structure View

I started the chapter by considering Okin's question to Rawls: if the family is part of the basic structure, and if the principles of justice apply directly to the

---

[41] Rawls, 'The Idea of Public Reason Revisited', p. 162.
[42] For further discussion, see Chambers, *Sex, Culture, and Justice*, along with its Bibliography.
[43] For further discussion, see Chambers, *Sex, Culture, and Justice*.

basic structure, shouldn't the principles of justice apply to the internal life of the family? We have seen that Rawls' insistence that the principles of justice do not apply to the internal life of the family must be because they do not apply to the internal life of any institution. Applying to the internal life of the relevant institutions cannot be what Rawls means when he says the principles of justice apply directly to the basic structure.

What, then, does Rawls mean by saying that the principles of justice apply directly to the basic structure? In this section, I consider an answer that Rawls might give, an answer that I call the *whole structure view*. Several commentators argue that the whole structure view is the right way to understand Rawls.[44] The whole structure view emphasises the *structure* part of the basic structure, and states that the principles of justice apply directly to the basic structure of society in the sense that that they apply directly to the way the major institutions *interact* with each other to form a *whole*. Justice must be considered as a virtue of this overall structure, not as a virtue of each institution considered in isolation. The principles do not apply to the internal life of the family (or any other institution) because that is only one institution among the many that together form the structure. The site of justice is the interactive whole, not the isolated component parts.

Amy Baehr argues that the whole structure view rescues Rawls from Okin. Whereas Okin "would have the family be directly subject to the two principles of justice", in fact "the principles of justice are not to be applied directly to any one institution but to the basic structure as a whole."[45] It follows, Baehr argues, that the family itself might be unproblematically unjust, since its injustice might be compensated for elsewhere:

> Rawls...points out that the system taken as a whole may be just even where some single institution is unjust.... This may be the case when relations in one institution make up for injustice in another. The claim of justice as fairness is that the system of institutions as a whole must be just.[46]

The example that Baehr gives is the difference principle. The difference principle does not apply internally to the family, in the sense that the family

---

[44] For example, see Lloyd, 'Situating a Feminist Criticism of John Rawls's Political Liberalism', p. 1327; Baehr, 'Toward a New Feminist Liberalism', pp. 49–52; Nussbaum 'The Future of Feminist Liberalism'; de Wijze, 'The Family and Political Justice', p. 274; Miriam Ronzoni, 'What Makes a Basic Structure Just?', *Res Publica* 14(3) (2008). I am very grateful to Chris Brooke, Jon Quong, and Andrew Williams, each of whom put forward versions of this answer in discussion and patiently responded to my queries.
[45] Baehr, 'Toward a New Feminist Liberalism', p. 51.
[46] Baehr, 'Toward a New Feminist Liberalism', p. 52.

does not have to distribute its resources so that any inequality benefits the worst-off family member. Baehr argues that this is not, contra Okin, because Rawls inconsistently forgets that the family is part of the basic structure, for the difference principle does not apply internally to *any* institution. There is one difference principle for the whole of society: inequalities are permitted if they benefit the least advantaged considered within society as a whole.[47]

The whole structure view is sometimes introduced so as to show that Okin wrongly interprets Rawls.[48] As a separate question we may ask: if Rawls does in fact hold the whole structure view, does this secure the distinctiveness of the basic structure as a unique site for the application of the principles of justice? In order for the whole structure view to rescue the distinctiveness of the basic structure, two further claims must hold. First, it must in general be true that justice is concerned with the structure as a whole, not any individual part of it; in other words, this claim must hold for each of the principles of justice. Second, it must also be true that only those institutions that are part of the basic structure institutions are relevant for the overall justice of society. Without this second claim there is no role for the basic structure: justice would be a feature of a society *tout court*, and the concept of the basic structure would be redundant.

Neither claim stands. First, it is not true in general that each of the Rawlsian principles of justice applies only to the basic structure as a whole, and not to its various individual institutions. Baehr is correct in arguing that a whole-structure view must be taken for the difference principle, and that is important. But of all the principles of justice the difference principle has the lowest priority, and is not a constitutional essential. The two more important principles are not secured by taking an overview approach that ignores the justice of individual institutions. Second, these two principles (the equal basic liberties and the equal opportunity principle) must apply directly not only to the individual institutions of the basic structure, but also to institutions that do not comprise it.

---

[47] Note, however, that the difference principle is not a good example of the claim that the family, specifically, could be unjust while the basic structure as a whole secures justice. For, as Okin has correctly argued, Rawls' insistence that the difference principle apply to heads of households rather than individuals is inconsistent with any defensible account of liberal values. In other words, the difference principle will have to reach inside the family to the individuals within it. This does not mean that the difference principle applies to the internal life of the family: the family does not have its own, self-contained difference principle. But it does mean that the difference principle cannot apply to the basic structure as a whole if it stops at the doors of the household. See Okin, *Justice, Gender, and the Family*, pp. 91–3.

[48] For useful discussion, see Abbey, *The Return of Feminist Liberalism*, pp. 62–5.

We have already seen that justice cannot be achieved if some institutions deny the basic liberties, so all institutions are subject to the constraints of the first principle.[49] A husband cannot prevent his wife from voting in the sense of imposing legal limits on her right. And these restrictions apply to all institutions, whether basic or not. Rawls states:

> The principles defining the equal basic liberties and opportunities of citizens always hold in and through all so-called domains. The equal rights of women and the basic rights of their children as future citizens are inalienable and protect them wherever they are.[50]

The equal basic liberty principle thus disproves each of the two claims essential to the whole structure view. Moreover, each claim is also undermined by the equal opportunity principle. The excerpt from Rawls just quoted also refers to the equal opportunity principle: this too cannot be realised for the basic structure overall if it is disregarded by some institutions. Imagine that one basic structure institution such as the department of health refuses to hire women, while another such as the department of education refuses to hire men. Even if there are the same number of equivalent jobs in the two departments, this is not a society characterised by equal opportunity—just as it is not if some state schools accept only white pupils while others accept only black pupils. Rawls appears to recognise this fact when he states that the equal opportunity principle governs "all sectors of society"[51] and indeed it could not be otherwise: if only some positions are allocated according to equal opportunity then it follows that there is not equal opportunity overall.

Moreover, Rawls agrees that non-basic structure institutions are also properly restricted by the demands of equal opportunity.[52] A society does not have equal opportunity if government departments hire according to sexist criteria, but it also lacks equal opportunity if private employers do the same. Indeed, the equal opportunity principle applies to institutions of the basic structure in *just the same way* as it applies to other institutions, posing further problems for the distinction between the principles applying 'directly' and applying 'internally'. Equal opportunity cannot exist in a society unless it applies to *internal* decisions made by institutions: most notably, employment

---

[49] This point is also made in Abbey, 'Back Towards a Comprehensive Liberalism?', p. 14.
[50] Rawls, IPRR, p. 161. [51] Rawls, *A Theory of Justice*, p. 73.
[52] Rawls, *Political Liberalism*, p. 261.

and promotion decisions of employing organisations. As I argue in another paper,[53] equal opportunity cannot be achieved or even respected merely by institutions failing to violate the equal opportunity that is somehow brought about elsewhere. Employers must make hiring decisions in accordance with the demands of equal opportunity (just as current anti-discrimination law requires that they must make hiring decisions without reference to certain characteristics such as race and sex). And although the economic order *is* part of the basic structure, Rawls suggests that organisations such as "business firms" within it are not.[54] So the equal opportunity principle must apply directly to the internal life of (some) non-basic structure institutions.

Rawls is not rescued, then, by the whole structure view. Rawlsian justice cannot be secured without individual institutions being just, and this includes the family. But we have not found a way in which membership of the basic structure determines the application of the principles of justice.

4.5 The Basic Structure and Coercion

My argument so far is twofold. First, I have argued that Okin is wrong to claim that Rawls' own theory requires that the principles of justice apply to the internal life of the family. Although Rawls does say that the principles of justice apply uniquely to the basic structure, he does not say that they apply to the internal life of the institutions of the basic structure. Second, I have argued that Okin's critique highlights a more general problem with Rawls' account: he does not, and possibly cannot, justify his claim about the specialness of the basic structure.

In *Rescuing Justice and Equality* G. A. Cohen makes an argument which has similarities to mine. Cohen argues, correctly, that it is "seriously unclear which institutions are supposed to qualify as part of the basic structure".[55] He locates this ambiguity in the question of whether the basic structure is comprised only of legally coercive institutions (or the legally coercive aspects

---

[53] Clare Chambers, 'Each Outcome is Another Opportunity: Problems with the Moment of Equal Opportunity', Chapter 9 in this volume.
[54] See Rawls, *Justice as Fairness: A Restatement*, pp. 10, 164. I say 'suggests' rather than 'states' because Rawls cites business firms as organizations to which the principles of justice do not apply directly in a list that also includes the family. But this interpretation is supported by consideration of what *is* in the basic structure, for which see the arguments earlier in this chapter and also Freeman, *Rawls*, pp. 101-2. I thus disagree with Stephen de Wijze, who places "business firms" within the basic structure in de Wijze, 'The Family and Political Justice', p. 274.
[55] Cohen, *Rescuing Justice and Equality*, p. 132.

of institutions), and rightly argues that it is wrong to care about coercive structures and not also "the ethos that sustains gender inequality and inegalitarian incentives".[56] Both, as Cohen rightly insists, are crucial to explaining the existence of injustice and to rectifying it. Cohen sees this fact as utterly undermining Rawls' insistence that the principles of justice apply uniquely to the basic structure.

As this chapter has shown, I agree with Cohen's conclusion that Rawls' statements about the uniqueness of the basic structure are problematic. I also agree that justice must be concerned with noncoercive phenomena as well as with what is coercive.[57] However, I do not agree with Cohen that the distinction between coercive and noncoercive institutions is the source of the instability in Rawls' account.

Cohen argues that Rawls faces a dilemma. Rawls could say that the basic structure is limited to the coercive aspects of institutions, but then he would face the objection that non-coercive aspects of society can also have the profound effects that justify restricting justice to the basic structure in the first place.[58] Or, Rawls could admit that justice is affected by non-coercive phenomena (such as whether citizens have an egalitarian ethos), but then the idea that justice applies uniquely to the basic structure collapses.[59]

Cohen illustrates his position with the example of the family, and the sexist expectations that may attach to the roles of husband and wife:

> [S]uch expectations need not be supported by the law for them to possess informal coercive force: sexist family structure is consistent with sex-neutral family law.... Yet Rawls must say, on pain of giving up the basic structure objection, that (legally uncoerced) family structure and behavior have no implications for justice in the sense of "justice" in which the basic structure has implications for justice, since they are not a consequence of the formal coercive order. But that implication of the stated position is perfectly incredible: no such differentiating sense is available.[60]

---

[56] Cohen, *Rescuing Justice and Equality*, p. 138.
[57] Chambers, *Sex, Culture, and Justice* is dedicated to arguing precisely that.
[58] Cohen, *Rescuing Justice and Equality*, p. 136.
[59] Cohen, *Rescuing Justice and Equality*, p. 137. Cohen could specify the first horn of the dilemma more precisely. Presumably it is open to Rawls to say that all those features that have profound effects on people's life chances are part of the basic structure, and that justice applies to that structure. Cohen's objection would then be not that justice cannot be restricted to the basic structure, but that the basic structure is more or less everything.
[60] Cohen, *Rescuing Justice and Equality*, p. 137.

I agree with the tenor of Cohen's remarks. But I do not think they are as crushing for Rawls as he, Cohen, thinks, for two reasons.

The first is that, contra Cohen, Rawls does have a "differentiating sense available" to distinguish the justice of the basic structure from justice in other spheres. In his later work he distinguishes three kinds of justice: local justice, domestic justice, and global justice. The distinction which Cohen thinks is impossible would be characterised by Rawls as a distinction between "local justice (principles applying directly to institutions and associations)" and "domestic justice (principles applying to the basic structure of society)".[61] Whether this distinction is a good one is difficult to say, since Rawls refuses to discuss local justice any further. But Cohen does not provide sufficient argument to show that the justice of the basic structure must be exactly equivalent, in form, content, and implication, to local justice.

Indeed, one initially plausible way of cashing out the distinction between local and domestic justice is through the idea of coercion. Domestic injustices (those of the basic structure) might be suitable candidates for coercive intervention, whereas local injustices (those of informal associations or individual choices) might not.[62] This hypothesis leads to my second objection to Cohen: it is a mistake to think that an institution's coerciveness is decided *before* it is incorporated into the basic structure. Although I have cast doubt on what it means to say that the principles of justice apply to the basic structure, surely at least one thing it must mean is that an institution to which the principles apply *thereby* becomes a candidate for legal coercion. If some aspect of the family, for example, is part of the basic structure *then it follows* that it might appropriately be the site of laws to ensure that it is structured in such a way as to instantiate the principles and ensure justice. Cohen has things the wrong way around: it does not make sense to think that we know there are going to have to be laws before we know what they must be about. A liberal society enacts laws only if they are needed for justice. So an institution that is part of the basic structure might therefore become a legitimate candidate for the application of coercion; it is not part of the basic structure because it was always, inevitably, the site of legal coercion.

Return to the example that Cohen gives: the sexist expectations that might attach to the roles of husband and wife. This injustice could be responded to in a coercive or noncoercive way. Coercive responses could include legally

---

[61] Rawls, *Justice as Fairness: A Restatement*, p. 11.
[62] Support for this view is found in Brettschneider, 'The Politics of the Personal'.

mandating certain sorts of equality (for example, entitling a housewife to one half of her husband's salary, or requiring fathers to take compulsory paternity leave), changing the legal definition of marriage (removing any reference to obedience from any state-recognised marriage, or even requiring all state-recognised marriages to include vows of equality), or measures that, while not directly coercive, are funded by coercive taxation (state campaigns in favour of marital equality, or compulsory sex equality teaching in schools). Noncoercive responses would not involve the state; they might include private citizens, voluntary groups, or campaigning associations actively working to break down sexist stereotypes and offer support to couples trying to escape them. It would be possible for Rawls to maintain that the former, coercive options involved aspects of the family that were thereby part of the basic structure, and thus that the equality they brought about was part of domestic justice. The latter, noncoercive options would not be part of the basic structure and would belong to the domain of local justice.

The problem for Rawls, then, is not that there can be no meaningful distinction between justice secured by coercion and justice secured through other means. The problem is rather that whether justice is secured coercively does not depend on whether an institution is part of the basic structure. It is not because the family is or is not 'part of the basic structure' that it becomes an appropriate or inappropriate site for justice 'applying directly' to it. On this interpretation, whether or not something is part of the basic structure is the result, not the cause, of its being an appropriate site of coercion.

This interpretation is meant to defend Rawls only from one specific part of Cohen's critique. As I noted at the outset I agree with Cohen that Rawls' version of the basic structure distinction is doomed, and I agree with him also that noncoercive factors are crucial to justice.[63] But I do not agree that the latter explains the former. The basic structure distinction is doomed because the family must be part of the basic structure, and because Rawls allows no way for the principles to apply 'directly' to the family that he does not also allow for non-basic structure institutions such as churches and universities.

---

[63] The purpose of Cohen's argument is to show that justice must require an egalitarian ethos from its citizens, such that incentive payments of a certain sort are not required. My remarks here do not touch upon that question. For further discussion, see Clare Chambers and Phil Parvin, 'Coercive Redistribution and Public Agreement: Re-Evaluating the Libertarian Challenge of Charity', *Critical Review of International Social and Political Philosophy* 13(1) (2010).

4.6 Reconstructing Okin's Critique

Return to the formalisation of Okin's argument that I gave earlier:

1. The family is part of the basic structure.
2. Rawls states that the principles of justice should apply internally to institutions that are part of the basic structure institutions (but not to others).
3. Therefore: for Rawls, the principles of justice should apply internally to the family.
4. Rawls states that the principles of justice should not apply internally to the family.
5. Therefore: Rawls' position on the family is inconsistent

We have now seen that Premise 2 is false, and so Conclusion 3 does not follow. Premise 4 is true but, without Conclusion 3, Conclusion 5 also fails.

Nonetheless I have not exonerated Rawls. We are in a position to substitute the following critique:

1*. The family is part of the basic structure.
2*. The principles of justice should apply directly to basic structure institutions.
3*. Rawls states that the principles of justice apply differently to basic structure v. non-basic structure institutions.
4*. Therefore: the principles should not apply directly to non-basic structure institutions.[64]
5*. Rawls gives various examples of how the principles apply to the family, but these examples apply equally to non-basic structure institutions such as churches, religions, and cultures.
6*. Therefore: Rawls is inconsistent.

Okin is right that Rawls' claims about the family are deeply confusing. As this chapter has shown, the only way to make sense of Rawls' claims about the

---

[64] The move from 3* to conclusion 4* could be questioned: it is possible that there is some other difference, not considered here, between the way the principles apply to the basic structure and elsewhere. However, Rawls provides us only with the two ideas I have considered here: direct and internal application. Since the idea of internal application does not provide the necessary distinction we are left with no viable alternative to the idea of direct application.

family puts catastrophic pressure on the fundamental Rawlsian idea that the principles of justice apply to the basic structure of society only, or uniquely. Okin's work has successfully demonstrated that, if the idea of the basic structure is to have any weight, the family must be considered part of it. If Rawls wishes to maintain his claims about the limits of interference in the family, then, he can do so only at the expense of the claim that the basic structure is uniquely the subject of justice.

5
Liberalism, Feminism, and the Gendered Division of Labour

Who looks after the children?
Who cleans the house?
Who takes responsibility for the children and the household?

These three questions—so simple, so straightforward—are radical, revolutionary, and painful.[1] They are key to feminism, and to women's equality, precisely because the answers to them have been so obvious as to be unstated, the work they describe so significant and yet unvalued.

The first two questions ask who *does things*. Who takes the hours needed to perform tasks like changing nappies, preparing and serving food, washing and buying clothes, hoovering, shopping, waiting at the school gates, getting up in the night, ringing the doctor, dusting, wiping? These tasks are numerous and relentless, everlasting and exhausting. They can also be satisfying—there's nothing like the calm of a clean house—and, particularly when they concern children, suffused with love and joy. Some of these tasks are highly visible, the demands they place unmissable. The school run must be performed twice a day; it cannot wait for a convenient moment or be fitted in around other commitments. Mealtimes come around with depressing regularity and everyone knows when they're hungry. The laundry piles up, and clothes are needed every day.

Other tasks are less obvious. The third question asks who *takes responsibility*—who bears the mental load, who remembers, who plans, who worries? This is perhaps the heaviest burden of all, because much of it is invisible and yet unavoidable. Someone must notice that the children's trousers are too short or their t-shirts too tight, they need new PE kit or uniform or fancy dress, prescriptions need ordering, appointments must be

---

[1] This chapter is new to this volume. Earlier versions of it were presented at two events on Gina Schouten's book *Liberalism, Neutrality, and the Gendered Division of Labor* (Oxford: Oxford University Press, 2019): a manuscript workshop at Georgia State University in Atlanta, GA, and an Author Meets Critics session of the American Philosophical Association in New York, NY. I also presented this paper at the conference on the Philosophy of Love, Intimacy, and Relationships at the University of Cambridge. I am grateful to participants at all those events for their comments and discussion.

made, emails from school must be read and actioned, the gutter is leaking, a birthday needs planning, where will we vacation, has the insurance been renewed?

Once, after a female friend had been telling me about how she bore the entirety of the mental load, I asked her what she thought her male partner would do if she died. How would he cope with all the tasks she did, tasks on which their family depended? My friend was in a happy relationship, bore no malice or suspicion towards her partner, but she didn't hesitate. "He'd find someone else, and she'd do them," she said.

The gendered division of labour, according to which women take on the majority—often the vast majority—of these tasks, with men specialising in paid labour outside the home, has been a feminist issue since feminism began. For early feminists like Mary Wollstonecraft and John Stuart Mill the issue was women's forced exclusion from the world of education, politics, and professional life, as compared with men of their own class and wealth. For early working-class and black feminists such as Sojourner Truth and Leonora O'Reilly, the issue was a patriarchal system that denied women the vote on the grounds that their place was in the home, while ignoring the millions of women working in fields and factories, mines and mills, and the homes of others.[2] For mid-twentieth-century feminists like Betty Friedan the issue was the loneliness, despair, and financial dependence of the suburban housewife, denied a career of her own and reliant on her husband for social status. Black feminists such as bell hooks pointed out the racialised aspects of Friedan's analysis: for many black women, during and after slavery, work was compulsory or coerced and family a longed-for and often-denied refuge.

More recently, feminists have analysed the persistence of the gendered division of labour even in families where both partners work outside the home. Arlie Hochschild's landmark 1989 work *The Second Shift* highlighted the fact that women in heterosexual relationships did the vast majority of housework even when they also worked outside the home. Women thus worked a first shift for their employer, followed by a second shift of unpaid domestic labour. In her previous book *The Managed Heart* Hochschild had coined the term 'emotion work' to describe the work women put in to managing others' emotions, both in careers such as flight attendance and nursing, and within the family. This emotion work affects the careers women have; the way they are expected to act as peacemakers, facilitators, service-providers

---

[2] Angela Yvonne Davis, *Women, Race and Class* (New York, NY: Vintage Press, 1983), p. 143; Sojourner Truth, *Ain't I a Woman?* (London: Penguin, 2020).

and caretakers within those careers; and their role in family dynamics as bearers of the mental load.

These multiple perspectives on the gendered division of labour ensure that it remains both an urgent and a complex site of feminist analysis. This complexity is captured by Patricia Hill Collins in her discussion of the institution of motherhood from a black feminist perspective. "Some women view motherhood as a truly burdensome condition that stifles their creativity, exploits their labour, and makes them partners in their own oppression," she wrote in 2000. "Others see motherhood as providing a base for self-actualization, status in the Black community, and a catalyst for social activism. These alleged contradictions can exist side by side in African-American communities and families and even within individual women."[3]

So, the gendered division of labour is multifaceted. It refers to the traditional distinction between man-as-breadwinner and woman-as-housewife. It refers to the unequal distribution of domestic and caring labour even in dual-earner couples. It refers to labour market specialisation, according to which men and women tend to cluster in different roles and industries. It refers to the additional burden of emotion work that women take on, often unconsciously. And it must be analysed as an institution that reflects and reinforced wider gender norms.

The challenge of the gendered division of labour is thus the challenge of combining domestic duties with paid employment within a family in a way that allows family members to be equals. This is a challenge for individual families, and a challenge at the level of public policy. What can a liberal state do to facilitate gender equality when there is always so much housework?

Public policy in some liberal states, notably the UK and the USA, has been to push mothers into paid employment by making many state benefits dependent on employment or job-seeking status. These policies are easy to understand as part of a neoliberal capitalist ideology that views only paid work as productive work, and that values citizens only insofar as they contribute directly to the market economy. But some theorists defend these policies on the grounds that they are feminist or egalitarian. One recent example is Gina Schouten, who argues that the gendered division of labour should be attacked by policies that incentivise men to perform *more* carework and *less* paid work, and that conversely incentivise women to perform *less* carework and *more* paid work. As I'll show, this leads Schouten to advocate measures that penalise women for specialising in carework. Remarkably, Schouten

---

[3] Patricia Hill Collins, *Black Feminist Thought* (New York, NY; London: Routledge, 2000), p. 191.

argues that state action to push mothers into paid work and discourage the gendered division of labour is justified from the perspective of *political liberalism*. In this chapter, I argue against these approaches.

Women have always worked outside the home, even if they have not had access to work with the elevated status of a *career*. Enslaved women had no choice at all. In wartime, women have taken on jobs previously reserved for men. Poorer women have no realistic choice but to earn money to support themselves and their dependents. Economic necessity means that every adult must work to support themselves unless they are provided for by someone else, whether through an inheritance, a family business, a partner whose wealth or wage is enough for two, or state benefits.

Once children are born, the economics shift. Children need full-time care for many years, and that care must be provided either by parents or wider family members sacrificing their earning power, or by professionals whose wages must be paid. Many families struggle to choose between these two options, since both are problematic. Sometimes the accounting makes things simpler. If the cost of childcare outweighs the wages of one parent—usually, because of the gender pay gap, the mother—then a traditional gendered division of labour may seem the rational choice. Whether this situation pertains depends on wage levels and government policy: whether there is a minimum wage and at what level, whether low-income families are supported by benefits, whether government support is dependent on both parents being in paid employment or is available to stay-at-home parents, the cost and availability of professional childcare.

As just mentioned, many liberal democracies tie welfare benefits or childcare support to employment status: parents must either be in paid employment or actively seeking work to be eligible for government assistance. Such measures can make stay-at-home parenting an option only for the wealthy. Lower-income parents are locked into a gruelling cycle of working at low-paid jobs so as to pay for professional childcare which costs a lot but pays low wages to its (mostly female) employees, thus creating more low-income families. One straightforward public policy measure in this context would be to enable low-income families with young children to access government support when the family includes a stay-at-home parent. This has not been the preferred policy solution of liberal states or of liberal feminists, for reasons I interrogate in this chapter.[4]

---

[4] In the UK, the main benefit payment is Universal Credit. To be eligible for Universal Credit claimants must be on a low income, or unable to work due to disability or health condition, or 'out of work'. To remain eligible when out of work, claimants must be seeking work, with increasingly stringent requirements as the child grows up. For example, a parent whose youngest child is two years old

Once women have access to professional careers, paid employment becomes more than a financial necessity. The prospect of career development and professional specialisation, alongside personal fulfilment and financial independence, gives women a reason to maintain their careers after motherhood even if the finances don't add up at first. Thus the desire to maintain a professional career, combined with economic necessity, means a great many women return to work after maternity leave, creating families in which both parents must juggle career and childcare.

Nancy Fraser's 'After the Family Wage: A Postindustrial Thought Experiment', published in the late 1990s, charts the development of feminist theorising of the gendered division of labour as women's careers became more mainstream. According to Fraser, feminists first advocated what she calls the 'Universal Breadwinner' model: the idea that, in order to be equal with men, women should have access to careers of the same sort and on the same terms as men. According to the Universal Breadwinner ideal, women should be able to hold down demanding, full-time jobs requiring hours and availability that are incompatible with childcare and household management. In other words, women should be able to act as men do under patriarchy.

Men's career structures (which is to say, career structures in general) have rested on the assumption that workers are either single men, or else have a wife at home taking care of the children and domestic tasks. If women are to enter into similar careers they need to pass on those burdens to others. (Or, as the existence of the second shift shows, they pass those burdens on to others for at least *some* of the time.) Thus the Universal Breadwinner model prioritises the provision of full-time, high-quality childcare covering working hours, alongside the availability of domestic help for cleaning and housekeeping tasks. Salaries must either rise to cover these additional household costs, or else these services must be subsidised.

The Universal Breadwinner model has been a key demand of feminists, one that has been accepted by mainstream political movements. It has resulted in feminist advances such as legislation against sex discrimination and sexual harassment in the workplace, mandatory reporting on the gender pay gap, and efforts to increase the numbers of women in senior leadership roles.

---

must be making active steps to prepare for work; once the child is three the parent must be working or looking for work for sixteen hours per week in order to claim Universal Credit. Carer's Allowance is also available, but to be eligible a claimant must be caring for an adult, or a child who is in receipt of Child Disability Benefit at the middle or highest rate, meaning that they need much more looking after than other children of the same age, throughout the entire day and with help or supervision also needed at night. Parents who are caring for children with less demanding disabilities or no disabilities are not eligible for Carer's Allowance. See http://www.gov.uk and https://huutimoney.com/can-stay-at-home-mums-get-universal-credit/.

However, while *necessary* to move towards women's equality, Universal Breadwinner is not *sufficient* as a feminist movement. Women's widespread entry into the workplace has meant that most families now rely on two incomes: the stay-at-home mother and housewife is now a luxury many families cannot afford. But not all women want to return to professional careers rather than care for their children, and doing so is not always beneficial to them. Childcare and housework are, it turns out, extremely expensive when they must be paid for at market rates—even when a sexist market shamefully undervalues 'women's work'. And women's work it remains: the vast majority of professionals providing childcare and domestic cleaning services are women, meaning that the gendered division of labour has not been disrupted so much as relocated.

Feminists noticed all of this, and asked why childcare and domestic work should be presumed to have value only when performed for a wage. Childcare in particular is work, but it is not a mere chore that can be performed by just anyone: it is a job both skilled and personal, requiring emotional commitment, even love, if it is to be done well. Children *care* who is looking after them; in most cases, they prefer their parents over other care-givers. Similarly, many parents—especially mothers, for reasons both biological and social—feel a great pull to be with their children, finding it enormously difficult to return from maternity leave and place their babies in others' care for long stretches (even if they also value having time to themselves). Why then, some feminists asked, should childcare be paid only if the children being cared for are not one's own? Why should a woman not be supported financially, and valued socially, if she looks after her own children full-time? In this vein, what are sometimes called 'difference feminists' argued that the solution to the gendered division of labour was not to push all women into paid work. Rather, the aim should be to make difference costless, through wages for housework and childcare, and through a social commitment to *value* the work that mothers do. Fraser named this feminist response to the gendered division of labour 'Caregiver Parity'.

For Fraser, neither Universal Breadwinner nor Caregiver Parity were adequate responses to the gendered division of labour, since neither adequately disrupted the idea that caring and domestic work was for women. As she puts it memorably,

> we have examined – and found wanting – two initially plausible approaches: one aiming to make women more like men are now; the other leaving men and women pretty much unchanged, while aiming to make women's

difference costless. A third possibility is to induce men to become more like most women are now, namely, people who do primary carework.[5]

This third possibility, a radical vision of a world in which everyone combines some paid work and some care work, Fraser named 'Universal Caregiver'. The Universal Caregiver model envisions a society in which everyone cares for others—whether children or the elderly, whether in one's immediate family or in the wider community—and in which paid employment is structured around those universal caring responsibilities.

But how to achieve it? As we moved into the twenty-first century several writers tackled the dilemma faced by women who maintain careers and have children. Joan Williams' outstanding 2000 book *Unbending Gender: Why Family and Work Conflict and What to Do About It* identified a tragic clash between two norms, both of which women are expected to meet. The first is *the norm of the ideal worker*. An ideal worker is someone who is dedicated first and foremost to their work: able to cover the hours the employer needs or wants, able to stay until the job is done, able to devote their time and energy to their employment. An ideal worker is the model of work for breadwinning men with a wife at home. As women have entered the workplace, Williams argues, the norm of the ideal worker hasn't shifted: women have been at pains to demonstrate that they can meet it, just like men do.

Of course women are capable of acting as ideal workers just as men are; in this respect women without children are much like men without children, and women with children can always take a career-focused attitude like men do, relying heavily on paid childcare and housekeeping services. Especially in the upper echelons of professional life, there are many examples of women excelling in their careers by fitting into the ideal worker model, exemplified by Sheryl Sandberg's bestselling 2013 book *Lean In: Women, Work, and the Will to Lead*.

The problem is that women face another, conflicting norm, one not applied to men with anything like the same force. This second norm, Williams argues, is *the norm of parental care*. The norm of parental care is the idea that children should enjoy the focused care and attention of their parents, particularly their mothers. In contrast to 'latchkey kids', 'free-range parenting', or models of parenting common in previous generations which involved sending children outside to play with friends with instructions to return at dinner time,

---

[5] Nancy Fraser, *Justice Interruptus: Critical Reflections on the "Postsocialist" Condition* (London: Routledge, 1997), p. 60.

contemporary parenting requires constant nurture and hands-on attention. Children are actively supervised for much longer than before; after-school time is more likely to involve clubs, pursuits, or homework requiring parental involvement; today's parents take a much more active interest in their children's development, social lives, and schooling than their parents did for them in the 1970s and 1980s.

It is beyond the scope of this chapter to evaluate the pros and cons of the norm of parental care. It seems superior in many ways to the more neglectful aspects of previous generations' parenting, but raises legitimate concerns about whether today's children are over-scheduled and over-supervised, lacking independence and playtime and suffering from pressure and anxiety. Either way, and regardless of the impact of the norm of parental care on children's well-being, one thing is clear. *It is simply impossible to fulfil both the norm of parental care and the norm of the ideal worker.* There are not enough hours in the day, and it is impossible to prioritise two competing demands at once. Do you attend the school play or the board meeting; take time off to care for a sick child or spend long hours in the office; travel frequently for work or be there at the school gates? Do you attend the second day of the academic conference or spend Saturday with your children?

Men traditionally solve this conflict by being ideal workers, sacrificing the norm of parental care. Some women try the same, often at significant personal cost, as chronicled in Anne-Marie Slaughter's 2015 book *Unfinished Business*, a kind of riposte to *Lean In*. Slaughter was an American academic who become an immensely successful public servant: the first female Director of Policy Planning in the US State Department. Taking that job had meant a move away from the city where she, her partner, and her two school-aged children were based, adjusting from "a world in which my office was a ten-minute walk away from home to a world in which I left the house at five A.M. Monday morning and came back late Friday afternoon or evening. This schedule", Slaughter continues, "was not unusual among political appointees in the Obama administration." But "the change was wrenching.... for our sons, the costs were immediate and large."[6]

Ultimately Slaughter decided to leave her high-powered Washington job and return to her much more flexible and family-friendly academic career. Even though that career was prestigious and well-paid in its own right, Slaughter describes how her decision devalued her in the eyes of many of her

---

[6] Anne-Marie Slaughter, *Unfinished Business* (London: Oneworld, 2015), p. xi.

colleagues, particularly those of her own generation or older. "In short," she writes,

> even as a woman who was still working full-time as a tenured professor, I had suddenly become categorized and subtly devalued as just another one of the many talented and well-educated women who showed great promise at the start of their careers and reached the early levels of success but then made a choice to take a less demanding job, work part-time, or stop working entirely to have more time for caregiving. I continually sensed that I had disappointed the expectations of the many people in my life.[7]

Slaughter's book is a manifesto for shifting our cultural expectations, for allowing women—and men—to value their family, to prioritise spending time with children, to let their careers at least sometimes take a backseat, without being branded as failures.

In this context came philosopher Gina Schouten's 2019 book *Liberalism, Neutrality, and the Gendered Division of Labour*. Schouten starts with three claims: that the gendered division of labour persists; that, as a matter of empirical fact, it harms women; and that, as a normative imperative, this must change. Moreover, she argues that changing it is a legitimate matter not merely for enabling policies but for *coercive governmental action*. And, finally, she argues that coercive state action in pursuit of what she calls 'gender egalitarianism' can be justified from within the philosophical framework of Rawlsian political liberalism.

Schouten's normative conclusion—which effectively functions both as conclusion and as premise—is that states should engage in coercive action to *promote* gender egalitarianism and *discourage* the gendered division of labour. To this end, Schouten argues, governments should enact policies that impose burdensome costs on those who conform to the gendered division of labour. This means imposing costs on *women* who choose to stay at home with their children, and on *men* who choose to specialise in paid work. Moreover, governments should give benefits and rewards to couples who divide caring and paid work equally, in ways that undermine the gendered division of labour. In practice, this means rewarding *women* for going out to paid work and rewarding *men* for taking care of the children.

Already we can see that Schouten's argument is unusual, from a feminist perspective, because it advocates rewarding men and punishing women for

---

[7] Slaughter, *Unfinished Business*, pp. xvii–xviii.

caring work. Or, to put it more starkly, punishing women *still further* for specialising in caring work, adding to the existing disadvantage they face. Yet more starkly, Schouten advocates giving the highest rewards for caring work to highly paid men, lower rewards for low-paid men, and rewards that are lower still, or are even negative, to women. These are recommendations that should trouble feminists.

Perhaps this is unsurprising. Schouten recognises that the claims of political liberalism and feminism can conflict. Where they do, on her analysis, it is feminism that must give way. Thus she describes her central question as "In order to justify promoting gender egalitarianism as a social ideal, must we invoke feminist values that political liberalism rules out as illegitimate bases on which to justify social policy? Or is a neutral justification available?"[8] Moreover, Schouten argues that the gendered division of labour is *not* primarily a distributive injustice, and thus her argument is not primarily aimed to appeal to traditional resource-focused egalitarians, either. Instead, she seeks to show that the gendered division of labour is a problem *for political liberals*. Her claim is that the gendered division of labour violates comprehensive autonomy, and that this violation of comprehensive autonomy is a legitimate political liberal concern.

Consider a thought experiment that Schouten introduces: the case of a heterosexual couple named Dave and Karen. This couple fall into a pattern whereby she ends up specialising in caring and domestic work while he specialises in paid work. This specialisation emerges from a series of uncoerced, autonomously considered, and rational choices. Karen and Dave are a loving married couple who support each other's goals and work together to do what is best for the family. Their gendered division of labour is not the result of abuse or coercion. It does not create disaster for Karen or make a monster out of Dave. It results in a happy, harmonious family—but one that is gender unequal.

What does it mean to say of two people that they are gender unequal? One difficulty is this: if we are dealing with a different-sex couple, won't that couple always be gender unequal unless they are identical? We might think that gender inequality is something that makes sense only in a wider social context: we need more than one man and one woman to know whether gender inequality obtains. Gender equality is a feature of groups, not individuals. And this is Schouten's view too. She describes Karen and Dave as gender

---

[8] Gina Schouten, *Liberalism, Neutrality, and the Gendered Division of Labor* (Oxford: Oxford University Press, 2019), pp. 16–17.

unequal not merely because they do different things from each other, but because their differences correspond to social norms about the proper behaviour for *all* women and *all* men. Karen fulfils the social role advocated for women, and Dave fulfils that advocated for men. If they switched roles so that Karen were the main breadwinner and Dave the main caregiver they would still be specialised, and they would still be unequal, but on Schouten's terms they would not be *gender unequal* in a way that should concern us.

Schouten uses the case of Karen and Dave "to illustrate the apparent innocence of the domestic choices that gender egalitarian interventions target".[9] Since there is no coercion or unjust discrimination that explains their situation, "nothing about Karen's and Dave's arrangement seems to call for redress".[10] They are generally happy, and their family life works well. Schouten frames cases like this as "hard cases for feminist liberals",[11] because it is difficult to find arguments to justify intervention in them.

So *why* we should be looking for such arguments? Why not conclude that these are precisely cases that do not merit intervention? It is true that Karen and Dave's situation is gendered, in that it follows gendered patterns. But is that really such a problem? Why should we think it would be preferable if Karen and Dave's positions were reversed, so that their division of labour ran counter to gender norms?

One possibility is that the situation is somehow *bad for Karen*. There are various ways that being in the situation of primary caregiver can be bad for women, even when it is chosen and wanted. It can be a position of financial vulnerability and dependence, especially on divorce or separation. It can be a position of restricted future choices, and the inability to return to the workforce, and a contribution to the gendered pay gap. It can be a position of frustration and unfulfillment.

But these sorts of problems can be mitigated by policies that do not try to discourage women from full-time caregiving: wages for housework, strong financial rights for caregivers on separation or divorce, increased opportunities for adult education, a shift in employers' attitudes to women returning to the workplace after absence. These changes do not try to prevent any gendered division of labour; instead, they aim to mitigate its costs for women. But Schouten advocates only those policies that aim "to erode the gendered division of labor by inducing more families to choose gender-egalitarian

---

[9] Schouten, *Liberalism, Neutrality, and the Gendered Division of Labor*, p. 74.
[10] Schouten, *Liberalism, Neutrality, and the Gendered Division of Labor*, p. 75.
[11] Schouten, *Liberalism, Neutrality, and the Gendered Division of Labor*, p. 75.

arrangements in the short term, thus eroding the social norms and reforming the gendered institutions that sustain the gendered division of labor in the long run."[12] In other words, she explicitly does *not* want policies that aim to make life easier for women who specialise in caring work, because anything that encourages or enables women and men to live according to the gendered division of labour is bad. In other words, for Schouten the gendered division is not unjust primarily because it is bad for women, and so making women better off or even just reducing their disadvantage is not a priority. She does not see the gendered division of labour as a problem of distributive justice, meaning that it cannot be solved by distributive measures. And so, in Schouten's narrative, Karen is frequently described as happy, choosing, and fulfilled.

An alternative option is that the problem with Karen and Dave's situation that it is *bad for Dave*. He is losing out on perhaps the most vital part of human life: parenthood, nurturing, and family relationships. He is alienated from a significant part of human flourishing. Undoubtedly one of the lesser-documented costs of the gendered division of labour is the fact that it has impoverished many men's family lives, rendering fatherhood far less emotionally fulfilling than motherhood. But Schouten does not want to advocate a perfectionist account that values family life above career. And so Dave's choices are little focused on in Schouten's narrative; he is not the victim.

Some people might criticise Karen's situation because they view a life devoted to care and family at the expense of career development as less valuable than one devoted to career. Many people do make such judgments, as Slaughter found when talking to people about her resignation from politics. In the UK, government policy focuses on pushing even single mothers into paid employment, seeing paid employment even in low-skilled jobs as preferable to paid motherhood. But this is not Schouten's argument either, because the judgment that paid employment or a professional career is superior to being a stay-at-home mother is not compatible with political liberalism and cannot justly influence political liberal state policy.

The hallmark of a political liberal society is that people are free to reach their own conclusions about the good life. This includes the relative merits of care and career. Having made their own value judgments, people should be free to structure their own lives accordingly. The state cannot legitimately make or act on value judgments of this sort, since to do so would be to posit a controversial conception of the good as the model for others to follow. The

---

[12] Schouten, *Liberalism, Neutrality, and the Gendered Division of Labor*, p. 49.

view that a life that prioritises family, children, and home over and above career advancement is inferior cannot be endorsed by the politically liberal state, or feed into its policies.

Family, children, and home are matters of deep value for many people. A deep emotional commitment to one's children is, thankfully, almost universally felt. And, while career is an important part of many people's conception of the good, there are many people for whom the available career options are not particularly fulfilling in either monetary or personal terms. "While it does not in any way diminish the importance of women resisting sexist oppression by entering the labor force, work has not been a liberating force for masses of American women", wrote bell hooks in 1982:

> White middle class and upper class women like those described in Betty Friedan's *The Feminine Mystique* were housewives not because sexism would have prevented them from being in the paid labour force, but because they had willingly embraced the notion that it was better to be a housewife than to be a worker. The racism and classism of while women's liberationists was most apparent whenever they discussed work as the liberating force for women.[13]

The situation is scarcely different forty years later. For some women, those privileged enough to have fulfilling and well-paid careers, maternity is an interruption into their earning power, a setback to success—even if, as with Slaughter, it is also a fulfilling vocation. But for countless other women motherhood and family life is a welcome break from drudgery, infinitely more rewarding than employment in sectors that are increasingly repressive, rigid, exhausting, and underpaid. Work that is also one's vocation, as it is for many professionals, is not the same as taking whatever job one has to take to avoid poverty or benefits sanction. The autonomy of academic life is utterly unlike the intensely monitored and routinised work in a call centre, delivery vehicle, or Amazon warehouse.[14] The security and promotion prospects of a career contrast sharply with zero-hours employment in retail and restaurants and with the fluctuating fortunes offered by work in the gig economy. It is hard to see why such work should be considered more fulfilling from an individual perspective or more valuable from a social one.

---

[13] bell hooks, *Ain't I a Woman*, p. 146.
[14] Elizabeth Anderson, *Private Government: How Employers Rule Our Lives (and Why We Don't Talk about It)* (Princeton, NJ: Princeton University Press, 2017).

The overwhelming value of family life, coupled with the highly variable value of paid work, means that there are a great many people for whom family reasonably trumps career. Denying this possibility would be to violate political liberal neutrality, and in an implausible way—resting on exclusionary assumptions and maintaining a classist and racist perspective.

So, what is wrong with the gendered division of labour, if it is neither a problem of coercion nor a problem of distribution? If liberalism is about freedom and equality, and if Karen and Dave are choosing freely and contentedly, what makes their situation unjust?

Schouten's answer is that the gendered division of labour is unjust because it instantiates social norms that make it more difficult for people to choose non-gendered patterns. The gendered division of labour does violate equality, but the equality it violates is not primarily distributive. As such, Schouten is not primarily concerned to alleviate disadvantage.

Gender egalitarian policies, as Schouten sees them, do not aim to alleviate disadvantage or increase choices for those women who wish to specialise in carework; they aim to make it easier and more rewarding for women to perform paid work, specifically, and they aim to make it easier and more rewarding for *men* to perform carework. This is because Schouten's main concern is not to make women in general better off, but rather to undermine gendered social norms. Undermining gendered social norms may make *some* women better off—in particular, those who do not wish to specialise in carework—but it will reduce the choices and well-being of others.

"Effective reform", Schouten writes, "requires *both* support provisions to make social institutions more family friendly *and* policy inducements to encourage families to behave in more gender-egalitarian ways in using those provisions."[15] In other words, the state should aim to restrict options.[16] Time and again this desire to undermine social norms will lead to the state penalising women who specialise in carework, even as it rewards men who make the same choice.

Schouten advocates three sorts of policy interventions aimed at disincentivising the gendered division of labour: work time regulation, family leave initiatives, and subsidised caregiving provision. She is clear that various sorts of policy measures could work—her examples are not prescriptive—but common to all of them is the aim to treat women and men differently so that men are encouraged to care and women are encouraged to work outside the home.

---

[15] Schouten, *Liberalism, Neutrality, and the Gendered Division of Labor*, p. 44.
[16] Schouten, *Liberalism, Neutrality, and the Gendered Division of Labor*, p. 57.

Consider the example of family leave policies. In most liberal democracies women take far more family leave than men do. This inequality starts with the first weeks of maternity leave that are necessary for gestational mothers and then continues with additional leave taken, predominantly by women, to enable caring for an infant. Since women take the bulk of family leave at present, for Schouten's gender egalitarianism the aim of family leave policies should be to encourage or force women to take less family leave than they do now so that men take more.

Family leave should be short, Schouten argues, because otherwise employers might not want to hire parents.[17] Of course, as we all know, it is *women* whose careers and hiring prospects are at risk; if the aim were to benefit women then the appropriate policy would be strict sex discrimination legislation to protect women's employment and maternity leave rights, not a reduction in leave. Since Schouten aims not to benefit women who are engaged in caregiving but rather to disincentivise the gendered division of labour, she proposes further measures to take family leave from women and give it to men. "If leave is allocated to the household as a unit," she writes,

> then one member can take the full amount, and social norms and household economic incentives will generally favor women taking the bulk of it. But if leave is allocated to parents individually, this generates an incentive effect, referred to by some as a 'daddy quota': Each parent's leave, if not taken up by that parent, is forfeited.[18]

Here Schouten is straightforwardly advocating a reduction in women's choices and entitlements, forcing them back into the workplace earlier than they might wish so that reluctant men get their turn.

Even more starkly, it might be desirable on Schouten's account to actively reduce a mother's *own* leave if the father refuses to take all of his.[19] She writes approvingly of "a policy that allocates three months to each parent of a newly born or adopted child, but each parent's second and third months are conditional on their partner taking his own corresponding months of leave."[20] The clear implication here is that such a policy is needed to incentivise men who

---

[17] Schouten, *Liberalism, Neutrality, and the Gendered Division of Labor*, p. 45.
[18] Schouten, *Liberalism, Neutrality, and the Gendered Division of Labor*, p. 45.
[19] Schouten, *Liberalism, Neutrality, and the Gendered Division of Labor*, p. 46.
[20] Schouten, *Liberalism, Neutrality, and the Gendered Division of Labor*, p. 45. She continues: "Such a policy plausibly will induce more men to take leave, and in so doing, help erode norms against male leave-taking, promote parental comfort and attachment to children among both leave-takers, promote labor market attachment among women, and, plausibly, promote gender-egalitarian behavior in future generations" (pp. 45–6).

do not really want to take paternity leave. So, a mother of a newborn would be entitled to just one month of maternity leave in her own right; she would then have to return to work. She would be permitted to take a second month of maternity leave only if her male partner reluctantly agreed to hold the baby for a bit, overriding his own preference for staying in the office.

These policies would not benefit mothers at all. Even a mere three months of maternity leave seems quite barbaric from a non-US perspective, let alone one month; six months to a year would be more normal. Three months is nowhere near enough leave to enable mothers to follow the WHO guidelines of exclusive breastfeeding for the first six months (breastfeeding not being reducible to breastmilk). The proposal to share leave for the first year, even alternating it month on month, either precludes natural-term breastfeeding (or any breastfeeding at all beyond the first period of leave), or else it imposes the burden of expressing milk on breastfeeding mothers, something that takes a significant amount of time and equipment, and which many women find painful and difficult. And the proposal to punish mothers by withdrawing their leave if fathers choose not to take theirs is appalling for women: worst of all for women whose partners are actively abusive and controlling, and who can use this measure as a threat or punishment, and terrible too for women whose partners are simply old-fashioned sexists.

Consider another policy measure that Schouten advocates: work time regulation. Schouten initially sets this up in a straightforwardly egalitarian way: "Work time regulations would limit the length of the work day and week, thereby enabling workers to reallocate time from paid labor to domestic and caregiving work."[21] Put this way, this sounds like a policy that could benefit women who want to specialise in caregiving. But the devil is in the detail. "Like the other policy initiatives," Schouten warns,

> work time regulation carries some risk of further entrenching the gendered division of labor if it is not implemented carefully. Improving the conditions of part-time work might encourage many women who would otherwise work full time to cut back. On the other hand, improving the pay and status of part-time work could draw more men into part-time work who would otherwise work full time.[22]

The message is clear: it is good to improve the pay and status of part-time work for *men*, but not for women.

---

[21] Schouten, *Liberalism, Neutrality, and the Gendered Division of Labor*, p. 47.
[22] Schouten, *Liberalism, Neutrality, and the Gendered Division of Labor*, p. 48.

My point is this: policies that look gender-neutral are not really gender-neutral if their aim is to disrupt highly gendered patterns. An apparently neutral policy that awards equal amounts of family leave to men and to women has gendered effects when applied in the context of existing gender inequality: it takes leave away from women and gives it to men. An apparently neutral policy that limits family leave so that careers are not undermined does nothing to harm men's lives, since (as Schouten points out) they already prioritise career over care and often decline to take up their full leave entitlement. But it does seriously set back the lives of women who are typically the main caregivers, putting family first, since they will no longer be entitled to take adequate leave while keeping their jobs.

So, Schouten is not primarily concerned to end disadvantage. Her target is, instead, *specialisation* and *social construction*. Schouten's real concern is not that caregivers are disadvantaged. Her concern is that *social norms push women into caregiving*. Gendered social norms mean, Schouten argues, that specialising in caregiving cannot properly be described as an autonomous choice for women. And this is where political liberalism comes in: according to Schouten, political liberals should create the conditions for people to frame, revise, and pursue their conception of good, and the social norms that sustain the gendered division of labour undermine that form of free choice. Political liberals should pursue "gender egalitarianism", which "undertakes to break the association of women with caregiving so that social institutions no longer assume entitlement to employees unencumbered by caregiving demands, and so that caregiving is no longer associated with femininity."[23]

Schouten's gender egalitarianism is not primarily about making things better for actually existing women. Instead, her gender egalitarianism is opposed to (unjust) *social construction*. Schouten's main claim is that it is problematic if the existence of sexist social norms means that people are encouraged to enact a gendered division of labour, because such social construction undermines both equality and autonomy.

This is the sort of argument I make in my 2008 book *Sex, Culture, and Justice*. I argue there that injustice results from the combination of what I call the 'disadvantage factor', which is a question of whether a choice disadvantages the chooser, and the 'influence factor', which is a matter of identifiable norms and pressures that encourage people to make choices that disadvantage them. When both the disadvantage and the influence factor occur together, I argue, injustice results. Now, concerns along these lines clearly do

---

[23] Schouten, *Liberalism, Neutrality, and the Gendered Division of Labor*, p. 57.

motivate Schouten. She ably shows that women are still disadvantaged by the gendered division of labour, by marshalling an array of empirical studies, and she also indicates that social construction is largely to blame. Insofar as this combination of disadvantage and influence is her target, her project mirrors mine.

But if what matters to gender egalitarianism is that *gendered social construction* should not cause a gendered division of labour, then the appropriate remedy is a rigorous programme of norm reform to break down sexist ideology. If that programme is successful then gendered patterns might shift—but they will not necessarily do so. What matters for justice, on this account, is not *what* people choose but *why* they choose it. The reduction or removal of sexist norms may reduce many of the gendered patterns we observe, but there is no reason to think that they will be destroyed completely.

Why not? Well, if carework becomes more valued than it is now, in terms of resources and status, there is no reason to think that women will autonomously shift out of it. Indeed, that is precisely Schouten's critique of the Caregiver Parity model. She is concerned that it will do nothing to dislodge women's association with caregiving and men's association with marketised labour. Instead, she advocates something closer to Fraser's Universal Caregiving model, according to which women and men must both combine paid work and caregiving.

It seems, then, that Schouten's gender egalitarianism is at least partly opposed to the mere fact of *specialisation*. Specialisation is the phenomenon whereby some people focus mainly on some sorts of work and other people focus on other sorts of work. Specialisation is another word for a division of labour.

Capitalism generally is built on specialisation. At the most general level, people have different jobs, and one person cannot generally do another person's job. I am an academic, and I could not (currently, without significant retraining) do the work of a bricklayer, or a company director, or a cinematographer, or a surgeon. Specialisation occurs even within an industry. A worker in factory will typically work on one particular point on an assembly line, making parts of a product over and over again rather than making the entire product. I am an academic philosopher not an academic physicist; I am a political philosopher not a logician.

Specialisation has much to recommend it. It is efficient; it allows for expertise; it allows people to play to their strengths; it allows people to find jobs they enjoy. It also has drawbacks. It can be alienating; it perpetuates class distinctions; it traps some people in dead-end roles while it rewards others with fulfilling ones. Karl Marx famously thought that specialisation was an evil of capitalism that would end in communism, with people being able "to do one thing today and another tomorrow, to hunt in the morning, fish in the afternoon, rear cattle in the evening, criticise after dinner, just as I have a mind, without ever becoming hunter, fisherman, herdsman or critic."[24]

Specialisation is problematic if it contributes to social norms that reduce freedom. But a thorough-going rejection of specialisation on these lines would hit far more than just the gendered division of labour. It would hit capitalist labour in general, as Marx recognised. Perhaps that's a good thing. But Schouten's target is not capitalist specialisation in general, not least because so much of her argument is aimed at pushing women into capitalist labour markets, not protecting them from them.

Instead, Schouten's concern is for the specific specialisation of the gendered division of labour. It's specific in two ways: it's about the division of labour between carework and marketised work, and about that division as undertaken along traditional gendered lines. Schouten is not (at least, not in this book) worried about gendered positions within employment (female nurses and male bricklayers), and she does not seem to be worried about families where women specialise in marketised employment and men specialise in carework. Her concern is the traditional gendered division of labour, and not just because it brings about disadvantage or because it results from social construction, but because *conforming to the gendered division of labour makes nonconformity more difficult for others*. If a couple choose to arrange their family life in accordance with the gendered division of labour, they undermine others' autonomy by implicitly implying that they should do likewise.

There is strength in this analysis. All social norms depend on widespread compliance if they are to survive. Any act of compliance may reinforce a social norm; any act of non-compliance has the potential to weaken it. The question is what follows from this observation in terms of the duties of individuals and the role of the state.

Contra Schouten, I suggest that a liberal cannot compel an individual to resist social norms so as to increase the autonomy of others to resist, for (at least) three reasons.

First, it is inconsistent to use some individuals as means to others' freedom. It can be a reasonable liberal policy to prevent individuals from complying with some norm or practice, if that norm or practice reaches a threshold of

---

[24] Karl Marx, *The German Ideology*, in David McLellan (ed.), *Karl Marx: Selected Writings* (Oxford: Oxford University Press, 1977), p. 169.

harmfulness. There can, in other words, be cases of legitimate paternalism.[25] But it would not be legitimate to prevent people from following some norm or practice merely on the grounds that their compliance sets an example and thereby makes it more difficult for others to choose. Such an approach would treat some individuals as means to others' autonomy, and would make individual freedom to choose a way of life contingent on the choices of others. If a woman is unable to make her own choice about work and family that is a violation of her autonomy—and it makes little difference whether that limited autonomy is the result of a norm of the gendered division of labour, or the prohibitions of a state seeking gender egalitarianism.

Second, when we contemplate using the state to compel resistance to a social norm or to punish compliance we risk targeting the already-disadvantaged. If a social norm is inegalitarian it will generally advantage some and disadvantage others; in a widely inegalitarian context the costs of non-compliance will be unequally distributed. In the case of the gendered division of labour, costs imposed for compliance with gendered norms inevitably hit poorer people more than richer ones, entrenching still further the fact that being a stay-at-home parent is a luxury that only some can afford. Making this choice a choice available to the privileged does nothing to undermine its appeal.

Thirdly, if the purpose is to manipulate social conditions such that norms do not develop, there is no principled end to state action. There are a great many norms about which we exercise little autonomy: norms of dress and deportment, norms of etiquette and manners, norms of bodily presentation, norms of health and hygiene. If the problem is that the mere existence of strong social norms undermines our autonomy in a way that merit punitive state measures, the scope for such action becomes worryingly wide.

At this point, Schouten might object that her concern is not with social norms in general, but with gendered norms in particular. Gendered norms might seem particularly inimical to autonomy because, in their dominant form, they attach to the unchosen characteristic of sex. As Schouten puts it, "The institutional design that presumes specialization, and thus makes it so costly to avoid specializing, results from and is sustained by this assumption that families consist of a male breadwinning specialist and a female caregiving specialist."[26] So perhaps it would make a difference if our institutions

---

[25] See Chambers, *Sex, Culture, and Justice*, ch. 7 for discussion.
[26] Schouten, *Liberalism, Neutrality, and the Gendered Division of Labor*, p. 202.

continued to rely on specialisation between caring work v. paid work, but without gendered norms that stipulate who should be in each category.

Indeed, in some socioeconomic demographics this is precisely what is happening. The combination of more generous paternity leave and a commitment to gender egalitarian ideology means that in some sectors we are seeing a shift in norms away from the implication that women should be caregivers and men should be breadwinners. However, this shift has not typically undermined the norm of the ideal worker, available to work at all hours at the employer's service. As Williams deftly shows, this norm is applied to female breadwinners just as much as to male ones.

But the norm of the ideal worker is a problem in itself, even if it applies to all workers regardless of gender. Caring responsibilities are essential to human life and human flourishing. Children cannot survive, let alone flourish, without secure attachment to caregivers with time to care for them properly. Parents suffer greatly if they are forcibly separated from their children, and this suffering may apply particularly strongly to gestational mothers forced to separate from their newborn babies too soon. For these reasons, strong objections remain to forced specialisation in the form of the norm of the ideal worker, even if women are held to that standard equally with men. But Schouten's account cannot explain why.

The priority for feminist and egalitarian liberalism cannot ultimately be to remove all social influence. As social creatures we inevitably influence each other all the time. That our actions are affected by social norms, that we choose things with a significant eye on the question of what others are doing, can scarcely be avoided for social creatures such as ourselves. 'Everybody else is doing it' may not be adequate reason to follow suit, but nor is it reason to condemn those who do. Instead, we should work to remove *influenced disadvantage*. And influenced disadvantage can be alleviated by shifting *influence*, or by shifting *disadvantage*.

It seems clear to me that the better political liberal strategy (and also the better feminist strategy) in dealing with the gendered division of labour is to mitigate *disadvantage*. We should not try to make the lives of women who specialise in carework impossible or more costly. Quite the opposite. We should aim to make their choice *less* costly. This may mean making it easier for mothers and housewives to return to work. But it could also mean making it easier for them to continue their specialisation in domestic and caring work. After all, this work must be done by someone, and it has always been undervalued. Giving caregivers independence, security, and status would be an immensely laudable aim. It might, also, encourage more men to be caregivers. But we should value caregiving even—especially—when it is done by women.

It has been a crucial part of feminism to secure women's access into professional and breadwinning life. But black feminists had it right when they pointed out that employment is not a surefire path to liberation. Perhaps we've had things entirely the wrong way around. Rather than suggesting that *women* are unreasonable or deluded, suffering from false consciousness or adaptive preferences, if they want to devote a portion of their lives to their children at the expense of their careers, why shouldn't we say that *men* are unreasonable and deluded when they want to devote their lives to career success at the expense of their children and domestic life? Rather than bemoan the delusion of the happy housewife, why not lament the false consciousness of the career-driven man?

Why punish *women* (by withholding their leave) if fathers refuse to take caring leave? Why not punish *men*? Rather than following Schouten's suggestion of using taxpayers' money to pay large sums of money to high-income men to take time off work (time which, studies show, many men use for leisure or career advancement rather than carework[27]), why not impose a significant tax on any high-earning man who does *not* take caring leave, and use that tax to pay for wages for (other, poorer) carers: a version of the second-wave feminist demand of wages for housework? Why allow men not only to shirk their own family responsibilities but also to prevent women from gaining their leave in the process? Why pay paternity leave at high levels to high-earning men, but not pay full-time mothers (including single mothers) a high wage for caring for their own children? Why should the state value childcare, by paying handsomely for it, only when it is performed by wealthy men?

An approach that addresses gender inequality by punishing women and rewarding men for taking on traditionally feminine roles is neither liberal nor feminist. Nor is it just.

In an ideal world, Fraser's vision of universal caregiving is indeed the right one. But in our actually-existing world it is merely utopian. We need to re-examine the idea of caregiver parity, recognising the reality for most

---

[27] For example, a study by Heather Antecol et al. found that "the adoption of gender-neutral tenure clock stopping policies substantially reduced female tenure rates while substantially increasing male tenure rates." This effect occurred because mothers used the stopped-clock time to look after their children, whereas fathers used it to further their careers. See Heather Antecol, Kelly Bedard, and Jenna Stearns, "Equal but Inequitable: Who Benefits from Gender-Neutral Tenure Clock Stopping Policies?", in IZA Institute of Labor Economics Discussion Papers No. 9904 (April 2016).

contemporary families. We are living in a transition period in which the traditional constraints on women have been removed—but so have the traditional supports. For many families, extended kinship networks in which childcare and domestic work are shared no longer exist.

Modern life is mobile. Modern mobility includes gendered mobility, as women progress into higher education and professional life; upward mobility, as people move to further professional careers; labour mobility, including migration, as people move to find better-paid jobs or any jobs at all; housing pressures, requiring many young families to move away from their home town as there is no affordable housing; family flux, as relationships break down and new, blended families are formed with diverse step-parenting and custody arrangements; and senior mobility, as many in the grandparental generation enjoy financial stability and a potentially lengthy healthy retirement filled with their own projects. For all these reasons, many families must be self-sufficient, relying on the money and time that the parents can provide themselves, without daily support from wider family. In this context, many parents are hopelessly over-stretched, juggling career, care, and housework. 'Having it all' means doing it all. And doing it all means always feeling that none of it is being done well.

Modern mobility means that we need to return to the idea of Caregiver Parity. We need to recognise that care work and domestic work, alongside the mental load of running a household and family, are burdensome and time-consuming. They cannot be borne by one person alone if that person is also in full-time employment, without that person sacrificing her own leisure time and well-being. So, until such time as paid work radically shifts and the norm of the ideal worker is dispelled, there are two options. Either domestic and care work must be *radically* shared, in a way that runs counter to gendered socialisation and to career ambition and expectations. This solution is only possible in those few households where all adults have equally progressive attitudes and equally-paid and equally-flexible careers. Some dual-academic couples may be like this, but by no means all—and dual-academic couples are hardly representative. Failing that, the only alternative that is compatible with feminist and egalitarian principles is to value care work and domestic work properly, even when it is performed outside of the capitalist market.

The solution to the gendered division of labour is not to elevate paid employment above unpaid care work. The solution starts with recognising that the gendered division of labour depends upon the systematic, enduring devaluation of care and domestic work. It depends on representing this work—women's work—as unskilled and economically unproductive. It depends on valuing work only when it is done by men. And it depends on rewarding women only to the extent that they replicate how men act under patriarchy. In this context, pushing mothers into paid employment by threat of economic punishment is not radical resistance to the gendered division of labour; it is compliance with it. For the gendered division of labour truly to be undermined, *women must be valued for what they do*.

6
The Marriage-Free State

Feminists have long criticised the institution of marriage.[1,2] Historically, it has been a fundamental site of women's oppression, with married women having few independent rights in law. Currently, it is associated with the gendered division of labour, with women taking on the lion's share of domestic and caring work, and being paid less than men for work outside the home.[3] The white wedding is replete with sexist imagery: the father 'giving away' the bride; the white dress symbolising the bride's virginity (and emphasising the importance of her appearance); the vows to obey the husband; the minister telling the husband 'you may now kiss the bride' (rather than the bride herself giving permission, or indeed initiating or at least equally participating in the act of kissing); the reception at which, traditionally, all the speeches are given by men; the wife surrendering her own name and taking her husband's.

Despite decades of feminist criticism the institution resolutely endures— though not without change. The most significant change has been in the introduction of same-sex marriages and civil unions in countries such as

---

[1] This chapter was originally published in *Proceedings of the Aristotelian Society* 113(2) (July 2013). I worked on material relating to that paper while a Visiting Scholar at the Center for the Study of Law and Society (CSLS) in the Boalt School of Law at the University of California, Berkeley, and while an Early Career Fellow at the Centre for Research in the Arts, Social Sciences and Humanities (CRASSH) of the University of Cambridge. I benefitted hugely from the support of both CSLS and CRASSH. I presented earlier versions of this chapter, and of material that relates to it, at the University of York Morrell Conference on Children, Schools and Families, the University of Cambridge Workshop in Political Philosophy, the Nuffield Political Theory Workshop at the University of Oxford, the Philosophy Graduate Workshop at Birkbeck College, the Political Theory Project Research Seminar at Brown University and the University of Warwick Philosophy Seminar. I am very grateful to all the participants for their comments.

[2] See, for example, Mary Wollstonecraft, 'A Vindication of the Rights of Woman', in Janet Todd (ed.), *A Vindication of the Rights of Woman and A Vindication of the Rights of Man* (Oxford: Oxford University Press, 2003 [1792]); John Stuart Mill, *On Liberty and the Subjection of Women* (Ware: Wordsworth, 1996 [1868]); Simone de Beauvoir, *The Second Sex* (New York, NY: Bantam, 1952); Betty Friedan *The Feminine Mystique* (Harmondsworth: Penguin, 1983); Shulamith Firestone, *The Dialectic of Sex: The Case for Feminist Revolution* (London: The Women's Press, 1979); Carole Pateman, *The Sexual Contract* (Cambridge: Polity Press, 1988); Susan Moller Okin, *Justice, Gender, and the Family* (New York, NY: Basic Books, 1989). Additional recent feminist contributions are discussed later in this chapter.

[3] Jane Lewis, *The End of Marriage? Individualism and Intimate Relations* (Cheltenham: Edward Elgar, 2001).

the UK, the Netherlands, Belgium, Spain, Canada, and parts of the USA. In the USA in particular, same-sex marriage was introduced only after a fiercely contested and central part of political debate, with many states alternately allowing and forbidding it as the issue passed between the legislature, the judiciary, and the electorate.[4] The 2015 Supreme Court decision *Obergefell v. Hodges* established same-sex marriage as a constitutional right, decided on a slim majority of five votes to four; with the election of Amy Coney Barrett in 2020 the Supreme Court included six justices who believe the ruling in *Obergefell* was wrong.[5] In other liberal democracies, such as those in Western Europe, the recognition of same-sex marriage is widely accepted and no longer a live political issue.

If marriage exists as a state-recognised institution then it must, as a requirement of equality, be available to same-sex couples. There is a great deal to celebrate in recent moves to widen marriage, and it is hard not to be touched by the scenes of same-sex couples rejoicing as they are finally allowed to marry.[6] In this chapter, though, I argue that even these welcome reforms do not go far enough to address egalitarian concerns.

Feminists have been the main critics of the institution of marriage, and in the first part of the chapter I discuss feminist arguments. I show that feminists attack marriage from several different angles, which can leave the feminist position somewhat conflicted on whether reforms such as same-sex marriage render the institution just. I argue that the way to reconcile feminist accounts is to support the abolition of state-recognised marriage. In the second part of the chapter I discuss options for regulating intimate relationships in a marriage-free state.

---

[4] In the 2012 US elections, citizens of Maine, Maryland, Minnesota, and Washington voted to allow same-sex marriage or civil union. President Obama publicly endorsed gay marriage during the campaign. Previously several states, such as Hawaii and California, had voted against same-sex marriage.

[5] John F. Kowal, 'Is Marriage Equality Next Target for SCOTUS Conservative Supermajority?', Brennan Center for Justice (14 June 2022), available at https://www.brennancenter.org/our-work/analysis-opinion/marriage-equality-next-target-scotus-conservative-supermajority.

[6] One contemporary example was Matt Stopera, '60 Awesome Portraits of Gay Couples Just Married in New York State', *BuzzFeed* (25 July 2011), available at http://www.buzzfeed.com/mjs538/portraits-of-gay-couples-just-married-in-new-york. Most of those images are no longer available, but similarly inspiring images can be seen in Madeline Wahl, '12 Iconic Photos from When Same-Sex Marriage Was Legalized', *Reader's Digest* (23 June 2022), available at https://www.rd.com/list/iconic-photos-when-same-sex-marriage-was-legalized/.

6.1 Feminist Critiques

> My current position on marriage is that I am against it.... Politically, I am against it because it has been oppressive for women, and through privileging heterosexuality, oppressive for lesbians and gay men.[7]

In this quote, and in feminist argument more generally, we can identify two distinct critiques of marriage. Both are common and yet in tension. The first states that traditional marriage is bad because it oppresses women. The implication of this critique is that being married makes women *worse* off. The second critique is that traditional marriage is bad because it privileges heterosexuality. The implication is that being married makes people, both men and women, *better* off: it provides benefits that are unjustly denied to same-sex couples. But these critiques seem contradictory. If marriage oppresses at least some of its participants, why would lesbians and gays want to participate in it? On the other hand, if marriage ought to be extended to same-sex couples because it confers privilege, what have feminists been complaining about all this time? And yet the two critiques are found together in the writings of many feminists.

These two critiques can be divided into what I call practical and symbolic effects. This distinction is not rigid but indicates the difference between ways in which marriage might affect individuals' material or legal status and ways in which it consolidates or instantiates social norms or ideological values. This four-way split in common feminist critiques of marriage explains why it can seem so difficult to develop a coherent feminist position and to be sure which sorts of reforms are progressive and which are reactionary. It explains, that is, the troubling ambiguities expressed by Merran Toerien and Andrew Williams, who label themselves a 'feminist couple'. "In short," they write, "we want to get married and we do not."[8]

The first feminist critique of marriage is that it has practical effects on women that make them worse off. Practical, empirical harms to women resulting from marriage include the contingent facts that marriages tend to

---

[7] Virginia Braun, 'Thanks to my Mother...A Personal Commentary on Heterosexual Marriage', *Feminism & Psychology* 13(4) (2003), p. 421; see also Sarah-Jane Finlay and Victoria Clarke, '"A Marriage of Inconvenience?" Feminist Perspectives on Marriage', *Feminism & Psychology* 13(4) (2003), pp. 417–18.

[8] Merran Toerien and Andrew Williams, 'In Knots: Dilemmas of a Feminist Couple Contemplating Marriage', *Feminism & Psychology* 13(4) (2003), p. 435.

reinforce the gendered division of labour, which itself means that women earn less and are less independent than men; that they reinforce the idea that women do most of the housework, even if they work outside the home, which saps their energies and dignity; and that domestic violence may be exacerbated by marital concepts of entitlement and ownership.[9]

The force of these critiques of marriage depends on particular laws and sociological facts. In past incarnations of marriage, when the institution left women with few or no rights over their bodies, possessions, children, and lives, practical feminist critiques were particularly salient. Janet Gornick argues that truly feminist marriages must involve an egalitarian division of household and caring labour, and suggests state action to enable and encourage both partners to work fewer hours outside the home than is currently normal, devoting their remaining time to domestic labour.[10] Such changes are not easy. Changes to marriage law in favour of gender equality are hard-won victories resting on the suffering of many women, and changes in social norms concerning domestic labour are extremely hard for even feminist women and would-be egalitarian couples to achieve.[11] Nonetheless, these sorts of critiques can in principle be overcome.[12]

But feminists also argue that marriage disadvantages women symbolically, by casting women as inferior. Thus Susan Moller Okin argues that "marriage has earlier and far greater impact on the lives and life choices of women than on those of men, with girls less likely to aspire to prestigious occupations or feel able to contemplate being happily independent."[13] Pierre Bourdieu describes this form of symbolic effect as 'symbolic violence'. Symbolic violence affects thoughts rather than bodies, and is inflicted upon people with

---

[9] Anne Kingston, *The Meaning of Wife* (London: Piatkus, 2004), pp. 158–61.
[10] Janet C. Gornick, 'Reconcilable Difference: What it Would Take for Marriage and Feminism to Say "I Do"', *The American Prospect Online* (7 April 2002).
[11] Pepper Schwartz, *Love Between Equals: How Peer Marriage Really Works* (New York, NY: The Free Press, 1994); Arlie Russell Hochschild and Anne Machung, *The Second Shift: Working Parents and the Revolution at Home* (London: Piatkus, 1990).
[12] Celia Kitzinger and Sue Wilkinson adopt this optimistic view in 'The Re-branding of Marriage: Why We Got Married Instead of Registering a Civil Partnership', *Feminism and Psychology* 14(1) (2004), p. 135. Card is more sceptical. On her analysis, the very idea of marriage as a state-awarded license giving claims over another person's property and person is profoundly problematic, for it exposes individuals to each other and puts in place legal barriers to separation. In doing so, marriage inevitably leaves its participants (largely its female participants) vulnerable to abuse. As she puts it: "For all that has been said about the privacy that marriage protects, what astonishes me is how much privacy one gives up in marrying.... Anyone who in fact cohabits with another may seem to give up similar privacy. Yet, without marriage, it is possible to take one's life back without encountering the law as an obstacle" (Claudia Card, 'Against Marriage and Motherhood', *Hypatia* 11(3) (1996), p. 12).
[13] Okin, *Justice, Gender, and the Family*, p. 142. See also Kingston, *The Meaning of Wife*.

their complicity.[14] In other words, symbolic violence occurs when, through social pressures, an individual feels herself to be inferior or worthless.

One particularly pernicious form of symbolic violence that marriage enacts on women in contemporary Western societies is the sense that they are flawed and failing if unmarried. Research shows that many heterosexual women see single life as a temporary phase preceding marriage, and that being single for longer or when older is construed as sad and shameful, and at least partially the fault of the single woman herself.[15] A particularly striking example of this sort of pressure can be found in *The Rules*, the mid-1990s best-selling self-help book that instructs women to secure marriage by following a strict set of guidelines such as not telephoning men, not describing their own sexual desires or asking them to be met, and not minding when men are angry. Women wishing to ignore, let alone criticise, *The Rules* are sharply admonished:

> If you think you're too smart for The Rules, ask yourself 'Am I married?'. If not, why not? Could it be that what you're doing isn't working? Think about it.[16]

More recently, a series of reality TV shows take on the theme of bringing about marriage by any means necessary. *Married at First Sight*, based on a Danish programme format from 2013, is now broadcast in the USA, the UK, and around the world. Participants agree to be matched up by relationship experts and, as the name implies, marry when they first meet. This format weakens the solemnity of marriage (participants can choose divorce on a scheduled 'Decision Day') but reinforces the idea of marriage as a goal.

We might ask, however, whether it would matter if women felt pressure to enter into marriage if it were the case that the practical aspects of marriage were egalitarian. In other words, if marriage no longer disadvantaged women practically, would it matter if they were pressured to enter it symbolically? We might have a number of autonomy- and diversity-based objections to such

---

[14] Pierre Bourdieu, *Masculine Domination* (Cambridge: Polity Press, 2001); Pierre Bourdieu and Loïc Wacquant, *An Invitation to Reflexive Sociology* (Cambridge: Polity Press, 1992).
[15] Anna Sandfield and Carol Percy, 'Accounting for Single Status: Heterosexism and Ageism in Heterosexual Women's Talk about Marriage', *Feminism & Psychology* 13(4) (2003); Jill Reynolds and Margaret Wetherell, 'The Discursive Climate of Singleness: The Consequences for Women's Negotiation of a Single Identity', *Feminism & Psychology* 13(4) (2003).
[16] Ellen Fein and Sherrie Schneider, *The Rules: Time Tested Secrets for Capturing the Heart of Mr Right* (London: Thorlens, 1995), p. 120. For a feminist who is not too chastised to criticise *The Rules*, see Petra Boynton, 'Abiding by The Rules: Instructing Women in Relationships', *Feminism & Psychology* 13(2) (2003).

pressure, which would apply to both women and men. But one way in which pressure to enter into even reformed marriages might particularly harm women (and thus be of particular concern to feminists) is through the simple fact that marriage has *historically* been an extremely sexist institution. Even if these historical oppressions have been reformed, such that wives are equal to husbands in all areas of law, marriage remains an institution rooted in the subjection of women.[17]

This question, of whether the patriarchal history of an institution continues to taint its modern incarnations even if the explicitly patriarchal aspects have been reformed, is a vexed one.[18] It seems obvious that institutions need not remain unjust forever, beyond the abolition of that which initially made them unjust. For example, cotton-picking and chimney-sweeping are jobs that were once done by slaves and children, respectively, both unjust forms of labour; and democratic participation was denied to women in the UK until the extension of the suffrage in the early twentieth century. But cotton-picking, chimney-sweeping, and democracy need not remain unjust once slavery, child labour, and sex discrimination are abolished: the injustice does not outlive its concrete manifestation.

What makes marriage different is that it is an institution entered into largely because of the meanings it represents. Couples may marry so as to obtain various practical benefits, but a key aspect of most marriages is the statement the couple makes about their relationship. For the marrying couple, and for society in general, the symbolic significance of marriage is at least as important as its practical aspects, as demonstrated in debates about same-sex marriage, discussed next.[19]

Thus the state recognition of marriage is state intervention in, and control of, the meaning of marriage. This being the case, it is impossible to escape the

---

[17] Pateman, *The Sexual Contract*; Card, 'Against Marriage and Motherhood'; Torien and Williams, 'In Knots', p. 434; Sheila Jeffreys, 'The Need to Abolish Marriage', *Feminism & Psychology* 14(2) (2004); Richard H. Thaler and Cass R. Sunstein, *Nudge: Improving Decisions About Health, Wealth and Happiness* (New Haven, CT: Yale University Press, 2008), p. 219.

[18] A particularly influential argument that the history of marriage pervades its present is found in Pateman, *The Sexual Contract*. Pateman's focus in that book is on marriage as a form of contract, and she strongly implies that no reform could render marriage non-patriarchal since the very idea of contracting parties is deeply embedded in insurmountably patriarchal concepts (pp. 184–5).

[19] The public nature of the symbolism, the state's control over the meaning of marriage, is demonstrated in the difference between the legal requirements of civil marriages and civil partnerships in the UK. At a marriage the officiating Registrar is required to say: 'Before you are joined in matrimony I have to remind you of the solemn and binding character of the vows of marriage. Marriage, according to the law of this country, is the union of one man with one woman, voluntarily entered into for life to the exclusion of all others.' There is no equivalent required legal declaration of the meaning of a civil partnership.

history of the institution. Its status as a *tradition* ties its current meaning to its past. This feature of marriage makes the issue of what the institution really does represent, what meanings it carries, particularly pertinent.

The second strand of feminist critique of marriage is that it is heterosexist. According to this critique marriage *benefits* those who enter into it. Thus feminists, who favour gender equality and oppose discrimination on the grounds of both sex and sexuality, must oppose marriage as long as it is denied to same-sex couples.[20] Many feminists campaign for the extension of marriage to same-sex couples, and some argue that extending marriage to same-sex couples would transform the institution. Margaret Morganroth Gullette writes that she was transformed from "a rebellious critic of the institution into a vocal and explicit advocate" as the result of "recognizing and honoring the growing desire of some of my lesbian friends and relatives to enjoy the protections that marriage now extends only to heterosexuals".[21]

Once again, this line of argument can be separated into practical and symbolic strands. Practically, marriage privileges heterosexuality if the law is structured so as to give married couples particular rights that are denied to unmarried couples. Such laws discriminate against both same-sex couples and all unmarried individuals (whether single or in a relationship). In the UK, for example, spouses do not have to pay inheritance tax when inheriting each other's property, unlike those in any other form of relationship. Material benefits such as this lead Thomas Stoddard to advocate same-sex marriage "despite the oppressive nature of marriage historically, and in spite of the general absence of edifying examples of modern heterosexual marriage".[22]

Heterosexual-only marriage also has discriminatory *symbolic* effects. By recognising heterosexual marriage the state confers legitimacy and approval

---

[20] Torien and Williams, 'In Knots', p. 434.
[21] Margaret Morganroth Gullette, 'The New Case for Marriage', *The American Prospect Online* (5 March 2004).
[22] Thomas B. Stoddard, 'Why Gay People Should Seek the Right to Marry', in Mark Blasius and Shane Phelan (eds), *We Are Everywhere: A Historical Sourcebook of Gay and Lesbian Politics* (London: Routledge, 1997), p. 754. It is worth noting that the existence of tax and other benefits for married couples does not simply mean that unmarried individuals cannot access a benefit. When that benefit is a tax break or similar it imposes a measurable *cost* on those who do not receive it, since their tax burden will necessarily be higher than it would be if the benefit did not exist for others. In other words, the move from tax equality to tax breaks for the married cannot be Pareto-optimal: the benefit for the married can be achieved only at the expense of the unmarried. David Estlund emphasises this point, and argues that pro-marriage campaigns are also coercive ('Commentary on Parts I and II', in David Estlund and Martha C. Nussbaum (eds), *Sex, Preference, and Family: Essays on Law and Nature* (Oxford: Oxford University Press, 1997), p. 163). Since marriage is unjust in both its effects on women and its unavailability to homosexuals, it follows that those who are married are benefitting from injustice.

on such partnerships and denies it to homosexual ones. Thus Maria Bevacqua, a feminist lesbian, argues:

> The exclusion of a portion of the population from a major social institution creates a second-class citizenship for that group. This is a humiliating experience, whether as individuals we feel humiliated or not.[23]

Bevacqua's insistence that the humiliation is independent of the feelings of the humiliated emphasises the deeply symbolic nature of the institution. Marriage presents and represents a particular symbolic meaning that transcends individuals' subjective self-understandings and experiences. Instead, it appeals to supposedly shared social understandings of value, understandings that can fail to respect minority and historically oppressed groups. In particular, marriage reinforces the idea that the monogamous heterosexual union is the (only) sacred form of relationship.

Stoddard argues that marriage is "the centrepiece of our entire social structure" and notes that the US Supreme Court has called it "noble" and "sacred".[24] Understandably he "resents" and "loathes" the fact that, according to the Court and US policy, lesbians and gays are not deemed able to enter into such noble and sacred relationships.[25] Like Bevacqua, Stoddard believes that legalising same-sex marriage is a crucial egalitarian step, even if many lesbians and gays have no desire to marry. Indeed, Stoddard argues that same-sex marriages would also benefit heterosexual women, as they would serve the feminist purpose of "abolishing the traditional gender requirements of marriage" and thus divesting the institution of "the sexist trappings of the past".[26]

According to these feminist critiques, then, marriage oppresses both those heterosexual women who do or could participate in it and those lesbians and gay men who could not; and it does so in ways that are both practical and symbolic. But these criticisms can conflict in their implications for marriage reform, rendering the debate exceedingly complicated.

From the perspective of these diverse feminist critiques, before same-sex marriage was widely recognised it was not clear whether such recognition would be desirable. Restricting marriage to different-sex couples is symbolically oppressive to women (straight and lesbian) and to gay men. If same-sex

---

[23] Maria Bevacqua, 'Feminist Theory and the Question of Lesbian and Gay Marriage', *Feminism & Psychology* 14(1) (2004), p. 37.
[24] Stoddard, 'Why Gay People Should Seek the Right to Marry', p. 756.
[25] Stoddard, 'Why Gay People Should Seek the Right to Marry', p. 756.
[26] Stoddard, 'Why Gay People Should Seek the Right to Marry', p. 757.

couples are allowed to marry, it is not clear whether the oppressiveness of marriage will rub off onto lesbians and gay men, making them worse off, or whether the progressiveness of gay and lesbian inclusion will rub off onto marriage, making all women better off. As we have seen, Stoddard argued that progressiveness would prevail. Paula Ettelbrick, on the other hand, predicted the triumph of patriarchy and reaction: "marriage will not liberate us as lesbians and gay men. In fact, it will constrain us, make us more invisible, force our assimilation into the mainstream, and undermine the goals of gay liberation," she writes.[27]

We can identify similar ambiguities in the issue of allowing same-sex couples to enter into civil partnerships but not marriages (as was the case in the UK between 2004 and 2014). Such a policy has two advantages from the feminist point of view: first, same-sex couples are given access to the practical benefits of marriage; second, the idea of a civil partnership breaks away from the patriarchal symbolism of historically oppressive marriage. Some feminists also argue that same-sex civil partnerships will benefit heterosexual women, whether married or not, by undermining both the hegemony of marriage and the idea that traditional gender roles must prevail within it. Indeed, one way of breaking away from the patriarchal history of marriage is to offer civil partnerships to different-sex couples as well as to same-sex ones, an option made available in the UK in 2019, after activism by the Equal Love Campaign, a successful legal challenge by Rebecca Steinfeld and Charles Keidan, and a Private Members' Bill sponsored by Tim Loughton MP.[28] The status of civil partnership can thus be doubly egalitarian: it emphasises equality between different-sex and same-sex couples since both can enter into it, and it emphasises equality between men and women by breaking from patriarchal history and by imposing equal terms on each member of the partnership.

However, the policy of distinguishing civil partnership from marriage also has disadvantages. When the title 'marriage' was reserved for different-sex relationships the institution of civil partnerships *entrenched* the gendered nature of marriage, since the idea that marriage must be between a man and a

---

[27] Paula L. Ettelbrick, 'Since When Is Marriage a Path to Liberation?', in Mark Blasius and Shane Phelan (eds), *We Are Everywhere: A Historical Sourcebook of Gay and Lesbian Politics* (London: Routledge, 1997), p. 758; see also Card, 'Against Marriage and Motherhood'.

[28] Rebecca Steinfeld and Charles Keidan of The Equal Civil Partnerships Campaign won their case in the UK Supreme Court, with the Court ruling that it is discriminatory for civil partnerships to be available to same-sex couples only. Subsequently, the Civil Partnerships, Marriages and Deaths (Registrations Etc.) Bill, a Private Members' Bill by Tim Loughton MP, was passed by Parliament with government support in 2019. See Equal Civil Partnerships Campaign Group at http://equalcivilpartnerships.org.uk and *R (Steinfeld and Another) v Secretary of State for International Development* UKSC 32 (2018), 3 WLR 415 (2018).

woman was reinforced, and with it traditional gender roles. Moreover, the fact that marriage symbolically oppresses lesbians and gays remains, since the discriminatory and hierarchical distinction between same-sex and different-sex couples is unchanged if only different-sex couples may marry. Finally, such a move does nothing to challenge the hierarchy that marriage enacts between being partnered and being single, since rights are even more forcefully allied to the former and denied to the latter. Thus Celia Kitzinger and Sue Wilkinson argue:

> By re-branding as 'civil partnership' a union that is otherwise identical to opposite-sex civil marriage, civil partnerships achieve the symbolic separation of same-sex couples from the state of 'marriage'. They grant same-sex couples the possibility of legal conformity with institutional arrangements which formally recognize heterosexual intimacy while effectively excluding us from that very institution. The irony is that this separation is positively valued by many feminists and LGBT activists because it is the *symbolism* of marriage – and not the civil institution itself – that is the target of their critique.[29]

The question of how, from a feminist standpoint, we can best understand and interact with the institution of marriage is thus incredibly complex, and this complexity is mirrored in the diversity of feminist positions on the issue. One way of understanding this diversity is by returning to the idea that marriage is an *institution*.[30] I have highlighted a puzzle, which is that feminists argue that marriage is both oppressive to its (female) participants and oppressive to its non-participants. These two oppressions seem in tension, but the tension might be resolved if we take a broader view. It is possible that, *if the institution of marriage exists*, it is better to be married than not, but that the *very existence of the institution* is oppressive. In other words, it might be that women are better off if marriage does not exist at all; but if marriage does exist they are better off married than unmarried. On this account, juxtaposing marriage's oppressiveness to women and to lesbians and gays fails to compare like with like: marriage is oppressive to women as compared to a world without marriage; it is oppressive to deny same-sex couples marriage only insofar as that institution does exist.

---

[29] Kitzinger and Wilkinson, 'The Re-branding of Marriage', p. 144.
[30] I am grateful to Fabienne Peter for pressing me on this point.

This analysis fits with some of the examples of oppression just given. The symbolic pressure on women to marry, and the idea that they are worthless if unmarried, means that *if marriage exists* women are better off married than unmarried. This view is compatible, then, with the idea that it is harmful to be denied access to marriage *if the institution exists for others* and confers practical or symbolic benefits. But there is no necessary harm if the state refuses to recognise marriage at all.[31]

The natural implication is that women and gay men are better off, and justice is served, if marriage ceases to exist as an institution. Abolishing the institution satisfies all feminist critiques, and is thus a policy implication around which feminists should unite.

6.2 The Marriage-Free State

I advocate, then, the abolition of state-recognised marriage and the institution of what I call a Marriage-Free State. The state recognises marriage in the relevant sense when it applies a *bundle* of rights and duties to married people *because* they are married.[32] The italics highlight the two parts of the claim. In a society with state-recognised marriage the members of a marrying couple thereby acquire a *bundle* of rights and duties that they did not previously have. For example, they may acquire rights to inheritance without tax, next-of-kinship rights, rights to financial support from each other, rights concerning children, and so on. These rights are given to the couple *because* they are married, not because they have chosen each right in turn (for they have not), and not because there is some other feature of their relationship

---

[31] The European Declaration of Human Rights protects the right to marry, a right which has also been seen as fundamental in US constitutional law. Insofar as the right to marry is a genuine right it is best understood as the right to form committed partnerships, and to enjoy protection from undue legal interference in those relationships, rather than as a right to have one's marriage recognised as a special and privileged legal status.

[32] This idea of state recognition does not exhaust the ways in which a state might take an interest in marriage. A state may also take an interest in marriage by defining and setting limits on it: stating who may and may not enter into a marriage and which procedures must be followed for a relationship to become a marriage. A marriage-free state might refrain from showing this sort of interest in the institution but it is not a requirement of a state counting as marriage-free that it so refrains, for a marriage-free state might take an interest in setting limits on even private marriages. For example, the state might make it illegal for religions to marry children. Even if the state refuses to recognise marriages, religious or secular, it still has an interest in protecting children and thus in setting limits on what non-state individuals and groups may do to them.

Another important way the state might interact with marriage is by registering and enquiring about its existence, for example on official forms. I take it that a marriage-free state will not do this for any purposes other than monitoring the prevalence of private marriage, or applying such regulations to private marriage as may be required by justice (such as a prohibition on marrying children).

that merits them (for non-married couples living in identical circumstances will lack some or all of these rights).

Abolishing state-recognised marriage means that the state no longer provides a bundle of rights and duties to people because they are married. It does not mean making it illegal for people to participate in the symbolic institution of marriage or to call themselves married. Without state-recognised marriage, people could still engage in private religious or secular ceremonies of marriage, but these would have no legal status.

Even if marriage is abolished as a legal category the question of how to regulate personal relationships remains. Personal relationships still have to be regulated so as to protect vulnerable parties, including but not only children; so as to regulate disputes over such matters as joint property; and so as to appropriately direct state benefits and taxes.

Some argue that personal relationships should be regulated on a contractual basis.[33] The contractual model has various problems, which I discuss in *Against Marriage*. But even if relationship contracts are permitted there is a need for an additional regulatory framework for personal relationships. Such regulation is required for several reasons. Even if contracts are allowed, the state must set limits on contracts that would be unjust for the contracting parties (such as contracts amounting to slavery) or for third parties such as children, and must provide guidance for disputes that arise between people in personal relationships who have not made a contract. There is also a need for regulation to protect legitimate state interests and to provide clarity on matters that must be determinate in law. So relationship contracts cannot replace marriage. There must still be a regulatory framework, a series of state directives, applying to personal relationships.

It is useful to distinguish two general models for state regulation of relationships: holistic and piecemeal. Most advocates of non-marital regulation of personal relationships take a holistic approach; I argue here in favour of piecemeal regulation.

Holistic regulation of relationships involves creating a *status*, such as marriage or an analogous alternative, which brings with it a bundle of legal rights and responsibilities. Both existing marriage and civil unions are examples of holistic regulation. When entering into these relationships individuals take

---

[33] Advocates of regulating relationships on a contractual basis include Marjorie Schultz, 'Contractual Ordering of Marriage: A New Model for State Policy', *California Law Review* 70(2) (1982); Martha Albertson Fineman, 'The Meaning of Marriage', in Anita Bernstein (ed.), *Marriage Proposals: Questioning a Legal Status* (New York, NY: New York University Press, 2006); Lenore J. Weitzman, *The Marriage Contract: Spouses, Lovers and the Law* (London: Free Press, 1983).

on a bundle of rights and responsibilities covering multiple areas of life such as property ownership, tax status, inheritance, next-of-kinship, child custody, and immigration. On a holistic model of marriage reform, the state continues to award some people a bundle of special rights and duties. It simply awards that bundle on the basis of a status other than marriage.

Civil unions are the most familiar alternative to marriage on the holistic model, but they are not the only one. Several progressive thinkers have proposed new holistic statuses to replace marriage. Some advocate versions of civil unions that differ in some way from the existing legislative models.[34] Other theorists advocate completely new statuses, usually replacing the marital focus on adult sexual partnership with an emphasis on care. For example, Tamara Metz proposes disestablishing marriage and replacing it with a state-recognised Intimate Care-Giving Union (ICGU) status, one that could apply to any relationship of intimate caregiving.[35]

All of these models—civil union, ICGU status, and minimal marriage—improve on the state recognition of traditional marriage by breaking from the patriarchal, exclusionary, and controversial meaning of that institution. In other words, each is to be preferred to marriage symbolically. Their practical advantages depend on their particularities. British civil partnerships afford the partners much the same legal rights as are afforded to married spouses. So British civil partnerships are neither better nor worse than marriage in terms of the practical support they provide to personal relationships; their advantage is that they counteract the symbolic inequalities of traditional marriage.

Metz proposes a more radical alternative status which, unlike marriage, "would be expressly tailored to protecting intimate care in its various forms".[36] She makes the convincing case that caregiving is a better basis for public policy than marriage since care is a more fundamental activity: a primary good essential to human flourishing that nevertheless brings with it risks and vulnerabilities. For Metz, state recognition and protection of caregiving status therefore protects the vulnerable and allows all to access vital human goods.

I endorse the claim that caregiving is crucial and worthy of state protection. However, I suggest that holistic regulation, implementing a new status, is not the best replacement for state-recognised marriage. Holistic regulation

---

[34] Thaler and Sunstein, *Nudge*; Andrew F. March, 'What Lies Beyond Same-Sex Marriage? Marriage, Reproductive Freedom and Future Persons in Liberal Public Justification', *Journal of Applied Philosophy* 27(1) (2010).
[35] Tamara Metz, *Untying the Knot: Marriage, the State, and the Case for their Divorce* (Princeton, NJ: Princeton University Press, 2010).
[36] Metz, *Untying the Knot*, p. 135.

involves a *bundle* of rights and duties. Holistic approaches thus tend to assume that all the most important functions of life are met within one core relationship. This is the model behind civil unions. Of course many people, such as most married people, do centralise activities such as intimate coupledom, childrearing, property-sharing, next-of-kinship and inheritance. For such people, the bundling feature of holistic regulation is unproblematic, even convenient. But the state should recognise that many individuals' arrangements are more wide-ranging. Separated couples with children may continue to co-parent but share no other relationship. Others maintain a nuclear family unit but also share property or care with an elderly parent or sibling. Bundling caring activity into one privileged status does not capture the complexity and diversity of real lives.

Bundling is also problematic for political or non-perfectionist liberals, since a holistic bundled status involves the state in making value judgments about better and worse ways of life and in marking one type of relationship out as the most fundamental.[37] Indeed, as Metz herself notes, special expressive status akin to the symbolic significance of marriage might become attached to ICGU status, and the conferral of such status does involve the state in "acting in a way that reflects particular political commitments".[38]

Instead I propose *piecemeal* regulation, which rejects bundling. Piecemeal regulation involves the state regulating the different practices or activities of a relationship separately. By 'relationship practices' I mean an activity or area of life which is carried out in a personal relationship. So relationship practices include things such as property ownership, financial interdependence, emotional interdependence, care, parenting, cohabitation, next-of-kinship, sexual intimacy. Under piecemeal regulation there is no assumption that all relationship practices coincide in one relationship. Thus there would be separate regulations for property ownership and division, child custody, immigration, and so on. Not all relationship practices need regulation, but those that do should be treated in a piecemeal way.

Elizabeth Brake proposes an alternative to traditional marriage that avoids bundling. On Brake's scheme, each individual can be 'minimally married' to more than one person at a time, assigning different rights (which Brake calls

---

[37] Metz explicitly acknowledges that "Both marriages and ICGU status reflect value judgements" (Metz, *Untying the Knot*, p. 148.) Her argument is that ICGU status is preferable since caregiving is a legitimate area of state interest. Elizabeth Brake argues that political liberals should endorse minimal marriage since care is a primary good; I address her account in Clare Chambers, *Against Marriage* (Oxford: Oxford University Press, 2017).

[38] Metz, *Untying the Knot*, p. 148.

'minimal marriage rights') to different people.[39] Brake's proposal is therefore a form of piecemeal regulation. But Brake's account is still vulnerable to a further problem, one that affects most alternative forms of personal relationship regulation: people must *opt in* to receive legal protection. People who have not, or not yet, chosen to acquire the status of minimal marriage, ICGU, or civil union are left unprotected—*even if they are in relationships that are functionally identical to those who have acquired such status*.

The Law Commission offers a compelling example to explain what is wrong with this situation, in the context of current British marriage law:

> Take the position of cohabitants who have children and have been living together for a long time. The mother stays at home to look after the children and has no real prospects of re-entering the job market at a level that would enable her to afford the child-care that her absence from home would require.... In order to obtain any long-term economic security in case of the relationship ending, she would first have to persuade him that he should take steps to protect her position. It might well be that he is quite happy with the status quo, which favours him.
>
> Even if she were able to overcome this initial hurdle and persuade her partner that something should be done, they would then have to decide what steps were appropriate. It might be thought that the obvious answer is that they should marry. But research suggests... that many cohabitants think it wrong to marry purely for legal or financial reasons. The alternative would be for them to declare an express trust over their home or enter into a contract for her benefit. However, such arrangements may be complex and require legal advice. The couple may simply conclude that the issue is not sufficiently pressing to take any further, and that they have other spending priorities.[40]

The outcome is that if the couple separate the woman is left without the financial protection afforded to divorcing spouses, despite the fact that their relationship is functionally identical to many marriages.

The same problems occur with any proposed alternative status to marriage. There must be a difference in law between those with that status and those

---

[39] Elizabeth Brake, *Minimizing Marriage: Marriage, Morality, and the Law* (Oxford: Oxford University Press, 2012), p. 303.
[40] The Law Commission, 'Cohabitation: The Financial Consequences of Relationship Breakdown', *LAW COM No 307* (2007), p. 33.

without that status, for otherwise the status is purely symbolic and affording it is outside the state's purview. But then the existence of that status means that legal protection is denied to those who are engaged in caring relationships but have not acquired the protected status.

Instead of regulating relationships by *status*, the state should regulate by *practice*. The state should set a regulatory framework that stipulates the non-voluntary, default rights and duties that apply to everyone who participates in a given relationship practice: anyone who is the primary carer of a child, any people who share in purchasing their main home, and so on. Alternative statuses such as minimal marriage or ICGU status mean that there will be differences between those who have, and do not have, those statuses even if there is no functional difference in their relationship. In contrast, practice-based regulation starts by working out what justice requires in any given area of human life and relationship, and secures that requirement for everyone.

The content and form of the ideal practice-based regulations is beyond the scope of this chapter. Separate arguments would be needed both to identify each area of state interest and to specify what the just regulations should be. Such arguments would proceed as follows. For each relationship practice we ask first whether, and second why, the state has a legitimate interest in regulation. The answers to these questions indicate the content of that regulation. Crucially, the arguments are separate for each proposed area of regulation.

Consider, for example, immigration rights for partners. Advocates of open borders will argue that the state should not control immigration at all, so there is no justification for any relationship-based immigration rights. Others will argue that states do have a legitimate interest in controlling immigration, in which case an argument must be provided as to what sorts of immigration should be allowed and what that implies for rights of immigrants to bring others with them. Depending on the outcome of that argument we might be left with a defence of immigration only for solitary, economically necessary workers, or with a defence of allowing all immigrants to bring a certain number of people of their choice with them (regardless of relationships between them), or any number of other possibilities. The point is that no status such as marriage settles these arguments in advance.

Or, consider the example of inheritance tax. Current UK law awards a privilege to spouses and civil partners that is not awarded to others, in the form of an exemption from inheritance tax for transfers between partners. Citizens in general are not allowed to nominate a person who is exempt from inheritance tax; they can opt in to the exemption only by marrying or entering a civil partnership. Inheritance tax exemptions might not be justified at all. But if they are justified this cannot be because married people are somehow more in need, or more deserving of, exemptions than others.[41] Exemptions might be justified on the grounds that if one cohabitant dies it is unfair or undesirable to require the other cohabitant to leave their home in order to raise the money to pay tax on the inherited portion of the home. If this is the justification then the tax exemption should be awarded to all people who inherit a portion of their primary residence. Alternatively, an exemption from inheritance tax might be justified on the grounds that it is good public policy to allow people one tax-free heir (perhaps because doing so encourages saving and hard work, since people know that what they save will pass to their nearest and dearest rather than to the Treasury). If this is the justification for the policy then *all* people should be allowed to nominate one tax-free heir of their choice, for the incentive will work regardless of whether that heir is a spouse, child, friend, or charity.

Finally, consider parenting. It is clear that the state has a legitimate interest in regulating how adults care for children so as to protect those children. Some such regulations, such as the duty not to physically abuse a child, apply to any adult interacting with any child, whether that adult is a stranger, a professional caregiver, a relative, or a parent. Other regulations might legitimately apply to professional carers but not to parents, perhaps because to apply them to parents would be an unjust interference in family life and parental privacy. For example, nurseries and childminders have to adhere to stricter health and safety standards than do private family homes. It is not my argument, then, that there should be no legal recognition of the differences between different sorts of relationships. But these differences should be based on the functional differences between strangers, professional carers, and intimate carers—and perhaps between primary carers (such as parents or guardians) v. non-primary intimate carers (such as wider family members). The crucial point is that there should be no difference between primary caregivers based on whether or not those caregivers have sought some special state-recognised status, such as marriage, civil union, ICGU, or minimal marriage. Piecemeal regulation thus has the advantage that it targets all relevant people, and does not miss those who have not sought the relevant status.

One potential objection to my argument is that it undermines liberty. A marriage regime allows people to choose whether to marry, and one reason

---

[41] Doubtless some defend exemptions for married people as an incentive to marry. Such arguments fail on two counts: first, there is no legitimate state interest in incentivising people to marry (as opposed to incentivising stable relationships, or care, or some other good); and second, few proponents of this argument would actually want people to marry purely for the money.

people choose not to marry is to avoid the consequent legal regulations. Should it not be possible to form a relationship without incurring extensive legal duties?

The answer to this question depends on the relationship activity in question. Some relationships, such as parenthood, rightly bring duties that cannot be avoided except in the most extreme circumstances. Other relationships, or relationship activities, seem more suitable for variation. I do not take a stand here on what those areas of legitimate diversity might be, or even if there are any; in general the liberal state should regulate only when there is a pressing need to do so. But *if* there are areas of relationships that need regulation but in which there can be legitimate diversity then the right approach is to allow people to *opt out* of the default regulations (which must be designed with justice in mind), rather than to leave people unprotected unless they *opt in* to some privileged status.

Opting out would be a matter of drawing up a contract or trust expressly setting out how the relationship deviates from the default. The law would stipulate when opting out is possible, and any limits that might apply. So the legal complexity and expense described by the Law Commission above would fall on those wanting to escape the protection offered in law, not on those wishing to be protected.[42]

Piecemeal regulation has many advantages, then. It is more flexible, allowing a variety of ways of life to receive appropriate state attention. It can meet the needs of caring relationships but does not assume that all caring relationships are attached to other forms of intimacy or that people have only one sort of caring relationship. And it dispenses entirely with one special status to which special recognition and thus endorsement is attached. Instead, the importance of many different forms of relationship is recognised, and each is provided with the legal recognition, rights, and responsibilities appropriate to it.

Freedom and Equality: Essays on Liberalism and Feminism. Clare Chambers, Oxford University Press.
© Clare Chambers 2024. DOI: 10.1093/9780191919480.003.0007

---

[42] As J. S. Mill argues, "laws and institutions should be adapted, not to good men only, but to bad" (Mill, *On Liberty and the Subjection of Women*, p. 149).

PART III
THE LIMITS OF LIBERALISM

7
Should the Liberal State Recognise Gender?

What should the state recognise?

In my 2017 book *Against Marriage* I argue for an end to the state recognition of marriage. State-recognised marriage, so I argue there, violates both freedom and equality. It violates freedom in the political liberal sense, because state-recognised marriage is a policy that can be justified only by appeal to a controversial conception of the good with which many people inevitably and reasonably disagree. It violates equality because it is based on a system that is traditionally and symbolically hierarchical, and because it creates an unjustified inequality between people who are and are not married. In this chapter, I argue that the same considerations apply to the state recognition of gender, meaning that liberals should not support it.[1]

The state recognition of gender is a live political issue. Many countries are grappling with the question of whether and how to allow people to change their legal sex as recorded at birth so that it reflects their gender identity. Sweden was the first country in the world to allow people to change their legally recorded sex to reflect their gender, through its 1972 Gender Recognition Act.[2] That Act was both progressive, since it was the first of its kind in the world, and regressive, since anyone wishing to use it had to be both unmarried and sterilised. Those restrictions were removed in 2013 and, since 2018, anyone who submitted to mandatory sterilisation under the 1972 Act can apply for compensation. However, Swedish trans advocacy groups would like the Gender Recognition Act to be reformed further. RFSL, the Swedish Federation for Lesbian, Gay, Bisexual, Transgender, Queer and Intersex rights, argues that "Changing your legal gender should be as easy as changing your first name; through a form from the Swedish Tax Agency."[3]

---

[1] Versions of this chapter, which has not previously been published, were presented at the Social Rights Conference at the University of Warwick, the University of Cambridge Seminar in Contemporary Political Thought, and the Philosophy Seminar of Umeå University, Sweden, where I was a Visiting Professor in 2021. I am very grateful to all participants for comments, and to the philosophers of Umeå, particularly Kalle Grill, for their hospitality.

[2] Ministry of Employment, 'Chronological Overview of LGBT Persons Rights in Sweden', Government Offices of Sweden (12 July 2018), available at https://www.government.se/articles/2018/07/chronological-overview-of-lgbt-persons-rights-in-sweden/.

[3] RFSL, 'Why Do We Need a New Gender Recognition Act?' (20 March 2020), available at https://www.rfsl.se/en/lgbtq-facts/gender_recognition/ (accessed 9 September 2022).

The current Swedish position resembles that of the UK. In the autumn of 2018 the UK government ran a public consultation about proposed changes to the Gender Recognition Act 2004. The UK Gender Recognition Act (GRA) enables a trans person to acquire legal recognition and documentation in their preferred gender, including having the sex recorded on their birth certificate changed to the gender with which they identify. Anyone wishing to make use of this provision must meet various conditions and submit to a process of clinical oversight. Trans activists and lobby groups argue that this process of legal transition is too onerous and invasive.[4] Like RFSL in Sweden, pressure groups such as Stonewall want people to be able to change their legal gender on the basis of self-identification only, without any medical documentation or gatekeeping. They argue that easier transition is a necessary part of respecting what they see as a right to determine one's own gender identity, and have that identity recognised by the state.[5] In response, the Gender Recognition Reform (Scotland) Bill was passed in 2022, introducing a new process for Scotland. The most significant changes were that obtaining a Gender Recognition Certificate would no longer require a supporting medical diagnosis of gender dysphoria, and the process would be available to 16- and 17-year-olds. According to official government documentation, "The Scottish Government considers that the current system [pre-reform] is intrusive and can take a long time, which can have a negative impact on applicants."[6]

A variety of activists, women's organisations and gender-critical feminists take an opposing view, arguing that recognising legal gender on the basis of self-ID would have harmful consequences.[7] For example, Fair Play For Women argue that GRA reform would make it impossible to protect single-sex services and spaces, for two reasons. First, easier legal transition would mean that many more trans women than at present could choose to become legally female, including those who have not and do not intend to undergo any physical transition (hormonal or surgical). This is significant, on their view, because the fundamental character of same-sex services and spaces will

---

[4] Organisations that argue for the liberalisation of legal gender recognition include Stonewall, Gendered Intelligence, Mermaids, and Pink News.

[5] See, for example, 'Stonewall Statement on Labour's Gender Recognition Act Reform Proposals' (24 July 2023), available at https://www.stonewall.org.uk/about-us/news/stonewall-statement-labours-gender-recognition-act-reform-proposals.

[6] See 'Gender Recognition Reform (Scotland) Bill', available at https://www.parliament.scot/bills-and-laws/bills/gender-recognition-reform-scotland-bill/overview.

[7] Organisations that argue against making it easier to change one's legal gender include Fair Play For Women, LGB Alliance, Transgender Trend, and Women's Place UK.

change significantly if access to them is opened to an increasing number of people who retain what most people regard as male biology and anatomy. As Fair Play For Women put it, "Women's single-sex spaces have been made mixed-sex, and women have not been consulted."[8] Second, even if there were not a significant increase in the numbers of people choosing to change their legal gender, GRA reform would mean that it would be possible for any apparently male person to be legally female. This possibility means, gender-critical groups argue, that it would become culturally taboo to question any male person's right to be in a female-only space. As a result, men who are not trans would be able to enter with impunity, and the protection and privacy supposedly offered by female-only spaces would become meaningless.

There are real tensions here, both philosophical and political. In January 2023 the UK government announced that it would take the highly unusual step of blocking a piece of Scottish legislation by declining to submit the Gender Recognition Reform (Scotland) Bill for Royal Assent. In a statement to Parliament, the Scottish Secretary Alister Jack said:

> The Government has looked closely at the potential impact of the Bill and I have considered all relevant policy and operational implications, together with the Minister for Women and Equalities. And it is our assessment that the Bill would have a serious adverse impact, among other things, on the operation of the Equality Act 2010. Those adverse effects include impacts on the operation of single-sex clubs, associations and schools, and protections such as equal pay. The Government shares the concerns of many members of the public and civic society groups regarding the potential impact of the Bill on women and girls. The Bill also risks creating significant complications from having two different gender recognition regimes in the UK and allowing more fraudulent or bad faith applications.[9]

Scotland's First Minister Nicola Sturgeon "accused UK ministers of 'using trans people as a political weapon'" and said that the Scottish government would contest the decision.[10] Soon afterwards she resigned, citing the

---

[8] Fair Play For Women, 'GRA Reform', available at https://fairplayforwomen.com/campaigns/gra-reform/.
[9] Alister Jack, Scottish Secretary, 'Statement: Gender Recognition Reform (Scotland) Bill' (17 January 2023), available at https://www.gov.uk/government/speeches/statement-gender-recognition-reform-scotland-bill.
[10] Jennifer Scott and Sophie Morris, 'UK Government Blocks Scotland's Gender Reform Bill in Constitutional First', Sky News, available at https://news.sky.com/story/uk-government-blocks-scotlands-gender-reform-bill-in-constitutional-first-12787916.

pressures of the job after many years in post. Her resignation was widely understood as a response to the criticism she had faced for her firm support of GRA reform.

There are many ways the state could respond to the problem of securing the rights of trans people while protecting the specific protections and rights of women. In this chapter, I do not survey the range of legislative and social options for balancing women's rights and trans inclusion, and I do not attempt to develop a solution to the controversy. Instead I engage with the specific claim that it is important to provide trans people with legal documentation that recognises their preferred gender.

This claim raises three subsidiary questions. First, should the state legally recognise people's sex at birth? Second, should the state also recognise people's gender identity? Third, should the state allow people's legally recognised birth sex to be *replaced* by their gender identity?

The long-standing legal position in countries like the UK and Sweden is that everyone has a legally recognised sex, recorded at birth, but that a limited number of people—those who have a clinical diagnosis and also meet social criteria—are permitted to replace their legally recognised sex with their gender. In other words, state recognition proceeds on the basis of sex, not gender, for most people. Trans advocacy groups like Stonewall and RFSL would like this system of state-recognised sex to become a system of state-recognised sex *or* gender, since they would like anyone to be able to replace their state recognised sex with their preferred gender without going through any process of clinical diagnosis or regulated social transition.[11] And so, effectively, the question becomes: should 'gender' become a state-recognised category? The answer I will argue for is 'no'.

7.1 Sex/Gender Distinction

In order to see the issues in play it is easiest to use a traditional sex/gender distinction. According to this distinction, 'sex' refers to the natural biological

---

[11] In a statement to the UK government, Stonewall wrote: "Stonewall welcomes the move to a nominal fee but calls for it be removed entirely; as well as the removal of the requirement for a gender dysphoria diagnosis, of the two year waiting period, and of the additional requirement to provide two medical reports. Stonewall believes a system of self-determination is a sensible approach to gender recognition, including a statutory declaration as the only legal requirement. Stonewall believes that 16- and 17-year-olds should be able to achieve legal gender recognition using the same process as trans people aged 18+, with a system based on parental consent available to under-16s." See Stonewall, 'Response to *Reform of the Gender Recognition Act*' (November 2020), available at https://committees.parliament.uk/writtenevidence/17743/html/.

features of a person that make them a member of the sex class male or the sex class female. It includes features like external genitals and secondary sex characteristics, internal reproductive organs, and chromosomes. Typically the external genitals are observed and recorded at or before birth, a process that determines the baby's legal sex. In the vast majority of cases, a baby's observable external genitals also correspond to his or her chromosomes and internal sex organs, meaning that a baby who is sexed male at birth will develop into an adult male capable of reproduction at puberty, and a baby sexed female at birth will develop into an adult female.

'Gender', on the other hand, refers to the cultural or identity-based features of a person. In this chapter, I take no position on what gender is, more precisely than that: whether it is fundamentally about social norms, or socialisation, or personal identity, or something else. There are a great many competing accounts of what gender is, as we'll see, and this is part of the problem with state recognition.

The status of the sex/gender distinction is controversial. Having been an essential part of feminist theory and activism for decades, even centuries (albeit not using those terms) some theorists and activists now argue that the distinction is untenable.[12] But the sex/gender distinction is necessary for the purposes of this chapter, because the question of whether the state should recognise gender is the question of whether it is legitimate for the state to switch from recognising sex to recognising gender: in other words, whether it should recognise those aspects of gender which are *not* biological. The existing Gender Recognition Acts of Sweden and the UK, and the reformed versions which trans advocates want, give legal status to a person's gender *instead of* or *in place of* their sex. They seek to supplement or replace the legal recognition of sex with the legal recognition of gender. Without using a traditional sex/gender distinction we cannot express these demands clearly.[13]

Using the traditional sex/gender distinction does not skew my argument against those who reject it. Quite the opposite: if the sex/gender distinction

---

[12] For extensive discussion, see Clare Chambers, *Intact: A Defence of the Unmodified Body* (London: Allen Lane, 2022), ch. 3.

[13] It follows that my use of the terms 'sex' and 'gender' in this chapter does not necessarily follow the use of the terms in law, since jurisdictions differ in their terminology. Even within UK law there is ambiguity and inconsistency in the use of the terms; for discussion, see S. Cowan, 'Gender is no Substitute for Sex: A Comparative Human Rights Analysis of the Legal Regulation of Sexual Identity', *Feminist Legal Studies* 13 (2005); R. Sandland, 'Feminism and the Gender Recognition Act 2004', *Feminist Legal Studies* 13 (2005); Andrew N. Sharpe, 'Endless Sex: The Gender Recognition Act 2004 and the Persistence of a Legal Category', *Feminist Legal Studies* 15 (2007); and Mary Leng, 'Amelioration, Inclusion, and Legal Recognition: On Sex, Gender, and the UK's Gender Recognition Act', *Journal of Political Philosophy* 31 (2023).

turns out to be untenable then my argument has even wider scope that I claim for it. The most plausible argument against the sex/gender distinction is that even sex is cultural, a claim made most memorably by Judith Butler. "Because 'sex' is a political and cultural interpretation of the body, there is no sex/gender distinction along conventional lines; gender is built into sex, and sex proves to have been gender from the start," Butler writes.[14] Following Butler, critics of the sex/gender distinction tend to argue that biology is of minimal or no significance to gender, because all features of sex/gender, including the body, are socially structured or mediated through identity. On that point of view, all we know about a newborn baby is what their genitals are like, and by recording this fact we are recording our social expectations about the gender we expect them to have. Since we may be wrong about a baby's gender, people ought to be able to change their official gender if it does not align with that assigned to them at birth.

For an advocate of this view, if I am right that the state should not recognise gender, it follows that the state should not record anything at all at birth. In other words, if the sex/gender distinction is untenable, then my argument will imply that the state should not recognise any sex/gender markers at all. On the other hand, if the sex/gender distinction is coherent, my argument against the state recognition of gender leaves it open whether the state should continue to recognise sex. I'll return to that question later on.

If the reforms that groups like Stonewall and RFSL advocate were implemented, an official designation of male or female would in some cases refer to a person's sex, and in other cases to their gender. For people whose gender and sex are in alignment (sometimes referred to as *cisgendered* or *cis* people), their official designation would reflect both their sex and their gender. For people whose sex and gender are not in alignment (trans people, broadly conceived, as well as those who reject the concept of gender identity), there would be ambiguity. For some—those who had changed their state-recognised gender—their official designation would reflect their gender but not their sex. For others—those who had not changed their state-recognised gender—their official designation would reflect their sex but not their gender. It would not be possible to tell, in any particular case, what the designation referred to.

This muddled situation would be unsatisfactory. It would not provide reliable information, meaning that its relevance to state purposes is doubtful. Data gathering and statistical analysis would not provide consistent information,

---

[14] Judith Butler, *Gender Trouble* (Cambridge: Polity Press, 1999), p. 144; see also Anne Fausto-Sterling, *Sexing the Body* (New York, NY: Basic Books, 2000).

meaning that it would not be possible to understand either sexed or gendered trends. The state would not be able to gather information about whether there were sex- or gender-based differences in matters such as health outcomes, pay and employment, criminal behaviour, or caring responsibilities. Since it could refer to *either* sex *or* gender, and need have no correspondence whatsoever to *either* the person's gendered presentation *or* their anatomy, the official designator would have limited use in confirming a person's identity on documents such as passports or driving licenses. And there is a risk of arbitrariness if some people's official designation recorded their sex whereas other people's documents recorded their gender, with no stable justification for the difference.

Instead, the best version of this position would advocate *replacing* state recognition of sex with state recognition of gender, for everyone. But that would not be a reasonable liberal policy, as I show here.

7.2 What is State Recognition?

State recognition, in the sense I'm interested in, is more than merely acknowledging that something exists out there in the world. For example, the British state acknowledges that cohabiting partners exist: in 2021 the House of Commons Women & Equalities Select Committee engaged in an Inquiry into the Rights of Cohabiting Partners, and the Law Commission of England and Wales produced a report on cohabitation in 2007. But cohabiting partnerships cannot achieve state recognition as such, because the UK state does not *recognise* cohabitation in the same way that it recognises marriage. Couples cannot get a certificate from the state to show they are cohabiting. They cannot attend a state-sanctioned cohabitation commitment ceremony. And their cohabitation status does not affect their legal rights.

State recognition, as I am using the concept, has six main features.[15]

1. *Definition*. When the state recognises a characteristic or status, it must provide a definition of that characteristic or status. The state's definition then becomes authoritative; literally, it becomes law. This definition may be explicitly stated or it may be derived from case law. 'Sex', for example, is explicitly defined in the UK Equality Act 2010 as being

---

[15] This section draws on analysis of the state recognition of marriage in my book *Against Marriage: An Egalitarian Defence of the Marriage-Free State* (Oxford: Oxford University Press, 2017).

(biologically) male or female.[16] In England and Wales the statutes and case law show us that 'marriage' is defined as a voluntary, monogamous, sexual, and financial union between two adults. Similarly, if the state were to recognise gender, in my sense, it must define what gender is. It would have to stipulate what genders there were (man, woman, any alternatives) and what it would be to be a man, or a woman, or any alternatives.[17]

2. *Gate-keeping*. If the state recognises a status or characteristic it must also stipulate the criteria for entry: who is eligible for that status or characteristic? Eligibility criteria are related to definitional criteria but are distinct from them. To be eligible for marriage, a person must be an adult who is not already married.[18] If it were to recognise gender the state would have to stipulate things such as: whether there is a minimum age for having a gender at all, whether there is a minimum or maximum age for registering a change of gender, whether there are any capacity requirements for registering a gender or a change of gender, whether there is a limit to the number or frequency of gender changes someone can register, and whether there are any circumstances in which persons cannot legally change gender (e.g. while in prison). The state would also have to stipulate, whether by statute or case law, whether specific criteria were required for access to any particular gender (e.g. whether being a woman entails not being a man) or whether one can have several genders at once (e.g. whether being non-binary is compatible with holding an additional gender identity such as genderqueer).

3. *Recording*. State recognition of a status typically involves the state recording relevant facts. In the case of marriage, the state keeps public records of all marital relationships and these records are open for anyone to consult; it does not do the same for cohabiting relationships. The state records sex on documents such as birth certificates, driving

---

[16] UK Equality Act 2010 section 212 'General Interpretation'. This position is complicated by the Gender Recognition Act, which introduces the concept of 'legal sex'. See Leng, 'Amelioration, Inclusion, and Legal Recognition' for discussion.

[17] This stipulation may be given at the time of legislation or it may emerge from case law. For example, the legal position in the UK at the time of writing is that there are only two recognised genders, male and female, because the Gender Recognition Act 2004 provides only for those two options (with no option to be registered as non-binary, for example).

[18] Part I of the Marriage Act 1949 is titled 'Restrictions on Marriage' and it sets out the requirements for eligibility, including age, marital status, and impermissible family relationships. Similarly, the Gender Recognition Act 2004 sets out the eligibility requirements of being over 18, of 'living in the other gender', and being affirmed by a medical panel in Part 1 'Applications'.

licenses, and passports. In the case of gender, state recognition might involve (re-)issuing official documentation such as birth certificates and driving licenses in the person's preferred gender, and it might mean making people's official gender information publicly accessible in at least some contexts. It would also likely involve data gathering and statistical analysis on the basis of gender. State recognition of gender would mean that one's gender became the business of the state, not merely a private matter. It would indicate that the state expected everyone with a gender to disclose that gender in a legally binding and public way.

4. *Approval.* State recognition of any status indicates official approval for the existence of that status as a conceptual category. It indicates, in other words, that the category is *significant for the purposes of the state.* Additionally, state recognition of a status may (but need not) indicate approval in an additional sense, that the state particularly approves of people who have that status.[19] Both features are present in the state recognition of marriage: by recognising marriage, the state signals that it deems marital status to be the business of the state, and that it deems marriage to be a worthy status. State recognition of gender would indicate at the very least that the state judged gender to be a significant category, relevant for state purposes. It would indicate that any genders not recognised by the state were not deemed to have equivalent status, or any status at all. And it might also indicate that the state approved of gender as a concept, allocating respect to the concept of gender or to people who had a gender.

5. *The demand for third-party recognition.* When the state recognises a status it thereby indicates not only that *it* recognises that the relevant subjects have that status, but also that *others* should recognise that they have that status. When it recognises marriage, the state also places obligations on third parties (such as hospitals, insurance companies, or foreign countries) to recognise that relationship status. If the state were to recognise gender then individuals could use their state recognition as

---

[19] State recognition of marriage indicates approval in both senses: the state approves of the category of marriage existing as a category, and it also approves of the state of being married. State-recognised categories that do not indicate approval in this second sense include categories such as 'criminal' and 'sex offender'. In both cases the state does not indicate approval of those who are criminals or sex offenders, but it does indicate approval of those categories existing as significant categories. It indicates, in other words, that there is something significant for state purposes about having or lacking the statuses in question. To take another example, the state does not recognise the status of 'sports fan' not because it disapproves of loving sports, but because it does not recognise that there is anything significant for the purposes of the state about being or not being a sports fan.

evidence or proof of their membership of a particular gender, and could demand that others must recognise that membership too.[20] State-recognised gender is thus a protection against exclusion and an affirmation of membership. It might also be used to require accommodations of others, such as the use of particular pronouns or other language.

6. *Rights and duties.* State recognition of a status may bring with it special rights and duties. For example, married people gain rights such as inheritance tax relief and duties such as a liability to share assets on separation. If the state were to recognise gender, rights and duties might follow. For example, people legally recognised as women might gain access to women-only spaces, opportunities, or competitions, such as women's prisons, women's colleges, women-only shortlists, women's prizes, and women's sports. People legally recognised as men might gain access to boys' schools, hereditary peerages, and membership in men-only clubs and societies (golf clubs, social clubs, Masonic lodges). And people recognised as non-binary might thereby lose access to gendered spaces and opportunities, such as gendered prizes or sports teams; alternatively, they might gain the special privilege of having access to multiple facilities or services.

At this stage it should already be clear how enormously controversial any state position on these questions would be. *Any* answers given to the questions raised so far would be counter to the deeply held views of a great many people; in Rawlsian terminology, they would inevitably conflict with some reasonable conceptions of the good.

This deep disagreement is why religion is typically not recognised by liberal states, in the sense I have outlined. Liberal states may have legislation that affects or references religion, such as measures against discrimination on religious grounds. But liberal states do not determine who counts as a member of a religion, or what the defining doctrines of any particular religion are. Liberal states do not issue certificates of religious membership, providing documentation that proves someone is a true Jew, Christian, or Muslim. When states do act in this way, they are to that extent no longer acting as liberal states. They might be protecting an established religion, such as Judaism in Israel or Anglicanism in the UK, by gatekeeping access into membership of a

---

[20] This is the sort of demand that Graham Mayeda defends in 'Who Do You Think You Are? When Should the Law Let You Be Who You Want To Be?', in Laurie J. Shrage (ed.), *"You've Changed" – Sex Reassignment and Personal Identity* (Oxford; New York, NY: Oxford University Press, 2009).

dominant group. Or they may be enacting fascist policies, labelling members of religions that are demonised as inferior, as was done to Jewish people in Nazi Germany. But state-recognised religion, in the sense I have set out, is not the practice of liberal states, because state recognition of religion would conflict with the key liberal values of freedom and equality.

I return to the case of religion later in this chapter. First, I'll argue that state recognition of *gender* also conflicts with liberty.

7.3 Liberty and Reasonable Disagreement over Gender

If it is to recognise gender, then the state must define gender and act as gatekeeper for gender identities. Few people will find this idea appealing. Feminists will note that the state has traditionally enforced gender *in*equality, by translating sex differences into gender norms and hierarchies. Feminists thus have reason to be wary of any moves to strengthen the concept of gender in law. Trans people will note the ongoing history of oppression of gender-diverse people and have reason to worry that the state will lack the will and the capacity to reflect a truly progressive stance on gender. It is also unlikely that the state has the flexibility to keep up with changing concepts and terminology. And liberals of all varieties, but perhaps especially political liberals, will wonder how the state can define gender while protecting individual autonomy.

Defining gender is notoriously difficult. What does it mean to be a woman, as distinct from being a member of the female sex? This problem has vexed philosophers, and there is no clear answer in the non-philosophical world either. In public discourse, disagreement is rife. For some, self-identity is necessary and sufficient for being a woman, for others it is necessary but not sufficient, for others it is neither. Some people hold that anyone born female is a woman, regardless of their current identity. Some people hold that womanhood depends on one's presentation and public persona.

The answer is no clearer when we turn from public opinion to the philosophy of gender.[21] Available answers to the question 'what is a woman?' in the philosophical literature include that being a woman is to have a particular

---

[21] Moreover, Anca Gheaus argues that existing concepts of 'gender identity' cannot meet feminist and trans theorists' requirements. See Anca Gheaus, 'Feminism without "gender identity"', *Politics, Philosophy, and Economics* 22 (2023).

place in an eroticised hierarchy of sexual domination and subordination,[22] to be discriminated against on the basis of one's presumed genitalia,[23] to have an internal map that orients oneself towards feminine norms,[24] to be a member of a resemblance type having a sufficient number of a cluster of characteristics,[25] to engage in a performative category within a discursive heteronormativity,[26] to have a particular relationship to embodied phenomenology,[27] or simply to identify as one.[28]

Whether in public discourse or in philosophy, people disagree profoundly on questions of gender. And this disagreement is reasonable, in the Rawlsian sense.[29] Disagreement about gender is subject to what Rawls calls the burdens of judgment, meaning that disagreement is likely permanent, and cannot be dismissed as the result of faulty reasoning.[30] And, since disagreement about gender is likely permanent, and since it is not a requirement of justice to uphold any particular view about gender, reasonableness requires that gender not become a state-recognised category. For Rawls, one holds a view that forms part of a conception of the good reasonably if one does not seek to impose it on others using the coercive power of the state.[31] Reasonableness is not the same thing as truth, plausibility, or rationality. One can hold a true

---

[22] Catharine A. MacKinnon, *Toward a Feminist Theory of the State* (Cambridge, MA: Harvard University Press, 1989). For discussion, see Clare Chambers, 'Judging Women: 25 Years Further Toward a Feminist Theory of the State', Chapter 12 in this volume.

[23] Sally Haslanger, *Resisting Reality: Social Construction and Social Critique* (Oxford: Oxford University Press, 2012). For discussion, see Clare Chambers, 'Judging Women' and 'Ideology and Normativity', Chapters 12 and 13, respectively, in this volume.

[24] Katharine Jenkins, 'Gender Identity and the Concept of Woman', *Ethics* 126(2) (2016). For discussion, see Chambers, *Intact*.

[25] Natalie Stoljar, 'Essence, Identity, and the Concept of Woman', *Philosophical Topics* 23(2) (1995).

[26] Judith Butler, *Gender Trouble* (Cambridge: Polity Press, 1999). For discussion, see Clare Chambers, 'Judith Butler's *Gender Trouble*', in Jacob T. Levy (ed.), *Oxford Handbook of Classics in Contemporary Political Theory* (Oxford: Oxford University Press, online first 2017).

[27] Beauvoir, *The Second Sex*. For discussion, see Chambers, *Intact* and 'Judging Women'.

[28] Talie Mae Bettcher, 'Trans Identities and First-Person Authority', in Laurie Shrage (ed.), *"You've Changed": Sex Reassignment and Personal Identity* (Oxford: Oxford University Press, 2009). For discussion, see Chambers, *Intact*.

[29] For further discussion of the concept of reasonable disagreement, see Clare Chambers, 'Reasonable Disagreement and the Neutralist Dilemma: Abortion and Circumcision in Matthew Kramer's *Liberalism with Excellence*', Chapter 8 in this volume.

[30] As Jonathan Quong glosses them, the burdens of judgment are: "(a) empirical and scientific evidence is often complex and conflicting; (b) we may reasonably disagree about the relative weight of different considerations; (c) concepts are vague and subject to hard cases; (d) the way we assess evidence and weigh values can be shaped by our total life experience; (e) different normative considerations on different sides can make overall assessment difficult; and (f) the number of values any social institution can incorporate is limited..." (Jonathan Quong, 'Public Reason', *Stanford Encyclopedia of Philosophy*, 20 May 2013), available at https://plato.stanford.edu/entries/public-reason/). Each of these undoubtedly applies to questions of what gender is.

[31] For Rawls it is, of course, permissible to use the state to impose principles of justice, coercively, even on those who disagree with them. See Chambers, 'Reasonable Disagreement and the Neutralist Dilemma', Chapter 8 in this volume.

view unreasonably—for example, believing that the earth is round (true) but seeking to outlaw groups who believe that the earth is flat (unreasonable). And one can hold a false view reasonably, as when adherents to incompatible religious doctrines (which cannot all be true) defend each other's rights to follow those doctrines (acting reasonably).

The key to whether one's views are reasonable in this sense is whether one wishes to use the state to impose them on others who disagree. So long as the state does not recognise gender, any of the competing views of gender can be reasonable. But as soon as any one of those is codified in law, that reasonableness is lost. Any state position on what the defining features of gender identity are would inevitably conflict, in quite serious ways, with deeply held, reasonable conceptions of the good. A liberal society can accommodate a wide variety of conceptions of gender; what it cannot do is make some of them official.

Not everyone is liberal, certainly not in the sense of Rawlsian political liberalism. But it is still obvious that no state definition of gender identity can possibly hope to please everyone. Certainly it will not satisfy both sides of the debate between trans activists and gender-critical feminists. In fact, it seems unlikely that either side of that debate would be satisfied, whatever the state definition of gender, for any state-recognised definition of gender will either be so diverse as to be meaningless, or it will be meaningful yet overly restrictive, unable to accommodate all gender identities. In this respect, state-recognised gender is like state-recognised marriage: it involves the state taking a side on disagreements about the good, matters on which a liberal state should remain neutral.

Of course, not all liberals are political liberals and not all egalitarians are liberals. So I turn next to the argument that the state recognition of gender is incompatible with equality.

7.4 Equality Before the Law

The present system in countries like the UK and Sweden, whereby only trans people who undergo a process of clinical diagnosis and social transition can have their gender recognised by the state, does not treat people equally. Trans people who do not meet the official criteria are prevented from having the state recognise the gender with which they identify. People whose gender does not differ from that traditionally associated with their sex also cannot have a state-recognised gender, because the state recognises only their sex. And people whose gender identity falls outside of official categories (for example, people who identify as non-binary or genderqueer) cannot have their gender recognised by the state. For a liberal to support the state recognition of gender, this inequality would have to be rectified and gender recognition made available to all.

Equality, in its most simple sense of equality before the law, requires one of two options. Either *everyone's* gender should be recognised by the state, meaning that having one's gender recognised would be compulsory. Or, everyone could have their gender recognised by the state if they wished, meaning that recognition would be optional. Neither alternative is satisfactory. Consider both in turn, starting with compulsory recognition.

7.4.1 Compulsory State-Recognised Gender

The problems of definition and gatekeeping just described would be particularly pressing if state recognition of gender were compulsory. But they are not the only problems with such a system. How would compulsory registration of gender be implemented? Gender is either formed or discovered (depending on one's point of view) in the course of one's life. It is not evident at birth, and it is not necessarily fixed. So at what point would compulsory gender registration apply, and how would the system cope with gender fluidity?

Children are usually socialised into one gender, and the socialisation is usually pretty extensive;[32] however, many people reject aspects of their gender socialisation. For many trans people, this rejection takes the form of disavowing one gender and embracing another; for gender non-conforming people, non-binary people, and gender-critical feminists this rejection takes more complex forms and may include embracing a variety of gender markers and identities or alternatively rejecting the idea of gender identity completely. (Some people think of non-binary as a gender; others regard it as the absence of gender.) Some people reject the gender into which they are being socialised even as children, some people reject their gender socialisation later in life, some people take time to decide or discover which if any of the letters of LGBTQ+ apply to them, some people transition and then change their mind.

If a system of compulsory gender registration were to avoid oppression it would have to take account of this diversity of experience, and provide options to allow for self-discovery and experiments in living. It follows that such a system would have to allow for one's official gender to be changed,

---

[32] Cordelia Fine, *Delusions of Gender: The Real Science Behind Sex Differences* (London: Icon, 2010).

perhaps several times, and it would have to allow for a diversity of gender categories, for ambiguity in categories, and for waiting periods for people who are unsure what gender they are. It would also have to allow for people who consciously reject gender identity for themselves, such as non-binary and gender-critical people. But a system of compulsory gender registration for everyone would be either oppressive, or unworkable, or both.

At present, both sex and gender are binary in UK law. Even if a person qualifies for a Gender Recognition Certificate, the only gender designations open to them are *male* and *female*.[33] This is because gender is currently used as a proxy for sex, which is legally binary. The sex binary could be carried over into a system of state-recognised gender, meaning that the only available gender identities were *man* and *woman*. This binary approach would have the benefit of simplicity and clarity but the serious disadvantage of clashing with many people's reasonable conceptions of the good and their own gender identity. If everyone were required to register as gendered *man/masculine* or *woman/feminine*, with limited or no opportunities for deviation, ambiguity, or alteration, the system would be clear and enforceable but oppressive and unjustified. It would be clear and enforceable because it would contain only two categories with widely understood social meanings, which could be further codified in law. Moreover, this official documentation might be of use for official identity documents, at least if there were some correlation between one's official gender and one's gendered presentation. But these very features would also make this scheme oppressive, since it would require everyone to fit themselves into rigid, sexist categories. Both gender-critical feminists and trans advocates can agree that such a legal regime would be undesirable.

Alternatively, if people were able to register any of a wide variety of gender identities, including being non-binary or rejecting gender completely, with ample opportunities to register ambiguity or uncertainty, the system would not be oppressive. It would be better suited to responding to diversity and the complexity of lived experience. However, this very flexibility would make compulsion and enforcement unworkable, since it would be very difficult to know whether a person had complied with the law and registered their gender correctly.

---

[33] Even the trans-friendly Gender Recognition Reform (Scotland) Bill (2023) retains the gender binary. It states: "A person of either gender may apply to the Registrar General for Scotland for a gender recognition certificate on the basis of living in the other gender." See clause 2(1) of the Bill, available at https://www.parliament.scot/-/media/files/legislation/bills/s6-bills/gender-recognition-reform-scotland-bill/stage-3/bill-as-passed.pdf.

An advocate of the state recognition of gender might find this conclusion untroubling, and might appeal to Yogyakarta Principle 31. The Yogyakarta Principles are a set of human rights principles proposed by LGBTQ+ experts and advocates. Principle 31, 'The Right to Legal Recognition', states that, if sex and gender are recognised, states should:

i. Ensure a quick, transparent, and accessible mechanism that legally recognises and affirms each person's self-defined gender identity;
ii. Make available a multiplicity of gender marker options;
iii. Ensure that no eligibility criteria, such as medical or psychological interventions, a psycho-medical diagnosis, minimum or maximum age, economic status, health, marital or parental status, or any other third party opinion, shall be a prerequisite to change one's name, legal sex or gender;
iv. Ensure that a person's criminal record, immigration status or other status is not used to prevent a change of name, legal sex or gender.[34]

This principle meets all the requirements of state-recognised gender I set out above in an expansive and unrestricted way: imposing no gatekeeping eligibility criteria for initial registration or for changes to one's recognised gender, and defining gender with a 'multiplicity' of labels.

Perhaps a system along these lines could be adopted. It might run along the following lines. A baby's gender could be assigned at birth, on the assumption that the baby's gender will conform to gender norms and 'align' with their sex. Parents could then change their child's gender whenever they felt it appropriate (the Yogyakarta Principle stipulates no minimum age for a change of gender). At the earliest possible age the child could change their gender for themselves, and this process of revision could be repeated whenever the person felt it necessary. Every identity document (birth certificate, driving license, passport, etc.) could be revised to record a change of gender with no restriction. What would be the problem with that?

The more pertinent question is: what would be the *purpose* of that? If all this diversity were permitted, what use would having a state-recognised gender be? What legitimate state purpose would it serve? If gender can be fluid and flexible, with no limitations or requirements for changing it, what would

---

[34] Yogyakarta Principle 31, 'The Right to Legal Recognition', available at https://yogyakartaprinciples.org/principle-31-yp10/.

state recognition prove? What would state recognition show that mere self-declaration could not?

Even if there were some state purpose, some reason why it would be important for the state to register and authorise a person's gender identity even in this fluid and flexible way, how could we be sure that the law were being complied with? The Gender Recognition Reform (Scotland) Bill 2023 includes the clause that it is "it is an offence to knowingly make a statutory declaration under this section which is false in a material particular", and this clause is intended as a safeguard against insincere or frivolous registrations, but if there are no legal prerequisites for having any given gender then there is no standard against which a declaration of one's gender for the purposes of obtaining certification could be false.[35] How could the state distinguish between honest and dishonest gender registrations, and ensure that everyone's records were kept up to date?

If the categories were fluid and flexible, as Yogyakarta Principle 31 advocates, a system of compulsory gender registration would lack adequate purpose. It would be an act of unjustified state coercion, akin to requiring people to register their interests or beliefs with the state. A fluid system of gender recognition would be of no use to legitimate state purposes, since nothing could be concluded from a person being registered as one particular gender at any point in time, beyond that bare fact. One's official gender would not be useful information for identity documents, because it would not necessarily correspond with anything visible about the person, neither their physical embodiment nor their gender presentation. There would be no reason to think that official gender would be a statistically significant predictor of important information, such as criminality, health, or economic status, since state-recognised gender would mean something different for everyone. State-recognised gender could not be used for safeguarding purposes since it need not correlate with categories significant to safeguarding (men could register as women with no penalty); similarly, it would have no stable connection to discrimination, (dis)advantage, or opportunity. And the documentation itself would serve no purpose: if the state imposed no checks, balances, or regulatory control on the registration process, then proving that the state had

---

[35] Gender Recognition Reform (Scotland) Bill 2023 clause 4. The Bill also requires applicants to affirm that they intend "to continue to live in the acquired gender permanently", and it would be theoretically possible for applicants to lie about this fact. However, the law gives no explanation of what it means to "live in" a gender, and so it would be very difficult to prove that a person was not doing so or that they had no intention of doing so. Moreover, this requirement would be ruled out by Yogyakarta Principle 31.

recognised one's gender would in practice be no different from simply affirming it oneself.

Perhaps for these reasons, the Yogyakarta Principles do not in fact recommend the state recognition of gender. The fluid system of recognition I quoted above is the ameliorative approach the Principles call for "while sex or gender continues to be registered", a second-best option. Their preferred approach is the abolition of the state recognition of both sex and gender. Principle 31 is called 'The Right to Legal Recognition' but this proposed right is explained as follows:

> Everyone has the right to legal recognition *without reference to, or requiring assignment or disclosure of*, sex, gender, sexual orientation, gender identity, gender expression or sex characteristics....
>
> STATES SHALL: A. Ensure that official identity documents only include personal information that is relevant, reasonable and necessary as required by the law for a legitimate purpose, and thereby end the registration of the sex and gender of the person in identity documents such as birth certificates, identification cards, passports and driver licences, and as part of their legal personality.[36]

So the Yogyakarta Principles actually align with my own position to this extent: ideally, we both agree, the state would not recognise gender.

The compulsory state recognition of gender is not good policy. It would either be oppressive or unworkable, and it lacks adequate purpose. Leading trans voices are not calling for it, and nor are gender-critical feminists. So we can safely leave this option behind and consider whether there are grounds for the state to institute an *optional* regime of state-recognised gender.

7.4.2 Optional State Recognition of Gender

State recognition of gender should not be compulsory, but perhaps it should be an option available to those who want it. Under this alternative proposal, no one would be *obliged* to register their gender with the state, but everyone would be *able* to register their gender with the state if they so wished. State-recognised gender would then be like state-recognised marriage: no one is

---

[36] Yogyakarta Principle 31. Emphasis added.

obliged to get married but everyone is able to do so (if they can find a willing partner).[37] Just as people might marry only if they endorsed the goals and meanings of marriage, so too people might register their gender only if they endorsed the goals and meanings of the state-recognised system. No one would be forced to reveal personal information about their gender identity that they wished to keep private, and no one would be forced to participate in a gender system that they did not believe in.[38] This system would be particularly beneficial for those trans people seeking official affirmation of their gender identity for symbolic or practical purposes.

Such a system would be a deviation from the status quo, according to which only a subset of trans people can gain state recognition of their gender, and people who are not trans cannot register their gender at all. Optional registration of gender for everyone would rectify this inequality by allowing *everyone* to register their gender, not just their sex, with the state.

But this proposal is subject to the same objections as state-recognised marriage. As I show in the following sections, even an optional system of state-recognised gender raises problems for equality.

7.5 What's Good About Gender?

State recognition of a status implies *approval* of that status. Gender is unquestionably a concept with an extremely unequal past and present. This is a claim that both trans advocates and gender-critical feminists can agree on. Both have reason to criticise the gender binary, according to which all people are normatively required to assume a gender that is socially dictated to 'correspond' to their sex. Both will point to the long history of gender-based discrimination and oppression, whether that consists in oppression of trans people, requirements on women to comply with deeply sexist gender norms, or the entire system of gendered inequality that has been and continues to be so harmful to everyone, especially women, girls, and gender non-conforming

---

[37] In my book *Against Marriage: An Egalitarian Defence of the Marriage-Free State*, I argue that state-recognised marriage, even if reformed to include same-sex marriage, necessarily violates freedom and equality. Many of the arguments in this section are drawn from that analysis.
[38] For the argument that people should be able to keep their gender identity private, see Brian Earp, 'On Sharing Pronouns', *The Philosopher* 109 (2021). For the argument that gender is an ideology that runs counter to deeply held beliefs, see the judgment in the Maya Forstater case: Employment Appeal Tribunal Appeal No. UKEAT/0105/20/JOJ (2021), available at https://assets.publishing.service.gov.uk/media/60c1cce1d3bf7f4bd9814e39/Maya_Forstater_v_CGD_Europe_and_others_UKEAT0105_20_JOJ.pdf.

people. As with marriage, gender is associated with a legacy of inequality that makes state recognition and thus approval of it fundamentally unappealing. Many people find this aspect of gender so problematic as to reject it entirely. They include some gender-critical feminists, who refuse to identify themselves as having a gender (they might say they are women as a sex class but not women as a gender), but also some people who identify as non-binary or genderqueer. Thus the notion that the state should recognise a person's gender because gender is a noble category would conflict with many reasonable perspectives.

But perhaps gender can be reformed, and a revised version of the concept put to egalitarian use. An advocate of state-recognised gender might concede my point that gender has historically been used to subordinate, but argue that this gives even greater grounds for a revised concept of gender, one that can counter inegalitarian associations. By registering as non-binary or genderqueer, or by registering a gender that does not conform to one's sex, perhaps we can break down the oppressive associations between sex, gender, and hierarchy?

Perhaps. I do not want to say that such strategies can never be successful. However, I am sceptical that they can work as general programmes for egalitarian reform. Not everyone is, or wants to be, gender non-conforming, and it would be deeply regressive to say that the only route to securing equality for members of some particular sex or gender is to identify out of it. Truly egalitarian politics require that people are treated equally regardless of their sex and gender, whether they are trans or not. And so a system that allows people to escape gender hierarchy by registering a non-conforming gender does nothing for those left behind in genders that are traditionally denigrated. It may even make their symbolic subordination worse, by implying that it is chosen.

7.6 Recognition and Discrimination

Third-party recognition is very important to trans people, and this is often taken to be the strongest argument in favour of state-recognised gender. Indeed, some trans theorists and activists argue that the refusal to recognise a person's gender amounts to erasure, or even violence against them. I find that claim unconvincing, but even if it is true it does not adequately justify state-recognised gender. Our question here is not the general question of recognition but the specific question of *state* recognition. Must the state recognise a person's gender to ensure that other people also recognise it?

Graham Mayeda argues that there is an "ethical responsibility to acknowledge a person's self-stated gender identity"[39] and that state recognition plays an important part. "By issuing an identity document," he writes, "the state is not just saying that the state recognizes that this document describes you. It is also saying that others ought to recognize you as the state has."[40] Mayeda recognises that the state recognition of gender on the basis of self-ID can create conflicts, and allows that the ethical duty of recognition that the state has may be overridden where necessary to prevent harm to others, or an infringement of other people's "rights and entitlements".[41] Nonetheless, Mayeda argues that the ethical requirement to recognise gender is so significant that it should be respected even though "this will make personal identification documents less useful for the provision of state or private services that aim at ameliorating the disadvantaged position of women."[42] This demand for the state recognition of gender should be understood as the demand that the state enforce the ethical recognition of a trans person's self-identity by others. Mayeda wants the state to compel others to recognise (as opposed to merely tolerate) a trans person's chosen gender.

I do not support the idea that the state should act as enforcer for third-party ethical recognition of a person's identity. The state should ensure that people do not suffer unjust discrimination and oppression, but this legitimate aim does not require state recognition in the sense defined in this chapter.

There are a great many valuable and important statuses that are not subject to state recognition, including those that are quite properly the subject of legal protections against discrimination. My arguments on this point are in line with what I take to be the correct liberal position on the recognition of other identities, such as religion and belief. Religion is a matter of personal identity, community membership, everyday practice, law, and belief that is of fundamental importance to a great many people, both individually and collectively. It is also of great importance to many religious believers to be recognised as such by others, for example to be recognised as eligible for religious sacraments and statuses such as marriage. Religion and belief is a protected characteristic according to the UK Equality Act 2010, meaning that it is illegal to discriminate against someone on grounds of their religion. Some religions also ask for and receive exemptions from general legislation. In the UK, religions are exempt from various features of equality law, exemptions which enable them to discriminate on the grounds of sex and sexuality in

---

[39] Mayeda, 'Who Do You Think You Are?', p. 203.
[40] Mayeda, 'Who Do You Think You Are?', p. 205.
[41] Mayeda, 'Who Do You Think You Are?', p. 206.
[42] Mayeda, 'Who Do You Think You Are?', p. 206.

certain contexts. So religions are treated very seriously in law, given legal protections, rights, and exemptions.

However, as I noted earlier, liberal democracies do not generally engage in the state recognition of religion. Recall the six features of state recognition, italicised in what follows. First, liberal states do not *define* what any particular religion is, by saying what beliefs, practices, or heritage defines a person as Christian, Jewish, Muslim, Hindu, Buddhist, and so on. Second, they do not engage in *gatekeeping*, stipulating as a matter of law what a person has to do in order to be considered eligible as a member of any particular religion. Third, liberal states do not *record* a person's religion. They do not offer certification to prove that a citizen is a member of a particular religion, and they do not back that certification up with a demand, fourth, that other citizens *recognise* them as a member of their certified religion. They do not, fifth, indicate an *approval* of religion as relevant for state purposes. Even liberal countries with an established religion, such as the Church of England in the UK, do not engage in these aspects of state recognition. It is generally recognised that liberal principles require that the state refrain from recognising and certifying religion in these ways.

Nonetheless, the liberal state can and should protect people from religious discrimination. That is to say, sixth, the liberal state can allocate *rights and duties* on the basis of some identity or characteristic without giving full state recognition to that identity or characteristic. A liberal state such as the UK has a series of legislative measures in place to protect religious freedom, and sometimes to set out situations where religious membership is of significance in public matters. For example, religions may have exemptions from certain aspects of law (in the UK, the Catholic Church is allowed to discriminate against women when employing priests; Sikh men can wear turbans instead of motorcycle helmets); religions may be permitted to perform certain state functions (for example, set up and run state schools, or conduct legally recognised marriages).[43] The state therefore allocates and protects rights and duties to religions and their members.

Moreover, religion is one of the protected characteristics under the UK Equality Act 2010, meaning that it is illegal to discriminate on grounds of religion or belief. This law operates without the state recognition of religion in the sense set out in this chapter. In order to show that unlawful religious discrimination has occurred, it is not necessary for the victims of discrimination

---

[43] My point is not to endorse these functions of religion, but merely to show that, in practice as well as in theory, they do not require state recognition.

to provide official documentation proving that they are members of a religion. All that is necessary is to show that the discrimination was motivated by anti-religious sentiment. In other words, the state can protect people against discrimination on the basis of some characteristic without having a prior mechanism for the state recognition of that characteristic. As with religion, so too with gender: discrimination on the basis of gender identity could be legally prevented without gender being a state-recognised category, in the sense I mean here.

Defending the state recognition of a status such as gender requires much more than an argument that that status represents something of significance and value to people. The state should recognise a status only if its recognition fulfils a legitimate purpose: one that is needed to secure justice, and that can be performed without violating the freedom and equality of citizens generally. Gender, like marriage, does not meet this criterion.

I have argued that either a compulsory or an optional system of state-recognised gender would violate freedom and equality, in ways analogous to my critique of state-recognised marriage. It would violate freedom because it would involve the state in setting the terms of what gender is at the general level, which genders there are at the specific level, and what the criteria are for belonging to any gender. Regardless of how the state determined these questions, reasonable conceptions of the good would be contradicted: any system of state-recognised gender would necessarily violate reasonable pluralism. And state-recognised gender would violate equality because, like marriage, gender is a system that has been used to create and reinforce inequality over centuries. Forcing people to define themselves within it would be incompatible with respecting them as equals. Making state-recognised gender available just for some would lack adequate purpose, and would create an unjustified inequality between those with and without an official gender. And state recognition of gender is unnecessary. As the case of religion shows, trans and gender-diverse people can be protected from discrimination without gender being a state-recognised category.

7.7 What About Sex?

If gender should not be recognised by a liberal state, what about sex? Trans advocacy groups like Stonewall and RFSL argue that the state recognition of gender is required precisely as a counterpoint to the state recognition of sex. As long as sex is recognised by the state and used for official purposes then, they argue, it is necessary for justice that trans and gender-diverse people be able to change their officially recognised sex so that it aligns with their gender. Otherwise, trans and gender-diverse people will be subject to injustices and indignities, such as official documentation that outs them as trans or does not align with their gender, and being allocated to spaces that do not align with their gender identity (for example, trans women being placed in men's prisons). On this perspective, state-recognised gender is necessary to rectify the injustices of a system of state-recognised sex.

At this point, then, we must turn to the question I set aside earlier: should a liberal state recognise sex? Various options are available. The state could recognise only sex and not gender, as was the norm before gender recognition legislation (in 2004 in the UK and in 1972 in Sweden). Alternatively, the state could recognise only gender and not sex, a novel system that does not occur anywhere in the world at present. As a third option, the state could recognise both sex and gender, meaning that sex at birth would co-exist, legally speaking, with gender identity. Official documentation might display either sex or gender, both or neither, depending on purpose. Fourth, the state could recognise neither sex nor gender.

Different patterns of recognition would have different pros and cons. Any system that recognises either sex or gender but not both faces criticism. The first option, recognising sex and not gender, is subject to the objections raised by Stonewall and RFSL: trans people are officially labelled as members of the sex that was observed at birth, even if that does not correspond to their gender identity, gender presentation, or even their current physical embodiment. The indignity and irrationality of this system is what prompted countries to pass gender recognition legislation in the first place. But, as this chapter has shown, recognising gender and not sex leaves the state vulnerable to a myriad of objections from freedom and equality, and thus is not a viable solution.

To work through this problem we need to rethink the purposes to which state recognition of sex is put. Is it legitimate for the state to recognise sex at all or should states follow Yogyakarta Principle 31 and abandon state recognition of both gender *and* sex?

Sex is highly predictive of many phenomena that are of legitimate interest to the state. It is strongly correlated with criminal behaviour, including but not only sexual violence. Sex is relevant for many purposes relating to health and medicine: many diseases and clinical conditions are sex-specific, and others present differently depending on sex. Sex is highly predictive of economic factors such as the gender pay gap, patterns of full- and part-time working, and workplace specialisation. In her book *Invisible Women: Data Bias in a World Designed for Men*, Caroline Criado Perez powerfully shows how failure to consider sex-based differences leads to women being systematically forgotten and disadvantaged in a vast array of contexts, ranging from the design of safety equipment, town planning and public transport, public health messaging, clinical research, medical treatment, public service provision, and technology design. In fact, her book starts with a discussion of how snow-clearing in Sweden has been sexist, by starting on major roads and only then moving on to pavements and cycle paths. As Criado Perez points out, "this was affecting men and women differently because men and women travel differently."[44]

Is it sex or gender that is predictive? In some cases, it is clearly sex: factors such as body shape and size, reproductive capacity, and other sex-based characteristics affect the design of health and safety equipment, sport, technology, and many health conditions. Other cases, such as crime and economic inequality, are likely sex-based. But this is disputed. Until very recently states have collected this data according to sex not gender. Collecting information on both sex and gender would assist statistical analysis, enabling us to see whether sex or gender is more important in various contexts. Collecting that information accurately does not necessarily require a state-recognised status, but it does require clear, centralised, and widely understood definitions of each category, and it requires a reliable method for identifying which category someone fits into.

In the case of sex we already have a weight of evidence that tells us both that sex is statistically significant, and that women are systematically disadvantaged. Women are disadvantaged by being ignored (with male treated as default) and by being subordinated in gendered systems. Moreover, while there are debates about precisely what sex is, and how to classify people who are intersex or have differences of sexual development (DSD), there are clear, objective scientific criteria that can reliably sort the vast majority of people into one sex or another. Similarly, most people know what their sex is, even if they have never had a chromosome test: for the vast majority, their external physical features at birth are a reliable guide to their sex, and further confirmation of biological sex comes first at puberty and then later if conceiving a child. Categorisation according to sex, and the sex of an individual person, is not subject to reasonable disagreement in the same way as systems and classifications of gender.

It seems, then, that there are good grounds for the state continuing to record a person's sex, and to use that information for various official purposes

---

[44] Caroline Criado-Perez, *Invisible Women: Exposing Data Bias in a World Designed for Men* (London: Chatto & Windus, 2019), p. 29.

such as monitoring and addressing crime, health care, and sex discrimination. In some contexts, for example in medical care, a person's biological sex is vital information, and it may also be important to know if a person has undergone gender-affirming surgery or hormone treatments.

However, not all purposes for which a person's sex is currently used are justified. Yogyakarta Principle 31 is right when it calls for sex and gender to be recorded or used only when "relevant, reasonable and necessary as required by the law for a legitimate purpose". The move to make sex irrelevant for the purposes of marriage, for example, is a progressive one, benefitting people of all sexes and genders.

Identity documents are more complex. Perhaps official sex should not appear on them, especially since a person's sex may not align with their physical appearance if they are trans or gender non-conforming. However, since most people are gender conforming, and since sex characteristics are often identifiable even when they are not, perhaps sex remains sufficiently useful to identification to make it relevant.

The question of precisely when the state recognition of sex is necessary, and the purposes to which it can legitimately be put, is complex, and I cannot do justice to it here. It seems likely that the right answer will be piecemeal: that some legitimate state purposes require the continued use of official sex and some do not. Robust forms of equality legislation need to be used and enforced so that sex-based information is not used to discriminate, humiliate, or oppress trans and gender-diverse people.

Similarly, it is likely that some legitimate state purposes should take account of a person's gender as they themselves identify it. For example, it would be reasonable for some state services to record a person's preferred form of address, including gendered language such as title and pronouns. In these contexts, the state might legitimately register and respect what for some is best described as their gender identity.

So perhaps state recognition should apply to both sex *and* gender. Mary Leng advocates a version of this proposal. She argues in favour of separating the concepts of sex and gender in law, advocating "two separate legally protected characteristics. These would be *sex* (understood biologically...) and *gender identity* (which, if self-ID is accepted, would be by sincere self-declaration)."[45] Leng writes as though only trans people would register their gender, but there is no reason to think that this would or should be the case. Some people might wish to register a gender that corresponded with their sex

---

[45] Leng, 'Amelioration, Inclusion, and Legal Recognition', p. 153.

according to traditional gender norms, for example that they were sex: female and gender: woman. Some might wish to register a trans identity, for example that they were sex: female and gender: man. Some might not wish to register a gender at all, for example that they were sex: female and gender: none.

Leng notes that this proposal meets various desiderata: it allows for accurate data collection regarding both sex and gender identity, which in turn allows inequalities to be tracked and tackled, and it allows people to gain legal recognition for their gender identity. We might also think that recognition of both sex and gender provides information that could be useful for identification purposes. However, she notes that it raises an issue of privacy: by forcing to register both their gender and their sex, trans people would be 'outed' as trans in a way they might not prefer. Leng argues that this issue can be overcome by requesting information about sex only when necessary; furthermore, she looks forward to an enlightened future in which trans status is more accepted than it is at present. "With greater progress in this direction," she writes, "the felt need to hide the fact that one's gender identity differs from one's sex should be reduced."[46]

The problem here is that trans people's desire to conceal their birth sex is not merely a matter of privacy or fear of censure. For many trans people, it is an important part of their identity to be affirmed as having always or only been the gender they identify as. This is why the practice of 'deadnaming'— referring to a trans person's pre-transition name—is thought by many trans people and their allies to be a profound wrong, and why trans activists campaign not just for identity documents to record gender from the point of transition, but for reissued birth certificates. So a process of dual recognition of both sex and gender is likely to meet considerable pushback from trans advocacy groups and would need careful justification.

7.8 Conclusion

Any state-recognised status must be compatible with freedom and equality, and it must serve some legitimate purpose. I've argued that this bar is not met with regard to gender, just as it is not met with regard to marriage. This conclusion leaves open what legislative or other measures should be in place to protect the rights and equality of people in general, and trans people in particular.

---

[46] Leng, 'Amelioration, Inclusion, and Legal Recognition', p. 154.

I have not attempted to settle the question of how to best weigh the interests and rights of people with different sexes or genders. There are many ways of tackling discrimination and inequality that do not rely on a state-recognised status, as the case of the prohibition of racial and religious discrimination shows. There is much more work to be done on this question, and a variety of different policies might be considered at both the social and the state level. This chapter has argued that the state recognition of gender should not be one of them.

Freedom and Equality: Essays on Liberalism and Feminism. Clare Chambers, Oxford University Press.
© Clare Chambers 2024. DOI: 10.1093/9780191919480.003.0008

8

Reasonable Disagreement and the Neutralist Dilemma

Abortion and Circumcision in Matthew Kramer's *Liberalism with Excellence*

Liberal neutralism is the position that the state should remain neutral between reasonable conceptions of the good.[1] Reasonable conceptions of the good are those whose proponents are willing to cooperate fairly with others under conditions of diversity. In other words, reasonable people will not use the coercive powers of the state to impose their judgments on people who reasonably disagree, which is to say on those who similarly do not try to impose their own judgments.

Consider a standard neutralist case. There is reasonable disagreement between Christians and non-Christians as to whether Jesus is the Son of God and should be worshipped as such:

Reasonable disagreement about Christianity: whether Jesus is the Son of God and should be worshipped as such.

For the neutralist, the state should be neutral on matters of reasonable disagreement. It should proceed using public reason alone, without endorsing one conception of the good over another. If the state were to be non-neutral and take a side in the reasonable disagreement about Christianity, one of two unreasonable policies might result:

Unreasonable policy on Christianity I: the state should encourage Christian worship, because Jesus is the Son of God and should be worshipped as such.

---

[1] This chapter was originally published in *The American Journal of Jurisprudence* 63(1) (2018). I would like to thank the organisers and participants of the Symposium on Matthew Kramer's *Liberalism with Excellence*, including Matthew Kramer himself, as well as the participants in the University of Cambridge Workshop in Political Philosophy for their comments on earlier versions of this chapter.

Unreasonable policy on Christianity II: the state should discourage Christian worship, because Jesus is not the Son of God and should not be worshipped as such.

In contrast to these unreasonable policies, liberal neutralists advocate that the state refrain from making a judgment on a matter that is subject to reasonable disagreement that cannot be resolved using public reason.[2] Doing so will result in a neutral policy:

Neutral policy on Christianity: Jesus may or may not be the Son of God. The state should neither encourage nor discourage Christian worship.

This position is neutral because it does not take a stance on the matter of reasonable disagreement. It is also a reasonable policy, because it will appear as reasonable from both sides of the disagreement.

In the superbly argued *Liberalism with Excellence*, Matthew Kramer argues that liberal neutralism is not a convincing political philosophy. I agree with much of his analysis. Like Kramer, I am not an advocate of state neutrality all things considered. In this chapter, then, I will not be taking issue with Kramer's general critique of neutralism and I will not be attempting to defend neutralism as a political philosophy. Instead, I want to delve deeper into a particular type of debate that Kramer identifies, one that causes problems for liberal neutralists. I call this *the neutralist dilemma*.

The neutralist dilemma is a phenomenon, identified by Kramer but not named that by him, whereby the state cannot remain neutral on some question of reasonable disagreement. In a standard neutralist case both sides can agree that the neutral policy is reasonable. Both Christians and non-Christians can agree that it is reasonable for the state to neither encourage nor discourage Christian worship, because that neutral position does not depend on the state either affirming or denying the controversial claim that Jesus is the Son of God and should be worshipped as such. In cases of the neutralist dilemma, though, *any* state action requires the state to either affirm or deny one side of a reasonable disagreement, meaning that *any* state action looks unreasonable from one point of view. The neutralist dilemma applies when, of two options available to the state, one is unreasonable. It follows that the state should enact only the reasonable policy. However, in a neutralist dilemma the fact of reasonable disagreement due to the burdens of judgment

---

[2] The issue of what it means to resolve a dispute using public reason is discussed in more depth later.

means that it is not possible for the state to act at all (including by refraining from legislating) without deviating from neutrality.

This chapter discusses the neutralist dilemma as Kramer sets it out in relation to abortion, and then considers whether it is of wider application. In particular it considers whether another case Kramer discusses, that of circumcision, is properly described as a neutralist dilemma. I argue that, while there can be versions of the circumcision debate that are neutralist dilemmas, their most plausible resolution results in prohibition.

8.1 Two Sorts of Reasonable Disagreement

Before proceeding we need a clearer account of what it is for a disagreement to be reasonable. Kramer notes that there are various ways of understanding this idea.[3] Let us focus on two. Both are found in Rawls, though they are not always clearly distinguished. We can separate them by thinking of the adjective 'reasonable' as applying either to the disagreement itself, or to the way the disagreement is resolved and the policies that are reached and enacted.

The first version of reasonable disagreement uses the term 'reasonable' primarily to describe the disagreement itself. For a disagreement to be reasonable in this sense it must be *about* a matter on which it is reasonable to disagree. I label this version 'reasonable disagreement due to the burdens of judgment'.

The second version of reasonable disagreement uses the term 'reasonable' to apply to the conclusion of the debate, or to the way either side of a debate recommends treating others. For a disagreement to be reasonable in this sense, both sides must adopt positions or recommend policies that treat others reasonably. I label this version 'reasonable disagreement with respect to freedom and equality'.

Consider, first, reasonable disagreement due to the burdens of judgment. People may reasonably disagree about some issue because reaching a conclusion on that issue is extremely difficult. The burdens of judgment apply when some matter of debate is complex, rests on vague or competing principles, is of questionable empirical standing (empirical evidence can be offered on both sides and is not decisive for either), involves a variety of ethical values which must be traded off against each other, and when one's views on the matter are

---

[3] Matthew H. Kramer, *Liberalism with Excellence* (Oxford; New York, NY: Oxford University Press, 2017), p. 6.

likely shaped by one's social and cultural background.[4] Reasonable disagreement due to the burdens of judgment means that reasonable citizens recognise those burdens and are therefore tolerant of citizens who reach different conclusions.

Consider some examples. On this understanding of reasonable disagreement, it is reasonable to disagree about whether Britain should exit the European Union because that is a matter of enormous ethical and empirical complexity. It follows that the correct way to proceed on this matter, for neutralists such as Rawls, is for both sides of the debate to put forward public reasons for their view, and to vote if a consensus cannot be reached, with voters taking into account only the public reasons that have been advanced on both sides. The state legitimately takes a position on Brexit only when it implements the decision that has been reached through this process of public reason.[5]

On the other hand, there is not a reasonable disagreement due to the burdens of judgment about whether $2 + 2 = 4$, because that is a matter of basic mathematics that is simple to demonstrate. The state need not, then, be neutral on that question.

Some matters may move, over time, from being matters that are subject to reasonable disagreement due to the burdens of judgment to ones that are not. For example, the weight of scientific evidence means it is no longer reasonable to disagree about whether the earth is flat, even though disagreement on that issue was reasonable once. The balance of public reason lies overwhelmingly on one side and so the state need not reserve judgment.

The second category is reasonable disagreement with respect to freedom and equality. It applies when both sides of a debate advocate only those policies that are compatible with the freedom and equality of citizens. A disagreement that is reasonable with respect to freedom and equality is thus one in which all parties to a debate are willing to cooperate fairly under conditions of diversity.[6]

In the context of reasonable disagreement with respect to freedom and equality it *is* reasonable to disagree about whether $2 + 2 = 4$, so long as neither side proposes to impose their answer on others in a way that would undermine freedom and equality (for example, by jailing all those on one side of the

---

[4] This is a brief overview of John Rawls' burdens of judgment; a full account is given in Kramer, *Liberalism with Excellence*, pp. 8–12.

[5] As Rawls writes, when reasonable disagreement due to the burdens of judgment means that consensus cannot be reached "citizens should simply vote for the ordering of political values they sincerely think most reasonable." See John Rawls, *Political Liberalism* (New York, NY: Columbia University Press, 1993), p. lv.

[6] Kramer, *Liberalism with Excellence*, p. 8.

debate). But it is *not* reasonable to disagree about whether the state should prohibit homosexuality, because the policy advocated by the prohibitionists does not treat lesbians and gays as free and equal citizens. A debate is thus unreasonable with respect to freedom and equality if the resolution favoured by one or both of the sides violates the freedom and equality of (some) citizens.

These two sorts of reasonable disagreement intersect in complex ways, with correspondingly complex implications for neutrality. For example, there is reasonable disagreement due to the burdens of judgment as to whether homosexuality is compatible with receiving God's grace. Since theological reasons cannot be public reasons there is no way of engaging in this debate, let alone settling it, using public reason. The neutral state therefore should not take any position at all on this question. On the other hand, there is only *un*reasonable disagreement with respect to freedom and equality as to whether gay and lesbian people may be discriminated against. Therefore the state should not remain neutral on that issue and should not leave it open to public debate.

The question of whether the earth is flat is not a matter of reasonable disagreement due to the burdens of judgment. The evidence for one side is clear and compelling. It follows that the state does not have to be neutral on this question of fact: the view that the earth is flat does not need to be taught in public schools, and state geographers and astronomers can proceed on the basis that the earth is round. Nevertheless, it would be unreasonable with respect to freedom and equality to suppress and silence Flat-Earthers, so they must be allowed to express their views even if they cannot influence policy.

It is beyond the scope of this chapter to offer an exhaustive account of the two forms of reasonable disagreement. But these remarks and examples demonstrate that the question of whether some matter of disagreement is reasonable, and what that implies for neutrality, is not simple. The next section considers the particular problems that arise when an issue is a matter of reasonable disagreement due to burdens of judgment, but when there can be only unreasonable disagreement on that issue with respect to freedom and equality.

8.2 From Reasonable Disagreement to Unreasonable Policy: Abortion

In chapter 3 of *Liberalism with Excellence*, Kramer considers whether there can be a neutral account of abortion. He notes that most advocates of political neutrality claim that their neutrality allows them to endorse permitting first-trimester abortions. Kramer discusses the accounts of Ronald Dworkin, Thomas Nagel, and Jonathan Quong. Though these accounts are importantly different, Kramer argues that they all suffer from a common flaw: they attempt to demonstrate the permissibility of abortion without taking a stance on the controversial question of whether or not the foetus is a person. They need to refrain from taking a stance on this question since it is a matter of reasonable disagreement due to the burdens of judgment. But, as Kramer convincingly argues, neutrality on this question is impossible.

The problem is as follows: if foetuses are part of the Rawlsian category of full moral persons (henceforth simply 'persons'), then any conception of the good that permits abortion is unreasonable with respect to freedom and equality, because it denies equality to foetuses and thus to some persons. So permitting abortion is justifiable only if foetuses are *not* persons. But that view is itself incompatible with those conceptions of the good that assert that foetuses *are* persons. Thus, Kramer concludes, "[w]hen we ascertain whether the laws in a jurisdiction conform to the requirement of neutrality, we are consciously or implicitly adopting a position on the question whether foetuses are persons."[7]

According to Kramer, the state simply cannot avoid taking a stance on the question of whether foetuses are persons. If foetuses *are* persons then it would be utterly unreasonable for the state to permit abortion, since abortion would be murder. But if foetuses are *not* persons, then it is similarly unreasonable to prohibit abortion, because to do so would be to impose "major curbs on the freedom of women that are not paralleled by any curbs on the freedom of men...even though they are not necessary to avert the infliction of harm on other persons".[8] If foetuses are not persons, that is, then the principles of equality and autonomy require that the state permit abortion.

One way of interpreting Kramer's argument is to say that the debate about abortion contains matters of both reasonable and unreasonable disagreement. It starts from a matter of reasonable disagreement:

Reasonable disagreement on abortion: whether the foetus is a person.

This is a reasonable disagreement due to the burdens of judgment. Indeed, the burdens may be particularly heavy in this case. The concept of personhood relies partly on scientific facts about what constitutes life, humanity, and

---

[7] Kramer, *Liberalism with Excellence*, p. 110.   [8] Kramer, *Liberalism with Excellence*, p. 115.

so on, but relies most strongly on controversial philosophical, moral, and religious questions about the boundaries of personhood. So neutralism seems to require that the state remain neutral on the question of whether the foetus is a person. The question is, what policy follows?

Neutral policy on abortion: the foetus may or not be a person. Therefore the state should…?

The state cannot remain neutral on the question of whether or not abortion should be permitted: it necessarily picks a side by either legislating or not. Kramer's argument is that picking a side on the question of whether abortion is permitted requires taking a side on the question of whether the foetus is a person. This is because either answer to the question of whether the foetus is a person leads to one of the possible state positions on abortion being unreasonable with respect to freedom and equality. The state should not be neutral between a reasonable and an unreasonable position: it must choose the reasonable position. But to identify the reasonable position the state must reach a conclusion on the question of foetal personhood.

On Kramer's analysis, the state must choose one of the following:

Policy on abortion I: the foetus is not a person. Therefore the state should permit abortion because forbidding abortion would be to deny women's equality and autonomy.

Policy on abortion II: the foetus is a person. Therefore the state should forbid abortion because abortion is murder, which denies foetus's freedom and equality.

In response to Kramer, one might ask why the state cannot simply proceed via public reason. In other cases of reasonable disagreement due to the burdens of judgment, such as Brexit, neutralism recommends debating the matter using public reason and voting if consensus cannot be reached. And Rawls recommends this approach for abortion. He writes: "disputed questions, such as that of abortion, may lead to a stand-off between different political conceptions, and citizens must simply vote on the question."[9]

The problem with this solution, Kramer argues, is that in the case of abortion both policies are potentially *unreasonable* with respect to freedom and

---

[9] Rawls, *Political Liberalism*, p. lv.

equality. Policy I is potentially unreasonable because it succeeds only if the foetus is not a person. If the foetus is a person, the policy is an unreasonable act of murder. Policy II is potentially unreasonable because it succeeds only if the foetus is a person. If the foetus is not a person, the policy is an unreasonable violation of women's freedom and equality. There is thus no policy available that is neutral on the matter of foetal personhood. The same is not true of Brexit: while one side may be more advisable or plausible than the other, both sides can in principle be argued and implemented in a way that respects the freedom and equality of citizens.

Why have I described the two abortion policies as only potentially unreasonable? This is because the foetus must either be a person or not. It cannot be both person and non-person. So settling the matter of foetal personhood will show that one policy is in fact unreasonable and the other is reasonable. If the foetus is a person then policy I is unreasonable and policy II is reasonable. Since the state need not be neutral between unreasonable and reasonable positions, it should enact policy II. Alternatively, if the foetus is not a person then the opposite conclusion applies.

The problem in the case of abortion, of course, is knowing which position is unreasonable with respect to freedom and equality. We know for sure that one of the positions on abortion must be unreasonable in that sense, but we (collectively, as liberal citizens) do not know which one. We do not know which one is unreasonable because that depends on the question of whether or not the foetus is a person, and this is a matter on which there is reasonable disagreement due to the burdens of judgment.

In other words, abortion is a matter on which there is unreasonable disagreement with respect to freedom and equality, but this cannot be resolved precisely because there is reasonable disagreement due to the burdens of judgment:

Reasonable disagreement on abortion due to the burdens of judgment: whether the foetus is a person.

Unreasonable disagreement on abortion with respect to freedom and equality: whether abortion should be legally permitted.

There is no neutral way out here. Liberals cannot remain neutral on the question of abortion, and must instead commit to a position that will necessarily be deeply controversial and difficult to justify.

At this point, liberal neutralists might be tempted to defend their position by saying that neutrality can be preserved by allowing women to decide on the question of foetal personhood for themselves. Since that is a question on which there is deep disagreement, neutrality suggests that the state should permit but not advocate abortion, so that pregnant women may follow their own consciences. After all, neutralists might argue, there is a truth of the matter on other cases of reasonable disagreement too. Jesus either is or is not the Son of God. The fact that there is reasonable disagreement on that question does not mean that there is no true answer. Neutralism does not commit us to relativism or the view that there is no truth;[10] it merely commits us to liberty, to allowing people to decide these matters for themselves and live according to their own consciences.

The problem with this suggestion in the case of abortion is that the rights of third parties are involved. If someone chooses to live according to their own beliefs about Christianity and those turn out to be false, it is only or primarily they that bear the consequences. The same is not true of abortion. If the foetus is a person then allowing women to choose abortion allows them to commit murder, and so would be an unreasonable position for the state to take. But if the foetus is not a person then preventing women from choosing abortion violates their liberty and equality. It is reasonable to allow women to decide for themselves whether the foetus is a person only if the foetus is not, in fact, a person. And so once again the state would be failing to be neutral on a matter of reasonable disagreement.

8.3 The Neutralist Dilemma

The problem that Kramer has identified with abortion is of wider application. Call it the *neutralist dilemma*. For a debate on matter, belief, or principle X, the dilemma can be stated as follows:

1. There is reasonable disagreement due to the burdens of judgment as to whether *X* or *not-X*.
2. If *X*, then policy *P* is required so as to avoid violating freedom and equality.
3. If *not-X*, then policy *not-P* is required so as to avoid violating freedom and equality.
4. (From 2 and 3) Either *P* or *not-P* violates freedom and equality.

---

[10] See Kramer, *Liberalism with Excellence*, pp. 11–12; Rawls, *Political Liberalism*, p. 63.

5. (From 4) Disagreement as to whether *P* or *not-P* is required would be unreasonable with respect to freedom and equality.
6. (From 1) We do not know whether *P* or *not-P* violates the freedom and equality of (some) citizens.
7. Therefore there is no neutral policy available.

Not all disagreements are neutralist dilemmas. But a disagreement will be a neutralist dilemma whenever there is a reasonable disagreement due to the burdens of judgment about whether some individual or category of individuals count as members of the morally salient class. In the abortion case, the disagreement is about whether foetuses count as persons. But other debates can take the same form.[11] If we can reasonably disagree whether foetuses are full moral persons then perhaps we can reasonably disagree whether children are full moral persons; later in the chapter I consider whether there is a neutralist dilemma concerning children's rights. But first consider a more straightforward example:

Neutralist dilemma on animal rights

1. There is reasonable disagreement due to the burdens of judgment as to whether animals have the same moral status as human beings.
2. If animals do have the same moral status as human beings, then meat-eating must be prohibited so as to avoid violating animals' freedom and equality.
3. If animals do not have the same moral status as human beings, then meat-eating must be permitted so as to avoid violating humans' freedom and equality.
4. (From 2 and 3) Either permitting or prohibiting meat-eating violates freedom and equality.
5. (From 4) Disagreement about whether meat-eating should be permitted or prohibited is unreasonable with respect to freedom and equality.
6. (From 1) We do not know whether it is permitting or prohibiting meat-eating that violates freedom and equality.
7. Therefore there is no neutral policy available.

The neutralist dilemma is thus of wider application than the abortion case, and presents a serious challenge to liberal neutralism.

---

[11] It is possible that a neutralist dilemma might exist concerning the status of immigrants and other non-citizens, though it would need to be carefully formulated.

A neutralist dilemma can be resolved in any particular case by denying one of its premises. Casual reflection suggests that in the neutralist dilemma on animal rights the premise most likely to be denied by mainstream liberal neutralists is premise 1. Most liberal neutralists do not advocate the prohibition of meat-eating and therefore must rely on the assumption that it is not reasonable to think that the moral status of animals is equivalent to that of humans. However, this denial is problematic since many serious thinkers do argue that animals have a moral status that rules out meat-eating.[12] The standard way for a neutralist liberal to think about this case is that there is a reasonable disagreement due to the burdens of judgment as to whether or not animals are moral persons, but that there is only unreasonable disagreement on the grounds of freedom and equality about whether meat-eating should be illegal. On the standard neutralist line, meat-eating must be legal so as to protect the liberty of those who are not convinced by the case for ethical vegetarianism, and so as to remain neutral on the question of animals' moral status. Kramer's analysis shows that this position is untenable: permitting meat-eating is justifiable only if animals do not have a moral status equivalent to that of persons. The neutralist dilemma is a genuine one.

8.4 Taking Precautions

One strategy for preserving neutrality in the abortion case is suggested by Jonathan Quong, in an argument that Kramer labels the Precautionary Argument. Kramer reconstructs Quong's argument as follows:

P1. Reasonable comprehensive doctrines disagree about whether the foetus is a full moral person.

P2. In the face of such reasonable disagreement, we should adhere to a precautionary principle and should therefore acquiesce in the proposition that the foetus does have the status of a full moral person.

C. Ergo, whenever we argue in favor of the legal permissibility of abortion, we should assume that the foetus is a full moral person. We are not thereby committed to accepting that such an assumption is true.[13]

---

[12] That there is genuine debate about the moral status of animals is evident; see, for example, Cass R. Sunstein and Martha C. Nussbaum (eds), *Animal Rights: Current Debates and New Directions* (Oxford; New York, NY: Oxford University Press, 2004) and Sue Donaldson and Will Kymlicka, *Zoopolis: A Political Theory of Animal Rights* (Oxford: Oxford University Press, 2011).
[13] Kramer, *Liberalism with Excellence*, p. 115.

This argument is precautionary because it proceeds by taking precautions against the most serious potential harm, which is committing murder. The implication of the Precautionary Argument is that it might be possible to justify the pro-choice position, as most liberal neutralists want to do, but only if one offers weighty reasons in favour of choice that can outweigh potential foetal personhood.

Kramer rejects this argument as a neutral way towards *justifying* abortion, not because it is non-neutral but because it is impossible. If we really did proceed on the assumption that the foetus is a moral person, the only acceptable policy would be to prohibit abortion. As Kramer puts it:

> When appraising the moral bearings of acts of murder perpetrated against adults or children, we would be badly misguided if we perceived ourselves as needing to strike a balance between the interests of the victims in bodily integrity and the autonomy of the murderers in wielding their weapons as they see fit. Yet – from the perspective of anyone who believes that foetuses are Rawlsian persons with the same basic rights as those of other persons – that grossly ill-judged angle on acts of murder is comparable to Rawls's and Quong's insistence on striking a balance between a pregnant woman's autonomy and a foetus's interest in survival.[14]

On the other hand, Kramer argues, the Precautionary Argument does not in fact justify a supposedly neutral *prohibition* of abortion. This is because, if the foetus is *not* a moral person, then prohibiting abortion would be unreasonable. Preventing women from having abortions imposes great limitations on their freedom, bodily integrity, and autonomy, limitations that are not similarly levied on men. These limitations are justified if they are necessary to prevent murder of persons, but they are not justified otherwise. If the foetus is not a person, then the Precautionary Argument unreasonably undermines women's equality and autonomy. In other words, we should not proceed on the assumption that the foetus is a person unless it really is a person. The stakes are too high.

The general problem with taking precautions is that doing so incurs certain costs as insurance against a greater but uncertain harm. And there can, of course, be reasonable disagreement about the appropriate balance between cost and risk; between insurance premium and payout. It is both rational and reasonable to pay even a very high premium to avoid the risk of harm that is both serious and likely. But it is not rational to pay any premium at all, let

---

[14] Kramer, *Liberalism with Excellence*, p. 116.

alone an extremely high one, to avoid a risk that is non-existent, and it would not be reasonable to require others to pay such a premium.

However, the strategy of taking precautions can be successful in some cases. It all depends on the likelihood and severity of the harm that is avoided by taking precautions, and the costs entailed in doing so. Kramer shows us that the only way for a state to proceed is by taking a judgment on these issues. It is for neutralists to show how the state can take such a judgment and remain neutral.

Kramer's conclusion is that the pro-choice position on abortion, favoured by most liberal neutralists, is permissible only if it can be adequately shown that foetuses are *not* persons. Showing this will, Kramer argues, necessarily entail grappling with issues that place neutralists directly in opposition to various comprehensive doctrines. In other words, before it is possible to engage in a debate on abortion that is confined to the constraints of public reason, it is first necessary to settle the deeply controversial question of whether a foetus is a person. And there is no way of having this debate that does not place us outside neutral territory and firmly within controversial, burdened judgment.

The abortion case is therefore an example of a reasonable disagreement on which the state cannot remain neutral, because one side and thus one of the two available policies must be unreasonable. The question is: which one?

8.5 Circumcision as Unreasonable

In this section, I discuss a debate with a similar structure to the abortion dilemma. However, I argue that in this case there *is* a neutral solution available. Moreover, the neutral solution that is available contrasts with both Kramer's own arguments and the practice of most liberal states.

The debate is whether the state should permit or prohibit the routine circumcision of babies and children. Kramer considers this case via a country he names Nosnipia. In Nosnipia the circumcision of babies and children is prohibited, and the prohibition is justified on what looks like neutral grounds. However, as with the case of abortion, Kramer argues that the purportedly neutral Nosnipian prohibition is actually not neutral at all.

In Nosnipia, a prohibition on circumcision is justified by a neutral appeal to public health. Nosnipian data indicates "that the net effect of male circumcision is mildly detrimental rather than mildly beneficial".[15] Since an appeal

---

[15] Kramer, *Liberalism with Excellence*, p. 85.

to public health is neutral between conceptions of the good, prohibition of circumcision appears similarly neutral. And yet Kramer is highly criticial of the Nosnipian officials:

> The people directly responsible for the legal interdiction of the practice of male circumcision in Nosnipia might not be aware of any biases on their part and might therefore be fully earnest in claiming that their issuance or sustainment of that interdiction is oriented purely toward public health. Nevertheless...those people are deluding themselves about their own intentions. Because the ritual of circumcising male infants is of such salience in Judaism and Islam, and because those two religions and that specific ritual have been subjected to ferocious bigotry in Western countries over the centuries, and because the detrimental effect of that ritual on male health in the counterfactual world which we are contemplating here is so mild [Kramer maintains that in the real world circumcision is *beneficial* to health], and because parents in Nosnipia are left with ample latitude to interact with their children in other ways which are more harmful and which are of no religious significance to the parents, we should conclude that the aim of the Nosnipian ban on male circumcision consists predominantly in the suppression of a religious practice that has long been an object of subrational antipathy. Although the proponents of that ban might *sincerely* disavow any such aim, they are thereby displaying a dearth of self-knowledge....
>
> In other words, the Nosnipian prohibition is not an instance of a law that is neutral in its intention but non-neutral in its effects. It is of course non-neutral in its effects, but its underlying intention is also non-neutral.[16]

Kramer's account suggests that the Nosnipians think of themselves as having a reasonable neutral policy:

Self-deluding Nosnipian supposedly neutral policy on circumcision: circumcision is bad for public health. Therefore, the state should prohibit it.

However, Kramer claims that their policy is actually non-neutral. It must rely on the decidedly non-neutral claim in the following description, placed in parentheses to show that the Nosnipian officials do not publicly avow it and may not be aware of its salience:

---

[16] Kramer, *Liberalism with Excellence*, p. 86.

Honest Nosnipian unreasonable policy on circumcision: circumcision is no worse for public health than many practices that are permitted. Circumcision is salient in Judaism and Islam. (Judaism and Islam should be suppressed.) Therefore, the state should prohibit circumcision.

Kramer argues that neutrality can be restored only by what Brian Barry would call a rule-and-exemption approach,[17] which would mean modifying the policy as follows:

Kramerian neutral policy on circumcision: circumcision is bad for public health. Therefore, the state could prohibit it. But circumcision is salient in Judaism and Islam, and those religions have been subject to ferocious bigotry. Circumcision is no worse for public health than many practices that are permitted. Therefore, even if the state prohibits circumcision generally, it should allow circumcision within Judaism and Islam.

Kramer's claim is that a blanket prohibition on infant circumcision would be unreasonable with respect to freedom and equality, even if apparently neutral public reasons were offered in its support. In this sense, circumcision resembles the abortion case.

I want to challenge Kramer's position. There is in fact an available neutral policy justifying the prohibition of infant circumcision. As with the abortion case, the state cannot avoid taking a side between those who advocate permission and those who advocate prohibition. But unlike the abortion case, the state can take a side on the matter of policy *without* taking a side on any matter on which there is reasonable disagreement. And unlike the abortion case, where neutralists tend to opt for permission, in the circumcision case the neutral policy would be to *prohibit* the practice.

I do not want to defend the legislators of Nosnipia (I've never met them) or any other polity. Kramer is right that the movement to proscribe circumcision can mobilise racism and religious bigotry.[18] But its justification need not be bigoted.

---

[17] Brian Barry, *Culture and Equality: An Egalitarian Critique of Multiculturalism* (Cambridge: Polity Press, 2001), pp. 40–50.
[18] For discussion, see Eric Rassbach, 'Coming Soon to a Court Near You: Religious Male Circumcision', *University of Illinois Law Review* 4 (2016), p. 1356; Ayreh Tuchman, 'Circumcision', in Richard S. Levy (ed.), *Antisemitism: A Historical Encyclopedia of Prejudice and Persecution* (Santa Barbara, CA: ABC-CLIO, 2005), p. 128.

First, it is important to note that the Nosnipian policy, and the policy that I am defending, forbids parents and doctors to forcibly circumcise *children*, who are too young to consent to the procedure; it does not forbid adult men to choose circumcision for themselves. Forbidding adults to choose circumcision for themselves would involve the state taking a side on a matter about which there is reasonable disagreement due to the burdens of judgment, as we shall see shortly. But since we are considering the circumcision of children, the debate is between the religious liberty and equality of *parents* (emphasised by the pro-circumcision side) and the bodily integrity and autonomy of *children* (emphasised by the anti-circumcision side). From the perspective of advocates of circumcision, such as Kramer, preventing the practice looks like an unreasonable restriction of parents' freedom and equality. From the perspective of critics of the practice, such as myself, permitting it looks like an unreasonable violation of the children's freedom and equality.

The debate about circumcision can thus be stated as a neutralist dilemma. Consider one version:

Neutralist dilemma on circumcision I

1. There is reasonable disagreement due to the burdens of judgment as to whether circumcision is harmful.
2. If circumcision is harmful then circumcision of children must be prohibited so as to avoid violating children's freedom and equality.
3. If circumcision is not harmful, then circumcision must be permitted so as to avoid violating parents' freedom and equality.
4. (From 2 and 3) Either permitting or prohibiting circumcision violates freedom and equality.
5. (From 4) Disagreement about whether circumcision of children should be permitted or prohibited is unreasonable with respect to freedom and equality.
6. (From 1) We do not know whether it is permitting or prohibiting circumcision that violates freedom and equality.
7. Therefore there is no neutral policy available.

However, this version of the neutralist dilemma on circumcision can be resolved. As we saw earlier, resolving a neutralist dilemma requires rejecting one of its premises. In this version of the dilemma, premise 3 fails, as I show shortly. First, I show that premise 1 succeeds.

Premise 1 states that there is a reasonable disagreement due to the burdens of judgment as to whether circumcision is harmful. There are two aspects to this disagreement: religion and public health. For some people, circumcision is justified on religious grounds, as Kramer notes. For such people, circumcision is not harmful precisely because it is a requirement of religion. The fact that circumcision is a religious tradition is for such people enough to outweigh any purported harms of the practice. Others might reasonably disagree in one of two ways. They might not be members of circumcising religions, and so might not endorse the idea that *any* of the tenets of the religion are properly understood as requirements or can have any justificatory weight. Or, people might be members of a circumcising religion and so agree in general that the tenets of that religion are requirements, but they might disagree on the question of whether circumcision really is a proper requirement of their religion.[19] Combining these options gives the following reasonable disagreement:

Reasonable disagreement on circumcision due to burdens of judgment I: whether circumcision is required or justified by religion.

Little discussion is needed to establish that this is a reasonable disagreement, since it very closely mirrors the standard neutralist case set out at the start of this chapter, and since disagreement on these questions is readily apparent.

The second aspect of the reasonable disagreement concerning circumcision is whether it is harmful in another way, which is to say whether removing a boy's foreskin constitutes an overall loss or gain to his health and well-being. Kramer himself argues that circumcision is mildly beneficial, and implies that there is not a reasonable disagreement on that question (although he is willing to concede this point for the sake of argument). He writes:

> On the one hand, bodies of experts such as the American Academy of Pediatrics and the American College of Obstetricians and Gynecologists and the Center[s] for Disease Control have in recent years concluded that

---

[19] For a historical discussion of the role of circumcision in Judaism, including dissenting voices, see Leonard B. Glick, *Marked in Your Flesh: Circumcision from Ancient Judea to Modern America* (New York: Oxford University Press, 2005). For discussion of different circumcision practices in Islam, see S. A. H. Rizvi, S. A. A. Naqvi, M. Hussain, and A. S. Hasan, 'Religious Circumcision: A Muslim View', *BJU International* 83(1) (1999), pp. 13–16.

the mildly beneficial effects of the circumcision of male infants outweigh the extremely small risks involved (Stobbe 2014; Task Force on Circumcision 2012). In light of those expert judgments, the crusades against male circumcision that are currently being conducted by some knights of the foreskin are especially dubious.[20]

In defence of Kramer's position note that most liberal states do not prohibit circumcision and in some, such as the USA, it is practised routinely. So there certainly are those who argue that circumcision is not harmful and may be beneficial to health and well-being.

However, while Kramer is right about the American Academy of Pediatrics (AAP), he gives a highly partial account of expert opinion. For one, while the AAP does judge that the benefits of circumcision outweigh the risks, it also states that the benefits are not significant enough to recommend the practice.[21] Other medical authorities take stronger positions against circumcision. The UK National Health Service (NHS) website describes circumcision as "a treatment of last resort" and states "It's rare for circumcision to be recommended for medical reasons in children. This is because other, less invasive and less risky treatments are usually available."[22]

With respect to therapeutic circumcision, the British Medical Association (BMA) advises "to circumcise for therapeutic reasons where medical research has shown other techniques to be at least as effective and less invasive would be unethical and inappropriate.... there is rarely a clinical indication for circumcision". With respect to routine or ritual circumcision, the BMA states:

> There is a spectrum of views within the BMA's membership about whether non-therapeutic male circumcision is a beneficial, neutral, or harmful procedure or whether it is superfluous, and whether it should ever be done on a child who is not capable of deciding for himself. The medical harms or

---

[20] Kramer, *Liberalism with Excellence*, p. 85.
[21] In Clare Chambers, *Intact: A Defence of the Unmodified Body* I examine the position of the American Academy of Pediatrics in detail. To summarise that analysis: the AAP's discussion of the medical complications and implications of circumcision is skewed strongly towards the practice, in contravention of its own stated recommendation; and it actively recommends that parents make the choice based on cultural and religious reasons rather than medical ones, even though it is a medical organisation not a religious or cultural one. The AAP's position on circumcision is comparable to the Nosnipian policy as Kramer interprets it: it is a policy that, whether intentionally and explicitly or not, reflects and furthers a particular cultural and religious conception above others.
[22] NHS Choices, 'Circumcision in Boys', NHS, available at http://www.nhs.uk/conditions/Circumcision-in-children/Pages/Introduction.aspx (accessed 20 December 2017). The most recent version of this page (accessed 6 September 2022) no longer refers to circumcision as a "last resort" but retains the other quoted statements.

benefits have not been unequivocally proven but there are clear risks of harm if the procedure is done inexpertly.[23]

The medical authorities of other countries concur with the BMA.[24]

It is also important to note that the medical benefits claimed by the AAP do not depend on circumcision being performed in childhood. Many of the benefits that the AAP claim for circumcision concern the prevention of diseases that do not generally present until adulthood, and so nothing is lost from a health perspective if circumcision is delayed until it can be consented to.[25]

As for men who have been circumcised, many of them are indifferent about or positively happy with being circumcised. However, there are a significant number of men who were circumcised as children who regret that fact, and some who experience severe mental distress or physical complications.[26] There is also a problem with evidence-collection since few men have experience of both conditions and there is a potential problem of adaptive preferences.[27]

In sum, there is ample evidence for the existence of a second reasonable disagreement:

Reasonable disagreement on circumcision due to burdens of judgment II: whether circumcision is beneficial or harmful to health.

---

[23] British Medical Association, 'The Law and Ethics of Male Circumcision', BMA (2017), available at https://www.bma.org.uk/advice/employment/ethics/children-and-young-people/male-circumcision.

[24] For example, the Canadian Paediatric Society states: "While there may be a benefit for some boys in high risk populations and the procedure could be considered as a treatment or to reduce disease, in most cases, the benefits of circumcision do not outweigh the risks" (The Canadian Paediatric Society, 'Canadian Paediatricians Revisit Newborn Male Circumcision Recommendations', Canadian Paediatric Society, 8 September 2015, available at https://cps.ca/en/media/canadian-paediatricians-revisit-newborn-male-circumcision-recommendations).

[25] The German Paediatric Association states "there is but one of the arguments put forward by the AAP that has some theoretical relevance in relation to infant male circumcision, namely the possible protection against urinary tract infections in infant boys, which can be easily treated with antibiotics without tissue loss. The other claimed health benefits, including protection against HIV/AIDS, genital herpes, genital warts and penile cancer, are questionable, weak and likely to have little public health relevance in a Western context, and do not represent compelling reasons for surgery before boys are old enough to decide for themselves" (Wolfram Hartmann, 'German Paediatric Association Criticises American Academy of Pediatrics, Circumcision Information Australia, n.d., available at https://www.circinfo.org/doctors.html).

[26] For discussion and testimony from men who reject their childhood circumcision, see Intact America at http://intactamerica.org; the National Organization of Circumcision Information Resource Centers at http://www.nocirc.org; 15 square at https://www.15square.org.uk/; and The Intactivism Pages at http://www.circumstitions.com. For discussion of the outcomes for men who are happy with their circumcision, see Clare Chambers, *Sex, Culture, and Justice: The Limits of Choice* (University Park, PA: Penn State University Press, 2008), ch. 1.

[27] Brian D. Earp, Lauren M. Sardi, and William A. Jellison, 'False Beliefs Predict Increased Circumcision Satisfaction in a Sample of US American Men', *Culture, Health & Sexuality* 20(8) (2018), available at http://www.tandfonline.com/eprint/EauVkp3YQe8KXU5qtyac/full.

Premise 1 of the neutralist dilemma on circumcision stands.

However, the existence of reasonable disagreement due to the burdens of judgment as to whether circumcision is beneficial or harmful does not mean that the state should permit the circumcision of babies and children. This is because the circumcision of babies and children violates their freedom and equality, whichever way you resolve the matter of reasonable disagreement due to burdens of judgment. The first version of the neutralist dilemma on circumcision can be resolved by rejecting premise 3. The disagreement due to burdens of judgment does not need to be resolved in order to identify which side violates the freedom and equality of (some) citizens.

In contrast to the abortion case, *the very fact that there is a reasonable disagreement about the harms of circumcision* means that it is a violation of freedom and equality to circumcise someone without his consent. The state must choose whether to permit or prohibit circumcision, but it can do so without taking a stance on the matter of reasonable disagreement due to burdens of judgment, because remaining neutral on that question would mean allowing men to choose *for themselves* whether to undergo circumcision.

Permitting circumcision of children is unreasonable with respect to freedom and equality. It undermines equality because in many liberal countries only boys, or even only boys belonging to particular cultures and religions, lack legal protection from unnecessary surgical modification of their genitals. It undermines freedom because it reduces a man's bodily autonomy and religious liberty. Permitting infant circumcision involves allowing parents to authorise the irreversible removal of a healthy, functioning part of their son's body.[28] It thus undermines that boy's bodily autonomy, since he will no longer be able to make his own decision about circumcision (on either religious or health grounds) and cannot choose to keep his foreskin. And it undermines his bodily integrity, since a healthy, functioning, erogenous part of his body has been removed without his consent. Since there is reasonable disagreement as to whether that removal is harmful, it follows that children should be able to decide the matter for themselves on reaching adulthood.

A neutral policy on circumcision would run as follows:

Reasonable neutral policy on circumcision: there is reasonable disagreement as to whether circumcision is harmful. Therefore each man should be able to decide this question for his own body for himself. Permitting the circumcision of children violates their freedom and equality.

---

[28] For a clinical description of the anatomy and function of the foreskin, see C. J. Cold and J. R. Taylor, 'The Prepuce', *BJU International* 20(83) (1999).

This reasonable neutral policy has the same conclusion as *Self-deluding Nosnipian supposedly neutral policy on circumcision* and *Honest Nosnipian unreasonable policy on circumcision*, but it is distinct from those policies and does not suffer from the same problems.

The reasonable neutral policy contrasts with two non-neutral policies:

Non-neutral policy on circumcision I: circumcision is beneficial. Therefore the circumcision of babies and boys should be permitted.

Non-neutral policy on circumcision II: circumcision is harmful. Therefore the circumcision of adult men should be prohibited.

These policies are non-neutral because they take a side on matters on which there is reasonable disagreement due to burdens of judgment (whether religion requires circumcision, and whether circumcision is good for public health) when it is possible to take a neutral stance on those questions. But notice that, *regardless of which side of the reasonable disagreement one lies*, it is unreasonable to impose that judgment on the babies and children who face circumcision without their consent. As adults those men could reasonably disagree with their parents about whether circumcision is justified by either religious or health considerations, but if they were circumcised as children then it will be too late for them to act on their own judgment. The decision will already have been taken for them—irreversibly and unreasonably—by their parents. It follows that it is unreasonable with respect to freedom and equality to permit the circumcision of children. Premise 3 fails. Circumcision is not a neutralist dilemma.

8.6 A Second Neutralist Dilemma on Circumcision

The conclusion of the previous section relies on the claim that one person's religious liberty cannot justify violating another person's freedom and equality, regardless of whether the violation is harmful or not. After all, religious liberty does not justify one adult forcing another adult to be circumcised against his will, even if the first adult does sincerely believe that her religion requires it. And this conclusion is generalisable, regardless of whether circumcision is harmful or beneficial. One adult cannot use her religious liberty to justify forcing another adult to have his hair cut, even if the haircut is not harmful to him and even if she sincerely believes that her religion requires her do the forcing. Similarly, one adult cannot use her religious liberty to justify coercing another adult to attend religious worship.

However, an objector might use these examples against me. They might point out that parents are generally permitted to force their *children* to have haircuts against their will, on the basis that haircuts are not harmful and parents have rights over their children. They might point out that parents are generally permitted to force their children to attend religious worship, justified by the parents' religious liberty. Thus, the objection proceeds, circumcision is a neutralist dilemma after all: if circumcision is not harmful then prohibiting it would be like prohibiting parents from choosing to cut their children's hair, and such prohibitions would violate parents' freedom and equality.

This objection suggests that the debate over circumcision can be turned into a neutralist dilemma by questioning the moral status of children. This version of the circumcision dilemma runs as follows:

Neutralist dilemma on circumcision II

1. There is reasonable disagreement due to the burdens of judgment as to whether children are full moral persons.[29]
2. If children are full moral persons, then it is unreasonable for parents to authorise circumcision of their children, since this denies the children's freedom and equality.
3. If children are not full moral persons, then it is unreasonable to prohibit parents from authorising circumcision, since prohibition would restrict the religious liberty of parents without being justified by the freedom and equality of other persons.
4. (From 2 and 3) Either permitting or prohibiting circumcision violates freedom and equality.
5. (From 4) Disagreement about whether circumcision of children should be permitted or prohibited is unreasonable with respect to freedom and equality.
6. (From 1) We do not know whether it is permitting or prohibiting circumcision that violates freedom and equality.
7. Therefore there is no neutral policy available.

---

[29] This argument could be framed in a variety of ways: whether children are full moral persons, whether children deserve full freedom and equality, whether they have the same moral status as citizens, whether parents have full authority over their children. Different framings will be differently plausible; what matters is that they be consistent throughout the dilemma.

Framed this way, the argument is once again a neutralist dilemma, and there is no way of settling it without engaging in the question of whether children are full moral persons.

If it is at least possible that foetuses are full moral persons then it must surely be possible that children are, and so the problem seems even more intractable than the abortion case. However, a defender of parents' right to circumcise their sons might argue that there is a disanalogy between abortion and circumcision. If foetuses are full moral persons then abortion certainly violates their freedom and equality because it kills them, but the harm of circumcision is not comparable. According to this objection, it is possible both to believe that children are full moral persons and that circumcision of children is permissible, because parents generally have the right to authorise medical procedures on their children, and because parents' religious liberty means that they can bring their children up according to their own religious beliefs, and because any harm entailed in circumcision is not serious.

Many issues are raised here, and it is beyond the scope of this chapter to engage them all fully, so a few remarks must suffice. First, it would be implausible to argue that parents may in general exercise their liberty via their children's bodies. The related principles of bodily integrity and bodily autonomy place limits on parental action. Parents should not be able to express their religious liberty by tattooing their children with religious symbols.[30] Parents should also not have complete authority to submit their children to surgical procedures: they may not authorise cosmetic surgery on their children so as to shape them to their own tastes. And parents should not be able to deny their children life-saving treatments on religious grounds.

So it is not plausible to say that there is reasonable disagreement on children's moral status of the sort that would truly leave open the possibility that children's freedom, equality, bodily integrity, and bodily autonomy, count for *nothing*.[31] Parents need to act as guardians, meaning that they can make decisions for their children when necessary to secure their children's interests. But they may not treat their children as accessories for their own interests.

---

[30] The claim is *not* that there is something particularly dishonourable about religious symbols: parents should similarly not be allowed to tattoo their children with symbols reflecting the parents' aesthetic taste, or parental allegiance to a sports team, or any other commitment. My claim is that *even* religious liberty, though weighty and important, does not justify allowing parents to undermine their children's bodily integrity and autonomy.

[31] Rawls describes full moral persons as "someone who can be a citizen, that is, a normal and fully cooperating member of society over a complete life" and that society must make room for "all the necessities and activities of life, from birth until death". These remarks are generally taken to indicate that children are persons in the relevant sense. See Rawls, *Political Liberalism*, p. 18.

Kramer's argument against Nosnipia invites us to weigh up bodily integrity v. religious liberty. Both bodily integrity and religious liberty are weighty values. However, in the case of circumcision of babies and children they are not symmetrical, because to permit circumcision is to value the religious liberty of parents against the bodily integrity and autonomy of children, and this is not a reasonable trade off. This conclusion does not depend on one's view about whether religious reasons favour circumcision. If circumcision were not required for religious reasons, then it would be unreasonable to circumcise babies and children since this would violate their bodily integrity and autonomy without justification. But if circumcision were required for religious reasons, it would still be unreasonable to circumcise babies and children since this would violate their bodily integrity and autonomy without contributing to *their* religious liberty.[32]

The practice of circumcision is particularly significant because it is a practice that undermines bodily integrity in an irreversible way. Forcing a child to have a haircut that he does not want violates his bodily integrity, and thus may sometimes be wrong, but hair grows back and so even a forced hair cut does not prevent the child from making his own decisions about his hair when he becomes an adult. But circumcision is irreversible: parents' decision to circumcise cannot be undone.

In one respect, everything a parent does to her children is irreversible: we cannot reverse time and create alternative childhoods. So irreversibility alone cannot be a barrier to parental action. But some sorts of parental action are irreversible not just in the time-travelling sense, but in the more interesting sense that they close future options: they prevent future choices, they remove capabilities, or they undermine autonomy. A boy who is not circumcised can choose circumcision for himself later; a boy who is circumcised cannot choose to be intact later.[33]

---

[32] A Rawlsian way of putting this point would be to say that using parental religious liberty to justify the circumcision of children violates the separateness of persons.

[33] One anonymous reviewer objected that circumcision is a requirement in Judaism, such that failing to circumcise a baby boy prevents him from having a properly Jewish childhood. In response, note first that not all Jewish people feel that circumcision is essential to a properly Jewish childhood. Some Jews support Brit Shalom as an alternative to circumcision, meaning that some Jewish boys are uncircumcised. For discussion and first-hand accounts, see http://www.beyondthebris.com. Nevertheless, Brit Shalom remains a minority practice and so many Jewish people may agree with the reviewer that an uncircumcised boy cannot have a properly Jewish childhood. On this account, not circumcising a boy *irreversibly* prevents him from accessing the value of a traditional Jewish childhood. However, there are a vast number of ways of preventing a child from accessing the value of a traditional or properly Jewish childhood, such as bringing him or her up in a different religion or without religion. Indeed, every parenting decision can be described similarly. Bringing up a child speaking only English

This consideration makes circumcision unlike other aspects of parents' religious liberty, such as attendance at religious worship. Parents may legitimately take their children to worship, since that choice serves the parents' religious liberty and does not prevent those children from making their own decisions about whether to worship as adults. Childhood acts of religious worship cannot be reversed, but childhood acts of worship do not prevent adult from choice about worship. And the same is true in reverse of an atheist upbringing.[34]

However, a challenger might claim that the circumcision of babies and children could be permissible if it improved public health. In this case, the objection would run, it is justifiable to circumcise babies and children even if that means violating their bodily integrity and autonomy, since we make a similar trade off in other cases. For example, we allow parents to submit their children to vaccination so as to improve public health. Moreover, Kramer notes that parents in Nosnipia remain at liberty to harm their children in other ways, such as by feeding them fattening food.

But circumcision is not a good analogy to vaccination, because while there *is* disagreement on the clinical benefits of vaccination it is *not* reasonable due to the burdens of judgment. Clinical judgment on the benefits of vaccination is overwhelming, whereas even the pro-circumcision AAP states that the benefits of the practice are not sufficient to *recommend* it. And vaccination does not involve the permanent removal of body parts.

Plying children with fattening food may or may not be a good analogy for circumcision, depending on its extent. It may well do damage to them and be wrong in various ways. Quite possibly, the freedom that parents have to feed their children unhealthy food should be constrained. For example, many state schools in the UK do not allow parents to include sweets and chocolate in packed lunches, or require that playtime snacks consist only of fruits and vegetables. Even more plausibly, parents who persistently restrict their children's diet despite damaging their health, particularly if the damage to health is so

---

irreversibly prevents her from accessing the value of a Spanish-speaking childhood; failing to teach a child piano from an early age irreversibly prevents her from accessing the value of being a child prodigy at piano-playing; bringing a child up in one country irreversibly prevents her from accessing the value of a childhood spent in a different country. So this objection cannot be decisive.

[34] Some parental actions prevent children from exercising some relevant liberty in the future, such as religious upbringings that amount to brainwashing and deny autonomy. It is an important aspect of liberalism that education should be autonomy-promoting, and so the liberal state may legitimately prevent parents from denying their children the opportunity to develop autonomously. See, for example, Meira Levinson, *The Demands of Liberal Education* (Oxford: Oxford University Press, 1999); Eamonn Callan, *Creating Citizens* (Oxford: Oxford University Press, 1997).

extreme as to be irreversible or to cause the loss of body parts, should be guilty of an offence. But simply giving one's child unhealthy food occasionally, or even frequently, is not analogous to the permanent removal of healthy body parts.

8.7 Taking Precautions Again

In the abortion case, Kramer argued convincingly that Quong's Precautionary Argument does not work. In the circumcision case, the Precautionary Argument is successful. A version of it applied to circumcision would go something like this:

P1. Reasonable comprehensive doctrines disagree about whether circumcision is required for religious or clinical reasons.

P2. In the face of such reasonable disagreement, we should adhere to a precautionary principle and should therefore acquiesce to the proposition that the foreskin is valuable and should not be removed. We are not thereby committed to accepting that such an assumption is true.

C. Ergo, since both bodily integrity and autonomy *are* generally-accepted political values, we should argue against the legal permissibility of the circumcision of children, so that adult men may decide for themselves whether circumcision is required for religious or health reasons.

This version of the Precautionary Argument is not subject to the objections that Kramer raises to its use in the abortion case. The values of bodily integrity and bodily autonomy are vital here. Even if one believes that the foreskin is valuable and should not be removed, one can also believe that bodily autonomy makes it reasonable for an adult man to choose circumcision for himself, whether for religious or health reasons. Even if one believes that circumcision is required for religious or clinical reasons, one can also believe that bodily autonomy makes it reasonable to preserve a man's right to make this choice for himself.

Indeed, as Kramer himself argues, the value of the freedom to choose is not dependent on the value of the thing one chooses. It is valuable simply to be treated as someone who is able to deliberate for oneself. In chapter 5, Kramer takes this point to grisly extremes, telling us that even the "freedom to disembowel oneself is important because it is typically a hallmark of respect for one's deliberative maturity.... Normally, then, a mentally sound adult who has been deprived of the freedom to resort to self-disembowelment should feel aggrieved."[35] There is no reason not to make a similar claim about the man who has been deprived of the freedom to keep his foreskin. After all, as Kramer argues about freedom in general, "Even when φ-ing is itself of no positive value, being free to φ is almost always of positive value."[36] For many men the foreskin is of great positive value, but even those who do not value it derive value from the freedom to choose its fate for themselves.

In order to believe that the law should permit circumcision of babies, which is what Kramer wants it to do, one must believe that bodily integrity and personal freedom is either not valuable at all, or that it is less valuable than the religious convictions of people whose body it isn't. As Kramer shows in the case of abortion, this would be an unreasonable position.

Kramer suggests that banning circumcision would be bigoted, because it would be a form of discrimination or oppression against those religions that practise it. This is an important consideration, and one of the greatest challenges for any anti-circumcision position. However, the fact that a view can sometimes mobilise racism or other unreasonable positions cannot be a decisive strike against it, because that would rule out many reasonable political perspectives.[37] It is also a challenge for the much more mainstream view that female genital mutilation (FGM) is wrong.[38] In countries such as the UK, FGM is illegal when performed for cultural reasons, even when performed on consenting adult women. But cosmetic surgery on the genitals (female genital cosmetic surgery or FGCS), including that which has surgical equivalence to

---

[35] Kramer, *Liberalism with Excellence*, p. 201.
[36] Kramer, *Liberalism with Excellence*, p. 231.
[37] For example, it is true that pro-Brexit opinion may mobilise racism. It would be wrong to endorse Brexit for racist reasons. But this does not mean that it is necessarily unreasonable to endorse Brexit for non-racist reasons. Similarly, it is possible to oppose pornography for oppressive reasons, but this does not mean that it is unreasonable to oppose pornography for feminist reasons. And it is possible to use support for abortion to mobilise anti-Catholicism, but this does not mean that all support for abortion is unreasonable.
[38] Female genital mutilation is sometimes referred to as female genital cutting (FGC), so as to avoid pre-empting questions of ethics, and so as to avoid denigrating women and girls' genitals as 'mutilated'. I have retained the phrase FGM for two reasons: first, it is referred to as such in the relevant legislation; second, many campaigners against the practice, including women who have themselves undergone it, argue that it is mutilating and use the phrase FGM themselves.

FGM, is permitted—including for children.[39] This position strikes many as discriminatory or racist.[40]

What policies would be needed to rectify any racism? Kramer's position on child circumcision is that racism could be avoided by forbidding it generally permitting it for Jewish and Muslim parents. Applying this logic to FGM might support a reversal in current practice: forbidding FGCS but allowing FGM members of practising cultures. But anti-FGM campaigners, including those who have experienced FGM themselves, would not advocate this position. They argue that any racism in the status quo comes from a *lack* of successful prosecutions of FGM, which amount to failing to protect black girls from abuse.[41]

Cultural and religious exemptions from laws are generally treated as benefitting the members of those cultures and religions. However, where the justification of a law is to protect the vulnerable or to secure freedom and equality, legal exemptions harm the vulnerable members of the culture or religion at the expense of the powerful.[42] Permitting only religious circumcision would

---

[39] FGCS is widely available in the UK, openly advertised, and sometimes provided by the NHS. This is possible because the UK Female Genital Mutilation Act 2003 states "no offence is committed by an approved person who performs a surgical operation on a girl which is necessary for her physical or mental health." There are restrictions on what sorts of things count as making surgery 'necessary': the Act stipulates "For the purpose of determining whether an operation is necessary for the mental health of a girl it is immaterial whether she or any other person believes that the operation is required as a matter of custom or ritual" (Crown Prosecution Service, 'Female Genital Mutilation Legal Guidance', available at http://www.cps.gov.uk/legal/d_to_g/female_genital_mutilation/#a01). However, the guidance notes for the legislation say that procedures that are necessary for mental health can include "cosmetic surgery resulting from the distress caused by a perception of abnormality" (UK Female Genital Mutilation Act 2003, 'Guidance', available at http://www.legislation.gov.uk/ukpga/2003/31/contents. For extensive discussion of the UK legal position on FGCS, see Clare Chambers, 'Choice and Female Genital Cosmetic Surgery', Chapter 11 in this volume; Clare Chambers, *Intact: A Defence of the Unmodified Body* (London: Allen Lane, 2022); Marge Berer, 'Labia Reduction for Non-Therapeutic Purposes vs. Female Genital Mutilation: Contradictions in Law and Practice in Britain', *Reproductive Health Matters* 18(35) (2010); Moira Dustin, 'Female Genital Mutilation/Cutting in the UK: Challenging the Inconsistencies', *The European Journal of Women's Studies* 17(1) (2010); B. Kelly and C. Foster, 'Should Female Genital Cosmetic Surgery and Genital Piercing Be Regarded Ethically and Legally as Female Genital Mutilation?', *BJOG: An International Journal of Obstetrics and Gynaecology* 119(4) (2012).

[40] See Moira Dustin, 'Female Genital Mutilation/Cutting in the UK'; Arianne Shahvisi, 'Why UK Doctors Should Be Troubled by Female Genital Mutilation Legislation', *Clinical Ethics* 12(2) (2017). For discussion of a racist double-standard in the Scandinavian context, see Birgitta Essén and Sara Johnsdotter, 'Female Genital Mutilation in the West: Traditional Circumcision Versus Genital Cosmetic Surgery', *Acta Obstetricia et Gynecologica Scandinavica* 83(7) (2004). For critique of the UN position, see Bronwyn Winter, Denise Thompson, and Sheila Jeffreys, 'The UN Approach to Harmful Traditional Practices', *International Feminist Journal of Politics* 4(1) (2002).

[41] British anti-FGM campaigner Hibo Wardere reports the words of fellow campaigner Waris Dirie: "If a white girl is abused, the police come and break the door down. If a black girl is mutilated, nobody takes care of her. This is what I call racism" (Hibo Wardere, *Cut: One Woman's Fight Against FGM in Britain Today* (London: Simon and Schuster, 2016), p. 215).

[42] For further development of this argument, see Clare Chambers, *Against Marriage: An Egalitarian Defence of the Marriage-Free State State* (Oxford: Oxford University Press, 2017), ch. 6.

be to selectively fail to protect the bodily autonomy of Jewish and Muslim boys. Similarly, many anti-circumcision campaigners argue that allowing male circumcision and forbidding FGM selectively fails to protect the bodily autonomy of boys as compared to girls.[43]

In *neutralist dilemma on circumcision II* the most plausible resolution of the dilemma is to deny premise 1. Children's moral status must be at least adequate to protect them from practices about which there is reasonable disagreement due to the burdens of judgment and which irreversibly undermine their bodily integrity and autonomy. To think otherwise would be unreasonable. And if premise 1 fails, then so does premise 3, and the dilemma is solved in favour of prohibition. One implication of this argument, which counters the charge of bigotry, is that infant circumcision should not be singled out for prohibition: states should legislate generally against all forms of non-therapeutic irreversible body modification on children.[44]

8.8 Conclusion

This chapter considered Kramer's argument about the impossibility of a neutral position on abortion and argued that it could be generalised into what I call a 'neutralist dilemma'. Neutralist dilemmas might occur in various forms. However, I argued that the case of circumcision is a neutralist dilemma only if there is a serious possibility that children are not full moral persons. If they are full moral persons, or at least have weighty moral status, then it is not justifiable to subject them to irreversible bodily procedures that are not clinically required treatments of a presenting health problem, and about which there is reasonable disagreement. It is much more plausible, I argued, to suppose that children have at least the moral status that would grant them protection against such procedures until they can decide for themselves.

Freedom and Equality: Essays on Liberalism and Feminism. Clare Chambers, Oxford University Press.
© Clare Chambers 2024. DOI: 10.1093/9780191919480.003.0009

---

[43] See, for example, Brian D. Earp, 'Female Genital Mutilation (FGM) and Male Circumcision: Should There Be a Separate Ethical Discourse?', *Practical Ethics* (2014), available at https://www.academia.edu/8817976/Female_genital_mutilation_FGM_and_male_circumcision_Should_there_be_a_separate_ethical_discourse.

[44] For an argument in favour of tougher legislation against cosmetic procedures being performed on children, see Nuffield Council on Bioethics, *Cosmetic Procedures: Ethical Issues* (Nuffield Council on Bioethics, 2017), available at http://nuffieldbioethics.org/project/cosmetic-procedures.

PART IV
EQUALITY OF OPPORTUNITY

9

Each Outcome Is Another Opportunity

Problems with the Moment of Equal Opportunity

Imagine two people, Jeremy and Jason, who have similar family backgrounds, similar educations and similar merit (in the Rawlsian sense, where merit means talent plus effort plus inclination) at eighteen years old.[1] Both apply to an elite university, such as Oxford, whose admissions tutors are (we assume) making decisions based on equality of opportunity. As places are scarce, only Jeremy is accepted. Jason studies a similar course at another university, one which is less prestigious and which devotes less time to undergraduate tuition. Both work equally hard (in other words, both display the same amount of effort and inclination to work). Both achieve 2:1 degrees, and both apply for graduate jobs at leading companies in a particular field.[2] Jeremy is more successful. Employers are impressed by his Oxford degree—not because they are wrongly prejudiced in favour of Oxford through something such as an old boy network, but because they believe that Oxford selects the best students in the first place, that it provides its students with a better education than other universities, and that its culture means that its students develop important skills such as confidence and initiative. In other words, employers prefer Oxford graduates because they believe that Oxford graduates are more likely to have qualities which *legitimately and genuinely* make better employees.[3]

---

[1] This chapter was originally published in *Politics, Philosophy and Economics* 8(4) (2009). The first draft of that article was presented at the workshop on Equality of Opportunity at the ECPR Joint Sessions in Granada in April 2005. I am extremely grateful to all the participants and particularly the workshop directors, Ian Carter and David Miller. Later drafts were presented at the Nuffield Political Theory Workshop, the University of Oxford Centre for the Study of Social Justice, the Political Theory Research Seminar at UCL, the *British Journal of Political Science*'s one-day conference at the British Academy, the Cardiff University Politics Research Seminar and the Philosophy Department Seminar at the University of Sheffield. I received very useful feedback at each event. I should also like to thank Chris Armstrong, Cécile Fabre, Marc Fleurbaey, Cécile Laborde, Phil Parvin, Avia Pasternak, Zofia Stemplowska, Adam Swift, Adam Tebble, and the reviewers and editors of *Politics, Philosophy and Economics* for written comments.

[2] British degrees are typically classified from best to worst as First Class, 2:1 (Upper Second), 2:2 (Lower Second), Third, or Fail. Many graduate employers and postgraduate courses require applicants to have achieved at least a 2:1.

[3] It might be asked here whether, for the purposes of this example, employers are correct in their beliefs. This question cannot be answered definitively without begging the questions that follow, but for now we may assume that at least some of their beliefs have at least some grounding. Certainly the beliefs are neither obviously wrong nor merely the result of prejudice.

So, Jeremy gets a top graduate job at a leading company, while Jason gets a less prestigious position at a less prestigious company. Both work equally hard. Jeremy's job develops his skills quickly. He is given important clients to work with, encouraged to try new things, sent on expensive training courses. Jason is also given opportunities to develop and sent on training courses, but his position and his company mean that he does not develop such impressive skills as Jeremy. In five years, each applies for a more senior position at another company. By this stage, Jeremy is the far better candidate. Not only does he have the advantages that his Oxford degree conferred upon him, he also now has a further advantage in terms of career experience, skills and the good name of a prestigious first employer. As a result, Jeremy gets the job. Jason has to wait until he is offered a less significant promotion at a less prestigious company. And here the process repeats itself. By the time they apply for their third jobs, Jason has no hope of competing with Jeremy: Jeremy's CV is far more impressive, and the experience he has enjoyed and skills he has developed make him clearly the more competent candidate. By retirement, Jeremy has achieved a much higher position in their industry than has Jason, and has earned much more money. Jason is neither poor nor unsuccessful, but his career has not reached the stellar heights of Jeremy's.

This story is by no means unusual. It is the general pattern of career development that we see in many industries—including academia, as Morris Zapp notes with glee in *Small World*, part of David Lodge's superb campus trilogy:

> The Villa Serbelloni proved to be a noble and luxurious house built on the sheltered slope of a promontory that divided two lakes, Como and Lecco, with magnificent views to east, south and west from its balconies and extensive gardens.
>
> [Professor] Morris [Zapp] was shown into a well-appointed suite on the second floor, and stepped out on to his balcony to inhale the air, scented with the perfume of various spring blossoms, and to enjoy the prospect. Down on the terrace, the other resident scholars were gathering for the pre-lunch aperitif – he had glimpsed the table laid for lunch in the dining-room on his way up: starched white napery, crystal glass, menu cards. He surveyed the scene with complacency. He felt sure he was going to enjoy his stay here. Not the least of its attractions was that it was entirely free. All you had to do, to come and stay in this idyllic retreat, pampered by servants and lavishly provided with food and drink, given every facility for reflection and creation, was to apply.

Of course, you had to be distinguished – by, for instance, having applied successfully for other, similar handouts, grants, fellowships and so on, in the past. That was the beauty of the academic life, as Morris saw it. To them that had had, more would be given.[4]

In this chapter, I ask whether the story of Jeremy and Jason is compatible with equality of opportunity. The inequality between them at the end of their lives can be traced directly back to the fact that Jeremy was admitted to Oxford while Jason was not. Does the fact that that decision was made in accordance with the ideals of equal opportunity legitimate the subsequent cumulative inequalities?

9.1 The Moment of Equal Opportunity

It has become commonplace for liberal egalitarians to interrogate the question of how people come to acquire certain skills and talents in childhood. Many, perhaps most, liberals argue that equality of opportunity cannot be realised unless advantages secured and disadvantages suffered during childhood are analysed and compensated for.[5] Egalitarian arguments of this sort often seem to be engaged in a genealogical project, tracing back the source of an individual's advantage through their educational, family and even genetic history. It is less common to encounter an egalitarian concern with the future, with what happens after the moment when equality of opportunity is secured.

The idea that equality of opportunity involves looking backwards is found explicitly in John Rawls, who states: "fairness depends on underlying social conditions, such as fair opportunity, extending backward in time."[6] An example of this backwards-looking reasoning can be found in Janet Radcliffe Richards' article 'Equality of Opportunity'. Richards parodies the literature on equality of opportunity by considering the headmaster of a sought-after boys' private school who is newly committed to the concept. The headmaster finds

---

[4] David Lodge, *Small World* (London: Penguin, 1985), p. 151.
[5] See, for example, Adam Swift, *How Not to Be a Hypocrite: School Choice for the Morally Perplexed Parent* (London: Routledge, 2003); Harry Brighouse, *School Choice and Social Justice* (Oxford: Oxford University Press, 2000); David Miller, 'Equality of Opportunity and the Family', in Debra Satz and Rob Reich (eds), *Toward a Humanist Justice: The Political Philosophy of Susan Moller Okin* (New York, NY; Oxford: Oxford University Press, 2009); Susan Moller Okin, *Justice, Gender, and the Family* (New York, NY: Basic Books, 1989); John Rawls, *Justice as Fairness: A Restatement* (Cambridge, MA: Harvard University Press, 2001), pp. 44, 167; James S. Fishkin, *Justice, Equal Opportunity, and the Family* (New Haven, CT: Yale University Press, 1983).
[6] Rawls, *Political Liberalism* (New York, NY: Columbia University Press, 1993), p. 267.

himself inexorably sliding down a slippery slope into straightforward equality of outcome, since he realises that equality of opportunity demands that he must compensate for disadvantages that occurred ever further in the past:

> Even equality of background could not give genuine equality of opportunity, since the children's different genetic endowments would still leave them with unequal chances of success. This seems to imply that genuine equality of opportunity requires the admission of everybody – the equality of outcome to which the headmaster always thought equality of opportunity was opposed – or, since this is impossible, either closing down the school or admitting pupils by lot. Neither of these is anything like what he had in mind when he started off in pursuit of equal opportunities, but he can now see no escape.[7]

A similar *reductio ad absurdum* argument is set forward in Bernard Williams' earlier article 'The Idea of Equality'. "One might speculate", Williams notes,

> about how far this movement of thought might go. The most conservative user of the notion of equality of opportunity is, if sincere, prepared to abstract the individual from some effects of his environment. We have seen that there is good reason to press this further, and to allow that the individuals whose opportunities are to be equal should be abstracted from more features of social and family background. Where should this stop? Should it even stop at the boundaries of heredity?[8]

Perhaps the first thing to note about these two *reductiones* is that the supposedly absurd resting-place at the end of each is in fact precisely what is argued for in much of the relevant literature. Radcliffe Richards' headmaster is asked to "wrestle with counterfactuals about what the children would have been like if they had had each other's backgrounds", to notice that "the children's different genetic endowments would still leave them with unequal chances of success", and to conclude as a result that either places must be allocated by lot or the school must be closed. These requirements do not seem so absurd in the light of contemporary egalitarian philosophy. For example, Ronald Dworkin states: "Unfair differences are those traceable to genetic luck, to talents that make

---

[7] Janet Radcliffe Richards, 'Equality of Opportunity', *Ratio* 10(3) (1997), p. 257.
[8] Bernard Williams, 'The Idea of Equality', in Louis P. Pojman and Robert Westmoreland, *Equality: Selected Readings* (Oxford: Oxford University Press, 1997), pp. 100–1.

some people prosperous but are denied to others",[9] and rules out inequality based on talent. "We must not allow the distribution of resources *at any moment* to be endowment-sensitive, that is, to be affected by differences in ability",[10] he cautions. To take another example, Adam Swift moves from the premise of equality of opportunity to the conclusion that " 'Family values' set limits on how far opportunities should be equalised, but respecting those values does not require us to permit private or selective schools."[11] It seems that, if the headmaster is not to distribute places by lot, he must indeed close down his school.

As this chapter shows, this kind of approach to equality of opportunity, one that reaches ever backwards into people's histories, investigating their backgrounds, the advantages they have previously enjoyed, and even their genetic endowments, obscures the fact that chains of equality-of-opportunity-upsetting events reach into the future as well as the past. The impression one gets when considering these accounts of equality of opportunity is of lives severed into two halves, with what I call a Moment of Equal Opportunity, or MEO, separating one from the other. In the first half of an individual's life, many things happen to her that *unjustly* make her different from her peers. As a foetus, she is unfairly formed with a particular set of genes, giving her particular propensities for particular talents. As a child, she is unfairly subjected to the influence of her parents, who add unjustly varying degrees of advantage to her genetic endowments according to their inclination for, and skill at, such activities as reading bedtime stories, playing Mozart in the home, taking her to Shakespeare plays, and asking her to count and name various everyday objects. As a schoolchild, she is unfairly benefitted or harmed by the skills of her teachers, the resources of her school (which may be unfairly determined by the resources of her parents) and the influence of her peers. These benefits or harms repeat themselves as she develops an unfair advantage or disadvantage as regards attaining places in other schools, or perhaps at university.[12]

---

[9] Ronald Dworkin, *Sovereign Virtue: The Theory and Practice of Equality* (Cambridge, MA: Harvard University Press, 2000), p. 92.
[10] Dworkin, *Sovereign Virtue*, p. 89. Emphasis added.
[11] Swift, *How Not to Be a Hypocrite*, p. 81.
[12] These phenomena can be described in a variety of different ways. One could argue that the very differences in upbringing and genes are unjust, or at least morally arbitrary (as Rawls would say). Alternatively, one could say that the differences in upbringing are compatible with justice but the ensuing (material) advantages are not. Or, one could take the approach discussed by Harry Brighouse and Adam Swift in 'Legitimate Parental Partiality', *Philosophy and Public Affairs* 37(1) (2009) arguing that some differences in upbringing such as bedtime stories do violate equality of opportunity but that this problem is outweighed by the benefits of family life. All methods of describing the issue share the idea that differences in upbringing in some way bring about injustice.

At some point in this process, equality of opportunity occurs. It is common to argue that this point should occur at age eighteen, when applications for universities or jobs are submitted. Harry Brighouse, for example, argues that education must give individuals equal opportunities at "the age of majority".[13] Progressive admissions tutors at elite universities such as Oxford tend to think that their decisions should take into account the unfairly different advantages that their applicants have enjoyed up until that point. So a public school boy whose use of the subjunctive is not quite perfect should be assessed more harshly than a boy from a state comprehensive who has never heard of the subjunctive.

Beyond this MEO individuals' lives go very differently, as the case of Jeremy and Jason illustrates. Unlike egalitarian admissions tutors, employers are generally not expected to take into account how candidates attained their skills. New recruits at investment banks or management consultancies are not usually selected on the basis of full historical equality of opportunity, and senior staff certainly are not. Instead, the presumption is that the candidate who has enjoyed the best education and been able to achieve the highest qualifications should be preferred, and this presumption intensifies the further in life people progress. An individual is *more* likely to be promoted, or appointed at senior level, if she has enjoyed great success in her previous career and has had (and used) many opportunities to develop her talents.

The crucial point is not merely that this severance of a life into two halves, one before and one after an MEO, *does in fact* occur. The point is that most advocates of equality of opportunity *accept* that it should occur. Despite the detailed burrowing into every aspect of an individual's history that might undermine equality of opportunity (the bedtime stories, the trips to the theatre, the piano lessons), the assumption prevails that at some point the attempt to compensate for previous advantage should stop.[14] We must ask, then, whether the final outcome and progress of Jeremy and Jason's lives are consistent with justice and with equality of opportunity.

Whether Jeremy and Jason's lives are deemed compatible with equality of opportunity depends on two things: the version of equality of opportunity one employs, and whether or not one endorses an MEO.[15] On some theories

---

[13] Brighouse, *School Choice and Social Justice*, p. 115.

[14] Examples are given throughout the chapter, but see also Brighouse, *School Choice and Social Justice*, pp. 114–15.

[15] Note that it is not necessary that any given version of equality of opportunity either does or does not employ an MEO. Take, for example, the idea that positions should be allocated to those who are best equipped to perform them—the version of equal opportunity that Rawls calls 'careers open to talents'. One could hold this view either with or without endorsing an MEO approach. Without an

of equality of opportunity, namely non-discrimination and careers open to talents, the increasing inequalities between Jeremy and Jason are unproblematic. In the next section, I briefly outline the response of these theories. However, most liberal egalitarian theorists advocate some more extensive, more egalitarian version of equality of opportunity. According to more extensive theories, I argue, the progress of Jeremy and Jason's lives is incompatible with equality of opportunity. In other words, equality of opportunity cannot consistently be restricted to an MEO, but must be applied throughout a person's life. However, it is not at all clear how equality of opportunity *can* be applied throughout a person's life, since doing so poses serious problems of epistemology, efficiency, and incentives, and leads to counter-intuitive results. Overall, my argument is that *liberal egalitarian theories of equality of opportunity are inconsistent if they support an MEO and unrealisable if they do not*.

9.2 Non-Discrimination and Careers Open to Talents

The most basic type of equality of opportunity concerns the absence of discrimination for certain ascriptive characteristics, most notably sex, race, and disability, and sometimes also age, religion, and sexuality. Although not without problems (such as those that arise when ascriptive characteristics are somehow relevant to the opportunity in question), this version of equality of opportunity is relatively uncontested as an ideal. It is also the version of equality of opportunity that is most likely to be thought necessary throughout a person's life. Equality of opportunity as non-discrimination should apply to every educational or career opportunity that an individual faces, regardless of her age or the seniority of the position. An advocate of non-discrimination as the sole measure of equality of opportunity would look at Jeremy and Jason and conclude that the growing inequality between them is fair, provided that Jeremy's success is not the result of racism or similar prejudice. In the rest of this chapter, I assume that equality of opportunity as non-discrimination is maintained and do not discuss it further.

MEO, careers open to talents would have to apply throughout a person's life. Jeremy and Jason's lives would be just only if every appointment decision had been made solely on the basis of merit. With an MEO approach, the requirements of justice are lower. Certain appointments would have to rely solely on merit—for example, admission to university—but future appointments (say to jobs) could legitimately be made on the basis of the employer's preference, even if that preference did not relate strictly to merit alone.

A somewhat less minimal version of equality of opportunity is what Rawls terms 'careers open to talents'. This version holds that cultural background should also not be permitted to count, and focuses instead on the idea of academic ability as the sole criterion for admissions. Whereas the first stage placed merely negative limits on the sorts of characteristics that may count as criteria for selection, this second stage introduces a positive normative requirement that only academic merit may count.

Is the story of Jeremy and Jason compatible with the careers open to talents version of equal opportunity? The answer to this question depends on the definition of 'merit'—or, more precisely, on which social endowments count. It is familiar to distinguish between natural and social endowments. Natural endowments are features such as innate intelligence, IQ, or ability to learn: things that remain constant throughout a person's life. Social endowments encompass things such as social class and wealth, along with the benefits that those can bring, such as private schooling.

However, there is an ambiguity in social endowments. Some social endowments give an individual an advantage in securing a position *without* enhancing that person's ability to perform well in that position. For example, a private education may give an individual better advice about which Oxford college to apply to, or contacts in a management consultancy who will offer an automatic interview, or friends who can lend an expensive suit for the interview. These social endowments give advantages without affecting the ability to perform once in the role. However, other social endowments (or other aspects of the same endowments) *do* affect an individual's ability to do the job or role in question. A boy from a private school who has learnt Latin and Greek will be better at a Classics degree than an equally intelligent state school boy who has not. Contacts made at private school may make one better at a job in consultancy, if one can use those contacts to get new clients. These options as they relate to Jeremy and Jason are shown Figure 9.1.

We then need to ask which sorts of social endowments may legitimately count when distributing positions. If we endorse equality of opportunity merely in the sense of non-discrimination, then any social endowment that is not discriminatory may count. So, employers may prefer candidates with expensive suits or good contacts even if those things in no way contribute to the candidates' ability to do the job. All four sections of the table may legitimately be considered and Jeremy clearly wins over Jason. Once we move to careers open to talents, however, it is clear that social endowments can count only if they contribute to an individual's ability to perform. On the simplest version of careers open to talents, this necessary condition is also sufficient:

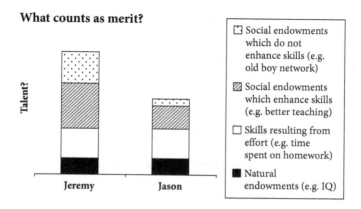

any social endowment that does make someone better at the job is a legitimate reason for awarding them that job. The 'talents' of 'careers open to talents' would therefore be *acquired* talents at any given moment, not innate talent or natural endowments. Assessors of Jeremy and Jason would then be permitted to take into account all the sections of the table except the top section. According to this measure Jeremy genuinely has more merit than Jason and it is compatible with equal opportunity to prefer him.

However, David Miller advocates a version of equality of opportunity which resembles careers open to talents but is not of this simple kind. Miller terms his approach 'meritocracy', defined as "the ideal of a society in which each person's chance to acquire positions of advantage and the rewards that go with them will depend entirely on his or her talent and effort."[16] Notice that it makes a great difference here whether 'talent' is interpreted to mean innate natural endowments, or talents as they have been shaped by social factors. If the latter, then meritocracy is reducible to the simple version of careers open to talents just described. 'Effort' merely serves as one possible way in which talent may be developed, and its specification is unnecessary. If the former, however, a far more radical theory emerges: positions may be allocated only according to natural innate endowments and the effort that individuals put in. The talents that individuals develop through *social* endowments, such as a better education or more stretching job, may not count.[17]

---

[16] David Miller, *Principles of Social Justice* (Cambridge, MA: Harvard University Press, 1999), p. 177.
[17] Meritocrats might wish to add some version of the requirement that there should be fair access to qualifications, perhaps by ensuring a minimum level of education for all. Criteria such as this are discussed in greater detail in the context of Rawlsian Fair Equality of Opportunity, later in the chapter.

On this second reading of meritocracy, Jeremy and Jason must be assessed on the basis of the lower two sections of the table alone. According to this measurement they are equal in merit, and remain so throughout their lives. In other words, it appears that the inequality that develops between them is incompatible with this version of equal opportunity as meritocracy and *pro tanto* unjust.

However, the case of Jeremy and Jason can be made compatible with this second reading of meritocracy, but only if an MEO approach is taken. An MEO version of meritocracy states that natural talent and effort are the sole permitted criteria *at only one particular point in time*. After that Moment, socially endowed talent may also count. Miller advocates this strategy. He writes:

> A person's opportunities have to be judged at some suitably chosen starting point, since each decision that is made to avail oneself of an opportunity, or not to do so, is likely to affect the opportunity set at a later point. For example, a person who decides to leave school at sixteen cannot later complain that she was denied the opportunity to go to university, if by staying on at school she could have achieved that goal.... The liberal ideal, then, is that *initial* opportunity sets should be equal, not necessarily opportunity sets at some later time when choices have already been made.[18]

Here, Miller seems to be advocating that the sixteen-year-old school-leaver should be judged according to simple careers open to talents as an adult, in the sense that the talents she has actually developed should be those that count, rather than those she could have developed had she gone to university. In other words, what Miller here terms 'equality of opportunity' should apply at one particular moment, 'some suitably chosen starting point', after which its demands need not be met (though the minimal versions of non-discrimination and simple careers open to talents may remain necessary). On this view, then, the case of Jeremy and Jason is compatible with equality of opportunity. At the MEO (their application to Oxford), only their innate talent and effort was permitted to count. Beyond the MEO, it is perfectly acceptable to prefer Jeremy since he has greater merit, even though his increased

---

[18] David Miller, 'Liberalism, Equal Opportunities and Cultural Commitments', in Paul Kelly (ed.), *Multiculturalism Reconsidered: Culture and Equality and Its Critics* (Oxford: Polity Press, 2002), p. 47. Emphasis in the original.

merit is the result of more fortunate *social* endowments and not more fortunate *natural* endowments, or greater *effort*.

9.3 Evaluating the MEO Approach

We can now consider whether this division of a person's life, into time before and time after the MEO, is justified. Let us consider what an advocate of the MEO might say in defence of this approach by looking at her possible defence of the growing inequalities between Jeremy and Jason.

First, she would want to look at the MEO embodied in the Oxford admissions process. If equality of opportunity really had been practised by the admissions tutors, she might say, then Jeremy must have been *better* than Jason. Although they had *similar* levels of merit, the fact that Jeremy and not Jason was allocated a place demonstrates that they were not *equal* in that regard. Jeremy had more merit, and so the subsequent inequalities that develop are entirely consistent with equality of opportunity. Alternatively, if the admissions tutors made a mistake and Jeremy was not the better candidate, we can criticise the unequal outcome simply by noting that equality of opportunity was not implemented at the start.

This first response highlights the problem with equality of opportunity outlined earlier in the chapter: egalitarian forms of equality of opportunity are either practically unrealisable or inadequate from the perspective of justice.[19] The requirements of justice are the focus of the next section; here I concentrate on issues of practical realisability. There may be a fact of the matter as to whether Jeremy and Jason's Oxford admissions process really did implement equal opportunity. However, unless we are able *both* to tell whether or not this was the case *and* to design procedures to ensure that it is the case, equal opportunity will be unrealisable. But a number of epistemological problems make it unlikely that the radically meritocratic form of equality of opportunity can be perfectly implemented. Simply assessing which of two candidates has more merit can be difficult enough. Moreover, it is *extremely* difficult for anyone accurately to judge which portion of an individual's ability results from merit and which from class or background. It is certainly unrealistic to suggest that this judgment can be perfectly made in all cases, particularly if

---

[19] By 'egalitarian forms of equality of opportunity' I mean those that go beyond non-discrimination and simple careers open to talents.

candidates are fairly evenly matched (as is the case with Jason and Jeremy). In other words, we cannot assume that any MEO is perfect.

This fact alone might be sufficient for us to question the MEO approach, and suggest that equality of opportunity should apply throughout a person's life if it is to apply at all. But let us set this objection aside, and assume for a moment that assessors can make accurate judgements about two individuals' relative merits. Even this assumption will only ensure equality of opportunity between candidates if we assume a strictly hierarchical ranking of candidates, with no two candidates on an equal footing. This too is very unlikely, unless the differences between candidates are so minute that the epistemological difficulties would be utterly overwhelming. It is implausible to think that no two candidates can ever be equally able, particularly when considering opportunities for which there are many applicants. Moreover, if a good is scarce such that it cannot be provided to all qualified persons, it follows that some qualified individuals will be denied it.[20] When dealing with a good such as an elite education or a prestigious job, it is highly plausible that some unsuccessful applicants will be as good as some successful ones.

Consider, for example, the case of Laura Spence. Spence was a British state school pupil who applied to study Medicine at Magdalen College, Oxford in 2000. She was rejected by Oxford but accepted by Harvard to study Biochemistry. Her case was publicised by her headmaster and a media frenzy ensued, based on the question of whether Oxford discriminated against state school pupils. The then Chancellor of the Exchequer, Gordon Brown, was among those who castigated Oxford for not implementing equality of opportunity. However, several Oxford dons wrote in their university's defence. One of those was Alan Ryan, who argued:

> Laura Spence's headteacher made a great to-do about her having 10 A and A* grades in GCSE; but every candidate for admission has 10 or more A and A* grades in GCSE and almost all of them will go on to get a minimum of three A grades at A level.... Short of offering places by lottery to anyone who shows up with 10 A or A* grades at GCSE, it is not obvious what the critics suppose we might try. (There is, in fact, something to be said for a lottery for half the places; the top 10 or 15% of applicants would walk in under any system, and the bottom 15% are, for all sorts of reasons, not going to thrive

---

[20] Indeed, Williams suggests that equality of opportunity is relevant only when distributing "goods which not all the people who desire them can have" (Williams, 'The Idea of Equality', p. 99).

at Oxford. What happens to the middle 70% is already closer to a lottery than most of us like to acknowledge.)[21]

If Ryan is right, then there are candidates for whom merit does not explain their success or failure. So, no matter how good the admissions tutors are at their task of implementing equality of opportunity, it simply will not be the case that the MEO is perfect and thus can render all subsequent inequalities irrelevant. Even an accurate ranking of candidates may result in many candidates at equal ranks. If this was the case with Jeremy and Jason, we cannot justify the inequality at the end of their careers simply by referring back to the MEO at the start.

It seems, then, that the first defence of the inequality between Jason and Jeremy will not work. We cannot plausibly argue that the MEO was perfect and thus renders all subsequent inequalities just, for two reasons: the difficulty of assessing merit, and the possibility that there may be several candidates with equal merit but not enough opportunities for all of them. Any realisable version of meritocratic equality of opportunity, then, will be inadequate in its achievement of justice. We must therefore look elsewhere if we are to justify refusing to assess Jason and Jeremy's applications for senior posts according to the radically meritocratic version of equality of opportunity.

A second possible answer appeals to efficiency, and runs as follows. It would be highly inefficient to allocate jobs, particularly senior jobs, on the basis of meritocratic equality of opportunity rather than simple careers open to talents, since that would require giving jobs to those less able to perform them. The more senior the post, the more disastrous the consequences. If Jeremy and Jason are in investment banking, for example, and Jason is less skilled than Jeremy as the result of his worse opportunities, then appointing Jason as Chief Executive of an investment bank will mean that the bank will not do so well as it would have done with Jeremy as its head. Profits will be down, management will be less competent, clients will be damaged. And the same goes for all other industries. University professors must be those with the best research and teaching records, surgeons must be those with the best

---

[21] Alan Ryan, 'Oxford Blues', *The Guardian* (24 May 2000). GCSE stands for General Certificate of Secondary Education, and GCSEs are usually taken at age sixteen. An average pupil would take nine GCSEs, with the most talented pupils taking ten or eleven. The government's 'threshold indicator', the minimum deemed necessary for a decent education, is five GCSEs at grade A* to C (or equivalent vocational qualifications). The top grade for GCSE is A*, a grade that was introduced fairly recently as an attempt to discriminate between the growing numbers of pupils gaining A grades, and the lowest is G. A ('Advanced') Levels are usually taken at age eighteen, and the top grade is A. Most pupils would take three A Levels, with the best taking four.

medical experience and skills, Permanent Secretaries must be those with the most experience of working in government departments. We cannot use equality of opportunity to allocate senior positions because the costs of having less-qualified people in those positions are too high. At the very least, lifelong meritocratic equality of opportunity would require that employers sometimes take on those who will need more training and will take longer to perform well in their post than alternative candidates. More likely, continuous equality of opportunity will require *enormous* expenditure on adult education, on-the-job training, and so on, for mitigating the cumulative effects of a lifetime's disadvantage will be extremely difficult. Indeed, if employers truly are to disregard the effects of cumulative disadvantage, they may well have to appoint candidates who simply lack the basic skills and experience needed to do the job.

Moreover, the ongoing use of fully meritocratic equality of opportunity could have some bizarre incentive effects. Until the time that an individual had reached her ultimate or major career goal it would be in her interests to fail in competitions and miss opportunities. For, if equality of opportunity were implemented throughout life, a privileged background and useful experience could be handicaps. Under ideal conditions, this would not be the case: assessors would accurately identify the effort and talent put in by all candidates regardless of background. In practice, however, this is unlikely. Imagine two extremely clever pupils, Melanie and Margaret, both of whom are able to gain high marks with little effort, and both of whom do actually achieve ten A*s at GCSE. Margaret attends a private school where most of her peers also gain ten A*s at GCSE, usually as a result of the intensive tuition they receive. Margaret's results, however, are the result of her superior merit: even if she had not attended the private school, she would have performed to the same standard. Melanie attends a state school, where ten A*s are extremely rare. Melanie outperforms her peers as a result of *her* superior merit; like Margaret, she is able to excel regardless of the standard of her schooling. A truly accurate system of fair equality of opportunity would judge Melanie and Margaret to be equal, but it seems likely that most university admissions tutors or employers attempting to implement equality of opportunity would judge Melanie's achievements more highly since they would not, and never could, have access to the relevant counterfactual information. It follows that attending private school is a handicap for some (the best) pupils, since it is harder for a private school pupil to prove that she has merit of the sort that is rewarded by fair equality of opportunity. Until the point at which further career advancement is not a priority (tenure or a professorship in academia, or partnership in law, for example), fair equality of opportunity could create an incentive for individuals to avoid, or fail to win, opportunities to develop their skills. In turn, this would mean that the most talented people in society were not performing to their full potential, instead deliberately holding themselves back. Such a situation would certainly be wasteful and inefficient. Efficiency concerns do, then, seem to require that fair equality of opportunity applies only at some initial starting-point (the MEO) and not beyond it.

This defence of the MEO approach has left us with two immediate problems. The first is that the value of equality of opportunity has been diluted. I have suggested that we should not appoint senior posts according to fully meritocratic equality of opportunity since it would be inefficient to do so. But, if the MEO approach is justified by concerns for efficiency rather than fairness, it follows that it will not adequately secure justice for those concerned. If fair equality of opportunity is an important component of justice, then abandoning it in the name of efficiency means sacrificing justice to efficiency. If justice is the first virtue of social institutions, this is a grave problem. But even if we are willing to sacrifice some justice for huge efficiency gains, it is important to be clear that there is indeed a sacrifice being made. Again, the dilemma for advocates of equal opportunity is highlighted: is the principle advocated as a practical guide to action that falls far short of what justice requires, or is it to be thought of as a fundamental principle of justice which is hopelessly unrealisable?

The second residual problem concerning the appeal to efficiency is that such an appeal could also be used to justify abandoning equality of opportunity for children. If efficiency trade-offs are justified, why should we not make them when allocating school or university places? If private schools really do create better pupils it might be far more efficient for universities to develop the superior talents of private school pupils, rather than waste resources trying to bring state school pupils up to scratch. Efficiency gains could justify selection at every stage of the educational process. But it is precisely this sort of selection that equality of opportunity is supposed to prevent. In other words, efficiency considerations lead us to question not only the application of equality of opportunity *after* the MEO, but its application *tout court*. As such, they prove too much.

9.4 Rawlsian Fair Equality of Opportunity

A consideration of Rawls' defence of fair equality of opportunity demonstrates that MEO approaches are inadequate from the perspective of justice. Like the contemporary liberal egalitarians who follow him, Rawls is not content with either of the first two stages of equal opportunity: both non-discrimination and unembellished careers open to talents are insufficiently egalitarian. Thus Rawls introduces the concept of 'fair equality of opportunity'. The concept aims to

> correct the defects of formal equality of opportunity – careers open to talents – in the system of natural liberty, so-called. To this end, fair equality of opportunity is said to require not merely that public offices and social positions be open in the formal sense, but that all should have a fair chance to attain them. To specify the idea of a fair chance we say: supposing that there is a distribution of native endowments, those who have the same level of talent and ability and the same willingness to use these gifts should have the same prospects of success regardless of their social class of origin, the class into which they are born and develop until the age of reason. In all parts of society there are to be roughly the same prospects of culture and achievement for those similarly motivated and endowed.[22]

This passage suggests that Rawlsian fair equality of opportunity must be judged at a key Moment in a person's life. The MEO to which Rawls refers is 'the age of reason'. His claim is that prospects of success must not depend on the class within which people develop 'until' this point, a claim that invites the question: 'what happens afterwards?' Rawls' formulation does not suggest that class is immaterial to a person's life after she has reached the age of reason. His argument is compatible with the extremely plausible view that class continues to have an effect throughout the whole of an individual's life. It is even compatible with the notion that differences akin to class can develop over the course of an adult working life, as occurs with Jeremy and Jason. Rawls does, however, imply that the relevantly unjust influences are those that occur in childhood, such that certain aspects of a person's talents that are developed in adulthood may justly be taken into account when selecting employees.

If Rawlsian fair equality of opportunity does include an MEO then it is vulnerable to the criticisms just made of the Millerian meritocratic MEO. Indeed, the two approaches would be very similar: equality of opportunity requires an in-depth investigation into and compensation for the process by which talent is developed up to the MEO, and careers open to talents after it. However, other

---

[22] Rawls, *Justice as Fairness: A Restatement*, pp. 43–4.

parts of Rawls' work give the impression that he would reject the MEO approach for reasons of justice. It is difficult to discern precisely how Rawls envisages the implementation of the equal opportunity principle, but there are several considerations that are compatible with the conclusion that Rawls either does reject the MEO approach, or at least recognises reasons that *ought to* lead him to reject it. First, Rawls explicitly rejects sacrificing fair equality of opportunity to efficiency.[23] Second, fair equality of opportunity is the second principle of justice full stop, not only at some initial starting point. Indeed, Rawls is deeply suspicious of what he calls an 'ideal historical process view', such as Robert Nozick's, that proceeds from an initially fair starting-point.[24] Third, the following passage criticising the injustice of the system of natural liberty is precisely directed against the cumulative effects of advantage such as that illustrated in the case of Jeremy and Jason:

> The existing distribution of income and wealth, say, is the cumulative effect of prior distributions of natural assets – that is, natural talents and abilities – as these have been developed or left unrealized, and their use favored or disfavored over time by social circumstances and such chance contingencies as accident and good fortune. Intuitively, the most obvious injustice of the system of natural liberty is that it permits distributive shares to be improperly influenced by these factors so arbitrary from a moral point of view.
>
> The liberal interpretation, as I shall refer to it, tries to correct for this by adding to the requirement of careers open to talents the further condition of the principle of fair equality of opportunity.[25]

This passage clearly indicates that equality of opportunity is meant to *remedy*, not legitimate, inequalities arising from 'chance contingencies' that develop the talents of some while leaving those of others unrealised. Here Rawls does not limit the scope of equality of opportunity to the time before an MEO, but heralds it as a tool to mitigate the ongoing injustices of chance and 'social circumstances', such as winning or losing in early competitions.

Rawls extends his idea that the principles of justice, including equality of opportunity, exist to adjust the unfair outcomes of social processes in *Political Liberalism*. Social processes, he notes, favour "an oligopolistic configuration of accumulations that succeeds in maintaining unjustified inequalities and

---

[23] Rawls, *A Theory of Justice* (Oxford: Oxford University Press, 1973), p. 84.
[24] Rawls, *Justice as Fairness: A Restatement*, p. 53.
[25] Rawls, *A Theory of Justice*, pp. 72–3.

restrictions on fair opportunity".[26] These accumulations must be remedied by the principles of justice:

> What the theory of justice must regulate is the inequalities in life prospects between citizens that arise from social starting positions, natural advantages, and historical contingencies. Even if these inequalities are not in some cases very great, their effect may be great enough so that over time they have significant cumulative consequences.[27]

Implementing fair equality of opportunity before but not after an MEO is not adequate, then. For historical contingencies of the sort that radically determine Jeremy and Jason's divergent lives occur at every stage in life, and have ramifications that, as Rawls notes, are significantly cumulative. Regardless of Rawls' actual intentions, we can at least say that the arguments of justice that favour Rawlsian fair equality of opportunity against careers open to talents also reject the MEO. And yet, if we wish to abandon the MEO and apply fair equality of opportunity throughout people's lives we have to confront the practical problems outlined earlier. Can we really endorse awarding senior posts to those who are less qualified, perhaps even unqualified, to perform them?

At this point Rawlsians might wish to remind us that the principles of justice are intended to apply only to the basic structure of society. It might be thought that this fact excuses advocates of fair equality of opportunity from having to deal with practical problems of hiring and firing, since employers do not have to act with the principles of justice foremost in their minds. Instead, equality of opportunity is secured by the basic structure. As long as they obey the law, citizens may go about their business freely, secure in the knowledge that justice is secured by the overall structure of society. And yet we still need to think about how the basic structure might be organised so as to ensure equality of opportunity overall.

One strategy for building equality of opportunity into the basic structure rather than the minds of employers is to enact legislation restricting the criteria which employers may use when appointing staff.[28] Employers may then

---

[26] Rawls, *Political Liberalism*, p. 267.

[27] Rawls, *Political Liberalism*, p. 271. One source of accumulation is over the course of several generations, a source which Rawls undoubtedly wishes to criticise; but another is over the course of a single life. The passage just quoted immediately follows a discussion of inequality occurring through the course of individual lives, so it is not far-fetched to interpret Rawls in this way.

[28] Richard Arneson notes these two understandings of Rawlsian fair equality of opportunity in Richard Arneson, 'Against Rawlsian Equality of Opportunity', *Philosophical Studies* 93(1) (1999). He understands the first option as a combination of careers open to talents and what he calls 'Fair

choose whoever they wish, as long as they conform to employment law (much as the difference principle is secured by allowing people to transfer money as they please, as long as they conform to taxation law). Rawls explicitly endorses this strategy to ensure non-discrimination,[29] and so it seems plausible that among those laws might be specific instructions for employers to take into account the requirements of fair equality of opportunity. For example, the law might lay down a points system to be used when comparing candidates for a job, with specific instructions on how many points should be added or subtracted for particular advantages or disadvantages that candidates have experienced. However, it should be clear that this option is identical in outcome to the idea that employers must have in their minds the full requirements of equality of opportunity, and is subject to the same objections. Even if such a scheme could be devised and implemented, it would still require inefficient and counter-intuitive hiring of those with less merit in the here-and-now. It would also exacerbate the problematic incentive effects, since candidates would have a clear incentive to manipulate the points system by refusing those advantages (such as an Oxford education) that carried a heavy points subtraction.

An alternative strategy is to think that the role of the basic structure is to adjust social conditions in general, such that employers may appoint on merit and yet retain fair equality of opportunity. This seems to be the strategy of those theorists such as Brighouse and Swift who criticise familial and educational advantages.[30] They distinguish between legitimate and illegitimate parental partiality according to whether a particular form of partiality is essential to realising the 'relationship goods' of parenthood. Their idea is that, as long as parents have access to essential relationship goods in their interactions with their children, "parents have no claim to the further freedoms that would be required for them to act on their loving motivation generally to further their children's interests, *where granting them those freedoms would undermine fair equality of opportunity.*"[31] It is therefore essential that society is structured in such a way as to protect a sphere in which parents can act to realise relationship goods *without* violating equality of opportunity, and the state may need to shape "the social environment so as to diminish the extent

---

Background'. The second violates careers open to talents since "candidates' merit scores are adjusted according to the social background" (Arneson, 'Against Rawlsian Equality of Opportunity', p. 81).
[29] Rawls, *Political Liberalism*, p. 363.
[30] Harry Brighouse and Adam Swift, 'Equality, Priority and Positional Goods', *Ethics* 116(3) (2006); Brighouse and Swift, 'Legitimate Parental Partiality'.
[31] Brighouse and Swift, 'Legitimate Parental Partiality', p. 74. Emphasis in the original.

of the influence of those attributes on children's prospects".[32] Only then can parents engage in activities such as helping their children with their homework without worrying that unfair advantages will be conferred by their activities.

The problem with this strategy is that it is not clear how it would work. The idea is that some activities, such as helping children with their homework, undermine equality of opportunity unless we reform the social environment so as to prevent them from doing so. But it is enormously difficult to see how we might secure equal opportunity if we cannot do so either by requiring employers and educators to take parental help into account when choosing between applicants or by banning the parental partiality that caused the problem in the first place. The only other available method seems to be to restrict the extra *resources* that follow from being successful as a result of parental homework help. This method, which I call the hybrid strategy, is discussed in the following section.

It seems, then, that Rawlsian fair equality of opportunity is incompatible with the MEO, so that fair equality of opportunity must be applied at each and every stage in a person's life.[33] However, an attempt to apply fair equality of opportunity without an MEO will face the practical problems of bizarre incentive effects (people will have an incentive to fail early in their lives), epistemological problems (the older people become, the harder it is to isolate the causes of their abilities), and efficiency problems (senior posts may have to be filled by drastically under-qualified candidates). An alternative is the hybrid strategy.

9.5 The Hybrid Strategy

The hybrid strategy uses the MEO approach (applying fair equality of opportunity only at one or more key starting points[34]) but supplements it with some other form of egalitarianism. According to this option, fair equality of

---

[32] Brighouse and Swift, 'Legitimate Parental Partiality', p. 73.
[33] Fleurbaey seems to have something of this sort in mind when he tries to imagine a "non-starting-gate-theory of equal resources", in which "every morning is a fresh start". He notes that such a theory "may obviously raise incentive problems" (Marc Fleurbaey, 'Equality of Resources Revisited', *Ethics* 113(1) (2002), p. 86).
[34] I say 'one or more' because it might be appropriate to have a separate MEO for different endeavours. The fact that Miller refers to a variety of different starting places for equality of opportunity suggests that he has something of this sort in mind. The key feature of an MEO is that, once it has been designated for a particular endeavour, it is not repeated for that same endeavour.

opportunity should be applied only at an MEO, but any unjust inequalities that develop must be rectified at a later stage. This rectification is done not by further use of fair equality of opportunity, but by an egalitarian compensation scheme. So, Jason and Jeremy's lives would run as they have been described, with Jeremy being more successful than Jason. However, the resulting inequalities would somehow be rectified, perhaps by a tax on Jeremy's higher salary that would be redistributed to Jason. Such redistribution would be justified by an alternative egalitarian principle, such as luck egalitarianism or the difference principle.

This sort of approach has been advocated by Richard Arneson. Arneson's concept, 'equality of opportunity for welfare', explicitly relies on an MEO. He defines it as follows:

> when an age cohort reaches the onset of responsible adulthood, they enjoy equal opportunity for welfare when, for each of them, the best sequence of choices that it would be reasonable to expect the person to follow would yield the same expected welfare for all, the second-best sequence of choices would also yield the same expected welfare for all, and so on through the array of lifetime choice sequences each faces.[35]

So far we have a straightforward MEO approach, with no additional egalitarian principle. However, Arneson recognises the force of an objection set out by Kasper Lippert-Rasmussen, an objection that echoes the case of Jeremy and Jason.[36] Lippert-Rasmussen points out that two people who have equal opportunity for welfare at the onset of adulthood might be rendered unequal when only one of them suffers unavoidable misfortune at a later date. Lippert-Rasmussen's example is two people who each live close to a different active volcano; only one of them actually experiences and suffers from an eruption. We can liken this example to Jeremy and Jason, who both choose to apply to Oxford and for high-powered jobs; only Jason experiences and suffers from rejection. Arneson notes that such situations are problematic for his approach. "[W]hy", he asks himself, "does sheer bad luck that befalls an individual after this canonical moment [of] redistribution demand no redress, while similar sheer bad luck that befalls an individual prior to the canonical moment

---

[35] Richard Arneson, 'Equality of Opportunity for Welfare Defended and Recanted', *The Journal of Political Philosophy* 7(4) (1999), p. 488.

[36] Kasper Lippert-Rasmussen, 'Arneson on Equality of Opportunity for Welfare', *The Journal of Political Philosophy* 7(4) (1999).

demands full redress?"[37] Arneson chooses to "avoid having to answer this question" by introducing an alternative concept: "equal opportunity for welfare in the strict sense".[38] According to this new concept, any windfall gains or losses occurring after the MEO must be compensated. Arneson's thought is that "strict equal opportunity can be fulfilled so long as the unavoidable misfortune that befalls people is fully compensable."[39] In other words, we are left with a combination of equality of opportunity at an MEO and a further luck egalitarian redistributive principle.

However, Arneson recognises a further problem: the principle that sheer bad luck should be compensated seems to imply that, if two people engage in high stakes gambling (thus both making the same choices) and only one wins, we must compensate the loser (who has suffered sheer bad luck) with the winnings of the former. However, this contradicts our intuition that people must take responsibility for the outcomes of choices such as gambling. In order to accommodate this intuition, Arneson shifts to a third refinement of his position: the revised equal opportunity principle. This version combines the key elements of the first two versions, but adds the caveat that "when individuals face an array that includes risky and satisfactory nonrisky alternatives (so that the choice of a risky alternative may be voluntary), the best risky life choice for each individual offers the same expected welfare."[40] This revision takes account of the gambling example, Arneson claims, since it "distinguishes between sheer good or bad luck that rains on a person in ways that are beyond his power to control and good or bad luck that individuals enjoy as they voluntarily pursue life choices that include lotteries".[41]

The gambling example is interesting since it could also be made to mirror the case of Jeremy and Jason. Rather than likening Jeremy and Jason to the volcano dwellers, we could say that they both *gamble* when applying for Oxford. We then need to ask whether this gamble is voluntary, and the answer is by no means clear. Jeremy and Jason do voluntarily choose to enter the particular competitions that concern us. They do not need to apply to Oxford or for high-powered graduate jobs: less competitive options are available. On the other hand, they cannot avoid all competition for jobs and qualifications, and in this sense they involuntarily take on risk. It is thus unclear whether they should be likened to the compensable volcano case or the non-compensable gambling case.

[37] Arneson, 'Equality of Opportunity for Welfare Defended and Recanted', p. 490.
[38] Arneson, 'Equality of Opportunity for Welfare Defended and Recanted', p. 490.
[39] Arneson, 'Equality of Opportunity for Welfare Defended and Recanted', p. 490.
[40] Arneson, 'Equality of Opportunity for Welfare Defended and Recanted', p. 491.
[41] Arneson, 'Equality of Opportunity for Welfare Defended and Recanted', p. 492.

This problem notwithstanding, Arneson's approach poses a prior question. Can we even say that Jeremy and Jason enjoy equal opportunity for welfare in Arneson's most basic sense, according to which their first-best preferences must yield the same amount of welfare, and their second-best, and so on? In other words, regardless of whether their final inequalities are compensable, did they ever enjoy an MEO? In one sense they did: both had precisely the same ordering of preferences and so, if each were to secure their first-best option (or second-best, and so on), each would have achieved the same level of welfare. But in another, crucial sense, Jeremy and Jason never did have equal opportunity for welfare, since the fact that they are in competition with each other means that it would always have been impossible for both to achieve their favourite preferences at the same time.[42] In other words, whereas the first best available option for Jeremy is 'attend Oxford', the first best available option for Jason *given the fact that he is in competition with Jeremy* is 'attend a less prestigious university than Oxford', and these two options do not yield the same expected welfare. The fact of competition for scarce resources means that two individuals who have the same preference and make the same choices simply cannot enjoy equal opportunity for welfare. Arneson's version of equal opportunity is incompatible with the fact of competition.

The redistributive principle accompanying equal opportunity does not have to be choice-based. It would be possible to supplement Arneson's compensation mechanism with the difference principle, for example. Jobs would be allocated according to equality of opportunity at an MEO, but any inequalities that developed subsequently would have to benefit the worst off. However, this option would not work for Rawls, for several reasons. First, it contradicts the actual wording of the principles of justice. In their most recent formulation, they state that social and economic inequalities must be "attached to offices and positions open to all under conditions of fair equality of opportunity". In other words, it is the offices and positions themselves that must be governed by equal opportunity, not merely the rewards that flow from them.

---

[42] It might be objected that it would be possible for both Jeremy and Jason to secure a place at Oxford, and a job with a major graduate employer, since there are more than two places and jobs available. This may be true, but of course the relevant group for consideration is all those people who have the same preferences (in other words, all those people who want to go to Oxford, and all those people who seek a job with a particular prestigious employer). Once this group is considered it becomes clear that it is impossible for all its members to secure their first-best (or second-best, and so on) preferences at the same time. In the following discussion the question of whether Jeremy and Jason have equality of opportunity should be taken as a shorthand way of talking about all those people who share their choice rankings.

Second, Rawls explicitly gives non-resource-based reasons for fair equality of opportunity. He states that those in Jason's position "would be justified in their complaint not merely because they were excluded from certain external rewards of office such as wealth and privilege but because they were debarred from experiencing the realization of self which comes from a skilful and devoted exercise of social duties. They would be deprived of one of the main forms of human good."[43] In other words, there is a need to distribute positions *themselves* according to equality of opportunity, not merely the resources that flow from them. Social primary goods, such as status and self-respect, are not determined merely by how much money a person has; Rawls seems to be arguing that one's job plays an important part.

Arneson states that this position contradicts Rawls' principle that there should be no social evaluation of competing conceptions of the good, since not everyone will find career success so crucial.[44] We can make two points in response. First, Rawls does not state that career success is in fact crucial for everyone. He states merely that it is unjust if people are deprived of the *opportunity* to develop themselves through their careers, since such development will be an important part of the good for many people. Think of the analogy of religion: one does not have to assert that religion is a crucial component of the good life for everybody in order to maintain that it would be a grave injustice to deny some people the opportunity to practise it. Second, recognising the intrinsic (non-resource-based) value of career success and fulfilment seems necessary for Rawls' position as a whole. Without it, fair equality of opportunity would be merely a job-allocation mechanism, but there would be no reason to care about the allocation of jobs. Since the difference principle takes care of distributive justice, fair equality of opportunity only has a role if there is more to one's career *that is relevant to justice* than money. Thus there are reasons to support Rawls' claim that equality of opportunity is not premised on resource considerations. But if equality of opportunity is important to justice in a way that is not exhausted by resource distribution, then the hybrid strategy with its MEO approach will not work.

The third reason for rejecting the hybrid strategy for Rawls is that equality of opportunity is lexically prior to the difference principle, meaning that no amount of the former can be sacrificed for any amount of the latter. It does not seem quite right, then, to abandon equality of opportunity at one point in time so that the difference principle may take over. Indeed, it is not clear what

---

[43] Rawls, *A Theory of Justice*, p. 84.
[44] Arneson, 'Against Rawlsian Equality of Opportunity', p. 98.

the justification for such a move could be. Rawls could not state that it is necessary to implement an MEO so as to benefit the worst off (the concern from efficiency), since the lack of equal opportunity after the MEO could not be justified by recourse to the lower-ranked difference principle. Indeed, using the difference principle as the egalitarian compensation mechanism would not rectify the inequality between Jeremy and Jason, since Jason is by no means a member of the worst-off group in society. Only a very few violations of fair equality of opportunity will be affected by subsequent application of the difference principle.

Finally, if the difference principle could supplant fair equality of opportunity, there is no clear reason why the difference principle could not sufficiently compensate for inequalities suffered in childhood and through education. If the difference principle is adequate for adults, why not for children? This question suggests one final chance to justify the MEO approach: a strong normative distinction between childhood and adulthood.

9.6 Childhood and Choice

If equality of opportunity is to apply only at key starting points in a person's life, it follows that it will most apply when that person is at the early stages of her life. In other words, equality of opportunity will be particularly relevant to the young. Miller puts this point explicitly, reiterating the sense in which equality of opportunity or, in this case, meritocracy divides a person's life into two. We should, he argues,

> see meritocracy as having two parts. One has to do with the formation of individuals' capacities and abilities in the early years of life, through the family and education system. The other part takes these abilities and capacities as given, and looks at the opportunities that are available to people from young adulthood onward, in higher education, in the job market, and in social life generally.[45]

This passage introduces the idea that abilities and capacities should be taken as given in adulthood. But it is not clear why this idea should have any moral force. As an empirical claim it is surely false. While once people might normally have had careers, and the corresponding skills, for life, the norm now is

---

[45] Miller, *Principles of Social Justice*, p. 181.

for far more fluidity. It is common for people to shift the emphasis of their career, or even their entire profession, later in life. The concept of 'lifelong learning' has gained currency, according to which adults are encouraged to develop their skills throughout their lives. It is no longer the case, if ever it was, that individuals acquire the experience and expertise that determine the shape of their lives only in formal education and only while children. Adults can re-enter formal education, perhaps gaining university degrees, long after their childhood education has finished.[46] Alternatively, specific formal qualifications are not required for many careers: people can shift jobs using the experience they have built up while working.[47] In other words, although childhood education plays a crucial role in affecting an individual's career progression and life chances, many factors in adulthood can be equally significant.

If capabilities and skills are not in fact set in stone early on but can develop throughout adulthood just as in childhood, what distinguishes the two phases of life? The idea that equality of opportunity is most important when considering young people might alternatively be motivated by a commitment to *choice* as necessary to legitimate inequality. As liberals tend to accept the idea that choice is necessary to justice, the absence of choice during childhood would be a relevant reason for more stringent monitoring and equalisation of the conditions of childhood.

Choice plays an important role in the luck egalitarian arguments offered by Arneson and theorists such as G. A. Cohen and Dworkin. But is clear, first, that choice cannot legitimate the inequalities between Jeremy and Jason. After all, it would be inaccurate to describe any of the inequalities that befall them as the result of choices that either makes, since both make the same choices throughout their lives. Both choose to apply to Oxford, both choose the same degree, both choose the same industry and apply for the same jobs. Both choose (if choice it is) to apply the same level of effort to their work. At no point in their lives are the differences between them attributable to choice. As a result, if choice is the only legitimator of inequality, the resulting inequality

---

[46] For a discussion of the proper egalitarian funding of adult education, see Alexander Brown, 'Access to Educational Opportunities – One-off or Lifelong?', *Journal of Philosophy of Education* 40(1) (2006).

[47] I have personal experience of several of these phenomena. My mother changed her career in her forties and became a university professor (without having a doctorate) at the age of sixty. My partner's father left school with few formal qualifications to follow the family career of shipbuilding. He changed career as an adult, eventually become a teacher in Further Education and gaining a university degree as a mature student in the same year as his son. My own career change, from civil servant to academic, occurred right at the start of my working life. Nonetheless, as a civil servant under the 1997 Blair government my first task was to research and develop the government's lifelong learning strategy.

between Jeremy and Jason is unjust, and luck egalitarians must also face the challenge of how to compensate. Andrew Mason notes that it is extremely difficult to allow only inequalities that result from choice, since "selecting people on the basis of their qualifications will entail rewarding them for their fortunate genetic endowments as well as their choice to make use of those endowments."[48] Mason is correct, but he understates the extent of the problem. It is not merely the unchosen genetic endowments that play a role in developing people's qualifications, but the experience they gain as the result of being successful or unsuccessful—lucky or unlucky—in previous competitions.

Advocates of the MEO approach must use the concept of choice in a different way, then: they cannot claim that the distinction between adulthood and childhood is justified because only chosen inequalities are just. For, firstly, children may make choices and, secondly, if an adult fails to win a job competition fought under conditions of fair equality of opportunity, it will not be true to say that she chose the resulting disadvantage. If choice is to motivate a distinction between adulthood and childhood, a different sort of argument is required. It might run as follows:

1. Children are absolutely unable to make choices about their lives, since either they are unable to make choices at all, or the choices that they do make cannot be considered as responsible or rational.
2. Inequalities cannot be legitimate if the disadvantaged individuals are absolutely unable to make choices about their lives.

Therefore, inequalities that result from childhood are unjust.

3. The best way to rectify inequalities resulting from childhood is through fair equality of opportunity.
4. If, after a starting position of fair equality of opportunity, individuals have some ability to make choices about their lives, the inequalities that result are just, subject to certain conditions.[49]

Therefore, fair equality of opportunity should be used to rectify an inequality if and only if that inequality results from childhood.

---

[48] Andrew Mason, 'Equality of Opportunity, Old and New', *Ethics* 111(4) (2001), pp. 765–6.
[49] I insert the phrase 'subject to certain conditions' since advocates of the MEO approach are unlikely to accept the justice of *all* inequalities. Constraints on legitimate inequalities might include non-discrimination, careers open to talents, minimum levels of income, and so on.

This argument focuses not on whether an individual has chosen this particular inequality, but rather on whether she is able to make choices in her life more generally. Premise 2 captures this idea and it is, I suggest, appealing. The idea that justice requires that individuals have *some* control over their lives, rather than complete control, is deeply plausible.[50]

One problem with the argument, however, is Premise 1. It is widely accepted, but it is called into question by some of the claims made by theorists of fair equality of opportunity (in support of whom the argument is made). Consider Miller's claim that "a person who decides to leave school at sixteen cannot later complain that she was denied the opportunity to go to university, if by staying on at school she could have achieved that goal."[51] This claim is made in support of the MEO approach, and yet it uses the example of an individual who would often be considered too young to be described as an adult, since many conceptions of adulthood start at age eighteen. This might seem like a trivial issue. After all, we can always say that adulthood starts at sixteen rather than eighteen. However, if we do say that then we will be unable to use fair equality of opportunity for university admissions, which take place at eighteen in Britain. And university admissions, as has already been noted, are often considered paradigmatically suitable for fair equality of opportunity. So it seems as though we do need to raise the age of adulthood to eighteen; but then Miller's sixteen-year-old can indeed complain of her lack of opportunity and seek remedy for it. Similarly, anyone will be able to complain that they lacked the opportunity to seek careers that require A Levels other than those they chose to pursue, since choices of A Level subjects are made before the age of adulthood. So a political theorist could justly complain that she lacked the opportunity to become a surgeon if, at sixteen, she chose to take no science A Levels. In general, since a great many important decisions are made by individuals between the ages of sixteen and eighteen, all adults will be able to complain of a great many denials of opportunity. One option would be to prevent people from making any choices that affect the course of their lives until they reach the decreed age of adulthood. However, even if this were desirable, it would be impossible: children will always be able to devote more effort to some subjects than others, or to devote less attention to their schooling than

---

[50] For a defence, see Matt Cavanagh, *Against Equality of Opportunity* (Oxford: Clarendon Press, 2002), p. 30.
[51] David Miller, 'Liberalism, Equal Opportunities and Cultural Commitments', in Paul Kelly (ed.), *Multiculturalism Reconsidered:* Culture and Equality *and Its Critics* (Cambridge: Polity Press, 2002), p. 47.

they could. Once again, the MEO approach is unsustainable: if it is to be realisable we need a determinate point from which to assign adulthood, but any such point faces normative problems that undermine the justice of the approach.

This problem is exacerbated by the ambiguity of the concept of inequalities that 'result from' childhood. An inequality that results from childhood does not necessarily need to have emerged during childhood. In other words, childhood could set conditions that cause an inequality to emerge much later in life. Fair equality of opportunity could be used to allocate first jobs on reaching adulthood, but attributes which are irrelevant to those first jobs could prove to be important later. For example, an employee who learned a particular foreign language while a child would be at a considerable advantage against a colleague who did not when, at middle management level, the opportunity for promotion overseas arose. If language proficiency had not been important until that point then differences in childhood language learning would not have figured in calculations of initial fair equality of opportunity. What this example shows is that, if we are concerned to remedy inequalities that result from childhood, it will not be enough to provide an MEO at the age of majority, since some inequalities will not reveal themselves until later. The overseas promotion should be awarded according to fair equality of opportunity, meaning that individuals who lacked the opportunity or chose not to learn the relevant language while children must be considered on equal terms with those who are proficient in it. Again, we reach the counter-intuitive conclusion that someone's basic lack of qualifications or experience for a job cannot be taken into account.

It is not, therefore, straightforward to justify the MEO approach by an appeal to the unchosen nature of inequalities that develop through childhood. Even if we can agree on a clear point at which adulthood commences, it does not follow that all childhood-related inequalities will have cashed themselves out by that point. Another way of expressing this point is to say that the ability to make choices about one's life does not suffice to justify unequal opportunities. So, once again, we are returned to the conclusion that fair equality of opportunity will have to be assessed repeatedly, throughout a person's life, with all the problematic consequences that entails; or, that fair equality of opportunity will have to give way to efficiency, with a concurrent sacrifice of justice.

9.7 Conclusions

As described at the outset, the aim of this chapter has been to show that *liberal egalitarian theories of equality of opportunity are inconsistent if they support an MEO and unrealisable if they do not*. They are inconsistent if they support an MEO because it does not make sense, from the point of view of justice, to divide a person's life into two halves with a Moment of Equal Opportunity. If there are good justice-based reasons to implement equality of opportunity at all, then there are good justice-based reasons to implement it throughout a person's life. That is to say, the injustice that equality of opportunity aims to prevent or remedy can occur at any time.

On the other hand, theories of equality of opportunity are unrealisable if they do not support an MEO. This conclusion is not true for the minimal approaches of non-discrimination and careers open to talents, which can realistically be applied throughout people's lives. However, it does apply to more egalitarian forms of equality of opportunity, since the attempt to assess how people would have performed if they had had the same chances will entail many counterfactual and counter-intuitive decisions.

It follows, then, that advocates of equality of opportunity need to be very clear about what the principle is trying to achieve: what is its strength and role? I have suggested that egalitarian approaches such as fair equality of opportunity cannot be strong enough adequately to remedy the injustice of certain forms of inequality unless they are so strong that they require radical changes in accepted practice, changes that compromise meritocratic and efficiency-based concerns. Since each outcome is another opportunity, such that successful candidates accrue skills while less successful individuals fall behind, equality of opportunity must be repeatedly re-applied if it is to take account of changing circumstances and potentially unjust differences. This repeated application means that the de facto best candidates very often will not be the right ones to appoint. Moreover, the gap between the competence of the best candidate (in a narrowly meritocratic sense) and the competence of the candidate that should be appointed (according to fair equality of opportunity) will only increase as positions become more senior and, presumably, more important. For the later in life an appointment is made, the more experiences and skills will have been developed by the most fortunate candidates, and the greater the contrast will be with those who have not enjoyed equivalent opportunities.

There will need to be a significant trade-off, then, between justice as secured by equality of opportunity, and meritocracy or efficiency. Advocates of either option must be open about the costs involved. So, advocates of the MEO approach need to acknowledge and account for the loss of justice, and advocates of the radical strategy of reapplying fair equality of opportunity throughout a person's life need to make similar concessions concerning efficiency and merit. The desire to compensate for past disadvantage, and to critically assess how individuals came to acquire their talents, remains worthy. However, this chapter has suggested that fair equality of opportunity is unable to satisfy it. The principle of equal opportunity can be either a workable mechanism for allocating jobs and other positions of privilege or a pivotal part of a theory of egalitarian justice. It cannot be both.

Freedom and Equality: Essays on Liberalism and Feminism. Clare Chambers, Oxford University Press.
© Clare Chambers 2024. DOI: 10.1093/9780191919480.003.0010

10

Equality of Opportunity and Three Justifications for Women's Sport

Fair Competition, Anti-Sexism, and Identity

A controversy has recently erupted: should trans women be eligible to compete in women's sport?[1] Some argue that women's sport should exclude trans women; others argue that it should include them. But a prior question is whether and why women's sport should exist at all.

In this chapter I investigate three potential justifications for women's sport. Each justification has merit in certain contexts; which justification is most apt depends on the social context (the social facts at play in any given time and place), the sporting context (elite competition, leisure sports, and school sports have very different requirements), and the specific sport in question. The justifications are in tension, and so choices must be made at key points.

This chapter starts from two premises. First, a key principle is equality of opportunity. Equality of opportunity is a generally accepted value in liberal and egalitarian theory generally, and it takes on particular importance in competitive sport. Thus any argument about the ethics and justice of sport must take full account of equality of opportunity.

Second, access to sport must be as near universal as possible. Sport is a valuable part of life for many reasons. Physical activity is needed for physical and mental health. Participation in sport is a valuable source of social interaction. Sport can be a gateway to other valuable resources and opportunities. And sport is an important part of many people's conception of the good.

Empirical research shows that women and trans people face barriers to sporting participation: physical factors and social norms that discourage or prevent

---

[1] This chapter is new for this volume. Earlier versions were presented at the King's College London Department of Political Economy seminar, the Queen's University (Canada) Colloquium in Legal and Political Philosophy, the Princeton University (USA) Philosophy Colloquium, and the University of Warwick Graduate Conference in Legal and Political Philosophy. In each of these settings I received pertinent and constructive comments for which I am very grateful. I should also like to thank Holly Lawford-Smith, Jon Pike, Adam Swift, and Lori Watson for providing extremely helpful feedback on previous drafts.

them from engaging in physical activity. These barriers include facilities, changing rooms, clothing, and equipment not well suited to their physical needs; physical discomfort; ubiquitous body-shaming from others or themselves, including feelings of dysphoria; and social norms that do not represent them as paradigm sportspeople.[2] The chapter proceeds on the assumption that access to sport and physical activity should be as close to universal as possible, and that formal and informal barriers should be lowered.

This chapter does not assume that women's sport must include trans women: that question remains open. Trans women must have access to sport, but access could be ensured by other means, including unisex sport (either as an alternative to, or a replacement for, women's sport), or the provision of trans sport, or allowing and encouraging trans people to participate in men's sport, or by breaking down formal and informal barriers against participation.[3] And so, while trans people's inclusion in sport will be assumed to be a requirement of justice, the method for inclusion is to be determined. The central question of this chapter is *Can women's sport be justified, and if so how?* The secondary question is *What does any justification for women's sport imply for trans inclusion?*

There are three distinct normative questions concerning women in sport.[4] The first is the issue of whether women should be permitted to participate or compete at all; call this *women's access to sport*. The second is the issue of whether there should be any sports reserved exclusively for women, sports

---

[2] For these experiences faced by women, see Heather Widdows, *Perfect Me: Beauty as an Ethical Ideal* (Princeton, NJ: Princeton University Press, 2018); Iris Marion Young, *On Female Body Experience: "Throwing Like a Girl" And Other Essays* (New York, NY; Oxford: Oxford University Press, 2005); Caroline Criado-Perez, *Invisible Women: Exposing Data Bias in a World Designed for Men* (London: Chatto & Windus, 2019); Shari L. Dworkin, ' "Holding Back": Negotiating a Glass Ceiling on Women's Muscular Strength', in Rose Weitz (ed.), *The Politics of Women's Bodies: Sexuality, Appearance, and Behavior* (New York, NY; Oxford: Oxford University Press, 2003); Susan K. Cahn, 'From the "Muscle Moll" to the "Butch" Ballplayer: Mannishness, Lesbianism, and Homophobia in U.S. Women's Sports', in Weitz (ed.), *The Politics of Women's Bodies*.

For these experiences faced by trans people, see Agnes Elling-Machartzki, 'Extraordinary Body Self-Narratives: Sport and Physical Activity in the Lives of Transgender People', *Leisure Studies* 36(2) (2017); Owen D. W. Hargie, David H. Mitchell, and Ian J. A. Somerville, ' "People Have a Knack of Making You Feel Excluded if They Catch on to Your Difference": Transgender Experiences of Exclusion in Sport', *International Review for the Sociology of Sport* 52(2) (2015); Thomas Page McBee, *Amateur: A Reckoning with Gender, Identity, and Masculinity* (Edinburgh: Canongate Books, 2018); Víctor Pérez-Samaniego, Jorge Fuentes-Miguel, Sofía Pereira-García, Elena López-Cañada, and José Devís-Devís, 'Experiences of Trans Persons in Physical Activity and Sport: A Qualitative Meta-Synthesis', *Sport Management Review* 22(4) (2019).

[3] Recent proposals include Jon Pike, 'Safety, fairness, and inclusion: transgender athletes and the essence of Rugby' in Journal of the Philosophy of Sport Vol. 48 No. 2 (2021) and Michael Burke, 'Trans women participation in sport: a feminist alternative to Pike's position' in Journal of the Philosophy of Sport Vol. 49 No. 2 (2022).

[4] For the purposes of this chapter, sport is taken to mean any non-instrumental physical activity, game, or endeavour. Sport can be played by teams or by individuals, and by amateurs or professionals. Its focus is usually competition, though it can also be pursued for intrinsic enjoyment or for the health benefits it brings.

which are closed to men; call this *women-only sport*. The third is the issue of whether, in sports that are played by both men and women, there should be separate competitions or events just for women; call this *women's sport*. This third issue is the one focused on in this chapter. Before turning to it, let us briefly consider *women's access to sport* and *women-only sport*.

Women's access to sport has taken considerable time and effort to secure. The Olympics are but one sporting competition, but they are the most prominent and illustrate the barriers to full participation in sport that women have faced. The modern Olympic Games, starting in Athens in 1896, were originally open to men only. Women were first allowed to compete in the Paris Olympics in 1900, when twenty-two women competed in five sports: tennis, sailing, equestrian, croquet, and golf.[5] In 1991 the International Olympic Committee (IOC) ruled that any new sport entering the Games had to include women's events, but existing men-only sports were not required to include women. Some sports were opened to women extremely late: table tennis and sailing in 1988, badminton and judo in 1992, bobsleigh in 2002, rugby in 2006. Securing women's access to sport has been part of the general feminist project of enabling women to access areas of social and professional life previously closed to them. Women's access to sport is a basic claim of sex equality and non-discrimination.

The Olympic Games also include *women-only sport*. Artistic Swimming (commonly known as synchronised swimming) is open to women only. Artistic Gymnastics includes different disciplines for men and women gymnasts. Other women-only sports exist beyond the Olympics: netball, not an Olympic event, is the sole women-only sport at the Commonwealth Games and is traditionally played only by women and girls.[6] Women-only sport can be objected to on grounds of sex equality: why shouldn't boys be able to play netball at school instead of rugby or football; why shouldn't men be able to compete in synchronised swimming?[7] The existence of women-only sport can be understood as a historically necessary counterweight to the prevalence of men-only sport. But there are no intrinsic objections to opening women-only sport to men, assuming that separate women's teams and competitions are maintained.

---

[5] Dates in this paragraph are from International Olympic Committee, 'When Did Women First Compete in the Olympic Games?' (2021), no longer online.

[6] World Netball, 'Olympic Games' (2018), available at https://netball.sport/events-and-results/olympic-games.

[7] Louise Radnofsky, 'Should Women-Only Olympics Sports Be Open to Men?', *The Wall Street Journal* (20 August 2016). For a discussion of men's netball, see Jo Gunston, 'England Men's Netball Captain Talks to Me About the Stigma He Faces', *Sports Liberated* (28 January 2015), available at https://www.sportsliberated.com/interview-england-netballer-gary-patrick-brown/. *Men Who Swim* is a documentary about the formation of the Swedish men's synchronised swimming team.

This chapter considers *women's sport*. Women's sport is the term I use to describe a sport that is played by both women and men, but that includes competitions, rankings, or teams that are open only to women. Women's sport can exist as the only alternative to men's sport, so that every sportsperson must fit into one of the two categories. But that is not a necessary feature of women's sport. Women's sport can exist alongside unisex (mixed-sex) sport, and alongside other options such as trans sport (discussed later).

Women's sport is often regarded as necessary for equality of opportunity. But at first glance this is surprising. Women's sport looks like a violation of equality of opportunity because it discriminates on grounds of sex. So why do most people think that equality of opportunity is compatible with women's sport, and may even require it?

Equality of opportunity aims to secure the conditions that enable people to compete fairly, without being burdened by an unfair disadvantage or boosted by an unfair advantage. Non-discrimination is the most basic version of equality of opportunity, in the sense that it is both the simplest and the most fundamental.[8] The principle of non-discrimination says that ascriptive characteristics should *not* be allowed to affect an outcome: they should not give an advantage or disadvantage in some competition. Ascriptive characteristics are ruled out as irrelevant to one's merit in that competition, at least partly because they are unchosen and thus undeserved. The paradigmatic ascriptive characteristics ruled out by non-discrimination principles are sex and race: the principle that sex and race discrimination are unjust, and that sex and race should not be relevant to a person's success or failure at some endeavour, underpins landmark legislation. More recently, many jurisdictions have extended the list of characteristics that are considered to fall under the principle of non-discrimination.

The principle of non-discrimination seems on the face of it to rule out the category of women's sport altogether, along with competitions reserved for disabled athletes such as the Paralympics. After all, if sex and disability are not legitimate bases for discrimination, how can it be permissible to have competitions that are open only to women or disabled people? However it is rare for people to argue against women's sport on the grounds that it discriminates against men,[9] and it is still rarer to see arguments that the Paralympics

---

[8] For further discussion, see Clare Chambers, 'Each Outcome is Another Opportunity: Problems with the Moment of Equal Opportunity', Chapter 9 in this volume.

[9] For the view that women's sport is discriminatory against women, see Dana Robinson, 'A League of Their Own: Do Women Want Sex-Segregated Sports?', *Journal of Contemporary Legal Issues* 9 (1998).

discriminate against those without disabilities. The general view is that the principle of non-discrimination does *not* mean that women's sport or the Paralympics are impermissible. The next section explains why.

10.1 The Fair Competition Argument

The principle of non-discrimination holds that ascriptive characteristics, such as sex, should not be used to justify inequality in most cases. 'In most cases' is needed because the principle of non-discrimination allows for exceptions when the protected characteristic is relevant to the opportunity in question.[10] In the case of sport, sex is a relevant characteristic insofar as it affects fair competition.

Thus, the standard argument for women's sport is that it is justifiable, and sometimes necessary, so as to secure fair competition. As philosopher of sport Sigmund Loland puts it, fairness in sport requires that we "eliminate or compensate for essential inequalities between persons that cannot be controlled or influenced by individuals in any significant way and for which individuals cannot be deemed responsible".[11] According to this argument there are sex-based physiological characteristics that affect sporting performance. Males are typically taller, heavier, and stronger than females. They have a different skeletal structure, different proportions of muscle and fat, different muscle types and composition, and different levels of testosterone. These various physiological differences combine to give males a natural advantage in most sports. Different sports make use of different features, meaning that females may be at a natural advantage in some sports, but in general the sports that are most highly rewarded, resourced, and esteemed are those in which males excel. While training and diet make a significant difference to athletes' strength and skill, they cannot eliminate sex-based advantage. It follows that

---

[10] Defence and discussion of this sort of argument in the equality of opportunity literature can be found in Andrew Mason, *Levelling the Playing Field: The Idea of Equal Opportunity and its Place in Egalitarian Thought* (Oxford: Oxford University Press, 2006), pp. 25–35; Brian Barry, *Culture and Equality: An Egalitarian Critique of Multiculturalism* (Cambridge: Polity Press, 2001), pp. 55ff.; Richard J. Arneson, 'Against Rawlsian Equality of Opportunity', *Philosophical Studies* 93(1) (1999); David Pannick, 'When is Sex a Genuine Occupational Qualification?', *Oxford Journal of Legal Studies* 4(2) (1984). See also Human Rights Commission, 'Circumstances when being treated differently due to sex is lawful', Equality and Human Rights Commission (19 February 2020), available at https://www.equalityhumanrights.com/en/advice-and-guidance/sex-discrimination#lawful and Court of Arbitration for Sport, 'Semenya, ASA and IAAF: Executive Summary', *TAS/CAS* (1 May 2019), available at https://www.tas-cas.org/fileadmin/user_upload/CAS_Executive_Summary__5794_.pdf, p. 4.

[11] Sigmund Loland, 'Fairness in Sport: An Ideal and Its Consequences', in Mike McNamee (ed.), *The Ethics of Sports: A Reader* (Abingdon: Routledge, 2010), p. 118.

females are not able to compete on a level playing field against males in most sports, and so fair competition requires women's sport.

The UK Equality Act 2010 explicitly lists sex-segregated sport as an exception to its general principle of non-discrimination, using the fair competition argument.[12] Sex discrimination in sport is permissible, according to the Act, because sex is a relevant difference in sport. Sex makes a difference to matters of fairness and safety. It could be unsafe for women if men, with their heavier, larger frames and greater strength, were allowed to compete against them in certain sports, particularly contact sports like boxing and rugby. And it would be unfair for women if men were allowed to compete against them in sports in which men have a natural advantage, which is most mainstream sport. The two considerations are related: a competition that is safe for some competitors and unsafe for others is an unfair competition.[13]

The Act emphasises that the relevant consideration for sport is sex, not gender, because it specifically allows trans people to be excluded from participation on the basis of their *sex*, not their gender identity, even though in other contexts there is a legal obligation not to discriminate on grounds of gender reassignment. The Equality Act 2010 therefore operates with a sex/gender distinction, where 'sex' is a biological category and 'gender' is a question of social role or identity. I continue that usage in this chapter.[14]

The Act also stipulates that the relevant comparators are the 'average' man and the 'average' woman. Its claim is that sex is a relevant difference in sport because the average male has a natural advantage over the average female. It does not state that there is a sex-based (dis)advantage that will be definitive in a competition between all males and all females, or between any two specific individuals. Serena Williams could beat the vast majority of men at tennis; Kelly Holmes can run faster than most men. But the average man has

---

[12] The relevant part is Equality Act 2010, 'Part 14: General Exceptions; Section 195: Sport', available at https://www.legislation.gov.uk/ukpga/2010/15/section/195. Similar exclusions are found in the UK Gender Recognition Act 2007. In the USA, sex-segregated sports are permitted under Title IX and the Equal Protection Clause. See Erin E. Buzuvis, 'Transgender Student-Athletes and Sex-Segregated Sport: Developing Policies of Inclusion for Intercollegiate and Interscholastic Athletics', *Seton Hall Journal of Sports and Entertainment Law* 21(1) (2011), p. 10.

[13] The risk of injury in some sports is so great that it is appropriate to have segregation additional to sex: weight categories in boxing being the most obvious example.

[14] The standard category for women's sport has been sex, meaning that to compete as a woman an athlete must be biologically female. The inclusion of trans women shifts the criterion from sex to gender, with significant consequences for the justification and practice of women's sport. For discussion of this shift, see Doriane Lambert Coleman, 'Sex in Sport', *Law and Contemporary Problems* 80(63) (2018). Unfortunately, the UK Equality Act 2010 does not use the terms 'sex' and 'gender' consistent with its own descriptions of the protected characteristics. For example, the provision allowing women's sport is confusing because the Act uses the term 'gender-affected activity' when referring to matters in which it means to stipulate that *sex* is relevant.

a natural physical advantage over the average woman. This natural advantage extends to elite athletes: male elite athletes significantly outperform female elite athletes in most sports. In the view of the law, this relevant sex difference makes unisex competition unfair, and so fair competition requires women's sport.[15]

The fair competition argument ties women's sport to women's access to sport. If unisex sport is unsafe for women then women face unreasonable barriers to participation. Women's sport is therefore necessary to ensure that women have genuine and equal access to sport. If unisex sport is safe yet unfair for women then women will find it much harder to win and are unlikely to make the top teams, competitions, or records, preventing women's access to elite sport. This inequality of access will trickle down to below-elite and amateur level.

In practice almost all sports are segregated by sex at competition level. In most events where winning requires speed, such as running, swimming, cycling, or rowing, the performance gap between men and women is about 10 per cent—a vast gap in elite sport. This means that a great many non-elite male athletes could beat even the very best record-holding women. For example, the female world record for the 100m is 10.49s, a time set by Flo Jo in 1988 and unbroken by a woman since then. But her time was beaten by 744 men in 2017 alone.[16] There are 9,000 males between the male 100m world record holder, Usain Bolt, and Flo Jo.[17] Paula Radcliffe holds the world record for women's marathon running, but her time of 2h 15m 25s is beaten by about 250–300 men each year.[18] Without women's sport there would simply be no elite female runners.

In tennis, the notorious 'Battle of the Sexes' match saw a retired male player beat the then world-champion woman: in 1973 Bobby Riggs, age fifty-five, beat world women's number one Margaret Court, age thirty. In 2013, Andy Murray tweeted that he would be willing to play Serena Williams, women's

---

[15] Notice that the UK legislation does not *require* equality of opportunity in sport: it does not stipulate that all sporting competitions must be fair. It simply permits organisations, including schools, businesses, voluntary groups, and charities, to segregate sports by sex if they wish, without falling foul of the legal requirements not to discriminate.

[16] Emma Hilton, writing as Fond of Beetles, 'Harder, Faster, Better, Stronger: Why We Must Protect Female Sports' (1 October 2018), available at https://fondofbeetles.wordpress.com/2018/10/01/harder-better-faster-stronger-why-we-must-protect-female-sports/.

[17] FPFW, 'Dr Emma Hilton Reviews the Science Supporting the IOC Decision to Let Male-Born Transgender Athletes into Female Competition', *Fair Play for Women* (14 July 2019), available at https://fairplayforwomen.com/emma_hilton/.

[18] Coleman, 'Sex in Sport', p. 88.

number one at the time. Williams responded, "That would be fun. I doubt I'd win a point, but that would be fun."[19]

So, in most sports, women's sport is a requirement of fair competition. Since sex makes a significant difference to sporting performance, women's sport is necessary to create a level playing field. This view is neatly summarised by Sebastian Coe, President of the International Association of Athletics Federations (IAAF): "The reason we have gender classification [he means sex classification] is because if you didn't then no woman would ever win another title or another medal or break another record in our sport."[20]

The fair competition argument for women's sport makes rules and policies on how to police the boundaries of women's competitions essential. Without such policing men can engage in sex fraud: deliberately cheating by pretending to be women.[21] Since the fair competition argument is based on the claim that men have an unfair natural advantage over women, sex fraud violates the fair competition that women's sport aims to secure.

The prevalence of sex fraud is contested. J. C. Reeser reports that sex fraud has been used systematically since the 1936 Berlin Olympics, often for political purposes.[22] In contrast, Lindsay Parks Pieper notes that there is only one confirmed instance of sex fraud in Olympic history, that of "German high jumper 'Dora' Ratjen, who finished fourth in the women's event [but] admitted two decades later to his male identity and name, Hermann Ratjen."[23] On Pieper's analysis, it is the *allegations* of sex fraud that serve political purposes, by undermining the success of athletes who are non-white, non-Western, or both. What is clear is that success in international sports competitions such as the Olympics brings glory not only to individual athletes but also to the countries they represent, creating high stakes and providing incentives for both one-off and systematic cheating. Moreover, the fair competition argument for women's sport relies on a clear division between female and male athletes, a division based on physiology rather than identity or social role.

---

[19] BBC Sport, 'Andy Murray: Serena Williams would face British Number One', BBC (27 June 2013).
[20] Press Association, 'Caster Semenya Accuses Sebastian Coe of "Opening Old Wounds"', *The Guardian* (27 March 2019).
[21] I use the phrase 'deliberate cheating' to indicate someone who is uncontroversially a man (including identifying as such when not engaged in deliberate cheating) pretending to be a woman for the purposes of gaining unfair advantage in a sporting competition. In 2019, tennis champion Martina Navratilova caused controversy by claiming that trans women competing in women's sports were cheating. Navratilova's attribution of cheating is controversial and not what I mean here.
[22] J. C. Reeser, 'Gender Identity and Sport: Is the Playing Field Level?', *British Journal of Sports Medicine* 39(10) (2005), p. 696.
[23] Lindsay Parks Pieper, 'Sex Testing and the Maintenance of Western Femininity in International Sport', *The International Journal of the History of Sport* 31(13) (2014), p. 1561.

There are a number of options for defining the physiological sex characteristics that qualify an athlete to count as female and therefore eligible to compete in women's sport. Choosing among them is partly a matter of developmental biology (which biological features determine biological sex), sports science (which biological features are key to explaining sex (dis)advantage in sport), and partly a matter of testing regimes (which biological features can reliably and decently be tested for while respecting athletes' dignity). The correct balance between rigorous testing to secure fair competition and respecting athletes' privacy will depend on the sporting context: elite athletes can reasonably expect to be subject to more rigorous testing, but in some sporting contexts (normal school sports, for example) testing would be inappropriate.

Whatever criteria are settled on must *necessarily* exclude some people from the category of 'female', and those excluded may suffer as a result. Excluded athletes may suffer simply by being unable to participate, but they may also suffer from stigma and invasion of privacy. Testing may 'out' some athletes as having Differences of Sexual Development (DSD, sometimes called 'intersex') or as being trans, and this outing may be unwanted or harmful. These considerations must be taken into account and may rule out testing in some contexts. But the mere fact of exclusion on physiological grounds cannot be avoided if the fair competition argument justifies women's sport.

In principle, the rules applying to athletes with DSD should be distinct from those applying to trans athletes. Having DSD and being trans are two different things and the experiences and challenges faced by trans people and people with DSD are often quite different. At present, however, they are often subject to the same regulations.

In 2011, the IAAF announced new rules that allowed females with hyperandrogenism, meaning they naturally produce high levels of testosterone, to compete in women's events provided their testosterone levels were 'below the male range'. In 2019, athlete Caster Semenya unsuccessfully challenged these IAAF regulations.[24] Semenya argued that it is unfair to require athletes to take hormone suppressants that interfere with their natural bodily processes, particularly since they might be bad for health.[25] Semenya's case rested on the claim "that the DSD Regulations unfairly discriminate against athletes on the

---

[24] CAS Arbitration, 'Caster Semenya, Athletics South Africa (ASA) and International Association of Athletics Federations (IAAF): Decision', *TAS/CAS* (1 May 2019), available at https://www.tas-cas.org/en/general-information/news-detail/article/cas-arbitration-caster-semenya-athletics-south-africa-asa-and-international-association-of-athl.html.

[25] Sean Ingle, 'Caster Semenya Case Verdict Postponed Until End of April', *The Guardian* (21 March 2019).

basis of sex and/or gender because they only apply (i) to female athletes; and (ii) to female athletes having certain physiological traits."[26]

There is a difference between testosterone naturally produced by the body and that artificially taken to enhance performance. Elite athletes, whether male or female, may not take performance-enhancing drugs, primarily anabolic steroids, since doing so would give unfair advantage. But Semenya's elevated testosterone levels are naturally produced. Why, then, should she be required to reduce them? Only in women's sport are athletes required to reduce their naturally produced testosterone levels. A man who naturally produces unusually high levels of testosterone compared to other men does not have to reduce his levels in order to compete in men's sport: he may simply reap the benefits of his natural advantage. So Semenya's case rested on the fact that she was being treated unequally to men who are fortunate enough to produce unusually high levels of endogenous testosterone.

The IOC and other sporting bodies could, in principle, implement different eligibility criteria for athletes with DSD and trans athletes. For example, it could allow women with DSD to compete in women's sport without restriction while imposing physiological criteria for trans women. But, in practice, guidelines adopted by the IOC in 2015 mean that Semenya's case has deep implications for trans athletes, and any ruling on her case had to take into account those implications.

Prior to 2015, the IOC required any trans woman wishing to compete in women's events to have undergone reassignment surgery (sometimes called 'bottom surgery') plus a minimum of two years of hormone therapy. These stringent physiological criteria meant that only a small minority of trans women were eligible to compete in women's sport. In 2015, the guidelines were changed. Trans women would be eligible to compete in women's events provided that their testosterone levels had been below 10 nmol/l for a minimum of one year prior to competition, and for the duration of the competition. In addition, an athlete competing as a woman must have "declared that her gender identity is female. The declaration cannot be changed, for sporting purposes, for a minimum of four years."[27] Trans men would be eligible to compete in men's events "without restriction", reflecting the IOC's judgment

---

[26] Court of Arbitration for Sport, 'Semenya, ASA and IAAF: Executive Summary', p. 2.
[27] IOC, 'IOC Consensus Meeting on Sex Reassignment and Hyperandrogenism November 2015', International Olympic Committee (November 2015), available at https://stillmed.olympic.org/Documents/Commissions_PDFfiles/Medical_commission/2015-11_ioc_consensus_meeting_on_sex_reassignment_and_hyperandrogenism-en.pdf, p. 2.

that trans men have no unfair advantage over men who are not trans. Indeed, they have a physiological disadvantage.

These guidelines have a number of consequences. First, they reinforce the consensus that male athletes have a natural, sex-based advantage over female athletes, largely based on testosterone levels, since they require trans women to reduce their testosterone levels before competing in women's events. Second, they assert that 'gender identity' is relevant to sex-segregated sport since they require a declaration of it; however, they give no definition or criteria for what it is to have a gender identity. No legal changes are required, no name changes are required, no lifestyle changes are required, and no anatomical changes are required. Identifying as 'female' for sporting purposes is therefore not burdensome. Third, despite affirming that testosterone levels give advantage in sport, the IOC guidelines allow trans women athletes to participate in women's events with testosterone levels nearly five times higher than the upper level of the normal female range.[28] Anti-doping rules forbid not-trans women athletes from taking steroids to increase their testosterone levels to the same levels permitted for trans women athletes competing against them.

In the context of these rules giving trans women easier access to women's sport, Semenya's case has implications beyond her own participation. Her case challenged the requirement for women athletes to limit their testosterone levels, a case that looks very plausible when compared with the fact that no men are required to limit their testosterone levels in order to compete in men's sport. But, since limited testosterone levels are the *only* physiological criteria for a trans athlete to compete as a woman under the IOC guidelines, removing testosterone limits for women athletes in general would mean that there would be *no* physiological restriction or criteria for participation in women's sport. Women would have to compete against athletes with significant sex-based physiological natural advantages over them. Such an outcome would effectively replace sex-segregated sport with gender-segregated sport, something not justified by the fair competition argument. As philosopher of sport Heather Reid puts it, "The sports question has nothing to do with an athlete's motives for wanting to compete in the women's category and everything to do with respecting the justification for that category, which is based on competitive advantage outside of one's control."[29]

---

[28] The normal level of testosterone for adult females is from 0.4 to 2.1 nmol/l; for adult males it is 10.2 to 39.9 nmol/l.

[29] Heather L. Reid, *Introduction to the Philosophy of Sport*, 2nd edition (London: Rowman and Littlefield, 2023), p. 219.

It is therefore unsurprising that a number of elite athletes are concerned about what they see as the threat to women's sport, or to fair competition within it, posed by more relaxed rules about trans women's eligibility to compete. If women's sport is a requirement of fair competition, necessary to offset men's natural physical advantage, trans women's participation seems unfair—an "intolerable unfairness" according to three bioethicists[30]—because trans women may retain male natural advantage, particularly if no physiological criteria are imposed.[31] This concern has led several elite sportspeople to raise objections against allowing trans women to compete in women's sport, including tennis player Martina Navratilova, middle-distance runner Kelly Holmes, long-distance runner Paula Radcliffe, swimmer Sharron Davies, rugby player Dan Leo, and runner Sebastian Coe. These athletes raise concerns based on fair competition: they argue that sex, not gender, is a relevant difference in sport, that men have a natural advantage over women on average, and that trans women retain male natural advantage. It follows that, if women's sport is justified by fair competition, it should not be open to trans women unless it is possible to remove any sex-based competitive advantage. Conversely, if women's sport *is* open to trans women, then it cannot be justified by the fair competition argument and an alternative justification must be found.

The views of the elite athletes just listed are strongly criticised by some trans activists.[32] Some defenders of trans women's participation in women's sport deny that trans women retain any natural male advantage.[33] In the current debate about trans athletes, there is controversy as to whether the biological advantage that males have is reducible to testosterone levels at the time of competition, which can in principle be reduced with testosterone-suppressing drugs, or whether anyone who has gone through male puberty has irreversible natural advantages relating to height, weight, muscular

---

[30] Taryn Knox, Lynley C. Anderson, and Alison Heather, 'Transwomen in Elite Sport: Scientific and Ethical Considerations', *Journal of Medical Ethics* 45(6) (2019).

[31] Since men's times, scores, and records generally beat women's, often significantly, it would not be an unfair violation of fair competition for women to compete in *men's* sports if they so wish, since they would gain no unfair advantage in doing so. However, objections to women and girls competing against men and boys are sometimes made on grounds of safety or decorum, considerations that are particularly salient in certain social contexts and historical periods. See Buzuvis, 'Transgender Student-Athletes and Sex-Segregated Sport', pp. 7ff.

[32] See Sean Ingle, 'Sports Stars Weigh in on Row Over Transgender Athletes', *The Guardian* (3 March 2019).

[33] See, for example, Sarah Teetzel, 'On Transgendered Athletes, Fairness, and Doping: An International Challenge', *Sport in Society* 9(2) (2006); John Gleaves and Tim Lehrbach, 'Beyond Fairness: The Ethics of Inclusion for Transgender and Intersex Athletes', *Journal of the Philosophy of Sport* 43(2) (2016).

composition, bone density, pelvic structure, and so on. Many athletes and scientists are sceptical that it is possible fully to neutralise any natural advantage that trans women have, since the physiological differences between post-pubescent males and females are numerous, extensive, and extend beyond testosterone levels at any one point in time.[34] At the time of writing there is significant flux in the regulations pertaining to women's sport, as various sporting bodies revise their eligibility rules for women's sport. But these are questions for sports science, and it is not my purpose to reach a conclusion on them here.[35]

We can now reach the following conclusions *from the perspective of the fair competition argument*:

1. If women's sport is justified by fair competition, then it must be true that there is a relevant difference between females and males.
2. The criteria for competing in women's sport should be based on physiology not identity.
3. Women who do not meet standardised biological definitions of femaleness[36] should be permitted to compete in women's sport only if it is possible to nullify any sex-based natural advantage they have, as determined by the best available sports science about the physiological characteristics that produce sex-based natural advantage.
4. If a woman does not meet standardised biological definitions of femaleness then she should be excluded from competing in women's events, regardless of gender identity. Excluded athletes should remain eligible to compete in unisex or men's events.

The fair competition argument is most appropriately prioritised in high-stakes sporting contexts, where winning is paramount or brings advantage.

---

[34] As well as the athletes and scientists already cited elsewhere in this chapter, see Reeser, 'Gender Identity and Sport'; Ross Tucker, 'On Transgender Athletes and Performance Advantages', *The Science of Sport* (24 March 2019), available at https://sportsscientists.com/2019/03/on-transgender-athletes-and-performance-advantages/; Coleman, 'Sex in Sport'; Doriane Coleman, 'On the Biology of Sex, Sex Differentiation, and the Performance Gap: Yes, It Is All About Testosterone', *The Volokh Conspiracy* (12 March 2019).

[35] There is at present inadequate scientific data on this question. See Michaela C. Devries, 'Do Transitioned Athletes Compete at an Advantage or Disadvantage as Compared with Physically Born Men and Women: A Review of the Scientific Literature' (2008), available at https://citeseerx.ist.psu.edu/viewdoc/download;jsessionid=B2304B2F5351EF127EE3FBAC14D9AF56?doi=10.1.1.546.8794&rep=rep1&type=pdf (accessed 6 September 2022).

[36] One option is that anyone who is female, as set out by standard and accepted biological definitions, should be eligible to compete in women's sport without further restriction, including females with DSD. However, this claim is not essential to the fair competition argument.

Elite sports, world record competitions, events that award significant titles, prize money, or scholarships will be strong candidates for sex-segregation on fair competition grounds. Fair competition concerns may be less relevant to sporting contexts focused on fun and fitness, and contexts where the harms of sex-based exclusion outweigh the harms of losing unfairly—a matter on which there can be reasonable disagreement. However, safety concerns will remain relevant in all contexts and so some sports should be sex-segregated at any level.

10.2 The Anti-Sexism Argument

The fair competition argument is a central justification for women's sport. But it faces a challenge: why think that unfairness results from natural advantages only when those advantages arise from sex?

Success in sport requires significant training and effort, but sports are strongly affected by natural advantage. It is advantageous for basketball players to be tall, or for jockeys to be small, or for runners to have long legs, and yet these are natural advantages. Should unusually tall basketball players be excluded from competitions? Most would think not. So why think that all males must be restricted to men's competitions, even if they lack natural advantage and thus have no hope of winning in those competitions? Why not have sex-neutral categories defined by other natural characteristics? For example, boxing is categorised by weight. Why not allow anyone of the relevant weight to compete together, regardless of sex? Why not have different basketball leagues for players of different heights? What is special about sex?

The anti-sexism argument helps us to answer these questions. It has similarities with justifications for affirmative action, although it is not precisely an affirmative action argument. The anti-sexism argument justifies women's sport as necessary to rectify historical and ongoing discrimination against women, in sport and elsewhere. According to this argument, women's sport serves two purposes. First, women's sport is needed to ensure that women can overcome the various explicit and implicit barriers to sporting participation and success. Without women's sport, this argument goes, women are unlikely to succeed at sport in direct competition against men. Unequal success is problematic in itself, and may also discourage women from entering sport. Moreover, there are sexist norms that discourage girls and women from physical activity. Only by providing sporting opportunities and rewards that are reserved for women can these barriers be overcome.

A recent international study of more than 14,000 women found that a significant number of girls reduce or stop their sporting activity in puberty. The reasons identified by the researchers combine those resulting from both biological sex and gender norms: "the impact of menstruation, bodily changes such as breast and body hair growth, embarrassment and low confidence, feelings of inadequacy, unflattering sports kit, a lack of enjoyment, and that sport was 'not cool'."[37] These findings bolster Simone de Beauvoir's argument that it is in puberty that a girl comes to realise that, "For the future, her muscular power, endurance, and agility will be inferior to those qualities in a man...and it is at just this time that the girl gives up rough games."[38] Sex is a relevant difference not just for determining which athletes will win: it also significantly impacts who will take part. When biological sex intersects with gender norms that prioritise girls' attractiveness, that shame them for menstruating, and that do not adequately cater for the shape and function of their bodies, girls' and women's ability to enjoy and maintain sporting activity is severely compromised.

Second, women's sport may be needed to ameliorate women's inequality in society more generally. Women's sport is one way of ensuring that women can succeed in prominent pursuits, providing inspiration and self-respect to all women. In 2019, the increased prominence given to women's football in the UK, the success of the USA team, and the publicity given to key players such as Megan Rapinoe, was inspiring for many women and girls, regardless of their personal interest in playing football. It also had an effect on men and boys, providing evidence that women can excel and inspire in sport. To quote Beauvoir again,

> in sports the end in view is not success independent of physical equipment; it is rather the attainment of perfection within the limitations of each physical type: the featherweight boxing champion is as much a champion as is the heavyweight; the woman skiing champion is not the inferior of the faster male champion: they belong to two different classes. It is precisely the female athletes who, being positively interested in their own game, feel themselves least handicapped in comparison with the male. It remains true that her physical weakness does not permit women to learn the lessons of violence; but if she could assert herself through her body and face the world in some

---

[37] Kate Rowan, 'Revealed: Two Out of Five British and Irish Girls "Shun Sport During Puberty" – Far More than Rest of the World', *The Telegraph* (26 March 2019).
[38] Simone de Beauvoir, *The Second Sex* (London: Vintage, 1997), p. 353.

other fashion, this deficiency would be easily compensated for. Let her swim, climb mountain peaks, pilot an aeroplane, battle against the elements, take risks, go out for adventure, and she will not feel before the world the timidity which I have referred to.[39]

Women's sport thus provides a service to women's equality in society as a whole.

Jane English makes a version of the anti-sexism argument. She distinguishes the 'basic benefits' of sport from the 'scarce benefits'. The basic benefits are "health, the self-respect to be gained by doing one's best, the cooperation to be learned from working with teammates and the incentive gained by having opponents, the 'character' of learning to be a good loser and a good winner, the chance to improve one's skills and learn to accept criticism—and just plain fun."[40] English notes that everyone ought to have access to these basic benefits, and this position may in some cases tell against women's sport.[41]

On English's analysis, the same considerations do not apply to the scarce benefits of sports, which she describes as "fame and fortune".[42] These benefits can be enormous. A notable example is American college sport. A US university's football or men's basketball coach is frequently its highest-paid employee, and is often the highest-paid public employee in the entire state.[43] Sports scholarships are a significant source of student income, and may be vital for students from poorer backgrounds. One scholarship-awarding body reports that it provides $2.9 billion in athletic scholarships to around 150,000 students each year, which it equates to 2 per cent of high school athletes in the USA.[44]

Where these scarce benefits of sports are concerned, English argues that the model of equal opportunity that should be used is "proportional attainment for the major social groups". In her words, "The justification for maintaining separate teams for the sexes is the impact on women that

---

[39] Beauvoir, *The Second Sex*, p. 357.
[40] Jane English, 'Sex Equality in Sports', *Philosophy and Public Affairs* 7(3) (1978), p. 270.
[41] As Reid notes, "Integrated sports – especially in youth competitions where sex-based performance differences are smaller – teach boys and girls not only that they can compete but also that they can work together as a team" (Reid, *Introduction to the Philosophy of Sport*, p. 217).
[42] English, 'Sex Equality in Sports', p. 271.
[43] According to ESPN, "In 2017, 39 of the 50 states' payrolls were topped by a football or men's basketball coach", an analysis that does not include the salaries of coaches at private universities. See Charlotte Gibson, 'Who's the Highest Paid Person In Your State', ESPN.com (20 March 2018), available at https://www.espn.com/espn/feature/story/_/id/22454170/highest-paid-state-employees-include-ncaa-coaches-nick-saban-john-calipari-dabo-swinney-bill-self-bob-huggins.
[44] National Collegiate Athletics Association, 'Scholarships', NCAA (2022), available at http://www.ncaa.org/student-athletes/future/scholarships.

integration would have. When there are virtually no female athletic stars, or when women receive much less prize money than men do, this is damaging to the self-respect of all women."[45] According to English, this consideration explains why sports can legitimately be segregated according to "major social groups" rather than "arbitrary sets of individuals": a group that is socially constituted, "singled out for distinctive treatment and recognized as a class[,] tends to develop feelings of mutual identification which have an impact on the members' self-respect".[46]

On the anti-sexism argument women's sport is justified because women as a group have been subject to historical and ongoing oppression, discrimination, and disadvantage. Unequal treatment of women has occurred within sport and more generally, and so remedial measures to rectify this disadvantage are justified. But women's sport is also justified simply because women are a salient social group. They identify with each other's successes and failures, gaining inspiration from other women role models. The anti-sexism argument thus has both a backward- and a forward-looking element, aiming both to compensate for past disadvantage and to provide a mechanism for ongoing social change.[47]

The anti-sexism argument explains why women's sports are justified even in cases where some particular man lacks natural advantage as compared to some particular woman. Women's sports are a mechanism for rectifying discrimination and unequal socialisation. The goal is not only to secure fair competition in some particular competition but to secure equal participation and success by different social groups against a background of unequal social treatment of those groups.

Thus the anti-sexism argument is distinct from the fair competition argument. This is because the anti-sexism argument can be used to justify separate women's competitions in sports or activities in which women do *not* have a natural disadvantage. For example, women's or girls' chess competitions may be justified not because women and girls are naturally worse at chess (I know of no evidence that they are), but because in a sexist society women and girls are less likely to be encouraged to play chess than are men and boys. A competition just for women and girls helps them to overcome the gendered norms of the activity and consider participating where they otherwise might not, and guarantees winners who can act as role models for other women and girls. Similar justifications can be made for having separate competitions for

---

[45] English, 'Sex Equality in Sports', p. 273.   [46] English, 'Sex Equality in Sports', p. 274.
[47] I am grateful to an anonymous reviewer for this point.

girls in STEM subjects, or for philosophy conferences such as PIKSI targeted at under-represented groups, or indeed for men's or boys' competitions or classes in activities that are gendered feminine such as dance or singing.

However, there is also the danger that women's competitions can *exacerbate* sexism. This worry is manifest in the affirmative action context, when sceptics argue that women-only shortlists or preferential hiring for minorities contributes to the impression that those groups cannot succeed on their own merits. So, a girls' chess competition may encourage girls to play chess, or it may imply that girls are naturally worse at chess than boys. This is an empirical question that depends on the context and social facts, such as how the competition is advertised and justified and how well the existence and operation of sexist norms is understood by the general population.

In the case of sport this worry is eased by the widespread acceptance of the fair competition argument. The anti-sexism argument is distinct from the fair competition argument, but they work together in two ways. First, the fair competition argument suggests that there will be few successful female athletes to act as role models for women without women's sport. As Coleman puts it, "Any other option that has males and females competing together works mainly to highlight, isolate and display male bodies and hierarchies."[48] Second, the anti-sexism argument shows why women are the relevant group for the fair competition argument, rather than a group distinguished by some other physical feature like height or weight. In all areas of life, including but by no means limited to sport, women and men are classified separately and treated differently. It thus makes sense, in a sexist society, to group people into sex categories for the purposes of assessing natural advantage, and to place even the strongest, most naturally athletic women—including women with DSD—into the women's category.[49]

In the case of women's sport the anti-sexism argument and the fair competition argument are mutually reinforcing. Neither is *necessary* to justify categories based on ascriptive characteristics: the fair competition argument alone is enough to justify age-based sporting competitions for children, for example, and the anti-sexism argument alone is enough to justify women's and girls' chess tournaments in favourable social contexts. But the arguments work together to create a strong defence of the existence of women's sport.

---

[48] Coleman, 'Sex in Sport', p. 86.
[49] The same arguments apply to affirmative action on grounds of race. Affirmative action programmes can be used to benefit all members of the targeted race, even those individuals who come from unusually privileged backgrounds, because the social treatment of people according to their race is entrenched and significant.

What does the anti-sexism argument tell us about trans women's participation in women's sport? Trans women—and trans men—face significant barriers to sporting participation and also face discrimination in society more generally.[50] The anti-sexism argument applied to trans people thus implies that measures must be taken to centre, celebrate, and encourage trans people within and beyond sport. But how this should be done is unclear. Trans people may benefit from anti-sexism gains by participating in the sport that matches their gender identity. Alternatively, the logic of the anti-sexism argument applied to trans people *as a group* is that trans sport should be created and supported, so as to provide the inspiration and prioritisation for trans people as a group that women's sport provides for women as a group.

Note that this argument for trans sport, one derived from a version of the anti-sexism argument, does not imply that trans women are not women. Some trans people are women and some are men, and this defence of trans sport neither denies that obvious fact nor says anything at all about which people are in which category. It simply points to the salience of being trans, that trans people share a social group or identity *at some level*, and that trans sport is justifiable to mitigate anti-trans discrimination and inspire trans people. It is fully compatible with an intersectional understanding of both sex- and gender-based oppression. Once again, whether trans sport or trans inclusion best serves anti-sexism concerns for all relevant groups will depend on the sporting and social context.

Some people argue that trans representation and equality is best secured not by trans sport but by allowing trans women to compete in women's sport and celebrating their success as visibly trans. They may even defend a hypothetical scenario in which trans women dominate women's competitions. For example, sports columnist Jonathan Liew writes in *The Independent*:

> Let's say the floodgates do open. Let's say transgender athletes pour into women's sport, and let's say, despite the flimsy and poorly-understood relationship between testosterone and elite performance, they dominate everything they touch. They sweep up Grand Slam tennis titles and cycling world championships. They monopolise the Olympics. They fill our football and cricket and netball teams. Why would that be bad? Really? Imagine the

---

[50] Bethany Alice Jones, Jon Arcelus, Walter Pierre Bouman, and Emma Haycraft, 'Sport and Transgender People: A Systematic Review of the Literature Relating to Sport Participation and Competitive Sport Policies', *Sports Medicine* 47(4) (2016). For a critique of this study, see note 61.

power of a trans child or teenager seeing a trans athlete on the top step of the Olympic podium. In a way, it would be inspiring.[51]

Liew's account, in which women's sport acts as a vehicle for trans representation, faces two questions. First, how will trans representation be secured if trans athletes are *not* prominent participants? Second, what are the implications for not-trans women if trans women *are* prominent participants?

One feature of inclusion and affirmative action in competitive contexts is that gains for one group are necessarily losses for another. Competitions are a zero-sum game. On the basic anti-sexism argument for women's sport, the costs should be borne by men. Men's sport must cede resources and attention to women's sport. Male athletes are denied the ability to beat female athletes. It is appropriate to require men to bear these costs because they enjoy the historic and current advantages of sexism, including greater levels of pay and funding for men's sport. The issue with including trans people in sporting categories that align with their gender identity is that there will likely be unequal gains for trans women as compared with trans men, and unequal costs for not-trans women as compared to not-trans men.

Trans women's success in women's sport is unlikely to be matched by trans men's success in men's sport. This is because trans men are at a double disadvantage in sport. They lack the natural advantage that is gained by having XY chromosomes, high levels of endogenous testosterone, and going through male puberty, meaning that their physiology is likely to make them uncompetitive in men's competitions. Moreover, if trans men are taking testosterone they will thereby gain some sporting advantage, but they will also be guilty of doping and thus ineligible to compete in either men's or women's sport under current rules.[52] Therefore, attempting to secure trans representation through existing men's and women's sport is less likely to work for trans men than trans women.

What of the situation for women and men who are not trans? There are two sorts of success at stake in the anti-sexism argument. Most obvious is success in the competition itself: gaining a place on a sports team, qualifying for a medal, winning a world record, being awarded a sports scholarship. These resources are scarce and so increasing the number of people eligible to

---

[51] Jonathan Liew, 'Why the Arguments Against Trans, Intersex, and DSD Athletes Are Based on Prejudice and Ignorance', *The Independent* (22 February 2019).
[52] For discussion of the comparison between trans women athletes and athletes who take steroids, see John William Devine, 'Gender, Steroids, and Fairness in Sport', *Sport, Ethics, and Philosophy* 13(2) (2019).

compete for them necessarily means that others lose out. In this very direct way, including trans women in women's sport makes it harder for all women to succeed in sport, whether trans or not, because the competition is greater. But this fact is not decisive, because the central point of the anti-sexism argument is to encourage more women and girls to take up sport, an aim which will necessarily increase competition. Exclusion of some cannot be justified merely so as to make things easier for others.

The second sort of success at stake in the anti-sexism argument is what we might call symbolic success: the inspiration and encouragement that is given to women and girls by the existence and visibility of women athlete role models. This symbolic success need not be a zero-sum game. It is possible for a trans woman athlete to inspire not-trans women and girls, and for a not-trans woman athlete to inspire trans women and girls. Indeed, it is possible for an elite athlete to inspire others regardless of both sex and gender. Nonetheless, there is a risk that the specific inspiration provided by role models with whom one can easily identify will be lost. If trans women compete in women's sport but are invisible within it, either because they are not identifiable as trans or because they are not significantly successful, then women's sport will not provide inspirational gains to trans people *as such*, as Liew hopes.

On the other hand, if trans women are visibly successful in sport then their success may inspire other trans women; however, it may demoralise women and girls who are not trans, particularly if it seems to them that sporting competition is unfair because of trans women's participation.[53] Now, the mere fact that some woman athlete does not inspire all women is not normatively significant. Audiences may not identify with successful athletes for all sorts of reasons, some of which are suspect. The anti-sexism argument does not imply that all feelings of non-identification must be given moral weight. But it does require that women's sport seems on balance to help women and girls, and to allow them to participate fairly.

For the anti-sexism argument to succeed as a justification for women's sport it must show two things. First, it must show that women are a salient social group, and one that suffers discrimination. This should not be

---

[53] Connecticut is one of seventeen states that allow trans athletes to compete in high school women's sport. Two trans girls, Terry Miller and Andraya Yearwood, have caused controversy by successive sprinting wins, including setting a new girls' indoor record for the fifty-five metre dash. One competitor, Selina Soule, spoke out against the inclusion of trans girls in girls' sport. "We all know the outcome of the race before it even starts; it's demoralizing," she said. "I fully support and am happy for these athletes for being true to themselves. They should have the right to express themselves in school, but athletics have always had extra rules to keep the competition fair" (Steve Warren, '"It's Not Equal": Parents Outraged as Transgender Athletes Continue to Dominate Girls' Sporting Events', CBN News (25 February 2019)).

contentious. Second, it must show that having separate competitions for women is a useful way of inspiring that group, and a useful counter to prevailing and historical sexism. If women's sport or some way of organising it exacerbate sexism, perhaps by strengthening the view that women are inferior or upholding sexist norms, the anti-sexism argument cautions against it. For example, the anti-sexism argument implies that it may not be a good idea to sex-segregate sport for pre-pubescent children, because anti-sexism gains might be better achieved by de-emphasising sex and gender norms at that age.

The anti-sexism argument is not decisive on whether trans women should be included in women's sport. It depends on empirical facts about whether trans women's participation undermines anti-sexism goals for women and girls in general, which in turn may depend on the perceived fairness of trans-inclusive competitions, and on the sporting context. It also raises concerns about a lack of equity between trans women and trans men, and between women's sport and men's sport. But if the anti-sexism argument is applied to trans people as a group, recognising them as oppressed in their own right, it justifies separate trans sport. Trans sport would guarantee that trans athletes would win, providing inspiration, role models, and self-respect to trans people. Trans sport could also be valuable in enabling trans people, especially trans men, to participate in competitive sport without falling foul of anti-doping rules, since in trans sport those rules could be designed around the specific medical needs and drug regimes of trans people.

Some feminists, and some trans people, have argued for 'third spaces' such as trans sport.[54] But many trans advocates are unhappy with this proposal, arguing that there remains a pressing need to include trans people in sport according to their gender identity.[55] The next argument explains why.

10.3 The Identity Argument

The identity argument starts with the claim that 'trans women are women'.[56] Call this the *identity claim*. The identity claim is understood as a claim of

---

[54] Holly Lawford-Smith in debate with Sophie-Grace Chappell, 'Transgender: A Dialogue', *Aeon* (15 November 2018), available at https://aeon.co/essays/transgender-identities-a-conversation-between-two-philosophers.

[55] For example, see Rachel McKinnon and Aryn Conrad, 'Including Trans Athletes in Sport' presented in lecture form (13 January 2018), available at https://www.youtube.com/watch?v=EImjVGxAlv4; Devine, 'Gender, Steroids, and Fairness in Sport'.

[56] One prominent advocate of the identity argument is Veronica Ivy, previously writing and speaking as Rachel McKinnon. See, for example, the lecture cited in the previous note. See also Lori Ewing, 'Canadian Cyclist Kristen Worley Blazes Own Trail as Voice for Gender Diversity in Sport', *The Globe and Mail* (19 April 2019).

equivalence: literally rather than rhetorically true.[57] The strength of the identity claim is important to understand. Many people are willing to accept that trans women are women in certain circumstances and for certain purposes: for example, that they should be treated as women in social interactions.[58] But the identity argument rests on the far stronger claim that there are *no relevant differences* between trans women and not-trans women. Increasingly, trans advocates take this identity claim to its logical limit, arguing that trans women are women not only socially but also biologically; that is, some argue that trans women are not only *women* but also *female*.[59]

If the identity claim is true, and trans women are women in any and all senses (or, more moderately, in all senses relevant to sport), it then follows that denying trans women access to women's sport is wrong because it involves denying the identity claim.[60] It is not acceptable from this perspective to say that trans women are not women in some sense relevant to sport, such as biologically. Crucially, the identity argument includes the idea that it is a very serious wrong to deny a trans woman's womanhood, meaning that it can outweigh fair competition or anti-sexism considerations.

The identity argument is not yet a justification for women's sport. According to a weak form of the identity argument trans women ought to be included in women's sport *if women's sport exists*. The weak identity argument gives no

---

[57] See Stonewall, 'The Truth About Trans', Stonewall (2022), available at https://www.stonewall.org.uk/truth-about-trans; Carol Hay, 'Who Counts as A Woman?', *The New York Times* (1 April 2019); Jennifer Wright, 'Transgender Women are Women. Transgender Men are Men', *Harper's Bazaar* (23 October 2018); Lori Watson, 'The Woman Question', *Transgender Studies Quarterly* 3(1–2) (2016).

[58] See Kathleen Stock, 'Changing the Concept of "Woman" Will Cause Unintended Harms', *The Economist* (6 July 2018); Holly Lawford-Smith's contribution to her and Sophie-Grace Chappell, 'Transgender: A Dialogue'; Kristina Harrison, 'A System of Gender Self-Identification Would Put Women at Risk', *The Economist* (3 July 2018); Sophie-Grace Chappell, 'Trans Women/Men and Adoptive Parents: An Analogy', APA blog (20 July 2018), available at https://blog.apaonline.org/2018/07/20/trans-women-men-and-adoptive-parents-an-analogy/.

[59] Mary Gregory, a trans woman powerlifter, had 'male anatomy' and had been taking hormone treatments for less than a year when she competed in a women's weightlifting event. "When Mary Gregory filled out the registration form to compete in a local weightlifting event, she checked the box that read 'female' without hesitation. 'I mean, that's my gender,' she said. 'I didn't even think about it. That's who I am'" (Rick Maese, 'Stripped of Women's Records, Transgender Powerlifter Asks, "Where Do We Draw the Line?"', *The Washington Post* (16 May 2019)). @PinkNews received 1,401 likes for its tweet 'Trans women are women. So trans women's bodies are women's bodies. So trans women's penises are women's penises', Pink News, Twitter (19 February 2019), originally at https://twitter.com/PinkNews/status/1098005566268547072 but no longer online. See also Julia Serano, 'Debunking "Trans Women Are Not Women" Arguments', *Medium* (27 June 2017), available at https://juliaserano.medium.com/debunking-trans-women-are-not-women-arguments-85fd5ab0e19c.

[60] For example, Athlete Ally state, 'Trans women are women, period.... Trans women athletes aren't looking to take over women's sport. They are women, and want to compete in the sport they love, just as any other athlete would' (Joanna Hoffman, 'Athlete Ally: Navratilova's Statements Transphobic and Counter to our Work, Vision and Values' (*Athlete Ally*, 19 February 2019), available at https://www.athleteally.org/navratilovas-statements-transphobic-counter-to-our-work-vision/).

reason why women's sport should exist. It is therefore not a justification for women's sport, and could be responded to by the abolition of women's sport.

Advocates of the identity claim who also support the existence of women's sport must therefore explain why. Some might defend the identity claim while also defending women's sport on fair competition or anti-sexism grounds. They must show that the moral weight of the identity claim is sufficient to *override* fair competition and anti-sexism concerns but does not fatally undermine them. The most promising strategy for doing this is with an empirical claim that few trans women will enter women's sport, that they will not enjoy disproportionate success, and that their participation will therefore not adversely affect women who are not trans.[61] A solution must also be found for supporting trans men.

Some make the very strong argument that trans women should be included in women's sport because they are women (the identity claim) but also because trans women have *no* natural advantage (denial of the fair competition argument).[62] This approach relies on claiming either that testosterone-suppressing hormone therapy removes any natural advantage gained from going through male puberty, or that there is no natural advantage from male puberty in the first place. Both claims are implausible, but they are also unnecessary if the identity claim is accepted. Natural advantages *within* categories or major social groups do not undermine fair competition. Tall

---

[61] For example, this argument is put forward by trans athlete and philosopher Rachel McKinnon in Alistair Magowan, 'Transgender Women in Sport: Are They Really a "Threat" to Female Sport?', BBC Sport (18 December 2018) and by trans athlete Cait Glasson, 'Sport Is a Human Right – So Let Trans Women Compete', *Arc* (1 June 2019), available at https://medium.com/arc-digital/sport-is-a-human-right-so-let-trans-women-compete-2db252184fe.

[62] For example, Athlete Ally insist, "There is no evidence at all that the average trans woman is any bigger, stronger, or faster than the average cisgender woman", in Hoffman, 'Athlete Ally: Navratilova's Statements Transphobic'.

An influential academic review of the literature on trans people in sport by academics at Loughborough University (full citation in note 49) concluded: 'Currently, there is no direct or consistent research suggesting transgender female individuals (or male individuals) have an athletic advantage at any stage of their transition (e.g. cross-sex hormones, gender-confirming surgery) and, therefore, competitive sport policies that place restrictions on transgender people need to be considered and potentially revised.' However, that literature review surveyed only eight papers, seven of which were qualitative rather than quantitative research: interviews with tiny numbers of trans people about their experiences in sport. Only one of the papers considered in the literature review was an experimental study of natural sex-based advantage. That study found that trans women *retained* muscular advantage even after hormone therapy: trans women's "muscle mass remained significantly greater than in transgender male individuals (assigned female at birth) who had not been prescribed cross-sex hormone treatment". In other words, the only study in the review that actually systematically assessed the question of natural advantage found that trans women retain "significant" natural advantage over other women. The authors' claim that there is a lack of evidence for athletic advantage is thus a result of their own survey methods rather than the science itself.

women do not need to be excluded from women's basketball teams; men with naturally high testosterone are not prevented from competing in men's sport. If trans women are women in all senses relevant to sport (the identity claim) then they should be included in women's sport, *even if* they have a residual natural advantage over not-trans women.

The identity claim thus implies that trans women should not have to take testosterone-suppressing drugs, or even that anti-doping rules might appropriately prevent them from doing so: if trans women are women then any natural advantage they have is immaterial to fairness, just as it is not unfair if a basketball player is unusually tall. The problem then is how to justify the continued existence of women's sport.

The fair competition argument is the most widely accepted argument for women's sport, but the identity claim undermines it. If sport is segregated by gender identity not biological sex then the group 'men' no longer has a sex-based natural advantage over the group 'women', and so women's sport is no longer justified by fair competition. Note that this point does not depend on the number of trans people participating in sport. The problem is *not* one of shifting average performance levels. Instead, the point is that if the identity claim is true then the category 'woman' ceases to be a biological or physiological category. If there is no physiology or body type that is necessary for being a woman then one can no longer say that women *as a group* have a category-based physiological disadvantage as compared to men. Any difference in performance between the two groups will be arbitrary, a matter of the average performance of the individuals who happen to populate each group at any one time, and not the result of physiological differences that constitute the groups as such.

Advocates of the identity claim who support women's sport thus need an alternative justification. One option is the strong form of the identity argument, which uses women's sport as a mechanism for affirming trans women's identity. It justifies trans women's participation in women's sport via the identity claim, as the weak version does, but then justifies the persistence of women's sport as a means of reinforcing the identity claim. In other words: trans-inclusive women's sport is justified as a way of showing that trans women are women.

John Gleaves and Tim Lehrbach make a version of the strong identity argument. They argue that "gender-segregated sport is best understood and defended as a tool for writing *gendered* meaningful narratives. Gender-segregated sport is a way for women and men to 'tell stories about themselves to themselves' that invoke and further inform their gendered identities."[63] On their account, gendered narratives can be about individual participants or about gender more generally: "all people can enjoy men telling gendered stories about masculinity and women telling gendered stories of femininity."[64]

The strong identity argument is most plausible when used in some limited contexts, to justify the existence of some gender-segregated activities. It would then be compatible with the existence of other sports segregated by sex not gender, and others not segregated at all. As an analogy, consider the Commonwealth Games, in which only countries who are part of the Commonwealth may compete. These Games plausibly strengthen solidarity and identity within the Commonwealth, and may be justified for that reason. However, that does not mean that it would be desirable to segregate *all* sports according to Commonwealth membership. Sometimes other national or trans-national identities should be emphasised instead, for example membership of the European Union; sometimes nationality should be irrelevant to sport so as to strengthen cosmopolitan feelings of common humanity.

There are three problems with the strong identity argument. The first is how to adjudicate between conflicting gendered narratives. Gender is an essentially contested concept, as the debate about trans inclusion in women's sport shows, and this contestation is at least in part about how we should properly understand gender categories for sporting purposes. So the strong identity argument does not tell us what to do when conceptions of gender conflict. These conflicting gendered narratives will also likely depend on the conception of sport that is held by the various participants: athletes and audiences who understand sport as being primarily about fair competition will see gender in sport as being fundamentally physiological, in contrast to those athletes and audiences who understand gender as primarily or solely a matter of self-identification. Whose gender narrative should be prioritised, and why?

The second problem is that the strong identity argument is not really about *sport*. It uses sport as a means to individuals' personal gender narratives: the fact that an activity is sport is far less important than that it is gendered. And so the strong identity argument provides no reason for confining gender-based segregation to sport. Indeed, it would legitimise extending gender segregation well beyond sport. If women's sport were justified only because it could affirm the identity of trans women, or allow them to tell their gendered

---

[63] Gleaves and Lehrbach, 'Beyond Fairness', p. 319.
[64] Gleaves and Lehrbach, 'Beyond Fairness', p. 320.

narratives, then other gender-based segregation that could serve the same end would also be justified: separate lectures for women, separate churches for women, separate exams for women, gender-segregated seating, and so on. Sport seems a weak place to start, given fair competition and anti-sexism concerns.

The third problem lies with the very idea of gendered narratives. Gender as a system has been profoundly oppressive: to everyone, but particularly to women, to lesbians and gays, and to gender non-conforming people (these categories overlap, of course, creating multiple intersections of gender-based oppression). Feminists, egalitarians, non-binary people, and some trans people argue against increasing society's gendered aspects, seeing them as repressive and harmful. The idea of increasing society's gendered spaces may well seem dystopian rather than liberatory.

The strong version of the identity argument for women's sport is therefore in tension with the logic of the anti-sexism argument. The strong identity argument requires continued distinction and segregation between women and men, whereas the anti-sexism argument seeks to dismantle such segregation. The ultimate goal of the anti-sexism argument is to make itself redundant: advocates of this argument want discrimination against women to stop and thus for anti-sexist measures eventually to become unnecessary or even unjustified.

The strong identity argument thus works best when used in some contexts: as *one* way of organising sports, rather than as *the* way of organising sports. It succeeds as a way of increasing solidarity in certain communities, as a mechanism for allowing some individuals to affirm their own particular gendered narratives and identities. But the existence of diverse conceptions of gender, as well as concerns of fairness and anti-sexism, suggests that there should be a diversity of sporting contexts: some open to all regardless of sex or gender, some sex-segregated according to the fair competition argument, and some gender-segregated according to multiple understandings of gender.

10.4 Conclusion

This chapter has reviewed three possible justifications for the existence of women's sport. First, fair competition always plays a role in sport. For some athletes and philosophers of sport, fair competition is the ultimate sporting virtue, and it is plausible to think that *unfair* competition is a serious sporting deficit.[65] The fair competition argument provides a strong justification for

---

[65] Jon Pike, 'Why "Meaningful Competition" is not fair competition' in Journal of the Philosophy of Sport Vol. 50 No. 1 (2023).

women's sport and implies excluding trans women unless they meet physiological criteria. The relevant data for this argument is the best sports science about the sex-based biological features that provide sporting advantage.

However, fair competition is not the only relevant value. In some cases, a broader conception of equality of opportunity means that it may be appropriate to subordinate fair competition to other considerations. The fair competition argument is most significant, and its prioritisation most apt, in sporting contexts focused on rewarding winners and allocating resources, such as professional competitions, elite athletics, and scholarship awards. It may become less important in contexts in which participation or solidarity are the dominant goals, such as leisure sports or casual school sports—although safety should still be secured, and considerations of fairness always remain relevant.

The anti-sexism argument provides a compelling justification for women's sport and could be applied, with appropriate changes, to the creation of sport reserved for trans people. It is compatible with trans women's inclusion in women's sport, but only if that inclusion does not undermine the anti-sexist goals of women's sport—a question that is largely empirical. In some cases, anti-sexism is harmed if trans women participate in women's sport, for instance if trans women win prizes or take spaces in teams in a way that undermines fair competition and discourages women from participating. In other cases, trans women's inclusion in women's sport helps anti-sexism goals by undermining the gender binary or disrupting gendered expectations. In another set of contexts, anti-sexism goals will be better served without women's sport, for example if women's sport perpetuates a perception of female inferiority. In these cases it might be preferable from an anti-sexism perspective to introduce mixed-sex sport, ideally alongside measures to ensure fair competition. For example, teams could be made up of a set number of women and men, or sports could be adapted in ways that mitigate sex-based advantage.

Intersecting the fair competition and anti-sexism arguments is the identity argument. The weak form states that trans women should be included in women's sport if it exists, even if fair competition or anti-sexism are undermined, because trans women are women and so their exclusion is a wrong in itself. However, the weak identity argument cannot show why women's sport should exist at all and is compatible with, or even strengthens, arguments for its abolition.

The strong version of the identity argument sees women's sport as a mechanism for affirming gender identity. This is a niche position. It is best suited to sporting contexts in which fair competition is less important than centring trans inclusion and affirming trans identities. There may be contexts where this prioritisation is appropriate, such as at Pride events or other community- and solidarity-building occasions. However, the argument is not confined to the sporting context; in that context, it must counter objections from fair competition and anti-sexism.

Freedom and Equality: Essays on Liberalism and Feminism. Clare Chambers, Oxford University Press.
© Clare Chambers 2024. DOI: 10.1093/9780191919480.003.0011

PART V
CHOICE

11
Choice and Female Genital Cosmetic Surgery

I google 'labiaplasty'.[1] The first result is for 'MYA Labiaplasty – Join 1000s of Happy Patients'. Clicking on the link, I learn:

Labiaplasty is MYA's most popular vaginal surgery and makes up 97% of procedures. For women after a quick procedure with effective results that will boost confidence and comfort, labia surgery is an excellent choice which forms part of our popular designer vagina surgery options.[2]

Back to Google. The next result is 'Labiaplasty Surgery – 40 min Out Patient Procedure'. This link takes me to The Surrey Park Clinic, who opens with:

Many women feel discomfort or embarrassment if the labia minora (the inner lips of the vulva) are enlarged. This can affect quality of life by causing worry about what clothes to wear and intimate relationships. Sometimes the fear of negative comments can affect the confidence of women and can even put them off starting a relationship. Surgical correction is a very straightforward procedure and the impact it can have on a woman's self esteem can be profound.[3]

---

[1] This chapter was originally published in Sarah M. Creighton and Lih-Mei Liao (eds), *Female Genital Cosmetic Surgery: Solution to What Problem?* (Cambridge: Cambridge University Press, 2019).
  Labiaplasty is not the only form of female genital cosmetic surgery (FGCS) but it is the most common and well-known. The Royal College of Obstetricians and Gynaecologists defines FGCS as follows: "FGCS refers to non-medically indicated cosmetic surgical procedures which change the structure and appearance of the healthy external genitalia of women, or internally in the case of vaginal tightening. This definition includes the most common procedure, labiaplasty, as well as others, such as hymenoplasty and vaginoplasty, also known as vaginal reconstruction and vaginal rejuvenation." See Royal College of Obstetricians and Gynaecologists Ethics Committee, *Ethical Opinion Paper: Ethical Considerations in Relation to Female Genital Cosmetic Surgery (FGCS)* (2013), p. 1.
[2] MYA Cosmetic Surgery, 'Labiaplasty', *MYA Cosmetic Surgery* (2022), available at https://www.mya.co.uk/procedures/body-procedures/labiaplasty#dqD4VLXScbtZAKUk.97.
[3] The Surrey Park Clinic, 'Labial Reduction', The Surrey Park Clinic (25 October 2017), originally at http://www.thesurreyparkclinic.co.uk/treatments/surgical-procedures-in-clinic/labial-reduction/?gclid=CM6_5frxodYCFcsW0wodp-sBhg but no longer online.

The third entry is for the Medico Beauty Clinic. Their information about labiaplasty also signals the normality of the procedure:

> Many women dislike the large protuberant appearance of their labia minora and wish to change their appearance. In some instances, women with large labia can experience pain during intercourse, or feel discomfort during everyday activities or when wearing tight-fitting clothing. Others may feel unattractive, or wish to enhance their sexual experiences by removing some of the skin that covers the clitoris.[4]

In each case, the providers of female genital cosmetic surgery (FGCS) signal the advantages of the procedure and give a number of reasons why it might be a desirable *choice*. Most prominently they cite the negative feelings that FGCS can remove: fear, worry, embarrassment, pain, discomfort, dislike, and feeling unattractive. Less prominent are the positives: boosting confidence and comfort, creating a 'designer vagina', increasing self-esteem, and enhancing sexual experiences. But the overall message, as MYA clinic concludes, is that "labia surgery is an excellent choice."

In this chapter, I challenge the idea that an appeal to choice exonerates FGCS. My argument proceeds in five stages. First, I consider the normative role that choice plays in liberal society and philosophy. Second, I note that UK law does not treat choice as adequate for accessing FGCS. Third, I consider the relationship between choice and the concept of normality. Fourth, I consider choice in the context of cosmetic surgery generally, and analyse the distinctive features of FGCS. Fifth, I consider the policy implications of my analysis.

11.1 Choice as a Normative Transformer

In liberal democracies there is a general presumption that individuals should be left free to choose whether to participate in practices that affect only themselves. One key proponent of this idea is philosopher John Stuart Mill, who writes: "The only part of the conduct of any one, for which he is amenable to society, is that which concerns others. In the part which merely concerns

---

[4] Medico Beauty and IVF, 'Labiaplasty', *Medico Beauty Clinic* (25 October 2017), originally at https://medicobeautyclinic.com/aesthetic-surgery/procedures/labiaplasty-labia-minora-reduction but no longer online.

himself, his independence is, of right, absolute. Over himself, over his own body and mind, the individual is sovereign."[5] This presumption of individual freedom of choice suggests the permissibility of cosmetic surgery. If people want to undergo surgical procedures to alter their body they should be free to do so, and it would be beyond the scope of the liberal state to forbid them. Prioritising choice thus supports the legalisation of all forms of surgical modification on everyone capable of exercising choice.

Mill is by no means the only philosopher to prioritise choice. Many political philosophers use choice as what I call a 'normative transformer'. A normative transformer is something that changes an outcome from normatively unacceptable to normatively acceptable.[6] Choice may be used to normatively transform an inequality from one that is unjust to one that is just. For example, some theorists argue that it is not an injustice if women are paid less than men so long as the reason for this pay gap is that women and men choose different jobs.[7] Or choice may be used to normatively transform a criminal assault into a legal act, as when rape is criminalised but even violent consensual sex is not, or when boxing is legal but GBH is not, or when consensual surgery is legal but non-consensual surgery is not. Choice may also be used as a normative transformer in a more general sense, indicating that a practice should be immune from moral or other judgment if it has been chosen. One example is the idea that feminism means not criticising women's choices, even if they choose to participate in gendered practices such as cosmetic surgery, wearing makeup, or removing body hair.[8]

Although Mill's principle of individual choice is extremely influential and generally accepted, it is usually thought to admit of exceptions. Most states do engage in some forms of paternalism, forbidding their citizens from making some choices for their own good. For example, it is common for even liberal states to require the use of seatbelts in cars or to forbid the use of dangerous recreational drugs. Paternalism in cases such as these may be justified by the seriousness of the harm that paternalism prevents, or by factors that undermine the extent to which individuals can really be said to be choosing freely.

---

[5] John Stuart Mill, *Utilitarianism, On Liberty, Considerations on Representative Government* (London: Everyman 1993 [1859]), p. 78.
[6] Clare Chambers, *Sex, Culture, and Justice: The Limits of Choice* (University Park, PA: Penn State University Press, 2008).
[7] Brian Barry, *Culture and Equality: An Egalitarian Critique of Multiculturalism* (Cambridge: Polity Press, 2001).
[8] Clare Chambers, 'Judging Women: 25 Years Further Toward a Feminist Theory of the State', Chapter 12 in this volume.

Elsewhere I have argued that there are grounds for state interference in individuals' choices if those choices are characterised by both *disadvantage* and *influence*.[9] The disadvantage factor applies if a choice disadvantages those who make it, relative to those who choose differently. This disadvantage may be physical or mental, such as the risk of bodily harm or emotional distress. Alternatively, the disadvantage may be economic or status-based, such as suffering financial cost or being regarded as inferior. The disadvantage factor alerts us to the fact that if people make choices that disadvantage them there is a prima facie reason to be concerned about that choice.

The second factor that prevents choice from properly acting as a normative transformer is the influence factor. The influence factor applies if there are identifiable pressures on the choosers to choose as they do. This influence may be direct and interpersonal, such as when a man repeatedly tells his partner that she would look better with breast implants. Or it may be more diffuse and capillary, such as when women live in a general climate of focus on their appearance, with magazines, adverts, and beauty products combining to portray an image of the ideal or even acceptable woman.[10] If the influence factor is present then we should question whether the choice really is a free one.

The influence factor on its own is not enough to render a choice suspect. All choices are made within a social context. All of us form our preferences and shape our choices around the norms and expectations of that context. But where there are identifiable ways in which people are pressured to make choices that disadvantage them—that is, where the influence and disadvantage factors are combined—there is reason to think that choice should not be regarded as a normative transformer. Choices that are characterised by disadvantage and influence are cases of injustice, and may justify intervention from the state and other actors.

11.2 FGCS and the Law

UK law does not grant women permission to undergo genital procedures whenever they choose. The practice of genital cutting known legally as female genital mutilation (FGM) is outlawed, even for consenting adult women, by

---

[9] Chambers, *Sex, Culture, and Justice*.
[10] Chambers, *Sex, Culture, and Justice*; Nuffield Council on Bioethics, *Cosmetic Procedures: Ethical Issues* (London: Nuffield Council on Bioethics, 2017); Fiona MacCallum and Heather Widdows, 'Altered Images: Understanding the Influence of Unrealistic Images and Beauty Aspirations', *Health Care Analysis* 26 (2018).

the UK Female Genital Mutilation Act 2003. The Act states: "It is a criminal offence to excise, infibulate or otherwise mutilate the whole or any part of a girl's labia majora, labia minora or clitoris."

The primary justification for this prohibition is that FGM is a harmful, dangerous, and destructive practice that paradigmatically involves the mutilation of young girls against their will in order to satisfy sexist cultural norms. Women and girls therefore need to be protected from the practice by legal prohibition. This case for outlawing FGM performed on girls under the age of eighteen can follow a simple choice-based logic, without invoking the analysis I offered above. Children are commonly not thought to have the ability to give consent on serious, irreversible, risky procedures such as FGM, for two reasons. First, children lack the mental capacity to gather adequate information and assess it rationally. Second, children lack the ability to withhold consent because they are under the effective control of parents and other adults, meaning that they are likely to cave into pressure to consent to procedures they do not want, or that they are vulnerable to sanction and abuse if they do manage to resist. So, an approach that prioritises choice is consistent with the illegality of FGM for children. Indeed, an approach of this kind has implications that extend far beyond the existing legal framework, since it implies the impermissibility of many cultural and cosmetic practices routinely performed on children such as male circumcision, otoplasty, and cosmetic dentistry.[11]

However, while the UK Female Genital Mutilation Act 2003 refers to 'girls', its provisions also apply to adult women. That is to say, the Act explicitly prevents any woman from choosing modification of their genitals without clinical indication. This prohibition includes labiaplasty and other similar procedures, since labiaplasty just is to "excise...part of a girl's labia majora [or] labia minora". Labiaplasty is thus explicitly covered by the definition of procedures that are presumptively illegal under the Female Genital Mutilation Act.[12]

---

[11] The Genital Autonomy movement includes groups that campaign against unnecessary genital cutting of children, whether male, female, or intersex. For a report criticising cosmetic procedures on children and calling for them to be banned outside the context of multidisciplinary healthcare, see Nuffield Council on Bioethics, *Cosmetic Procedures*.

[12] Speaking as Home Secretary, Teresa May stated in 2014 that FGCS is outlawed by the 2003 Act (Roisin O'Connor, 'Designer Vagina Surgery Could Be as Illegal as FGM, Theresa May Warns', *Independent*, 10 December 2014, available at https://www.independent.co.uk/news/uk/politics/designer-vagina-surgery-could-be-as-illegal-as-fgm-theresa-may-warns-9915466.html). Legal firm Mills & Reeve refers to female genital cosmetic surgery as "technically unlawful" (Mills & Reeve LLP, 'The Female Genital Mutilation Act and Its Relation to Female Genital Cosmetic Surgery', *Lexology*, 16 October 2013, available at https://www.lexology.com/library/detail.aspx?g=2afbc225-8ba6-4e83-80 3c-034c070529de). Marge Berer notes that, in the UK, "there is a law against female genital mutilation (FGM) which describes it in the very same terms as the procedure described by the Department of

However, FGCS is widely available in the UK, and openly advertised as we saw at the start of this chapter. This is possible because the Act allows an exception: "no offence is committed by an approved person who performs a surgical operation on a girl which is necessary for her physical or mental health." There are restrictions on what sorts of things count as making surgery "necessary": the Act stipulates "For the purpose of determining whether an operation is necessary for the mental health of a girl it is immaterial whether she or any other person believes that the operation is required as a matter of custom or ritual."[13] However, the guidance notes for the legislation say that procedures that are necessary for mental health can include "cosmetic surgery resulting from the distress caused by a perception of abnormality."[14]

This perception of abnormality does not have to be based on fact; it is legal to operate on genitals that are perfectly normal. For labiaplasty to be legal, all that is needed is that women choosing it should *think* that their labia are abnormal, so that this perception causes them sufficient distress as to constitute (or be portrayed as) a barrier to mental health. The result is that FGM is ruled out absolutely, even if genuinely freely chosen by an adult woman, but labiaplasty is permissible if it can be shown to be "necessary" for the patient's mental health. In practice, FGCS is performed without legal sanction not only on adult women but also on children, meaning that parents are able to authorise FGM on their daughters if it justified by aesthetics but not if it is justified by tradition.

Now, none of the adverts for FGCS described above explicitly refer to mental health, or state that they are able to operate only on patients with a mental health problem. The "distress caused by the perception of abnormality" wording allows women to access FGCS merely on the basis of choice, in practice. But that is not its intention. FGCS is legal in the UK only if the distress is sufficient to constitute diminished mental health. In other words, for FGCS to be legal women have to be suffering. But surgery does not have to be the only way to alleviate their suffering. The Act merely requires that women's distress be caused by the *perception* of abnormality; actual abnormality or pathology are not required. This wording may explain the predominance of negativity in the FGCS providers' marketing material. The joyous "designer vaginas" of MYA are on shakier ground.

Health as labia reduction" (Marge Berer, 'Labia Reduction for Non-Therapeutic Purposes vs Female Genital Mutilation: Contradictions in Law and Practice in Britain', *Reproductive Health Matters* 18(35) (2010), p. 106).

[13] Crown Prosecution Service, 'Female Genital Mutilation Legal Guidance', available at http://www.cps.gov.uk/legal/d_to_g/female_genital_mutilation/#a01.

[14] Explanatory Note to UK Female Genital Mutilation Act 2003, available at https://www.legislation.gov.uk/ukpga/2003/31/contents.

11.3 Choosing to Be Normal

The desire to be normal is a crucial part of many patients' decisions to undergo cosmetic surgery, whatever the procedure.[15] Commercial cosmetic surgery providers therefore benefit from encouraging prospective patients to think that their natural bodies are abnormal. They are ably assisted in this marketing strategy by a vast industry of beauty, fashion, media including social media, and pornography, all problematising the normal body—particularly if that body is female.[16] For FGCS providers the stakes are particularly high: the legality of the practice depends on women thinking they are abnormal, and on that perception causing them significant distress. Since a vast range in the size of the labia minora is in fact perfectly normal,[17] and the vast majority of women seeking FGCS fall within normal range,[18] commercial providers of FGCS rely on women being falsely persuaded that there is something wrong with their genitals.

As we saw at the start of this chapter, FGCS providers often market the procedure by encouraging prospective patients to think that there is something wrong with their genitals. The providers refer to the "many women" who are distressed by their labia and highlight the popularity of FGCS. The paradoxical nature of the idea that it could be normal to have abnormal genitals does not matter if all that is needed is a *perception* of abnormality. The providers of FGCS thus present the *surgery* as normal and the natural female *body* as abnormal.

What counts as normal thus becomes a matter of subjective rather than objective fact; a matter of social norms rather than anatomical reality. Choosing to be normal is thus about choosing to conform to social norms rather than choosing to rectify clinical abnormality. The choice to be normal, like choice more generally, is *socially constructed*.

---

[15] Chambers, *Sex, Culture, and Justice*; Nuffield Council on Bioethics, *Cosmetic Procedures*; Kathy Davis, *Reshaping the Female Body: The Dilemma of Plastic Surgery* (London: Routledge, 1995).

[16] Royal College of Obstetricians and Gynaecologists Ethics Committee, *Ethical Opinion Paper*; Gemma Sharp, Marika Tiggemann, and Julie Mattiske, 'Factors That Influence the Decision to Undergo Labiaplasty: Media, Relationships, and Psychological Well-Being', *Aesthetic Surgery Journal* 36(4) (2016).

[17] Jamie McCartney, 'The Great Wall of Vagina', *The Great Wall of Vagina*, 2022, available at http://www.greatwallofvagina.co.uk/home.

[18] Royal College of Obstetricians and Gynaecologists Ethics Committee, *Ethical Opinion Paper*; Rebecca G. Rogers, 'Most Women Who Undergo Labiaplasty Have Normal Anatomy; We Should Not Perform Labiaplasty', *American Journal of Obstetrics and Gynecology* 211(3) (2014); N. S. Crouch, R. Deans, L. Michala, L.-M. Liao, and S. M. Creighton, 'Clinical Characteristics of Well Women Seeking Labial Reduction Surgery: A Prospective Study', *BJOG: An International Journal of Obstetrics & Gynaecology* 118(12) (2011).

Social construction can be divided into two phenomena: the social construction of *options* and the social construction of *preferences*. Consider first the social construction of options. In order for an option to be chosen that option has to be available as an option in the social context of the chooser. Labiaplasty and other forms of FCGS are relatively new procedures and their popularity has risen rapidly.[19] Women can only choose to undergo FGCS if that procedure exists, technologically, and if surgeons are willing to perform it. The choice to undergo FGCS also requires GPs who are willing to recommend it and refer patients for it, or marketing to make commercial patients aware of it. It may also require the availability of finance for the procedure. All these factors are social: they depend on a particular social context in which FGCS is normalised and the natural vulva is pathologised.

The second aspect of the social construction of choice is the social construction of preferences. Women have to want FGCS if they are to choose it. In order for FGCS to be appealing then the benefits it offers or the problems it alleviates have to seem more important than the costs it entails. The costs of FGCS are fairly straightforward: they include financial cost; the time spent in consultations, surgery, and recovery; the pain caused by the procedure; the loss of highly sensitive erogenous tissue; and the risk of complications. The choice to undergo FGCS may involve an active attempt to minimise those costs—or, more precisely, to minimise patients' awareness of the extent of those costs. There is evidence that cosmetic surgery providers do not always adequately ensure that their patients are fully aware of the costs and risks of procedures and that, even where they do, the message does not always get across.[20] Certainly the value of intact labia is not emphasised. As an example, note the idea in the Medico Beauty Clinic website extract, quoted above, that labiaplasty removes skin that gets in the way of sexual pleasure, rather than that skin itself being a source of sexual pleasure.

But the choice to undergo FGCS also requires a sense that the procedure will be beneficial. For cosmetic surgery in general, and for FGCS in particular, the advantages are fundamentally socially constructed. FGCS has increased in popularity extremely rapidly, coinciding with the increased ubiquity of pornography, viewed online, and an accompanying strong norm that women

---

[19] Nuffield Council on Bioethics, *Cosmetic Procedures*; Crouch et al., 'Clinical Characteristics'.

[20] Nuffield Council on Bioethics, *Cosmetic Procedures*. Lauren Greenfield's photographs of women undergoing and recovering from cosmetic surgery allude to the fact that patients would rather not think about what the surgery actually involves. See Lauren Greenfield, *Generation Wealth* (London: Phaidon Press, 2017).

should remove all their pubic hair.[21] These very recent changes provide the social conditions for the perception of labial abnormality. It is not surprising that women develop the sense that their labia are abnormal only in social conditions in which it is easy to view many other women's labia, in pornography and unobscured by pubic hair.[22]

What is normal thus depends not simply on what is numerically common, or on what is non-pathological, or on what is well-functioning. The labia of women who choose labiaplasty are most likely neither uncommonly large, nor pathological, nor dysfunctional. What is normal is culturally relative. It may also depend on ignorance of the true prevalence of a particular trait, an ignorance that may be accidental or cultivated. Women *can* be concerned about the normality of their genitals without viewing pornography or adverts for cosmetic surgery: if a body part is deeply private, even taboo, then the lack of exemplars of that part can lead to ignorance, anxiety, and doubt. In these contexts, increased visibility leads to a broadening of the concept of normality. But the increased visibility of vulvas in ever-more-accessible pornography (including the vulvas of women who have had FGCS), the norm for complete pubic hair removal, and the intensive marketing of FGCS all lead to a narrowing of the concept of normal.[23] Self-esteem, confidence, and embarrassment are all emotions that relate intricately to social context.

Even those benefits of FGCS that relate to physical experience are socially dependent. Some women have FGCS to avoid the pain of tight trousers.[24] If

---

[21] Sharp et al., 'Factors That Influence the Decision to Undergo Labiaplasty'; Vanessa R. Schick, Brandi N. Rima, and Sarah K. Calabrese, 'Evulvalution: The Portrayal of Women's External Genitalia and Physique across Time and the Current Barbie Doll Ideals', *The Journal of Sex Research* 48(1) (2011); Virginia Braun, 'Female Genital Cosmetic Surgery: A Critical Review of Current Knowledge and Contemporary Debates', *Journal of Women's Health* 19(7) (2010).

[22] C. Moran and C. Lee, 'What's Normal? Influencing Women's Perceptions of Normal Genitalia: An Experiment Involving Exposure to Modified and Nonmodified Images', *BJOG: An International Journal of Obstetrics & Gynaecology* 121(6) (2014); Calida Howarth, Jenny Hayes, Magdalena Simonis, and Meredith Temple-Smith, '"Everything's Neatly Tucked Away": Young Women's Views on Desirable Vulval Anatomy', *Culture, Health & Sexuality* 18(12) (2016).

[23] For example, Gemma Sharp, Julie Mattiske, and Kirstin I. Vale found that the majority of women who had undergone labiaplasty in their study "tended to compare their own labial appearance with images they considered to be more valid representations. This was primarily the 'before' labiaplasty photographs on surgeons' websites. [One participant said:] 'I'd seen a lot on the internet like lots of "before" ones [photos]...I thought, oh my god, all these women are getting it done [labiaplasty]. Mine was still worse than theirs'" (Gemma Sharp, Julie Mattiske, and Kirsten I. Vale, 'Motivations, Expectations, and Experiences of Labiaplasty: A Qualitative Study', *Aesthetic Surgery Journal* 36(8) (2016)). A study by Howarth et al. found that "All participants identified a photograph of hairless female genitals with no visible labia minora as the societal 'ideal'" (Howarth et al., '"Everything's Neatly Tucked Away"').

[24] This reason was given by a respondent to the Nuffield Council on Bioethics Online Questionnaire (Nuffield Council on Bioethics, *Cosmetic Procedures: Ethical Issues—Online Questionnaire: Summary* (Nuffield Council on Bioethics, June 2017), available at https://www.nuffieldbioethics.org/wp-content/uploads/Survey-Monkey-Questionnaire-analysis.pdf, p. 8). Some researchers report that physical

tight trousers were not fashionable for women this problem would probably not arise. Once it does arise, the decision to solve it with FGCS rather than different clothes makes sense only in a social context in which women are encouraged to think of their bodies as naturally deficient, and in which women routinely are expected to place their appearance above their comfort and choose how they *look* over how they *feel* or how they *are*.

The fact that the benefits of FGCS are socially constructed does not mean that they are not real. That is to say, given the social costs and benefits of the practice in any particular context, it may be rational for an individual woman to choose FGCS. For her, it may be a surgery that makes sense to choose. But to make an assessment of the normative features of that choice—to know whether choice is properly treated as a normative transformer in this case—the question is: what social conditions have to be in place to make this choice a rational or comprehensible one?

In the case of FGCS, the social conditions required to make sense of the practice include the social value denied to women, the primacy attributed to women's appearance, the centring of the pornographic, the subordination of women's erogenous experience to their sexual confidence, the commercialisation of low self-esteem, and the conscious and cynical manipulation of anxiety. FGCS will be chosen by women if they are encouraged to see deformity rather than beauty, and to seek solace in the scalpel.

11.4 The Disadvantage and Influence of FGCS

FGCS is a choice that is characterised by both the influence and the disadvantage factors. It is a choice that women face significant pressure to make. This pressure comes from the images of vulvas they see in pornography and on the Internet, or from comments by men who have seen cosmetically modified vulvas in pornography, or from the normalisation of the practice when it is discussed in the mainstream media, or from parents who are concerned that their daughters' genitals look different, or from GPs and other healthcare providers who recommend FGCS as a 'solution' for genitals that are perfectly normal, or from the marketing materials offered by FGCS providers.[25]

---

reasons for FGCS are given as a way of disguising the fact that the primary motivation is cosmetic (Sharp et al., 'Motivations, Expectations, and Experiences of Labiaplasty').

[25] All these reasons were cited by respondents to the Nuffield Council on Bioethics Working Party on Cosmetic Procedures call for evidence (Nuffield Council on Bioethics, *Cosmetic Procedures*).

But it is also a choice that puts women at a disadvantage, compared to men or to women who do not undergo genital surgery. All surgery brings with it pain and the risk of side effects, and requires recovery time. FGCS is no exception, and also involves the removal of highly sensitive irreplaceable erogenous tissue. Like all commercial surgery, FGCS involves financial cost. All these costs of FGCS can be regarded as disadvantages that accrue to those who choose it.

But FGCS involves another disadvantage, which is that it requires the woman who chooses it to think that her natural body is deformed or deficient, and that surgery is required to rectify it. All cosmetic surgery may involve this feature. But FGCS is distinctive in that it requires the perception of one's own abnormality as a condition of legality of the surgery, and so it is a perception that providers are bound to encourage. It is a severe disadvantage of status to be encouraged to believe that one's own body is abnormal.

Moreover, since FGCS applies only to women it reinforces gender inequality more generally. Cosmetic surgery on men's genitals is far less common; many of the major commercial cosmetic surgery providers do not offer it. The fact that many women use images from pornography to identify the 'ideal' vulva also connects that ideal to the idea that women's bodies are primarily for the sexual satisfaction of men and should be appraised as a thing to be looked at by others rather than experienced from within.

FGCS is a procedure that can be chosen. But since the choice to undergo FGCS is affected by both the disadvantage and influence factors, it is a choice that should be questioned. The mere fact of choice is not enough to exonerate FGCS.

11.5 Policy Implications

Choices that are affected by the influence and disadvantage factors are unjust. Remedying that injustice can take several forms. It can involve reducing the costs of the practice, so that it no longer brings disadvantage. It can involve reducing the influence to undergo the practice, so that it can more honestly be described as an autonomous choice. It can involve regulating, restricting, or even banning the practice, so that it may not be chosen. These different methods can also be employed in combination.

Which option is best suited to FGCS? The disadvantage resulting from the practice is of three kinds: physical, financial, and psychosocial. The physical costs of FGCS cannot easily be reduced. Reputable cosmetic surgeons should already be practising safely and professionally, striving to provide the best possible clinical outcome. The commercial cosmetic surgery industry is plagued with poor practice and inadequate regulation, and there is room for improvement there, but little government appetite for reform.[26] But no matter how skilled the surgeon, FGCS necessarily involves the removal of sensitive, healthy tissue, and brings risks of side effects and complications.

Attempting to solve the problem by reducing the financial costs is not promising. There is no commercial incentive to make the procedure cheaper, and provision on the NHS would normalise the procedure further while taking resources from other areas. And normalising the procedure means increasing the psychosocial costs, in the sense of entrenching the social norm that many women have socially abnormal labia that should be corrected surgically.

The more promising strategy is thus to reduce the pressure to undergo FGCS. This can be done in a variety of ways involving a variety of actors. It can include education in schools and elsewhere—for girls and for boys—about the normal variety of bodily anatomy. It can involve educational programmes that seek to raise girls' and women's self-esteem and body confidence, and to reduce appearance-related anxiety. It can involve media, marketing, and advertising changes, either voluntarily or through regulators. The report *Cosmetic Procedures: Ethical Issues* contains many recommendations for reducing the pressures that lead women to demand cosmetic procedures of all kinds, and these apply to FGCS too.[27]

What of legal measures that tackle the practice directly? The most obvious and simple legal move would be for the UK government to enforce the provisions of the UK Female Genital Mutilation Act 2003 and prosecute those who perform FGCS when it is not necessary for the patient's physical or mental health. This measure would have the advantage of restricting provision of FGCS but would have the disadvantage of encouraging both patients and practitioners to think of their natural labia as causing serious distress. Instead, then, the guidance notes of the legislation should be revised so that they no longer include the asymmetry between FGM sought for 'cultural' reasons and FGM sought for cosmetic reasons. Since cosmetic considerations just are cultural considerations there is no philosophical basis for this distinction,[28] and it renders the law racist by effectively outlawing a practice for women from FGM-practising communities but not others.

---

[26] Nuffield Council on Bioethics, *Cosmetic Procedures*.
[27] Nuffield Council on Bioethics, *Cosmetic Procedures*.
[28] Clare Chambers, *Intact: A Defence of the Unmodified Body* (London: Allen Lane, 2022).

This move, interpreting the Act as ruling out both FGM and FGCS, was in fact the intention of Parliamentarians. For example, Baroness Rendell said in the House of Lords in 2003:

> When the 1985 Act was passed, it was not Parliament's intention to place any statutory limitation on operations that are genuinely necessary; nor is it the intention of the Bill. Such operations may well be rare, but they do occur, and it would be wrong to criminalise them. But unless they are medically necessary, any operations involving mutilation of the external genitalia—"designer vagina" or otherwise—are already illegal if carried out by a person in the UK. Under the Bill's provisions, they will also be illegal if carried out by a UK national or permanent UK resident outside the UK. That will be the case even if the woman on whom the operation is carried out consents.[29]

In the House of Commons debate Sandra Gidley MP made a similar point, and also pointed to the dangers of racism:

> That observation brings me to an important point, because my understanding of the Bill is that it will make cosmetic surgery to the vaginal area illegal. I have no problem with that, but the issue should definitely be explored in Committee. It is regarded as a choice issue. I do not think that we should make any exceptions for white women expressing a choice for fashion reasons, when we are stopping black women, who may have no choice, perhaps because they are children, from having surgery. We must ensure that no distinction is drawn between these two practices, and it should all be part of the same message.[30]

One issue raised by my analysis is whether FGCS is distinct from other forms of cosmetic surgery. In many ways it is not. All cosmetic surgery takes place in a social context, one that is highly gendered and that encourages women in particular to place high value on their appearance. There is an epidemic of appearance-related anxiety among young people and particularly

---

[29] Baroness Rendell of Babergh, speaking in the debate on the Female Genital Mutilation Bill in the House of Lords (Hansard HL Deb 12 September 2003 vol. 652 cc635-53, available at https://api.parliament.uk/historic-hansard/lords/2003/sep/12/female-genital-mutilation-bill).

[30] Sandra Gidley (Romsey), speaking in the debate on the Female Genital Mutilation Bill in the House of Commons (Hansard HC Deb 21 March 2003 vol. 401 cc1188-208, available at http://hansard.millbanksystems.com/commons/2003/mar/21/female-genital-mutilation-bill).

young women,[31] and all cosmetic surgery both contributes towards that anxiety and is made popular by it.[32] There is reason, in other words, to be concerned about cosmetic procedures in general, to enact stronger regulation on the industry itself, and to work to counter the emphasis on body image that is found in media of all sorts and exacerbated by social media, marketing, and youth culture.

But FGCS does have some distinctive features. In general, cosmetic procedures are more commonly performed on women than on men, but cosmetic genital surgery is still largely a procedure for women only. For example, major commercial providers such as Harley Medical Group and MYA Cosmetic Surgery offer cosmetic surgery on female genitals but not male ones, despite there being no legal restrictions on male genital cosmetic surgery. Moreover, the rapid and recent rise in popularity of FGCS, and the fact that the female genitals are otherwise so private and seldom seen, suggests its association with deeply sexist norms, connected with pornography and the fashion for complete hair removal. Several researchers note that the 'ideal' vulva that labiaplasty creates resembles that of a prepubescent girl.[33] Finally, its connections to FGM mean that a consistent approach to eradicating FGM must necessarily tackle FGCS as well.

I have argued elsewhere that there are grounds for much greater restrictions on cosmetic procedures in general. As a brief summary, there are grounds for regulating or even prohibiting those cosmetic procedures that are both seriously risky or harmful, and strongly connected to sex inequality.[34] And there are grounds for restricting *all* cosmetic procedures performed on children.[35] Objections to FGCS are not, therefore, unique to it. Nonetheless, FGCS remains a clear case of a practice that cannot be exonerated merely by an appeal to individual choice.

Freedom and Equality: Essays on Liberalism and Feminism. Clare Chambers, Oxford University Press.
© Clare Chambers 2024. DOI: 10.1093/9780191919480.003.0012

---

[31] Nichola Rumsey and Diana Harcourt (eds), *Oxford Handbook of Psychology of Appearance* (Oxford: Oxford University Press, 2012).
[32] Nuffield Council on Bioethics, *Cosmetic Procedures*.
[33] Rogers, 'Most Women Who Undergo Labiaplasty Have Normal Anatomy'; Schick et al., 'Evulvaluation'.
[34] Chambers, *Sex, Culture, and Justice*.
[35] Nuffield Council on Bioethics, *Cosmetic Procedures*.

12

Judging Women

25 Years Further *Toward a Feminist Theory of the State*

One cannot really overstate the importance of Catharine MacKinnon's work.[1] Its philosophical, political, and legal impact is huge. MacKinnon's legal work has improved the standing of women around the world, and her political philosophy is both a defining statement of feminism and a challenge that every theorist, feminist or not, must face.

Re-reading *Toward a Feminist Theory of the State* for the purposes of this special edition, I kept wanting to interrupt my reading. Every page, every paragraph, has a claim that I want to tell people about and discuss with them. So many of the sentences in the book are quotable: are in themselves

    complete,
        enlightening,
            provocative,
                so obviously right,
                    so fraught with difficulty,
                        at the same time the final word on one question,
                            and the thrown-down gauntlet on another.

Reading MacKinnon, in other words, is an exhilarating ride through philosophy and politics, a journey in which it is impossible to sit still and in which it is no use wearing a seat belt. There is going to be challenge, there is going to be danger, and there is, above all, going to be an emergency stop: a point at which everything sharply judders to a halt, silence descends, and you whisper

---

[1] This chapter was originally published in *Feminist Philosophy Quarterly* 3(2) (2017) as part of a symposium, edited by Lori Watson, to mark 25 years since the publication of Catharine A. MacKinnon, *Toward a Feminist Theory of the State* (Cambridge, MA: Harvard University Press, 1989). I am extremely grateful to Catharine MacKinnon for comments on an earlier draft, and to Lori Watson for extensive comments and invaluable guidance.

to yourself, *Can that really be true?* and, at the very same moment, *How could I not have seen this before?*

It is tempting, then, simply to proceed by quoting a selection of my favourite MacKinnon sentences. But I will resist that temptation and try to make a more sustained contribution.

One philosophical question with which I have been grappling for some time, and which *Toward a Feminist Theory of the State* tackles head-on, is how much significance we should grant to the fact of *choice*. The role of choice is problematic within the context of social construction generally and gender inequality specifically. In liberal theory, choice is treated as what I call a 'normative transformer', something that transforms a prima facie unjust inequality into a just one. I have argued that the fact of social construction prevents choice from playing this role.[2] We cannot assess the justice of a situation by reference to a choice that is itself, at the most profound and sometimes unconscious level, a result of that situation. This over-reliance on individual choice is a central problem for liberalism.

MacKinnon's work provides foundations for this critique. She writes that liberalism's "aggregation of freely-acting persons is replaced, in radical feminism, with a complex political determinism. Women and women's actions are complex responses to conditions they did not make or control; they are contextualized and situated. Yet their responses contextualize and situate the actions of others."[3] And, as she puts it in the chapter on consciousness-raising:

> The instrument of social perception is created by the social process by which women are controlled. But this apparent paradox is not a solipsistic circle or a subjectivist retreat. Realizing that women largely recognize themselves in sex-stereotyped terms, really do feel the needs they have been encouraged to feel, do feel fulfilled in the expected ways, often actually choose what has been prescribed, makes possible the realization that women at the same time do not recognize themselves in, do not feel, and have not chosen this place.[4]

MacKinnon here draws our attention to our situation as simultaneously recipients and transmitters of norms, victims and agents of oppression, conformists and rebels, apologists and malcontents. We are all trying to find ways to negotiate the social demands on us: how to fit in while remaining individual, how

---

[2] Clare Chambers, *Sex, Culture, and Justice: The Limits of Choice* (University Park, PA: Penn State University Press, 2008).

[3] MacKinnon, *Toward a Feminist Theory of the State*, pp. 46–7.

[4] MacKinnon, *Toward a Feminist Theory of the State*, p. 102.

to distinguish those preferences that are authentic from those that are distorted, how to live in a way that both we and others can accept, how to find a place that is both unique and human. Western liberal culture requires both conformity and individuality. The individual is exalted as a unit of analysis even while being expected to fit into recognisable social tropes. Culture urges us to assimilate and to differentiate, with predictably unpredictable effects.

An issue that arises from this analysis is the question of *judgment*. One feature of contemporary popular feminism is the rejection of judgment: the idea that it is somehow a violation of feminist ideals, and perhaps a general moral failing, to assess other women's behaviour and find it wanting. One encounters this conviction in discussions of parenting (which usually means mothering—the critique of judgment is most pointed in matters of breast- versus bottle-feeding), activism, domestic violence, *Fifty Shades of Grey-* inspired sadomasochism, beauty practices, and cultural difference.[5]

Consider some examples from the popular media. Jemma Wayne writes in the *Huffington Post* that the phenomenon of women who judge other women's parenting styles on online forums is "just as dangerous [a] trend undermining feminist values" as the sexualisation of children.[6] The risk, according to Wayne, is great: "with every wagging finger we are unravelling the victories of feminism." Jessica Wakeman in *The Frisky* writes that, for feminists, "there are a lot of areas where I think being judgmental is inappropriate, particularly when it comes to people's private choices that do not hurt anyone else and do not affect you."[7] Kiara Imani Williams, in the *Huffington Post* again, writes "You Know What Is Worse Than Donald Trump? Other Judgmental Women."[8]

Michaele Ferguson interprets critiques of judgment like these as part of choice feminism: the idea that feminism means respecting women's choices, whatever they may be, on the assumption that choice is the measure of freedom. Ferguson proposes that choice feminism is, inter alia, an attempt to neutralise three criticisms of (non-choice) feminism: it is too radical, it is exclusionary, and it is judgmental. Her analysis is that "feminism will

---

[5] Linda Zerilli discusses the question of whether feminists may judge those from other cultures in Linda Zerilli, 'Toward a Feminist Theory of Judgment', *Signs* 34(2) (2009), a title that invokes MacKinnon even though MacKinnon is not mentioned at all.

[6] Jemma Wayne, 'Mother Judgement: How Women are Undermining Modern Feminism', *Huffington Post* (4 April 2013), available at http://www.huffingtonpost.co.uk/jemma-wayne/women-undermining-modern-feminism_b_3006752.html.

[7] Jessica Wakeman, 'The Soapbox: On Feminism and Judging Other Women', *The Frisky* (19 June 2012), originally at http://www.thefrisky.com/2012-06-19/the-soapbox-on-feminism-judging-other-women/ but no longer online.

[8] Kiara Imani Williams, 'You Know What Is Worse Than Donald Trump? Other Judgmental Women', *Huffington Post* (18 August 2015), available at http://www.huffingtonpost.com/kiara-imani-williams/you-know-whats-worse-for-_b_8002682.html.

continue to provoke these three criticisms so long as it is deeply critical of existing institutions, or aims in any way to speak for or about a collectivity (such as women), or claims that the personal is political."[9] Ferguson suggests that, while it is both understandable and in some sense laudable for feminism to wish to "make feminism appeal to as many people as possible",[10] feminists should not shy away from judgment. "Without making judgments," she writes, "politics becomes vacuous relativism: we have no reason to prefer one course of action over another.... Political freedom requires that we make the best judgments that we can, without knowing for certain that the judgments we make are correct."[11]

Ferguson's analysis is helpful and perceptive. I agree with Ferguson that the concern to avoid judgment is a key feature of choice feminism; I agree with her (as I argued in Chambers, *Sex, Culture, and Justice*) that the focus on choice as the measure of freedom is ultimately not compatible with feminism as a political and philosophical project; and I agree with her that one must "resist the temptation to reject judgment".[12] Ferguson suggests that the concern to avoid judgment is a concern to make people *like* feminism and feminists. This may well be part of the matter. In addition, as evident in the examples from popular feminism given earlier, judgment is often rejected not just for being unappealing but for being in some way *normatively wrong*. In the first part of this chapter, I want to question this normative critique of judgment. Why is avoiding judgment seen by some as a central feminist concern?

Feminists might well worry about judgment that is directed *to* women, since one aspect of feminism is the need to listen to women rather than denigrate or silence them. But in wider patriarchal society, judgment is demonised when it is done *by* women. Women are not supposed to judge, not supposed to think themselves sufficiently qualified to have opinions or criticise others, particularly if those others are men. This is part of the reason why women in the public eye are subject to such vile online abuse,[13] particularly if they write about issues on which men feel themselves to be particular experts (which is to say: all issues). A woman is not supposed to have a controversial opinion (which is to say: any opinion). I don't think I've ever heard a man berate

---

[9] Michaele L. Ferguson, 'Choice Feminism and the Fear of Politics', *Perspectives on Politics* 8(1) (2010), p. 249.
[10] Ferguson, 'Choice Feminism', p. 250.   [11] Ferguson, 'Choice Feminism', p. 251.
[12] Ferguson, 'Choice Feminism', p. 252.
[13] See Becky Gardiner, Mahana Mansfield, Ian Anderson, Josh Hodler, Daan Louter, and Monica Ulmanu, 'The Dark Side of Guardian Comments', *The Guardian* (12 April 2016), available at https://www.theguardian.com/technology/2016/apr/12/the-dark-side-of-guardian-comments; and David Grimer, 'Men Read Mean Tweets About Female Sportswriters, and Are Shocked at How Dark It Gets', *Adweek* (26 April 2016), available at http://www.adweek.com/adfreak/men-read-mean-tweets-about-female-sportswriters-and-are-shocked-how-dark-it-gets-171064/.

himself or another man for being too judgmental. As MacKinnon might say, judgment is a male method.

I get the sense, from discussions with my students and others, that readers of MacKinnon often feel that *they* are being judged. I certainly feel that way. That feeling is, for me, part of the exhilaration that I referred to earlier: there is exoneration in MacKinnon's work, and explanation, and excitement, but there is also judgment. I think one of the reasons I have to keep stopping when I read her work is that I keep needing to introspect: *Do I do that?* And: *Should I stop?*

MacKinnon addresses this point directly:

> Feminism aspires to represent the experience of all women as women see it, yet criticizes antifeminism and misogyny, including by women. Not all women agree with the feminist account of women's situation, nor do all feminists agree with any single rendition of feminism. Authority of interpretation—here, the claim to speak for all women—is always fraught because authority is the issue male method is intended to settle. Consider the accounts of their own experience given by right-wing women and lesbian sadomasochists. How can male supremacy be diminishing to women when women embrace and defend their place in it? How can dominance and submission violate women when women eroticize it? Now what is women's point of view?[14]

For MacKinnon, the answer is neither subjectivism nor determinism. We must not assume that women are free, having what MacKinnon calls "considerable latitude to make or choose the meanings of their situation".[15] No individual is the final arbiter of the meaning of her action. But we must also not rely on an idea of false consciousness, according to which 'they' are hopelessly distorted by their situatedness while 'we' somehow remain magically isolated, perspectivally pure. Instead, the project of feminism "is to uncover and claim as valid the experience of women, the major content of which is the devalidation of women's experience".[16]

Judgment is thus particularly fraught. There is a serious qualm about claiming to speak for all women, to assert the authority of the authentic female voice. This qualm is both to be respected (after all, who are we to judge?) and rejected (why shouldn't we judge?!).

---

[14] MacKinnon, *Toward a Feminist Theory of the State*, p. 115.
[15] MacKinnon, *Toward a Feminist Theory of the State*, p. 116.
[16] MacKinnon, *Toward a Feminist Theory of the State*, p. 116.

Now, one sense in which it may be right to refrain from judgment is that it is not helpful to judge people for doing something that they cannot avoid doing, or for responding rationally to circumstances they cannot control. And so it does not make sense to judge women for participating in beauty practices in a world that judges them always and everywhere on their appearance; or to judge women for staying with abusive partners in a world that fails to protect them from violence whether they stay or whether they leave; or to judge women for enjoying sadomasochism in a world that teaches them from childhood that they will find romantic and sexual fulfilment in submission; or to judge women for participating in pornography and prostitution in a world that suggests that doing so is empowering, lucrative, and freely chosen, even at the same time as women and children by the thousands are forced into prostitution and pornography by poverty, violence, and powerlessness. Of course, we can praise the bravery and feminism of those who reject beauty practices, or who leave violent men, or who resist pornography, or who escape prostitution. But these things are difficult, often crushingly so, and feminism cannot write off women who do not achieve them.

Still, it surely must make sense to judge men who participate in and benefit from these practices. It is hard to envisage a feminism that lets abusive men off the hook. Although both women and men would be better off in a world without patriarchy, freed from the oppression of gender inequality, it is unpalatable to extend sympathy or even empathy to those men who actively brutalise, use, and exploit women and children. Perhaps the fact that abusive men *benefit*, in terms of power, wealth, and sexual gratification, makes them proper subjects of judgment. But then can we judge those women who deftly manipulate the position patriarchy gives them, those who find status and success, of sorts, through maintaining practices of gender inequality?

MacKinnon studiously avoids making what she terms a moral critique:

> This book is not a moral tract. It is not about right and wrong or what I think is good or bad to do. It is about what *is*, the meaning of what is, and the way what is, is enforced.[17]

Earlier I mentioned that *Toward a Feminist Theory of the State* is full of compelling arguments. In the interests of balance, let me state that the claim just quoted may be my least favourite part of the book. I dislike it for two reasons. First, I find it unconvincing. The idea that there can be a non-moral statement

---

[17] MacKinnon, *Toward a Feminist Theory of the State*, p. xii.

of what *is* seems to me to contradict MacKinnon's claims that "there is no Archimedean point",[18] no "purely ontological category", no "category of 'being' free of social perception".[19] The recognition that there is no authentic subject-position outside of social construction means that we must rely on normative critique if we are to have critique at all. We cannot be against rape and pornography because women *are not* objects for the sexual pleasure of men because, under patriarchy, they *are*. We cannot be against sexual harassment and female poverty because women *are not* unequal to men because, under patriarchy, they *are*. We are against rape and pornography and sexual harassment and gendered poverty because women *should not be* unequal to men, *should not be* objects for the sexual pleasure of men, and because it is *bad* to treat them in that way. And if it is bad to treat women in this way then it is bad for men to do it, and it is bad for women to do it, and it is at least sometimes right to judge those who do it.

The second reason why I dislike MacKinnon's refusal to declare "what I think is good or bad to do" is that I find it unsatisfying. I would like to know what she thinks is good or bad to do, not just in the legal struggles in which she is such a crucial participant, but in general. In our personal lives, in that space where the political is truly to be found, where *what is* is most significant and most entrenched, what should we do?

Now one answer that MacKinnon gives to this question is consciousness-raising, which she terms feminism's method. MacKinnon argues that consciousness-raising, namely systematic collective attention paid to the realities of women's everyday and personal lives, is politically significant because it is in our personal and everyday lives that male dominance is most located. As she puts it:

> Daily social actions are seen to cooperate with and conform to a principle. They are not random, natural, socially neutral, or without meaning beyond themselves. They are not freely willed, but they are actions nonetheless. From seeing that such actions have meaning for maintaining and constantly reaffirming the structure of male supremacy at their expense, women can come to see the possibility, even the necessity, of acting differently.[20]

This account of consciousness-raising offers hope. It tells us that there can be feminist activism in every action and every location: when thinking, when

---

[18] MacKinnon, *Toward a Feminist Theory of the State*, p. 117.
[19] MacKinnon, *Toward a Feminist Theory of the State*, p. 119.
[20] MacKinnon, *Toward a Feminist Theory of the State*, p. 101.

reading, when caring, when working, when living. We can do these things in an unconscious, habitual way, in a way that conforms to our social context with its explicit and implicit patriarchy. Or we can attempt to do these things in a more conscious way, in a way that is at least aware of, and ideally does something to subvert, gender inequality.

* * *

In the current political climate, one area of women's experience that has become profoundly invalidated relates to the question of who counts as a woman and thus what counts as women's experience. The question "What is a woman?" is a question that MacKinnon identifies as "implicit in feminism".[21] Her answer is developed in chapter 3 of *Toward a Feminist Theory of the State*. In this discussion, the distinction between moral judgment and political critique comes once again to the foreground.

MacKinnon notes that feminists have given a variety of answers to the question of what counts as a woman. She identifies two extremes. At one extreme, there is feminism in which womanhood is "almost purely biological, in which women are defined by female biology".[22] At the other, there is feminism that sees the category as "almost purely social, in which women are defined by their social treatment".[23] MacKinnon does not explicitly say where she stands on or outside this continuum, but we can draw some inferences about her view.

The first thing to note is that any feminist account must reject the association between women and inferiority, if it is to count as feminist at all. So any feminist account of womanness based on biology derives its feminism, on MacKinnon's analysis, from one of two places. Female biology might be seen as the source or cause of women's subordination. Alternatively, female biology might be seen as the terrain or subject-matter of contestation. MacKinnon certainly rejects the first option and seems to endorse the second.

MacKinnon rejects the idea that biology is 'the source' of women's subordination, an idea that she attributes to feminists such as Simone de Beauvoir and Susan Brownmiller.[24] MacKinnon argues that de Beauvoir sees childbirth and motherhood as necessarily natural functions involving no project, failing to realise that motherhood has no "universal invariant significance".[25]

---

[21] MacKinnon, *Toward a Feminist Theory of the State*, p. 54.
[22] MacKinnon, *Toward a Feminist Theory of the State*, p. 54.
[23] MacKinnon, *Toward a Feminist Theory of the State*, p. 54.
[24] MacKinnon, *Toward a Feminist Theory of the State*, p. 55.
[25] MacKinnon, *Toward a Feminist Theory of the State*, p. 58.

Similarly, MacKinnon critiques Brownmiller's claim that the difference between male and female genitals is what makes rape possible. This claim relies on seeing the penis as in some sense necessarily active with the vagina passive; coitus is thus an act of penetration that can be performed aggressively. MacKinnon notes that the mere fact of genital biology cannot do the work needed for Brownmiller's account, since it would be equally biologically possible for women to "lurk in bushes and forcibly engulf men".[26] We might think that this image is somewhat over-optimistic about women's ability forcibly to procure an erection or proceed with coitus regardless, but MacKinnon's general point is correct: rape and sexual assault do not necessarily involve what Brownmiller calls the "locking together" of penis and vagina, even when men attack women, and so the fact that women do not sexually assault men with anything like the frequency or ferocity that men attack women cannot be explained by their lacking a phallus. The existence of penises does not explain rape and sexual assault, and sexual assault does not require a penis or even a phallic object.

In the social context of women's subordination, to be sexually attacked is to be attacked by or as if by a penis. The penis itself is not an aggressive organ. It becomes one only when accompanied with physical strength, brute force, intimidation, or humiliation. But any of these features could, in a different social context, accompany sexual assault by or as if by vagina. MacKinnon demonstrates this alternate social possibility with her use of the language of engulfment. It is society, not biology, that determines that we do not fear aggressive vaginal engulfment (or smothering, flattening, compressing, devouring, the tropes of the *vagina dentata* that have been used by women to assert power and discourage rape[27]). Rape is explained by doctrines of masculinity and male supremacy, not the existence of penises. These doctrines portray the penis as a powerful instrument of dominance but they do not make it so. To paraphrase Andrea Dworkin, have you ever wondered why women do not frequently rape men? It's not because there's a shortage of dildos.[28]

Viewed in this way, Brownmiller's and de Beauvoir's accounts of biology as the cause of subordination are question-begging. They assert that biology

---

[26] MacKinnon, *Toward a Feminist Theory of the State*, p. 56.
[27] Catherine Blackledge, *The Story of V: Opening Pandora's Box* (London: Orion Books, 2003), pp. 190–4.
[28] I am paraphrasing Dworkin's speech to the Midwest Regional Conference of the National Organization for Changing Men: "I came here today because I don't believe that rape is inevitable or natural. If I did, I would have no reason to be here. If I did, my political practice would be different than it is. Have you ever wondered why we are not just in armed combat against you? It's not because there's a shortage of kitchen knives in this country" (Andrea Dworkin, *Letters from a War Zone* (London: Secker & Warburg, 1988), pp. 169–70).

causes social subordination, but in fact biology subordinates only if it is socially interpreted as subordinating. As MacKinnon puts it, "Social and political inequality begins indifferent to sameness and difference. Differences are inequality's post hoc excuse, its conclusory artefact, its outcome presented as its origin."[29]

Brownmiller's and de Beauvoir's accounts may be question-begging, but what makes them feminist is their insistence on applying normative critique to biology and nature. Feminism along these lines encourages a sharp line between nature and nurture, biology and culture: nature may make something possible or even likely, but it does not make it *right*. Normative critique, *judgment*, is crucial here. Brownmiller wants to recognise and prosecute rape as an illegitimate attack; de Beauvoir wants to free women from the fetish of motherhood that stifles their active creativity.

MacKinnon rejects these feminisms insofar as they are based on a normative critique of a biological reality perceived as autonomously, albeit not inevitably, producing subordination. These feminisms, which she identifies with liberalism, "construe evidence of women's subordination as evidence of women's difference, elevating the body of women's oppression to the level of a universal, a category beyond history".[30]

What we are left with is the idea that "women's biology is part of the terrain on which a struggle for dominance is acted out";[31] or, as she puts it earlier in the book, "A theory is feminist to the extent it is persuaded that women have been unjustly unequal to men because of the social meaning of their bodies."[32] But this, of course, returns us to the question we started with—what is a woman? Which bodies, and which bodily features, have had the social meaning that counts as legitimating inferiority? Again we are returned to the biology/culture divide. MacKinnon highlights various answers within feminism without directly identifying which, if any, she endorses:

> What, really, is a woman? Most feminists implicitly assume that biological femaleness is a sufficient index and bond because of what society makes of it: a woman is who lives in a female body. Others locate what women have in common within a shared reality of common treatment as a sex: a woman is who has been treated as one. A few define a woman as one who thinks of herself, or identifies, as one. Most consider women's condition to be a

---

[29] MacKinnon, *Toward a Feminist Theory of the State*, p. 218.
[30] MacKinnon, *Toward a Feminist Theory of the State*, p. 59.
[31] MacKinnon, *Toward a Feminist Theory of the State*, p. 54.
[32] MacKinnon, *Toward a Feminist Theory of the State*, p. 37.

descriptive fact of sex inequality: no woman escapes the meaning of being a woman within a social system that defines one according to gender, and most do. Women's diversity is included in this definition, rather than undercutting it. Once sameness and difference are supplanted by a substantive analysis of position and interest, women become defined politically: since no woman is unaffected by whatever creates and destroys women as such, no woman is without stake in women's situation.[33]

MacKinnon seems to be rejecting the first three options, or at least highlighting their incompleteness,[34] and endorsing the fourth. If that is right, then, for her, being a woman is not merely living in a female body, or merely being treated as a woman, or merely identifying as a woman. Instead—or perhaps additionally—MacKinnon seems to endorse the idea that "no woman escapes the meaning of being a woman within a social system that defines one according to gender." Woman becomes a political category, and one with deep ontological significance: "no woman is unaffected by whatever creates and destroys women as such."

We can get a handle on this idea by considering the concept of (biological) essentialism. This idea has two main components. First, it invokes the idea that there is something about women's biology that determines their social position. Second, it invokes the idea of commonalities between women: that women exist 'as women', in the sense of having some experiences that transcend other significant differences such as race and class. MacKinnon strongly defends the second idea, as discussed below. We have already seen that MacKinnon rejects the first idea, that biology determines women's social position. This rejection continues in *Women's Lives, Men's Laws*:

> While treating women as if they are a biological group is not necessarily easy to avoid, to say that a biologically determinist theory of gender is not very feminist is not very controversial. Contemporary feminism begins by resisting biology as destiny. If women's bodies determine women's inferior social status, the possibilities for sex equality are pretty limited. On this simplest level, one cannot be essentialist and feminist at the same time.[35]

---

[33] MacKinnon, *Toward a Feminist Theory of the State*, p. 38.
[34] For the argument that woman is a 'cluster concept', requiring resemblance rather than identity between its members, see Natalie Stoljar, 'Essence, Identity, and the Concept of Woman', *Philosophical Topics* 23(2) (1995).
[35] Catharine A. MacKinnon, *Women's Lives, Men's Laws* (Cambridge, MA: Harvard University Press, 2005), p. 86.

However, this first dimension of essentialism actually disguises two contrasting claims. While it is not true that biology *actually* explains or justifies women's oppression, it is true that biology is often *used socially* to explain or justify the oppression of women. Consider the claim that 'women are subordinated because women can get pregnant'. As a description of *social* reality, it is true. The fact or assumption that women and not men can become pregnant does lead to their subordination in many ways: it contributes to them being paid less, promoted less, and hired less than men; it allows women to be controlled through restrictions on the availability of birth control and abortion; and it can be a contributory factor in women's vulnerability to domestic violence. But this does not mean that the fact of pregnancy necessarily or essentially explains women's subjection. A feminist society would not use women's propensity to pregnancy in these ways. As a statement of *essential* reality, 'women are subordinated because women can get pregnant' is false.

Feminists and anti-feminists do not always expressly distinguish these meanings, which can lead to confusion. Feminism is in part the simultaneous *realisation of* and *resistance to* the fact that women's bodies are used to subject them. We need to be careful to distinguish feminist identification of a social reality with an anti-feminist identification of an essential reality. MacKinnon herself makes this distinction clearly and emphatically, but it is often missed by critics of feminism in general and of her work in particular.

For MacKinnon, it is the truth of the identification of social reality that explains the truth of the second aspect of essentialism: the idea of commonality between women. This idea of commonality between women can be understood in different ways. One answer to the question of what it is that women share 'as women' is that they share some biological feature. On this account, women share the experience of having female bodies, and female bodies have a variety of uniquely female experiences such as menstruation, gestation, childbirth, and breastfeeding. Many feminists[36] insist on the significance of these biological experiences both to individual women and to women as a group, and their work is vitally important.

But though these experiences are shared by many women they are not shared by *all* women. Some do not conceive, gestate, birth or breastfeed a child, and some do not menstruate. The fact that some women, including those who have what is commonly called 'female biology'[37] do not share some

---

[36] Iris Marion Young, *On Female Body Experience: "Throwing Like a Girl" and Other Essays* (New York, NY; Oxford: Oxford University Press, 2005) is a notable example.

[37] Many trans people and scholars reject references to 'female biology', since they argue that even sex categories are social and perhaps reject the very idea of a biological element to sex or gender. This is a live question within feminist and trans theory: how does biology itself interact with gender

or any of these experiences means that it is problematic to speak of them as phenomena that unite *all* women. It does not mean that it is problematic to speak of them as phenomena that unite women. A significant part of the ordinary everyday life that feminist consciousness-raising uncovers as significant and as political concerns bodily experiences and the way they are socially treated—for example, the shame and secrecy associated with menstruation, together with the ways that it is used as a trope to undermine women as irrational or unreliable. The demonisation of menstruation is an issue that affects *all* women by affecting their social and political status, regardless of whether they have ever menstruated or will do so in the future.

When feminists including MacKinnon insist on the commonalities between women they predominantly mean that women share the experience of being socially constructed and situated as women. They share the fact that they are treated as inferior to men because they are women. This shared experience applies even if they are also treated as superior to some other women and men because of their position in another dimension of privilege such as race and class.

Sally Haslanger's work seems to question that conclusion. She gives the example of a black man who is treated as a legitimate target for systemic police violence because he is both "Black and *male*", and argues that in cases like these "someone marked for subordination by reference to (assumed) *male* anatomy does not qualify as a woman, but also, in the particular context, is not socially positioned as a man."[38] Haslanger's account suggests that people who would usually be referred to as men on the basis of their "assumed male anatomy" do not necessarily share the experience of being dominant. But, for Haslanger, that experience of being dominant (an experience which accompanies being socially identified as male and thus accorded male privilege) is necessary for someone to be a man. It follows for her that a person with "male anatomy" who is being subordinated is, at that moment at least, not a man—even if common usage and his own gender identity would label him as one. By implication, a person with "female anatomy" in a position of dominance or power is not a woman and does not share the experience of womanness with other women, even those with the same anatomy.

---

experience and identity? I want to leave open the idea that, while sex categories are social, they are not *only* social. For an argument that sex categories have a biological basis at the group level, see Sarah S. Richardson, *Sex Itself: The Search for Male & Female in the Human Genome* (Chicago, IL: University of Chicago Press, 2015).

[38] Sally Haslanger, 'Gender and Race: (What) Are They? (What) Do We Want Them to Be?', *Noûs* 34(1) (2000), p. 41.

The problem with this aspect of Haslanger's analysis is that a black man's subordination as compared to white men is compatible with his dominance as compared to black women. It is thus problematic to say that in this interaction the black man loses his manliness. The dominance of masculinity does not translate into absolute dominance; it intersects with other hierarchies. But in male supremacist society there is no situation in which a woman is socially positioned as superior to a man of her own race, class, and so on. Even a woman in a position of great power, such as German Chancellor Angela Merkel, is subjected to sexist commentary that serves to mark her as other from and inferior to men in equivalent positions, and in some respects to all men.[39]

As MacKinnon writes in *Women's Lives, Men's Laws*:

> [Elizabeth Spelman writes about] "assumptions of feminism." These assumptions include "that women can be talked about 'as women,'... are oppressed 'as women,'... that women's situation can be contrasted to men's" and so on. Professor Spelman is wrong to call these assumptions. They have been hard-won discoveries. Calling feminism "essentialist" in this sense thus misses the point. Analysing women "as women" says nothing about whether an analysis is essentialist. It all depends on *how* you analyse them "as women": on whether what makes a woman be a woman, analytically, is deemed inherent in their bodies or is produced through their socially lived conditions.[40]

So feminism asserts that there is a reality to how women are treated as women, and that this does lead to a commonality between women. Moreover, this shared experience and treatment is often related to assumptions about their biology, to their socially perceived femaleness, in the sense that women's bodies are the terrain on which gender hierarchy is played out. But this is not to say that women's bodies produce their social position. Society dictates that women are to be subjected, and it also dictates that much of this subjection will be played out on their bodies, and it also dictates that women's bodies are to be fraudulently used as the apparent justification for their subjection.

* * *

---

[39] See Mary Dejevsky, 'If Even Merkel Attracts "Black Widow Spider" Sexism, What Hope Is There for the Rest of Us?', *Independent* (25 September 2013), available at http://www.independent.co.uk/voices/comment/if-even-merkel-attracts-black-widow-spider-sexism-what-hope-is-there-for-the-rest-of-us-8839577.html; Ngaire Donaghue, 'Gender Bias: Why Appearance Focus Fuels Sexism in Media', *Conversation* (13 April 2013), available at http://theconversation.com/gender-bias-why-appearance-focus-fuels-sexism-in-media-13325; and Amelia Hill, 'Sexist Stereotypes Dominate Front Pages of British Newspapers, Research Finds', *Guardian* (14 October 2012), available at http://www.theguardian.com/media/2012/oct/14/sexist-stereotypes-front-pages-newspapers.

[40] MacKinnon, *Women's Lives, Men's Laws*, p. 86.

What does this analysis of gender and essentialism mean about what we ought to do? What are the political implications? In a recent interview published on the *TransAdvocate* website, MacKinnon reiterates her distaste for morality and also, in some circumstances, for judgment. For example, she repeats several times her support for trans people and states that there is no need to justify what she calls "individual people's decisions about the social presentation of their bodies".[41] At the same time, she does make normative, political criticisms, some implicit and some more forthright. For example, she states:

> There is no relation between the biology of sex and the meanings socially enforced on it, other than the very real consequences of the social system of sexual politics that does that forcing. This does, of course, raise the question: if it is all a social construction, why intervene in the biology of sex? That is a real political question.[42]

This statement implicitly questions sex-reassignment surgery and other forms of medical intervention such as hormone treatments. The interviewer does not pick up on this point, and so we do not have a close analysis of why this "real political question" has no implications for "individual people's decisions about the social presentation of their bodies". But the comment is not a one-off: MacKinnon also raises questions that do seem directly to affect individual choices, such as when she states: "if [as I agree] 'sex creates oppression,' how does changing from one sex to another oppose that oppression? If 'there is no sex,' how do we describe the gain and stake in changing it?"[43]

The general political-philosophical issue is this: if biology is not the cause of oppression, what is its role, both actual and ideal? What significance should we attach to biology? How do changes in biology affect oppression? And what is the significance of shifting our definition of 'woman'—and, for that matter, of 'man'—so that it does, or does not, require certain biological features?

Viewed in this context, indeed in any recognisably feminist context, "individual people's decisions about the social presentation of their bodies" are *necessarily* political. After all, the personal is political. We cannot act without being at once the product and the producer of social meaning. Trans issues are paradigmatic examples of MacKinnon's claim that "women's biology is

---

[41] Cristan Williams, 'Sex, Gender, and Sexuality: The TransAdvocate Interviews Catharine A. MacKinnon', *TransAdvocate* (2015), available at https://www.transadvocate.com/sex-gender-and-sexuality-the-transadvocate-interviews-catharine-a-mackinnon_n_15037.htm.
[42] Williams, 'Sex, Gender, and Sexuality'.   [43] Williams, 'Sex, Gender, and Sexuality'.

part of the terrain on which a struggle for dominance is acted out."[44] Who counts as a woman? Which privileges does a trans person acquire and which do they lose? Who gets to speak for women or as a woman? If biology does not determine one's gender position, can men speak for women? If men can speak for women, can women speak for women? Can they speak at all?

In the TransAdvocate interview, the main target of MacKinnon's judgment is non-feminist women:

> Having been surrounded by born women who do not identify as women particularly, and reject feminism as having nothing to do with them, it has been inspiring to encounter transwomen who do identify as women, actively oppose violence against women including prostitution (in which those who engage have little choice), and are strong feminists. "Woman" can be, in part, a political identification. To be a woman, one does have to live women's status. Transwomen are living it and, in my experience, bring a valuable perspective on it as well.
>
> I have encountered transwomen with excellent, clear feminist politics. They are quite a contrast to the many privileged women I am often surrounded by who deny that sex discrimination exists or who assert that prostitution is a liberating choice for women. I've encountered transwomen who are prostituting who strongly oppose prostitution, who make clear that they would not be in prostitution if they could be paid to do anything else. And I'm supposed to conclude that the born women who support prostitution are my team?[45]

In these passages, MacKinnon praises feminists and judges non-feminists, with particular judgment implied for "born women" non-feminists, which is surprising. But what strikes me particularly is MacKinnon's praise for people who "identify as women".

Elsewhere MacKinnon is scathing about the focus on identity, describing it as a "shift away from realities of power in the world".[46] Identity, she writes, "is not women's problem. Reality is: a reality of group oppression that exists whether we identify with our group or not."[47] So why should it be praiseworthy to "identify as a woman", or problematic not to?

---

[44] MacKinnon, *Toward a Feminist Theory of the State*, p. 54.
[45] Williams, 'Sex, Gender, and Sexuality'. [46] MacKinnon, *Women's Lives, Men's Laws*, p. 90.
[47] MacKinnon, *Women's Lives, Men's Laws*, p. 90.

It would be implausible to interpret MacKinnon as suggesting that there is anything suspect about a woman not particularly identifying with *femininity*, since nonconformity to feminine practices such as passivity, beauty, and submissiveness has always been a central part of radical feminism. Alternatively, if the category 'woman' is a social category, and if women are socially defined as the sex that is subordinated, then 'identifying as a woman' seems to mean 'identifying as a member of a subordinate group'. But feminists have pointed out that there are many sensible reasons *not* to 'identify as women particularly', if that means identifying with one's position of subordination in a male supremacist world.[48] It is plausible in fact to think of feminism as the claim that one can identify as a woman in the sense of recognising the significance of one's embodied experience and socialisation as female, while rejecting women's subordinate position and thus refusing to identify as a woman in the sense of refusing to 'live women's status'. Feminists recognise that women are treated as subordinates and actively fight for the erasure of this subordination. If the end of male supremacy means the erasure of the social category of woman then it would seem right for feminists not to identify particularly as women, socially; instead, a feminist would identify as a *human* first and foremost, and would identify as a woman only in the sense of recognising the social meaning of her body and socialisation, and feeling solidarity with others whose bodies and socialisation rendered them similarly liable to subordination.

Alternatively, the sense of 'identifying as a woman' that MacKinnon is praising might be synonymous with 'identifying as a feminist'. But that identification has no direct relationship to sex or gender. Feminists can be male or female, gay or straight, masculine or feminine, trans or not. It would be clearer then if MacKinnon were to say that some people are feminist and some are not, regardless of biology or social position, and that it is better to be a feminist.

But the question then raised by MacKinnon becomes: who is on 'my team'? Is it women, defined however they are defined by patriarchy, as a subordinated group, the target of eroticised domination? Or is it feminists, however constituted: those who criticise male supremacy, even if they benefit from it? The notion that all feminists are on the same team seems initially attractive, but it is troubling if the team 'feminists' should somehow be pitted against those women who do not identify as women, or do not identify as feminists, if

---

[48] Rebecca Reilly-Cooper, 'Am I Cisgender?', *More Radical with Age* (2014), originally at https://rebeccarc.com/2014/08/04/am-i-cisgender/ but no longer online.

those are different categories. This image of teams means that women who are complicit with patriarchy are ranked lower than those people who critique it, even if those people are men who also benefit from patriarchy and to whom patriarchy grants the right to act as critic. Yet feminist analysis of male supremacy of the sort we find in *Toward a Feminist Theory of the State* provides us with ample resources to understand the complicity of the oppressed. And the image of opposing teams is also vulnerable to MacKinnon's own critique of the way that liberal feminism focuses on the individual woman and her actions rather than on women as a unified group or class.

One answer to this problem is consciousness-raising as a *collective* practice, as something that women do together. MacKinnon writes:

> If every woman's views are true, regardless of content, how is feminism to criticize the content and process of women's determination, much less change it? Regardless of the weight or place accorded daily life or women's insight, feminist theory probes hidden meanings in ordinariness and proceeds as if the truth of women's condition is accessible to women's collective inquiry. The pursuit of the truth of women's reality is the process of consciousness; the life situation of consciousness, its determination articulated in the minutiae of everyday existence, is what feminist consciousness seeks to be conscious of.[49]

It is thus the collective consciousness-raising of feminism that enables us to question any individual woman's perspective: together, we can uncover and seek to change the various ways in which we are determined. But, of course, even consciousness-raising need not produce consensus, and so we are still faced with the issue of how to deal, methodologically speaking, with the persistence of disagreements between women. We are also still faced with the problem of how to answer the prior question of who qualifies as a woman: whose consciousness counts?

Consciousness-raising's focus on the everyday, on ordinariness, shows us that feminists should be interested in someone's presentation of their own body. Bodily presentation is part of the ordinariness of daily life, part of how one fits in with or resists gender norms, how one fits in with or resists structures more generally. Recall MacKinnon's statement in *Toward a Feminist Theory of the State* that "a theory is feminist to the extent it is persuaded that women have been unjustly unequal to men because of the social meaning of

---

[49] MacKinnon, *Toward a Feminist Theory of the State*, p. 39.

their bodies."⁵⁰ This seems to make the social meaning of bodies a fundamental feminist question, and a person's use of their own body, and claims about its proper social place, a fundamental feminist or anti-feminist act.

Of course, one reason to refuse judgment of other people's use of their own bodies is that women, feminist or not, know all too well what it is to be subject to such judgment; and feminists recognise such judgment as a subordinating political act. What we wear is political, how we present ourselves as feminine or masculine is political, and the act of endorsing or critiquing clothes or presentation is political.

For example, wearing revealing clothes or high heels is to position oneself in a certain aspect of femininity. It is to say that one belongs there whether by choice or by necessity. Various responses to such dress are possible: one response from within male supremacy is to say that a person wearing such clothes deserves sexual assault, which is to affirm the male supremacist doctrine that to be feminine (or even just female) is to be worthy of such assault.

Wearing such clothes—wearing any clothes⁵¹—thus becomes a political action, because it is to situate oneself in the category of feminine, a category which is taken by many to indicate worthiness for assault. But the possible motivations and meanings for this action are multiple, and there is no stable correlation between motivation (which depends on the agent) and meaning (which does not). Consider some examples of possible motivations. Wearing feminine clothing might be a necessary or normal route to access certain sorts of resources, such as sex, or money, or power, experienced by the wearer as a necessary evil or just the simple cost of life. It might be a preference, perceived as freely chosen yet socially constructed as all choices are, and this preference might present itself as urgent, profound, and essential to oneself, or as frivolous, pleasurable, and peripheral. It might be a conscious act of rebellion against constraining gender norms, such as in the drag performance or the feminist SlutWalk. Or it might be a wholehearted endorsement of those very same norms. How one presents oneself is inexorably political, in that it cannot make sense outside of a particular context of power.

Moreover, how others respond to those presentations will depend on both their views about, and their position within, that context of power. Wearing feminine clothing might bring success or failure, acceptance or rejection, advantage or attack. When feminine clothes are worn by people whom

---

⁵⁰ MacKinnon, *Toward a Feminist Theory of the State*, p. 37.
⁵¹ Wearing *any* clothes is a political action because it is to situate oneself, or attempt to situate oneself, inside or outside any number of socially defined and politically significant groups: gender, race, class, religion, culture, age, and so on.

observers assume to be women the result is simultaneously beneficial and harmful: women benefit from the approval they receive by conforming to norms of femininity at the same time as they are harmed for indicating their membership of the subordinate sex. This simultaneous benefit and harm can be seen in any number of examples: the businesswoman who must wear makeup and high heels to be accepted professionally, but who is then marked out as less serious than a man, less suitable for hiring or promotion, and less deserving of her salary; the young woman who must wear revealing clothing on a night out so as to be considered attractive by her peers and by potential male partners, but whose clothes simultaneously render her physically and symbolically vulnerable to rape; the woman who gains authenticity, comfort, and integrity from rejecting certain feminine beauty ideas, but whose grey hair and natural features earn her derision or disregard.

The body and its presentation are thus deeply politically significant. But we can recognise this and still be wary of judging individuals. Women are damned if they do and damned if they don't, so maybe we should stop damning!

An example of this compassionate approach can be found in Andrea Dworkin's *Woman Hating*. Dworkin urges us to "refuse to submit to all forms of behaviour and relationship which reinforce male-female polarity, which nourish basic patterns of male dominance and female submission".[52] She advocates the wholesale rejection of feminine beauty practices: "The body must be freed, liberated, quite literally: from paint and girdles and all varieties of crap. Women must stop mutilating their bodies and start living in them."[53] She envisages a future in which "community built on androgynous identity will mean the end of transsexuality as we know it".[54] At the same time, while we are not in that future, Dworkin argues that a trans person is "in a state of primary emergency as a transsexual".[55] A world that violently enforces a gender binary is a world which is hostile to trans people (and, of course, to women). In response, Dworkin argues, "Every transsexual has the right to survival on his/her own terms. That means that every transsexual is entitled to a sex-change operation, and it should be provided by the community as one of its functions. This is an emergency measure for an emergency condition."[56]

Emergency measures for emergency conditions are understandable and may be the best we can do in any given situation. Dworkin herself was the

---

[52] Andrea Dworkin, *Woman Hating* (New York, NY: E. P. Dutton, 1974), pp. 192–3.
[53] Dworkin, *Woman Hating*, p. 116.   [54] Dworkin, *Woman Hating*, pp. 186–7.
[55] Dworkin, *Woman Hating*, pp. 186–7.   [56] Dworkin, *Woman Hating*, p. 186.

victim of the most vicious personal attacks, many of which focused on her refusal to participate in various norms and rituals of feminine appearance. As necessary as emergency measures are, though, we must be wary that they do not prolong the emergency situation for everyone even as they alleviate the emergency for some.

* * *

There is an intersection between the questions 'what is a woman?' and 'may women judge?' Feminists and women are increasingly wary of asserting a judgment about who counts as a woman because 'transphobia' has become a stick to beat women with, feminist women in particular. In 1997 (published in 2005), MacKinnon spoke of the way that the charge of essentialism was being used against feminism. In 2017, everything she says in the following excerpts from that talk could be said of transphobia. Replace 'essentialism' with 'transphobia' in the following paragraphs and you get a pretty accurate picture of the current climate:

> The "essentialism" charge has become a sneer, a tool of woman-bashing, with consequences that far outrun its merits. The widespread acceptance of the claim seems due more to its choice of target than its accuracy in hitting it. Male power is ecstatic; its defenders love the accusation that feminism is "essentialist," even though they don't really know what it means. They do know that it has divided women, which sure takes a lot of heat off.[57]
>
> Fear of being labelled "essentialist"... has far-reaching consequences. Those within and outside the academy who know that male power in all its forms remains entrenched also know they face defamatory attacks and potential threats to their economic survival if they say so. As "essentialism" has become a brand, a stigma, a contagious disease that you have to avoid feminism to avoid catching, it has become one more way that the connections and coherence of the ways women are oppressed as members of the group "women" can be covered up. It is silencing when women cannot tell the truth of what they know and survive.[58]

The charge of transphobia is so damaging to feminism because it can be used to conflate the legitimate demand for acceptance, consideration, and support of trans people with the illegitimate demands for uncritical acceptance of very

---

[57] MacKinnon, *Women's Lives, Men's Laws*, p. 88.
[58] MacKinnon, *Women's Lives, Men's Laws*, p. 89.

specific ways of thinking and speaking. Feminists who question some forms of trans theory and practice, particularly those feminists who want to reserve some significance for 'born women' and 'female biology', have been vilified and, sometimes, threatened with paradigmatic forms of male violence against women, namely rape and murder.[59] Trans people, including trans women, are also subjected to violence, including sexual violence.[60] Violence against trans people is abhorrent. But feminist analysis shows us that violence against trans people and violence against trans-critical feminists are versions of the same thing. They are Misogyny 101, proof that women may not judge, that women may not assert their opinions, that women's bodies and women's bodily appearance are a crucial site of their oppression, and that it doesn't much matter what sort of a woman you are or seem to be when susceptibility to male sexual violence is at stake.

* * *

The title of this chapter is 'Judging Women', a phrase that can be understood in three senses. First, when is it acceptable or necessary to make judgments about what women do? Second, when can women engage in the act of judging? Third, how are we to judge who counts as a woman? MacKinnon's work offers profound, sustained, rich analysis of these questions, but does not fully resolve them. This is not to say that full resolution is possible or desirable. It is simply to welcome ongoing discussion.

Freedom and Equality: Essays on Liberalism and Feminism. Clare Chambers, Oxford University Press.
© Clare Chambers 2024. DOI: 10.1093/9780191919480.003.0013

---

[59] Examples are documented at the website 'TERF is a slur' at https://terfisaslur.com . TERF stands for Trans-Exclusionary Radical Feminist.

[60] Rebecca L. Stotzer, 'Violence Against Transgender People: A Review of United States Data', *Aggression and Violent Behavior* 14(3) (2009).

13
Ideology and Normativity

In 'Culture and Critique', Sally Haslanger investigates what she calls "ideological oppression".[1] Like all oppression, ideological oppression involves unjust social practices. Its distinctive feature is that it is not recognised as oppression by either its victims, or its perpetrators, or both. It is not recognised as oppression because, in Haslanger's words, the "cultural technē... frames the straightforward possibilities for thought and action so that certain morally relevant facts are eclipsed and others distorted".[2] In other words, the oppressive behaviour is framed by the social norms and cultural context as normal and appropriate.

Wolf whistling illustrates this phenomenon. Feminist analysis and women's experience tell us that wolf whistling oppresses women by buttressing various aspects of male supremacy: the idea that women should be judged by their looks, the idea that women's bodies are public property, the idea that women are appropriate targets for sexual objectification, and the idea that woman both are and should feel unsafe on the streets.[3] As Laura Bates reports, this lesson is taught to girls from an early age. One of the contributors to her collection *Everyday Sexism* recalls: "When I was 9 a man asked 'the girl with the dick sucking lips' to come here."[4] Many women find the experience of being whistled at insulting, offensive, alarming, frightening, or upsetting. As another contributor states, "There are times I wish I wasn't female because I'm fed up

---

[1] This chapter was originally published in *Aristotelian Society Supplementary Volume* 91(1) (2017), following its presentation at the Joint Session of the Aristotelian Society and the Mind Association at the University of Edinburgh in 2017. I am very grateful to the Joint Session organisers for the invitation to be a symposiast, and to Sally Haslanger for conversation and feedback on the paper at the event.

[2] Sally Haslanger, 'Culture and Critique', *Aristotelian Society Supplementary Volume* 91(1) (2017), p. 168.

[3] Andrea Dworkin, *Life and Death: Unapologetic Writings on the Continuing War Against Women* (London: Virago, 1979); Catharine A. MacKinnon, *Sexual Harassment of Working Women* (New Haven, CT: Yale University Press, 1979); John Stoltenberg, *Refusing to Be a Man: Essays on Sex and Justice* (Harmondsworth: Penguin, 1990); Carol Brooks Gardner, *Passing By: Gender and Public Harassment* (Berkeley; London: University of California Press, 1995); Laura Bates, *Everyday Sexism* (London: Simon & Schuster, 2014).

[4] Bates, *Everyday Sexism*, p. 167.

of being scared of walking down the street on my own."[5] Many men would never engage in wolf whistling, recognising it as an oppressive act.[6]

And yet there are both men and women who find wolf whistling unproblematic, or even complimentary. "How can wolf whistling be offensive to women?", asked actor Joanna Lumley in 2016. "It's a compliment. They're saying 'cor you look all right, darling.' What's wrong with that?"[7] Two of the male participants on the reality TV show *I'm a Celebrity Get Me Out of Here!* were similarly confused, as reported in *Cosmopolitan* magazine. "Adam Thomas added:... 'I would like it if someone wolf whistled me. I would be like "hi guys!"' Joel Dommett also reckoned he'd be into it: 'I would absolutely love it.'"[8]

A positive appraisal of wolf whistling eclipses morally relevant facts: women's fear of and vulnerability to sexual violence by men; men's objectification of women; sex inequality in general. It frames thought according to the standards of male supremacy: women are to be objectified, so their objectification is appropriate; women should be judged by their attractiveness, so signs of judgment are to be welcomed. Moving beyond what Haslanger would call the cultural technē of the ideology of male supremacy has required women's consciousness and feminist analysis, which provide tools and grounds for critiquing the ideology and its sustaining practices, including renaming 'wolf whistling' as 'street harassment'.

In general I am very sympathetic to Haslanger's analysis. I certainly agree that ideological oppression exists and that we must resist it. As I have argued in my own work, using the concept of social construction rather than Haslanger's preferred concept of ideology, feminism as a social and philosophical movement has focused on critical analysis of the processes by which individuals are motivated to participate in practices that harm them.

I find it helpful to identify two main forms of social construction. First, there is the social construction of options: our social context determines not only which options are available, but also frames the available options as

---

[5] Bates, *Everyday Sexism*, p. 164.
[6] It is clear that many men who oppose street harassment have no idea how ubiquitous it is. For example, Tony Parson claims "It is a strange anomaly of male behaviour that builders are the only men who feel free to shout loudly at passing females", which just shows that he has never been a passing female. He centres men's experience still further when he writes that "there is no more ardent feminist in this world than the man with a growing daughter" (Tony Parsons, 'Is It Ever OK to Wolf Whistle?', GQ (13 October 2015), available at https://www.gq-magazine.co.uk/article/is-it-ok-to-wolf-whistle).
[7] Joanna Lumley in Emily Retter, 'Joanna Lumley Defends Wolf Whistling and Insists People Are Offended by "Everything"', *The Mirror* (4 October 2016), available at http://www.mirror.co.uk/3am/celebrity-news/joanna-lumley-defends-wolf-whistling-8980221.
[8] Anna Lewis, 'I'm a Celeb Campmates Are Divided on Whether Wolf Whistling Is Sexist or Not', *Cosmopolitan* (30 November 2016), available at http://www.cosmopolitan.co.uk/entertainment/news/a47701/im-a-celeb-campmates-wolf-whistling-sexist/.

appropriate or inappropriate for people like us. The second, more controversial aspect of social construction is the social construction of preferences. People generally *want* to conform to the norms of their social context. This desire to conform could take place at various levels of consciousness. It could be a politically conscious, rational assessment that conformity will offer greater payoffs than defection. Examples include a woman who wears uncomfortable high heels to work because she judges that it will help her career, or a woman who undergoes cosmetic surgery so as to counteract age discrimination at work. Alternatively, the desire to conform could be embraced as part of the person's genuine preferences. Examples include a woman who considers buying and wearing high heels to be a personal indulgence, a treat, or a woman who asks her male partner to pay for her breast implants as a gift—not for him but for *her*.

On my analysis, which draws on feminists and critical theorists such as Catharine MacKinnon,[9] Michel Foucault,[10] and Pierre Bourdieu,[11] social construction means that most of our practices rely on a social context to make sense.[12] Without a social context there is no meaning to many practices. High heels and breast implants are not functionally successful, practically useful, or objectively beautiful.[13] They gain their appeal and pleasure purely as carriers of beauty, status, and self-esteem: concepts that are inexorably social.

But analysis of what I call social construction and what Haslanger calls ideological oppression faces two key problems. The first problem is how to explain *why* ideological oppression is oppressive, if it is not recognised as such by those involved in it. The second problem is how to explain what gives the philosopher or the critic the ability and the right to judge that a practice that a culture endorses is wrong. These problems are closely related but not identical: if a culture or practice is oppressive then there is at least a prima facie case for critique, but we still need to know when critique is legitimate, especially

---

[9] Catharine A. MacKinnon, *Feminism Unmodified* (Cambridge, MA: Harvard University Press, 1987); Catharine A. MacKinnon, *Toward a Feminist Theory of the State* (Cambridge, MA: Harvard University Press, 1989).

[10] Michel Foucault, *Discipline and Punish: The Birth of the Prison* (Harmondsworth: Penguin, 1991).

[11] Pierre Bourdieu, *The Logic of Practice* (Cambridge: Polity Press, 1990); Pierre Bourdieu, *Masculine Domination* (Cambridge: Polity Press, 2001).

[12] It seems plausible that some of our practices are pre-social. Examples might include bodily functions such as sleeping, eating, and defecating, and the basic relationships of human life, such as sexual intercourse, birthing, breastfeeding, and mothering. But even these practices vary across societies and history in their particular form and meaning, such that they still get much of their character *as practice* from the social context in which they occur.

[13] Clare Chambers, *Sex, Culture, and Justice: The Limits of Choice* (University Park, PA: Penn State University Press, 2008); Clare Chambers, *Intact: A Defence of the Unmodified Body* (London: Allen Lane, 2022).

where critique aims to be action-guiding. In cases of ideology there is necessarily a disagreement about whether or not a practice is oppressive. The ideology critic claims that it is, but those who endorse and enact the practice claim that it is not. The critic may have the right to her opinion, but (why) does she have the right to try to enforce that opinion on others, or to attempt to end the practices that she and not they condemn?

These problems can be answered. But, as I have argued elsewhere, answering them requires a strong and unashamed commitment to substantive, controversial normative values—values that are themselves inevitably tied to particular social contexts.[14] Recognition of social construction should not lead us to a permissive cultural relativism. It is legitimate to use our own normative commitments to critique practices, including those of other cultures, as long as we use those same values to critique our own practices at least as forcefully.

13.1 Defining Ideological Oppression

Awareness of ideological oppression, and the problems it raises, is not new. It features strongly in feminist critiques of gendered practices and sex inequality, in Marxist and socialist critiques of capitalism and class, in rational choice and decision theory, in development work, in critical race theory, in poststructuralism, and in contemporary debates in the theory of liberal multiculturalism.

The diverse contexts in which the concept of ideological oppression has been considered has led, predictably, to a diversity of attitudes towards it. Ideological oppression has been thought of as false consciousness, as adaptive preferences, as being a victim or a cultural dupe; or alternatively as living an authentically situated life, as following tradition, as living according to the meanings of one's own culture. Similarly, the task for the philosopher has been alternatively described as being to liberate, to illuminate, to facilitate, to revolutionise, to save; or alternatively those attempting such moves have been described as racist, imperialist, colonial, as themselves the oppressors.

Strategies for ending ideological oppression also vary according to one's interpretation of it. Ending the oppression might seem to require extreme measures such as regulation, restriction, coercion, enforced liberation, or even invasion. More moderately, ending oppression might seem to require campaigning, education, raising awareness, or raising consciousness. But for

---

[14] Chambers, *Sex, Culture, and Justice*.

those who see ideological oppression as benign or even honourable (which is to say, not really as oppression at all) the correct response might be restraint, relativism, respect, and recognition of difference.

The first task is to define the concept clearly. At the start of 'Culture and Critique' Haslanger states that she will "embrace" Stuart Hall's account of ideology, according to which ideology can be both a feature of a dominant form of "power and domination" *and* part of "the processes by which new forms of consciousness, new conceptions of the world, arise, which move the masses of the people into historical action against the prevailing system".[15] This definition is vague, describing ideology as having something 'to do with' these phenomena. But it sets out a concept of ideology as politically or morally neutral: found in both status quo and resistance, used by both oppressors and their victims, and liberators.

A normatively neutral account of ideology makes sense of the phrase 'ideological oppression'. Since not all ideology is oppressive it makes sense to distinguish that which is. A neutral definition also raises the epistemological problem of the possibility of ideology critique: if ideology is always and everywhere part of our conceptual and social practices, how can we escape it, much less criticise it? If our thoughts and practices are always shaped by ideology, how can we know what is right or wrong, good or bad? Questions of the legitimacy of ideological critique are also raised here: if there is always ideology, what gives 'us' the right to critique 'theirs'?

However, later in the paper, Haslanger's usage shifts and the neutral term for the practices and systems that shape our thoughts and understanding is 'culture', sometimes further refined into the idea of the 'cultural technē'. Here ideology becomes normatively problematic by definition. Thus she writes: "whether a cultural technē is ideological is to be determined in terms of the injustice of its effects and the values it promotes.... Not every cultural technē is ideological."[16]

On this normatively charged definition the term 'ideological oppression' is somewhat tautological: all ideology is oppressive. The question of the legitimacy of ideology critique also seems to be answered immediately: we should critique ideology because, by definition, it creates and perpetuates injustice or other moral wrongs (concepts that Haslanger uses interchangeably). However, this answer to the question merely begs it. If the only difference between ideology and culture is normative (cultures good, ideologies bad) the real

---

[15] Quoted in Haslanger, 'Culture and Critique', p. 150.
[16] Haslanger, 'Culture and Critique', p. 20; see also p. 19.

question is not 'on what basis can we criticise an ideology?' but 'on what basis can we say that something *is* an ideology?' And this is not an easy question to answer, because the key feature of ideological oppression is that it is not recognised as such by those who are subject to it. The claim that the followers of an ideology are in the grip of oppression is precisely what they deny. Those who are subject to ideological oppression would describe themselves as subject to (mere) culture. And since we, and everyone, are also subject to culture, how can we criticise that?

Now, as Haslanger notes, there are two main solutions to this problem of how to go about a legitimate ideology critique. One is epistemological and the other is moral (more broadly, it is normative). The epistemological critique points to the ways in which the ideology "prevents us from valuing things aptly"[17] and relies on the idea that there are identifiable sources of non-ideological knowledge. The moral critique points to the way that ideology produces morally bad or unjust outcomes and relies on the idea that there is some agreement or non-ideological basis for identifying what counts as morally bad.

13.2 Epistemology and Normativity

The normatively charged definition of ideology implies that, even if there is always culture, there is not always ideology. We might say that a project of emancipation is a project not just of ideology critique but of ideology destruction.

The normatively charged definition also raises the question of how culture relates to ideology. Is 'ideology' simply the name of a culture that has gone wrong, such that there are some things that count as cultures and other things that count as ideologies, with both things being of the same phenomenological/ontological type but differing in their moral characteristics? Alternatively, is ideology one part of culture, such that within a culture there is or may be a subset of ideology? Either way, how general or large are cultures and ideologies? For example, should we be speaking of the culture/ideology of a country, or of a political party, or should we be dividing still further into wings of a political party or factions of a religion, or should we be looking at trans-national movements? In the examples that Haslanger describes is the relevant culture/ideology America, or Republicans, or Trump supporters,

---

[17] Haslanger, 'Culture and Critique', p. 165.

or the alt-right, or the more amorphous White Supremacy, or American values, or liberalism, or conservatism? Or should we speak of America as a culture which contains many ideologies, some of them overlapping, such as White Supremacy, the alt-right, male supremacy, and so on, but say that America or American values are not themselves ideological because there is a version of each that is not unjust?

If ideologies are subsets of cultures then situated criticism may answer some of the problems.[18] Critique becomes possible because even within a culture it is possible to identify alternative beliefs; there are easily accessible positions from outside an ideology but inside the same culture that provide both epistemological and moral challenges to the ideology, as well as providing the alternative practices that Haslanger says are necessary to critique.[19] To give an example, one can criticise the American alt-right by pointing to American political positions that are not the alt-right, and by highlighting tensions between the values of the alt-right and other American values, as enshrined in the Constitution, in legislation, and in the convictions and voting behaviour of millions of Americans.

The problem with the idea that ideologies are subsets of cultures is that it illegitimately assumes that the normatively acceptable culture is larger than the normatively bad ideology: that injustice is the exception and justice the rule, that oppressors are the minority and progressives the majority. This may or may not be true of any particular society. There is no reason to suppose it is always true. And the problem with the reliance on situated criticism is that it relies on the idea of shared traditions, which may in fact be traditions only of the dominant group.[20]

It is more plausible to say that ideology and culture are phenomenologically and ontologically equivalent, differentiated only by their normative features—or, as I would put it, that there is always social construction and the question is what *values* it reflects and maintains. This interpretation is more plausible but it makes the possibility and legitimacy of critique more problematic. Critique, on this perspective, is not possible from a position outside culture, because there is no such position. So this way of thinking about ideology and culture already suggests that ideology critique cannot be merely a matter of epistemology.

---

[18] Alasdair MacIntyre, *After Virtue: A Study in Moral Theory* (London: Duckworth, 1996); Michael Walzer, *Spheres of Justice: A Defence of Pluralism and Equality* (Oxford: Blackwell, 1985); Michael Walzer, *Thick and Thin: Moral Argument at Home and Abroad* (Notre Dame, IN: University of Notre Dame Press, 1994); Richard Rorty, *Contingency, Irony, and Solidarity* (Cambridge: Cambridge University Press, 1989).

[19] Haslanger, 'Culture and Critique', pp. 158–9.

[20] Susan Moller Okin, *Justice, Gender, and the Family* (New York, NY: Basic Books, 1989).

We cannot critique ideology by saying that it shapes the thoughts, concepts, and practices of its members, because culture does the exact same thing, and because we are necessarily speaking from within a culture ourselves. Instead, the critique has to be that ideology shapes knowledge *badly*, where this is a normative and not an epistemological bad.

In response, the defender of the epistemological critique might claim that even within an ideology there are some who have better access to the truth than others. This claim is deeply plausible; after all, in any group of people there will be some who are better epistemological agents than others. But two further problems arise. The first is how to *identify* the superior epistemological agents. The second is how to justify that assessment of superiority: how to *legitimate* their judgments.

First consider which subject-positions are best placed to produce knowledge and critique. It seems to be in the nature of ideology and culture that those who are members of it are not best placed to assess it. By definition, those whose way of thinking is shaped by an ideology or culture are less likely to be able to gain critical purchase on that ideology or culture. And yet Haslanger argues, somewhat surprisingly, that those who are 'in' an ideology or culture are actually well-placed—possibly even best-placed—to critique it. "Much of the discussion of cultural critique situates such critique as cross-cultural," she writes. "I suggest, however, that we take the paradigm of critique to occur *within* a culture."[21] The reason Haslanger gives for this judgment is "those directly affected by the practices in question" are "likely to have better access to morally relevant facts".[22] A crucial part of her analysis is the claim that people can have access to morally relevant facts without relying on moral principles or a theory of justice. For critique, Haslanger argues, "it is not necessary to *know what justice is*, or have a complete moral theory." Instead, critique can emanate from the knowledge that "a moral wrong or injustice is being done *to me* or *to us*."[23]

Now, while it is undoubtedly true that it is not necessary to have a *complete* theory of justice to identify injustice,[24] it does not follow that *no* objective (i.e. non cultural/ideological) normative knowledge is necessary. For without some theory or principles of justice we cannot justify why something being done to us is an injustice rather than merely something we don't like, and we have no way of justifying which facts are morally relevant.

---

[21] Haslanger, 'Culture and Critique', p. 166.
[22] Haslanger, 'Culture and Critique', p. 166.
[23] Haslanger, 'Culture and Critique', p. 21.
[24] Jonathan Wolff and Avner De-Shalit, *Disadvantage* (Oxford: Oxford University Press, 2007).

There are many claims to have suffered injustice that we should not take at face value. The obvious example is the child who insists 'it's not fair!' when what she really means is 'I don't like it!' But adults do this too. For example, Dan Turner, father of Stanford rapist Brock Turner, caused legitimate outrage with his claim that a jail sentence for his son would be "a steep price to pay for 20 minutes of action".[25] Dan Turner thought a prison sentence would be an injustice done to his son. He was wrong.

Moreover, some claims that an injustice has been suffered are incompatible with others. A member of a privileged group may claim that affirmative action towards minorities is unjust; others accuse universities of ingrained and institutional racism against minorities.[26] Anti-abortion campaigners may claim that abortion is unjust or immoral harm to the foetus; advocates of the woman's right to choose may claim that being denied an abortion is an injustice.[27] Not all claims that an injustice or moral wrong has been done are compatible, and they cannot all be true. Identifying a legitimate claim of injustice requires theory or principles of justice.

We need to be careful here. Since culture is everywhere, and since there is no pre-social consciousness, we are not looking for pre-social or non-social normative facts. Instead we are looking for normative facts that do not depend on a particular culture or ideology for their truth-value. Facts and judgments that depend on a culture for their truth include statements like 'crop tops are cool', or 'high heels are sexy', or 'pale skin is beautiful'. These will be true in

---

[25] Michael E. Miller, '"A Steep Price to Pay for 20 Minutes of Action": Dad Defends Stanford Sex Offender', *The Washington Post* (6 June 2016), available at https://www.washingtonpost.com/news/morning-mix/wp/2016/06/06/a-steep-price-to-pay-for-20-minutes-of-action-dad-defends-stanford-sex-offender/.

[26] For views on both sides, see Louis P. Pojman, 'The Case Against Affirmative Action', *International Journal of Applied Philosophy* 12(1) (1998); Toby Young, 'David Cameron is Plain Wrong About Oxford and Race. Here's Why', *The Spectator* (31 January 2016), available at https://www.spectator.co.uk/article/david-cameron-is-plain-wrong-about-oxford-and-race-here-s-why; the Student Union of SOAS campaign on Decolonising the University, 'What is Decolonising SOAS?', SOAS University of London (2018), available at https://blogs.soas.ac.uk/decolonisingsoas/what-is-decolonising-soas/; David Cameron's claim that "racism in the UK's leading institutions 'should shame our nation'", in Tim Shipman and Sian Griffiths, 'A Young Black Man is More Likely to be in Prison Than at a Top University', *The Times* (31 January 2016), available at https://www.thetimes.co.uk/article/a-young-black-man-is-more-likely-to-be-in-prison-than-at-a-top-university-mq699s0hdcb.

[27] For a view on each side, see John Piper, 'Why the Simple Right to Abortion is Unjust', *Desiring God* (15 January 1990), available at http://www.desiringgod.org/articles/why-the-simple-right-to-abortion-is-unjust, and Loretta Ross, 'Understanding Reproductive Justice', available at https://d3n8a8pro7vhmx.cloudfront.net/rrfp/pages/33/attachments/original/1456425809/Understanding_RJ_Sistersong.pdf. There are also first-person accounts on both sides, from people who were nearly aborted and claim that they would have suffered a moral wrong (see Faith Noah, 'I Was Nearly Aborted', *LifeTeen* (n.d.), originally at http://lifeteen.com/blog/nearly-aborted/) but no longer online, and from women who were denied abortion and who claim that as an injustice (see BBC News, 'Woman Denied Abortion in the Republic of Ireland Speaks Out', BBC (19 August 2014), available at http://www.bbc.co.uk/news/world-europe-28849058).

some cultures and false in others. Normative facts and judgments are not like this. Statements like 'sexism is unjust' and 'racial segregation is wrong' are accepted in some societies and not in others, but for ideology critique (not to mention justice) to have a chance, their truth or falsity must not depend on the culture in which they are asserted.

Once we accept that ideology critique requires theory, or access to normative claims that do not depend on a particular culture or ideology for their truth, it is then less clear who has access to such facts. It is in the nature of critique that claims are disputed: there are those who assert them and those who deny them. Haslanger's solution is to suggest "epistemic humility: we should listen to those directly affected by the practices in question because they are likely to have better access to morally relevant facts."[28] But it is not clear why this is true, or how it can be asserted without begging the question. Even if it is true, moral disagreement can occur between people who are directly affected by practices. Who has better access to morally relevant facts about affirmative action: the white man who did not obtain a place at university and blames it on unjust affirmative action, or the black man who did not obtain a place at university and blames it on unjust racism? There is no reliable way to determine who is correct from their subject position alone. Perhaps neither of them has the best access to the morally relevant facts: perhaps we should turn to the admissions tutor who made the decision, or the statistician who can contextualise the decision in the university's general admissions figures, or the academic who can theorise about general patterns and structures of racism. To take another example, who has better access to the morally relevant facts about abortion: the woman who was denied an abortion and claims she suffered an injustice, or the adult who was nearly aborted as a child and claims she narrowly escaped injustice? Both are directly affected by the practice.

Of course, sometimes people make judgments on matters of morality or justice while clearly lacking morally relevant facts. For example, Ohio Republican Jim Buchy, who supports legislation to reduce or ban abortion, "once admitted he had 'never thought about' why women have terminations".[29] It seems obvious that this man does not have (and has not sought access to) vitally important morally relevant facts. But even this judgment relies on a

---

[28] Haslanger, 'Culture and Critique', p. 166.
[29] Siobhan Fenton, 'US Politician Trying to Ban Abortion Says He Has Never Thought About Why Women Have Them', *The Independent* (9 December 2016), available at https://www.independent.co.uk/news/world/americas/politician-trying-to-ban-abortion-after-admitting-he-has-never-thought-about-why-women-have-them-a7466196.htm.

moral or political theory. The facts of why women seek abortions are morally relevant only if abortion is, at least in part, an issue about women's rights and sex inequality. If abortion is only about unjust harm to the foetus then women's motivations are not morally relevant. To take another example, the feelings and intentions of men who like to wolf whistle are not morally relevant to the question of whether wolf whistling is oppressive, even though those men are directly affected by the practice. But I can only make the claim that wolf-whistling men do not have superior epistemological access to the meaning of their practice via a feminist *theory* that gives a normative perspective on street harassment and its place in male supremacy.

There is no way of determining in advance of theory that some have better epistemological access to morally relevant facts merely by virtue of their subject-position. Instead, identifying the relevant subject-position is already the task of theory. This is not to say that theory can be developed without input from those who are directly affected by the practice: I agree with Haslanger that consciousness-raising is a vital critical tool.[30] But the only way to adjudicate between competing assertions of facts as morally relevant is via a theory of the justice of practices. And if we have that then we have the basis for a moral rather than an epistemological critique of ideology.

Note that it is not a solution to this problem to say that we should listen to victims rather than perpetrators, the oppressed rather than the oppressor. Since the whole point of ideological oppression is that it is not recognised by people who are subject to it, including its victims, we cannot identify who counts as oppressor and who counts as oppressed without a theory of justice. There is no non-normative answer to the question of whether it is the black or the white university applicant who has been oppressed, or whether the foetus or the women denied an abortion, or whether the prosecuted wolf whistler or the woman whistled at. In these examples oppression is claimed on both sides. In other cases, such as the willing wearer of high heels, oppression is denied.

Haslanger writes convincingly about the epistemological limitations that can prevent the *dominant*, those on the *advantaged* side of oppression, from recognising the oppression that they perpetuate. The idea that the dominant lack the tools to recognise their role in systems of oppression is currently in the cultural ascendant. It underpins the instruction to 'check your privilege'. It also informs concepts such as 'mansplaining', the slur 'trans-exclusionary

---

[30] Clare Chambers and Phil Parvin, 'What Kind of Dialogue Do We Need? Gender, Deliberation and Comprehensive Values', in Jude Browne (ed.), *Dialogue, Politics and Gender* (Cambridge: Cambridge University Press, 2013).

radical feminists' or TERFs, and the critique of the 'All Lives Matter' movement as racist. Some of these judgments are better than others,[31] but in general they share the idea that we must not be complacent in assuming that we are not perpetrators of injustice. Less in line with the zeitgeist is the idea that people might claim to suffer oppression unjustifiably. But both are possible.

Also out of fashion is the idea that people might suffer from oppression without themselves knowing it. It is not that this idea is unfamiliar, but rather that it has been explored in terms that are no longer in vogue. False consciousness is one long-standing version of the idea. False consciousness implies that there can be an objective distinction between consciousnesses that are true and those that are false: it relies, that is, on the idea of a pre-social consciousness that the critic and not the citizen can access. This idea is unappealing not only because there is no such thing as a pre-social consciousness, but also because it seems to offer two unpalatable options. Either false consciousness is described as so pervasive and impermeable, as such an inevitable consequence of social situatedness, that the fact that some claim to identify and criticise it undermines its very existence. Or, the fact that the critic is able to exist and thus remain immune from its distorting effects suggests an aloofness, that those who do suffer from false consciousness are weak-minded, irrational dupes. On the first option the critic is impossible, on the second, insufferable.

It seems clear that differently situated people have different epistemological access to practices. But it is not clear that we can say in principle or in advance which subject-positions are epistemologically superior. The key issue is not so much epistemology as *normativity*. We should be looking not for better *knowers*, but *better* knowers.

13.3 Sources of Value

Haslanger herself is not content with a mere epistemological critique. She writes:

> In contexts of ideological oppression, the cultural resources are inadequate to recognize the injustice for what it is. The problem is not that the

---

[31] This is not the place for an analysis of each of these claims, but my view is that the concept of mansplaining and the critique of All Lives Matter are illuminating and politically important, whereas the critique of TERFs is neither. I discuss the phenomenon of criticising feminists as transphobic in Clare Chambers, 'Judging Women: 25 Years Further Toward a Feminist Theory of the State', Chapter 12 in this volume.

individuals who participate in the injustice, i.e., who either suffer from, perform, or are complicit in it, are stupid or ignorant; even epistemic responsibility within the available cultural technē is insufficient to appreciate the wrongs in question.[32]

Her solution turns to critical theory and its embeddedness within a social movement. Epistemological critique is insufficient because it is not possible simply to describe ideological beliefs as false: "in the social domain, shared beliefs can make themselves true."[33] As she puts it later in the paper, "[t]he point is not just that culture shapes what we *take to be value*, i.e., our beliefs about value, but *what is valuable*."[34]

Beauty and appearance norms are an excellent example. As I have written elsewhere:

> High-heeled shoes aren't inherently, naturally sexy. On a man, even one with feminine, slender legs, the general consensus is that they look ridiculous. The distortions they produce in the male body are not seen as attractive – even though they are the same distortions that are revered in a woman. The fact that we find high heels attractive on a woman is entirely dependent on how our society constructs beauty, and this, in turn, is strongly affected by our social norms of gendered behaviour. Practices are contingent on the set of social norms (or power/knowledge regime) they support and from which they derive.[35]

In other work, Haslanger uses the similar example of crop tops, imagining a discussion between a twelve-year-old girl and her parents as to whether or not crop tops are cute.[36] According to what Haslanger calls the daughter's "milieu"—the community and beliefs of her schoolfriends—they do count as cute; according to the parents' milieu—the community and beliefs of adults with a certain outlook—they do not.

In the paper discussing this example, Haslanger considers two possible bases for critique. The first, which she ultimately rejects, is the idea that some *milieus* are superior either epistemologically, politically, or morally. This approach might say that the parents may justifiably critique the daughter because, as adults, they know more (including more about politics and

---

[32] Haslanger, 'Culture and Critique', p. 160.
[33] Haslanger, 'Culture and Critique', p. 150.
[34] Haslanger, 'Culture and Critique', p. 162.
[35] Chambers, *Sex, Culture, and Justice*, p. 29.
[36] Sally Haslanger, *Resisting Reality: Social Construction and Social Critique* (Oxford: Oxford University Press, 2012), ch. 15.

morality), because their critique is based on a political analysis of the gender and clothing that the daughter lacks, and because their critique is based on a moral perspective on bullying and peer pressure that is absent from the daughter's analysis.[37]

Now, on the face of it this seems clearly sensible to me (and doubtless to parents everywhere). So what is wrong with the idea that critique is justified based on epistemological, political, or moral superiority? There is what we might think of as a philosophical and a political answer to this question, and Haslanger focuses on the philosophical answer whereas my thoughts turn towards the political.

The philosophical answer looks again to the idea of epistemological superiority, and asks both how we can know that one perspective is superior to another, and also whether truth-conditions for practices such as fashion are necessarily relative. In other words, the truth of the question as to whether crop-tops are cute depends not just on the milieu but on differences as to which agents' views on cuteness truly do constitute the value of cuteness. As Haslanger puts it:

> suppose in the seventh grade milieu there is a norm that everyone should agree with Hannah (e.g., about what's cute, dorky, fun, boring…). If this norm is followed, there will be a coordination of beliefs and responses that constitute social facts which can be effectively known by following the Hannah-agreement norm. However, the hope, on this quasi-objectivist approach, would be to establish conditions on epistemic (or moral) norms, for example, of universality, that downgrade milieus governed by norms like Hannah-agreement. But we must ask: what makes such conditions objective?[38]

The demand for objectivity in matters of social norms is misguided. The goal of undermining norms like Hannah-agreement should not be to approach more objective milieus. I have no sense of what it would mean for a milieu (or a social context, set of social norms, social structure, community, call it what you will) to be objective, or of why this should seem to be a good thing. There is no such thing as objective fashion, objective criteria of cuteness or beauty. The issue is that we should not agree with something merely because some authority states it, and the problem with such agreement is not epistemic (perhaps Hannah is an extremely skilled knower) but *political*.

---

[37] Haslanger, *Resisting Reality*, pp. 424–5.   [38] Haslanger, *Resisting Reality*, p. 425.

The political answer points to the problem of inequality, power, and dominance. What is at stake in asserting that one point of view is superior? How does that silence further disagreement? Even if we can identify the epistemologically, morally, or politically superior view, how can we allow that view to prevail without engaging in further oppression? More pragmatically, *how* can the superior view (supposing there is one) overcome the morally, politically, or epistemologically inferior yet dominant one? This is a particularly pressing issue in the current political climate of Trump and Brexit.

Haslanger's preferred basis for critique offers some guidance, but again its focus is philosophical rather than political. She suggests that we

> develop a notion of critique that requires more than just truth relative to the milieu of the assessor. For example, suppose the assessor's claim is a genuine critique of a speaker's only if there is some common ground (factual, epistemic, or social) between the speaker's milieu and assessors' milieus, and the assessors' claim is true relative to the common ground. To say that a critique is genuine, in this sense, is not to say that it is the final word, rather, it is to say that a response is called for.[39]

What is striking in this version of critique is Haslanger's assumption that what makes a response called for is the existence of shared assumptions rather than, say, the need to live together or to seek compromise (what Rawls calls the circumstances of justice). She argues that if critique is based on shared assumptions then it can be transformative, for working through a critique becomes "a matter of forming or finding a common milieu".[40] But whether a common milieu can be found depends on whether one thinks of a milieu as primarily a conceptual or ideological phenomenon, to do with the ideas, concepts and ways of thinking one has, or as an institutional or communal phenomenon, to do with one's social context and location within that context. In some cases critique may succeed in shifting concepts but not community. Even if the daughter comes to agree with her parents' values she cannot shift from her schoolchild milieu into their lefty adult milieu. Other times, a shared community just is not enough to overcome differences of ideological milieu, as with the unreasonable people that even Rawls is unable to assimilate.

Often, we find it easier to see what is wrong with a practice from outside of our own culture or ideology than one from inside it, even where the two practices share all salient moral features. This means that critique of other

---

[39] Haslanger, *Resisting Reality*, p. 425. [40] Haslanger, *Resisting Reality*, p. 425.

cultures can be a vitally important route to critique of one's own culture. If another culture contains a practice that we find abhorrent, it is illuminating to consider whether our own culture contains practices with the same features. If so, rather than abstain from all critique as the cultural relativist would have us do, we have the tools for solid critique of our own culture.[41]

13.4 Agents of Change

Who are the agents of change? We might imagine a continuum of actors, ordered by size and strength. At one end stands the individual: solitary, vulnerable, noble, lauded. At the other end is the state: monolithic, awesome, power-laden; monstrous to some, benevolent to others. Between the two is culture. Close to individuals in terms of strength and reach are minority cultures: struggling against the tide, defending themselves from intrusion by the majority, but always including their own internal minorities. Closer to the state are majority cultures: sometimes merging almost seamlessly with it, other times drifting away. Majority culture spreads along the centre of the continuum and reaches everywhere: individual and state, majority and minority groups. Majority culture engulfs some individuals wholeheartedly, those who are situated firmly within it and who do not challenge its ideals, but its wispy tentacles infiltrate everyone. No one is immune.

Both Haslanger and I want to draw attention to the dimorphous inescapability of culture: its reach into individual and state, its creativity and constraint. We both want to critique those forms of political philosophy that focus attention on the ends of the continuum without adequately analysing the cultural mass in between. But while my work emphasises the problems with focusing on the individual, 'Culture and Critique' focuses on problems with the state.

Haslanger paints a bleak picture in which the state is as often the cause of oppression as its cure. She points to the example of racial desegregation in the USA, and reminds us that legislation for equal civil rights was insufficient to overturn entrenched practices of racial inequality and oppression, many of them perpetuated by agents of the state in the form of police officers and

---

[41] I have used this method, working from a generalised Western critique of the practice of female genital mutilation towards a critique of practices that are generally accepted in the West such as breast implants, other forms of cosmetic surgery including on the female genitals, and male circumcision. See Chambers, *Sex, Culture, and Justice*; Chambers, *Intact*.

courts. "[A]t this point in time," she concludes, "the idea that racism is going to be dismantled by state action is no longer credible."[42]

I agree entirely that state action does not exhaust the possibilities for change, and I share Haslanger's scepticism that the state will dismantle racism any time soon. "At this point in time", in particular, who could think otherwise? But it is instructive to question the scope of Haslanger's judgment of incredibility. Is the issue that state *won't* do what is needed to dismantle racism, or that it *can't*?

There are various levels of difficulty or impossibility here. Some relate to democratic and political processes. Can a political party standing on an anti-racism platform secure a democratic mandate? If it can, do the legislative processes and politics allow that party to pass a sufficiently radical legislative agenda? Once passed, does legislation come with adequate funds and provision for it to be upheld?

Other questions apply more directly to culture. Are police officers and judges adequately capturing and prosecuting offenders, or are their own cultural locations and views leading them to pursue leniency or even to facilitate lawlessness? Is the penalty of the law sufficient to deter ordinary citizens from acting illegally? Are other citizens inclined to report or tolerate the behaviour? Are victims empowered to resist? In some cases, we might even fear that state action has a counter-productive effect, if it creates backlash or if it encourages complacency.

Haslanger is undoubtedly right to suggest that state action is not sufficient to dismantle racism totally: the state does not exhaust the possibilities for change and state intervention may not always be the best option. But the efficacy and desirability of state action will depend in large part on the particular political and historical context of any given struggle. In some cases, state action is the central focus and aim of emancipatory activism. Examples include the women's suffrage movement, the equal marriage movement, and the pro-choice movement. In Haslanger's example, the civil rights movement, she is right to note that *Brown v. Board of Education* was insufficient to combat the "multiple factors – legal, economic, historical, cultural, psychological – relevant to explaining the phenomenon of racial segregation and the educational achievement gap in the United States".[43] But it does not follow that the solution does not at least include additional, more effective state action, such as a return to the court-enforced integration that ended in the late 1990s.

---

[42] Haslanger, 'Culture and Critique', p. 152.   [43] Haslanger, 'Culture and Critique', p. 152.

Behind these practical concerns, however, lies a normative one. Haslanger directs our attention to the fact that state action can fail to end oppression because, to put it simply, the majority or the powerful don't *want* to end oppression. As she puts it, "at the heart of these patterns is a structure of social relations that is ideologically sustained in spite of legislative, judicial, and individual efforts to change it."[44] In other words, the citizenry, viewed as a whole, acts so as to maintain the oppression because it believes that the oppression is *right*.

The belief that oppression is right may take one of two forms. First, one could believe that oppressive acts are not, in fact, oppressive (for example, anti-abortion legislators who see women's decisions to have an abortion as frivolous or selfish, failing to understand the complex clinical, personal, social, or economic reasons why women choose abortion). Second, one could believe that oppression is morally justified (for example, Trump supporters who believe that sanctions against American and immigrant Muslims is justified by the threat of terrorism). Depending on whether we conceptualise individual citizens and the citizenry in general as dupes/victims or as agents/aggressors, we might say that the citizenry is either in the grip of an oppressive ideology or is actively maintaining an oppressive ideology.

Either way, if social relations are "ideologically sustained in spite of legislative, judicial, and political efforts"[45] we can say that the would-be progressive state is out of sync with the ideological citizenry. The normative political question thus becomes not simply: '*how* can we change things?' but also 'to what extent are we *justified* in trying to change things?' and, even more problematically in a democracy, 'to what extent may the *state* legitimately try to change things?' Plausibly the state should adapt to the views of its citizens, rather than the other way around.[46]

Resisting this conclusion, as Haslanger and I (and progressives everywhere) want to do, relies once again on a normative theory of justice, and on defending the emancipatory potential of the state. Scepticism about the emancipatory potential of the state can too easily result in a rebound towards the *individual* as the actor who is expected to emancipate herself and as the only legitimate source of emancipation. In my own work, I begin with a critique of the liberal focus on the individual, and particularly the liberal focus on individual choice. Liberal political philosophy rests on twin foundations of liberty and

---

[44] Haslanger, 'Culture and Critique', p. 152. [45] Haslanger, 'Culture and Critique', p. 152.
[46] Haslanger warns of the need to avoid "normative overreach" (Haslanger, 'Culture and Critique', p. 165).

equality, but ultimately places liberty before equality. Within liberalism generally choice is used as what I call a 'normative transformer': it is something that transforms a morally bad outcome into a morally good or at least morally acceptable one. Most commonly, choice is used to normatively transform what would otherwise seem to be an unjust inequality into a just one. Inequality, with its oppressive ring, becomes mere difference.

Within liberal *political philosophy*, individuals who have chosen their own inequality are to be respected. Within liberal *societies*, individuals who have chosen their own inequality are just as likely to be blamed. In either case, there is no recourse for those who end up disadvantaged. The use of choice as a normative transformer leads to a number of fallacious conclusions. Women are to blame for the gender pay gap because they choose to prioritise children over career. Black men are to blame for their incarceration because they choose to commit crime. Muslims are to blame for prejudice against them because they choose to become terrorists. The poor are to blame for their disadvantage because they choose to live on benefits rather than to work. Women are to blame for being raped because they choose to go out at night, to drink alcohol, to wear clothes of some sort or another. The litany of victim-blaming is long.

The solution must be that individuals, state, and culture all must be taken into account. Each has its role to play in maintaining structures of dominance, and each plays a vital role in resistance. But behind all resistance there must be normative principles: a political theory.

Freedom and Equality: Essays on Liberalism and Feminism. Clare Chambers, Oxford University Press.
© Clare Chambers 2024. DOI: 10.1093/9780191919480.003.0014

References

15 square, 'Information, Education and Advice for Men With or Without a Foreskin (n.d.), https://www.15square.org.uk/.
Abbey, Ruth, 'Back Towards a Comprehensive Liberalism? Justice as Fairness, Gender, and Families', *Political Theory* 35(5) (2007).
Abbey, Ruth, *The Return of Feminist Liberalism* (Durham: Acumen, 2011).
Adichie, Chimamanda Ngozi, *We Should All Be Feminists* (London: Fourth Estate, 2014).
Ahmed, Sarah, *Living a Feminist Life* (Durham, NC: Duke University Press, 2017).
Anderson, Elizabeth, *Private Government: How Employers Rule Our Lives (and Why We Don't Talk About It)* (Princeton, NJ: Princeton University Press, 2017).
Anderson, Elizabeth, 'What Is the Point of Equality?', *Ethics* 109(2) (1999).
Antecol, Heather, Kelly Bedard, and Jenna Stearns, 'Equal but Inequitable: Who Benefits from Gender-Neutral Tenure Clock Stopping Policies?', in IZA Institute of Labor Economics Discussion Papers No. 9904 (April 2016).
Arneson, Richard, 'Against Rawlsian Equality of Opportunity', *Philosophical Studies* 93(1) (1999).
Arneson, Richard, 'Equality of Opportunity for Welfare Defended and Recanted', *The Journal of Political Philosophy* 7(4) (1999).
Baehr, Amy R., 'Liberal Feminism: Comprehensive and Political', in Abbey, Ruth (ed.), *Feminist Responses to John Rawls* (University Park, PA: The Pennsylvania State University Press, 2013).
Baehr, Amy R., 'Toward a New Feminist Liberalism: Okin, Rawls, and Habermas', *Hypatia* 11(1) (1996).
Baron-Cohen, Simon, *The Essential Difference: Men, Women and the Extreme Male Brain* (London: Allen Lane, 2003).
Barrett, Michelle, 'Words and Things: Materialism and Method in Contemporary Feminist Analysis', in Kemp, Sandra and Squires, Judith (eds), *Feminisms* (Oxford: Oxford University Press, 1997).
Barry, Brian, *Culture and Equality: An Egalitarian Critique of Multiculturalism* (Cambridge: Polity Press, 2001).
Barry, Brian, *Justice as Impartiality* (Oxford: Oxford University Press, 1995).
Bartky, Sandra Lee, 'Foucault, Femininity and the Modernization of Patriarchal Power', in Meyers, Diana Tietjens (ed.), *Feminist Social Thought: A Reader* (London: Routledge, 1997).
Bates, Laura, *Everyday Sexism* (London: Simon & Schuster, 2014).
Baumgardner, Jennifer and Richards, Amy, *Manifesta: Young Women, Feminism and the Future* (New York, NY: Farrar, Straus, and Giroux, 2000).
BBC News, 'Woman Denied Abortion in the Republic of Ireland Speaks Out', BBC (19 August 2014), http://www.bbc.co.uk/news/world-europe-28849058.
BBC Sport, 'Andy Murray: Serena Williams Would Face British Number One', BBC (27 June 2013), https://www.bbc.co.uk/sport/tennis/23087179.
Benhabib, Seyla, *Situating the Self: Gender, Community and Postmodernism in Contemporary Ethics* (Cambridge: Polity Press, 1992).

Benhabib, Seyla, *The Claims of Culture: Equality and Diversity in the Global Era* (Princeton, NJ: Princeton University Press, 2002).
Benhabib, Seyla, Butler, Judith, Cornell, Drucilla, and Fraser, Nancy, *Feminist Contentions* (London: Routledge, 1995).
Berer, Marge, 'Labia Reduction for Non-Therapeutic Purposes vs Female Genital Mutilation: Contradictions in Law and Practice in Britain', *Reproductive Health Matters* 18(35) (2010).
Berlin, Isaiah, *Four Essays on Liberty* (Oxford: Oxford University Press, 1969).
Bettcher, Talie Mae, 'Trans Identities and First-Person Authority', in Laurie Shrage (ed.), *"You've Changed": Sex Reassignment and Personal Identity* (Oxford: Oxford University Press, 2009).
Bevacqua, Maria, 'Feminist Theory and the Question of Lesbian and Gay Marriage', *Feminism & Psychology* 14(1) (2004).
Bindel, Julie, *Feminism for Women: The Real Route to Liberation* (London: Little Brown, 2021).
Blackledge, Catherine, *The Story of V: Opening Pandora's Box* (London: Orion Books, 2003).
Bordo, Susan, *Unbearable Weight: Feminism, Western Culture, and the Body* (Berkeley and Los Angeles, CA: University of California Press, 2003).
Bornstein, Kate, *Gender Outlaw: On Men, Women and the Rest of Us* (New York, NY: Vintage, 1995).
Bourdieu, Pierre and Wacquant, Loïc, *An Invitation to Reflexive Sociology* (Cambridge: Polity Press, 1992).
Bourdieu, Pierre, *Masculine Domination* (Cambridge: Polity Press, 2001).
Bourdieu, Pierre, *The Logic of Practice* (Cambridge: Polity Press, 1990).
Brake, Elizabeth, *Minimizing Marriage: Marriage, Morality, and the Law* (Oxford: Oxford University Press, 2012).
Braun, Virginia, 'Female Genital Cosmetic Surgery: A Critical Review of Current Knowledge and Contemporary Debates', *Journal of Women's Health* 19(7) (2010).
Braun, Virginia, 'Thanks to my Mother...A Personal Commentary on Heterosexual Marriage', *Feminism & Psychology* 13(4) (2003).
Brettschneider, Corey, 'The Politics of the Personal: A Liberal Approach', *American Political Science Review* 101(1) (2007).
Brighouse, Harry, *School Choice and Social Justice* (Oxford: Oxford University Press, 2000).
Brighouse, Harry and Swift, Adam, 'Equality, Priority and Positional Goods', *Ethics* 116(3) (2006).
Brighouse, Harry and Swift, Adam, 'Legitimate Parental Partiality', *Philosophy and Public Affairs* 37(1) (2009).
British Medical Association, 'The Law and Ethics of Male Circumcision' (BMA, 2017), https://www.bma.org.uk/advice/employment/ethics/children-and-young-people/male-circumcision.
Brizendine, Louann, *The Female Brain* (London: Bantam, 2007).
Brizendine, Louann, *The Male Brain* (London: Bantam, 2010).
Brown, Alexander, 'Access to Educational Opportunities—One-off or Lifelong?', *Journal of Philosophy of Education* 40(1) (2006).
Brownmiller, Susan, *Against Our Will: Men, Women and Rape* (New York, NY: Simon and Schuster, 1975).
Bunch, Charlotte, 'Lesbians in Revolt', in Phelan, Shane and Blasius, Mark (eds), *We Are Everywhere: A Historical Sourcebook of Gay and Lesbian Politics* (London: Routledge, 1997).

Burke, Michael, 'Trans women participation in sport: a feminist alternative to Pike's position' in Journal of the Philosophy of Sport Vol. 49 No. 2 (2022).
Burton, Tara Isabella, 'Poll: 48% of White Evangelicals Would Support Kavanaugh Even if the Allegations Against Him Were True' (*Vox*, 27 September 2018), https://www.vox.com/policy-and-politics/2018/9/27/17910016/brett-kavanaugh-christine-blasey-ford-white-evangelicals-poll-support.
Butler, Judith, *Gender Trouble* (Cambridge: Polity Press, 1999).
Butler, Judith, 'Performativity's Social Magic', in Shusterman, Richard (ed.), *Bourdieu: A Critical Reader* (Oxford: Blackwell, 1999).
Buzuvis, Erin E., 'Transgender Student-Athletes and Sex-Segregated Sport: Developing Policies of Inclusion for Intercollegiate and Interscholastic Athletics', *Seton Hall Journal of Sports and Entertainment Law* 21(1) (2011).
Cahn, Susan K., 'From the "Muscle Moll" to the "Butch" Ballplayer: Mannishness, Lesbianism, and Homophobia in U.S. Women's Sports', in Weitz, Rose (ed.), *The Politics of Women's Bodies: Sexuality, Appearance, and Behavior* (New York, NY; Oxford: Oxford University Press, 2003).
Califia, Patrick, *Sex Changes: Transgender Politics* (San Francisco, CA: Cleis Press, 1997).
Callan, Eamonn, *Creating Citizens* (Oxford: Oxford University Press, 1997).
Cameron, Deborah, *The Myth of Mars and Venus: Do Men and Women Really Speak Different Languages?* (Oxford: Oxford University Press, 2007).
Card, Claudia, 'Against Marriage and Motherhood', *Hypatia* 11(3) (1996).
CAS Arbitration, 'Caster Semenya, Athletics South Africa (ASA) and International Association of Athletics Federations (IAAF): Decision' (TAS/CAS, 1 May 2019), https://www.tas-cas.org/en/general-information/news-detail/article/cas-arbitration-caster-semenya-athletics-south-africa-asa-and-international-association-of-athl.html.
Cavanagh, Matt, *Against Equality of Opportunity* (Oxford: Clarendon Press, 2002).
Chambers, Clare, *Against Marriage: An Egalitarian Defence of the Marriage-Free State* (Oxford: Oxford University Press, 2017).
Chambers, Clare, *Intact: A Defence of the Unmodified Body* (London: Allen Lane, 2022).
Chambers, Clare, 'Judith Butler's Gender Trouble', in Levy, Jacob T. (ed.), *Oxford Handbook of Classics in Contemporary Political Theory* (Oxford: Oxford University Press, online first 2017).
Chambers, Clare, *Sex, Culture, and Justice: The Limits of Choice* (University Park, PA: Penn State University Press, 2008).
Chambers, Clare and Parvin, Phil, 'Coercive Redistribution and Public Agreement: Re-Evaluating the Libertarian Challenge of Charity', *Critical Review of International Social and Political Philosophy* 13(1) (2010).
Chambers, Clare and Parvin, Phil, 'What Kind of Dialogue Do We Need? Gender, Deliberation and Comprehensive Values', in Browne, Jude (ed.), *Dialogue, Politics and Gender* (Cambridge: Cambridge University Press, 2013).
Chappell, Sophie-Grace, 'Trans Women/Men and Adoptive Parents: An Analogy' (APA blog, 20 July 2018), https://blog.apaonline.org/2018/07/20/trans-women-men-and-adoptive-parents-an-analogy/.
Cohen, G. A., *If You're an Egalitarian, How Come You're So Rich?* (Cambridge, MA: Harvard University Press, 2001).
Cohen, G. A., 'Incentives, Inequality, and Community', in Peterson, Grethe B. (ed.), *The Tanner Lectures on Human Values* (Salt Lake City, UT: University of Utah Press, 1991).
Cohen, G. A., *Rescuing Justice and Equality* (Cambridge, MA: Harvard University Press, 2008).
Cold, C. J. and Taylore, J. R., 'The Prepuce', *BJU International* 20(83) (1999).

Coleman, Doriane Lambert, 'On the Biology of Sex, Sex Differentiation, and the Performance Gap: Yes, It Is All About Testosterone' (*The Volokh Conspiracy*, 12 March 2019).
Coleman, Doriane Lambert, 'Sex in Sport', *Law and Contemporary Problems* 80(63) (2018).
Collins, Patricia Hill, *Black Feminist Thought* (New York, NY; London: Routledge, 2000).
Cornell, Drucilla, *The Imaginary Domain: Abortion, Pornography, and Sexual Harrassment* (London: Routledge, 1995).
Court of Arbitration for Sport, 'Semenya, ASA and IAAF: Executive Summary' (n.d.), https://www.tas-cas.org/fileadmin/user_upload/CAS_Executive_Summary__5794_pdf.
Cowan, S., 'Gender is no Substitute for Sex: A Comparative Human Rights Analysis of the Legal Regulation of Sexual Identity', *Feminist Legal Studies* 13 (2005).
Creighton, Sarah M. and Liao, Lih-Mei (eds), *Female Genital Cosmetic Surgery: Solution to What Problem?* (Cambridge: Cambridge University Press, 2019).
Crenshaw, Kimberlé, *On Intersectionality: Essential Writings* (New York, NY: The New Press, 2023).
Criado-Perez, Caroline, *Invisible Women: Exposing Data Bias in a World Designed for Men* (London: Chatto & Windus, 2019).
Cronin, Helena, *The Ant and the Peacock: Altruism and Sexual Selection from Darwin to Today* (Cambridge: Cambridge University Press, 1991).
Crouch, N. S., Deans, R., Michala, L., Liao, L.-M., and Creighton, S. M., 'Clinical Characteristics of Well Women Seeking Labial Reduction Surgery: A Prospective Study', *BJOG: An International Journal of Obstetrics & Gynaecology* 118(12) (2011).
Crown Prosecution Service, 'Female Genital Mutilation Legal Guidance' (updated 2023), http://www.cps.gov.uk/legal/d_to_g/female_genital_mutilation/#a01.
Cudd, Anne E., *Analyzing Oppression* (Oxford: Oxford University Press, 2006).
Davis, Angela Yvonne, *Women, Race and Class* (New York: Vintage Press, 1983).
Davis, Kathy, *Reshaping the Female Body: The Dilemma of Plastic Surgery* (London: Routledge, 1995).
de Beauvoir, Simone, *The Second Sex* (New York, NY: Bantam, 1952).
de Wijze, Stephen, 'The Family and Political Justice—The Case for Political Liberalisms', *The Journal of Ethics* 4(3) (2000).
Dejevsky, Mary, 'If Even Merkel Attracts "Black Widow Spider" Sexism, What Hope Is There for the Rest of Us?', *Independent* (25 September 2013), http://www.independent.co.uk/voices/comment/if-even-merkel-attracts-black-widow-spider-sexism-what-hope-is-there-for-the-rest-of-us-8839577.html.
Delphy, Christine, *Close to Home: A Materialist Analysis of Women's Oppression* (Amherst, MA: University of Massachusetts Press, 1984).
Department of Gender and Women's Studies, 'History & Discoveries', UC Berkeley (n.d.), https://www.berkeley.edu/about/history-discoveries/.
Devine, John William, 'Gender, Steroids, and Fairness in Sport', *Sport, Ethics, and Philosophy* 13(2) (2019).
Devries, Michaela C., 'Do Transitioned Athletes Compete at an Advantage or Disadvantage as Compared with Physically Born Men and Women: A Review of the Scientific Literature' (2008), https://citeseerx.ist.psu.edu/viewdoc/download;jsessionid=B2304B2F5351EF127EE3FBAC14D9AF56?doi=10.1.1.546.8794&rep=rep1&type=pdf.
Donaghue, Ngaire, 'Gender Bias: Why Appearance Focus Fuels Sexism in Media', *Conversation* (13 April 2013), http://theconversation.com/gender-bias-why-appearance-focus-fuels-sexism-in-media-13325.
Donaldson, Sue and Kymlicka, Will, *Zoopolis: A Political Theory of Animal Rights* (Oxford: Oxford University Press, 2011).

Dupré, John, *Human Nature and the Limits of Science* (Oxford: Oxford University Press, 2001).
Dustin, Moira, 'Female Genital Mutilation/Cutting in the UK: Challenging the Inconsistencies', *The European Journal of Women's Studies* 17(1) (2010).
Dworkin, Andrea, 'Dworkin on Dworkin', in Diane Bell and Renate Klein (eds), *Radically Speaking: Feminism Reclaimed* (London: Zed Books, 1996).
Dworkin, Andrea, *Letters from a War Zone* (London: Secker & Warburg, 1988).
Dworkin, Andrea, *Life and Death: Unapologetic Writings on the Continuing War Against Women* (London: Virago, 1979).
Dworkin, Andrea, *Scapegoat: The Jews, Israel and Women's Liberation* (London: Virago, 2000).
Dworkin, Andrea, *Woman Hating* (New York, NY: E. P. Dutton, 1974).
Dworkin, Ronald, *Sovereign Virtue: The Theory and Practice of Equality* (Cambridge, MA: Harvard University Press, 2000).
Dworkin, Shari L., '"Holding Back": Negotiating a Glass Ceiling on Women's Muscular Strength', in Weitz, Rose (ed.), *The Politics of Women's Bodies: Sexuality, Appearance, and Behavior* (New York, NY; Oxford: Oxford University Press, 2003).
Earp, Brian D., 'Female Genital Mutilation (FGM) and Male Circumcision: Should There be a Separate Ethical Discourse?', *Practical Ethics* (2014), https://www.academia.edu/8817976/Female_genital_mutilation_FGM_and_male_circumcision_Should_there_be_a_separate_ethical_discourse.
Earp, Brian D., Sardi, Lauren M., and Jellison, William A., 'False Beliefs Predict Increased Circumcision Satisfaction in a Sample of US American Men', *Culture, Health & Sexuality* 20(8) (2018).
Elling-Machartzki, Agnes, 'Extraordinary Body Self-Narratives: Sport and Physical Activity in the Lives of Transgender People', *Leisure Studies* 36(2) (2017).
Elshtain, Jean Bethke, *Public Man, Private Woman* (Princeton, NJ: Princeton University Press, 1981).
English, Jane, 'Sex Equality in Sports', *Philosophy and Public Affairs* 7(3) (1978).
Equal Civil Partnerships Campaign Group (n.d.), http://equalcivilpartnerships.org.uk.
Equality Act 2010, 'Part 14: General Exceptions; Section 195: Sport' (2010), https://www.legislation.gov.uk/ukpga/2010/15/section/195.
Essén, Birgitta and Johnsdotter, Sara, 'Female Genital Mutilation in the West: Traditional Circumcision Versus Genital Cosmetic Surgery', *Acta Obstetricia et Gynecologica Scandinavica* 83(7) (2004).
Estlund, David, 'Commentary on Parts I and II', in Estlund, David and Nussbaum, Martha C. (eds), *Sex, Preference, and Family: Essays on Law and Nature* (Oxford: Oxford University Press, 1997).
Ewing, Lori, 'Canadian Cyclist Kristen Worley Blazes Own Trail as Voice for Gender Diversity in Sport', *The Globe and Mail* (19 April 2019), https://www.theglobeandmail.com/sports/article-canadian-cyclist-kristen-worley-blazes-own-trail-as-voice-for-gender/.
Faith Noah, 'I Was Nearly Aborted', *LifeTeen* (n.d.), http://lifeteen.com/blog/nearly-aborted/ (no longer online).
Fausto-Sterling, Anne, *Myths of Gender: Biological Theories About Women and Men* (New York, NY: Basic Books, 1985).
Fausto-Sterling, Anne, *Sexing the Body* (New York, NY: Basic Books, 2000).
Faye, Shon, *The Transgender Issue: An Argument for Justice* (London: Allen Lane, 2021).
Fein, Ellen and Schneider, Sherrie, *The Rules: Time Tested Secrets for Capturing the Heart of Mr Right* (London: Thorlens, 1995).

Feinberg, Leslie, *Trans Liberation: Beyond Pink or Blue* (Boston: Beacon, 1998).
Fenton, Siobhan, 'US Politician Trying to Ban Abortion Says He Has Never Thought About Why Women Have Them', *The Independent* (9 December 2016), https://www.independent.co.uk/news/world/americas/politician-trying-to-ban-abortion-after-admitting-he-has-never-thought-about-why-women-have-them-a7466196.html.
Ferguson, Michaele L., 'Choice Feminism and the Fear of Politics', *Perspectives on Politics* 8(1) (2010).
Fine, Cordelia, *Delusions of Gender: The Real Science Behind Sex Differences* (London: Icon, 2010).
Fineman, Martha Albertson, 'The Meaning of Marriage', in Bernstein, Anita (ed.), *Marriage Proposals: Questioning a Legal Status* (New York, NY: New York University Press, 2006).
Fineman, Martha Albertson, *The Neutered Mother, the Sexual Family, and Other Twentieth Century Tragedies* (New York, NY: Routledge, 1995).
Finlay, Sarah-Jane and Clarke, Victoria, '"A Marriage of Inconvenience?" Feminist Perspectives on Marriage', *Feminism & Psychology* 13(4) (2003).
Firestone, Shulamith, *The Dialectic of Sex: The Case for Feminist Revolution* (London: The Women's Press, 1979).
Fishkin, James S., *Justice, Equal Opportunity, and the Family* (New Haven, CT: Yale University Press, 1983).
Flax, Jane, 'Postmodernism and Gender Relations in Feminist Theory', in Kemp, Sandra and Squires, Judith (eds), *Feminisms* (Oxford: Oxford University Press, 1997).
Fleurbaey, Marc, 'Equality of Resources Revisited', *Ethics* 113(1) (2002).
Fond of Beetles, 'Harder, Faster, Better, Stronger: Why We Must Protect Female Sports', *FondofBeetles* (1 October 2018), https://fondofbeetles.wordpress.com/2018/10/01/harder-better-faster-stronger-why-we-must-protect-female-sports/.
Foucault, Michel, *Discipline and Punish: The Birth of the Prison* (Harmondsworth: Penguin, 1991).
FPFW, 'Dr Emma Hilton Reviews the Science Supporting the IOC Decision to Let Male-Born Transgender Athletes into Female Competition', *Fair Play for Women* (14 July 2019), https://fairplayforwomen.com/emma_hilton/.
Fraser, Nancy, 'After the Family Wage: Gender Equity and the Welfare State', *Political Theory* 22(4) (1994).
Fraser, Nancy, *Fortunes of Feminism: From State-Managed Capitalism to Neoliberal Crisis* (London: Verso, 2013).
Fraser, Nancy, *Justice Interruptus: Critical Reflections on the "Postsocialist" Condition* (London: Routledge, 1997).
Freeman, Samuel, *Rawls* (London: Routledge, 2007).
Friedan, Betty, *The Feminine Mystique* (Harmondsworth: Penguin, 1983).
Friedman, Marilyn, *Autonomy, Gender, Politics* (Oxford: Oxford University Press, 2003).
Galston, William A., *Liberal Pluralism: The Implications of Value Pluralism for Political Theory and Practice* (Cambridge: Cambridge University Press, 2002).
Gardiner, Becky, Mansfield, Mahana, Anderson, Ian, Hodler, Josh, Louter, Daan, and Ulmanu, Monica, 'The Dark Side of Guardian Comments', *The Guardian* (12 April 2016), https://www.theguardian.com/technology/2016/apr/12/the-dark-side-of-guardian-comments.
Gardner, Carol Brooks, *Passing By: Gender and Public Harassment* (Berkeley, CA; London: University of California Press, 1995).
Gheaus, Anca, 'Feminism without "gender identity"', *Politics, Philosophy, and Economics* 22 (2023).

Gibson, Charlotte, 'Who's the Highest Paid Person In Your State', ESPN.com (20 March 2018), https://www.espn.com/espn/feature/story/_/id/22454170/highest-paid-state-employees-include-ncaa-coaches-nick-saban-john-calipari-dabo-swinney-bill-self-bob-huggins.
Gilligan, Carol, *In a Different Voice* (Cambridge, MA: Harvard University Press, 1982).
Gilman, Charlotte Perkins, *Herland* (London: The Women's Press, 1979).
Glasson, Cait, 'Sport is a Human Right—So Let Trans Women Compete', *Arc* (1 June 2019), https://medium.com/arc-digital/sport-is-a-human-right-so-let-trans-women-compete-2db252184fe.
Gleaves, John and Lehrbach, Tim, 'Beyond Fairness: The Ethics of Inclusion for Transgender and Intersex Athletes', *Journal of the Philosophy of Sport* 43(2) (2016).
Glick, Leonard B., *Marked in Your Flesh: Circumcision from Ancient Judea to Modern America* (New York, NY: Oxford University Press, 2005).
Gornick, Janet C., 'Reconcilable Difference: What It Would Take for Marriage and Feminism to Say "I Do"', *The American Prospect Online* (7 April 2002).
Greenfield, Lauren, *Generation Wealth* (London: Phaidon Press, 2017).
Greer, Germaine, *The Female Eunuch* (London: Flamingo, 1991).
Grimer, David, 'Men Read Mean Tweets About Female Sportswriters, and Are Shocked at How Dark It Gets', *Adweek* (26 April 2016), http://www.adweek.com/adfreak/men-read-mean-tweets-about-female-sportswriters-and-are-shocked-how-dark-it-gets-171064/.
Gullette, Margaret Morganroth, 'The New Case for Marriage', *The American Prospect Online* (5 March 2004).
Gunston, Jo, 'England Men's Netball Captain Talks to Me About the Stigma He Faces', *Sports Liberated* (28 January 2015), https://www.sportsliberated.com/interview-england-netballer-gary-patrick-brown/.
Gutmann, Amy and Thompson, Dennis, 'Deliberative Democracy Beyond Process', *The Journal of Political Philosophy* 10(2) (2002).
Haider-Markel, Donald P. and Joslyn, Mark R., 'Beliefs About the Origins of Homosexuality and Support For Gay Rights: An Empirical Test of Attribution Theory', *Public Opinion Quarterly* 72(2) (2009).
Halberstam, Jack, *Trans*: A Quick and Quirky Account of Gender Variability* (Berkeley, CA: University of California Press, 2018).
Hampton, Jean, 'Feminist Contractarianism', in Baehr, Amy R. (ed.), *Varieties of Feminist Liberalism* (Oxford: Rowman & Littlefield, 2004).
Hansard HC Deb 21 March 2003 vol. 401 cc1188-208, 'Female Genital Mutilation Bill', http://hansard.millbanksystems.com/commons/2003/mar/21/female-genital-mutilation-bill.
Hansard HL Deb 12 September 2003 vol. 652 cc635-53, 'Female Genital Mutilation Bill', http://hansard.millbanksystems.com/lords/2003/sep/12/female-genital-mutilation-bill.
Harding, Sandra and Hintikka, Merrill B., *Discovering Reality: Feminist Perspectives on Epistemology, Metaphysics, Methodology, and Philosophy of Science* (New York: Springer, 2003).
Hargie, Owen D. W., Mitchell, David H., and Somerville, Ian J. A., '"People Have a Knack of Making You Feel Excluded if They Catch on to Your Difference": Transgender Experiences of Exclusion in Sport', *International Review for the Sociology of Sport* 52(2) (2015).
Harrison, Kristina, 'A System of Gender Self-Identification Would Put Women at Risk', *The Economist* (3 July 2018).

Hartley, Christie and Watson, Lori, 'Is a Feminist Political Liberalism Possible?', *Journal of Ethics and Social Philosophy* 5(1) (2010).

Hartmann, Wolfram, 'German Paediatric Association Criticises American Academy of Pediatrics', Circumcision Information Australia (n.d.), https://www.circinfo.org/doctors.html.

Haslanger, Sally, 'Culture and Critique', *Aristotelian Society Supplementary Volume* 91(1) (2017).

Haslanger, Sally, 'Gender and Race: (What) Are They? (What) Do We Want Them to Be?', *Noûs* 34(1) (2000).

Haslanger, Sally, *Resisting Reality: Social Construction and Social Critique* (Oxford: Oxford University Press, 2012).

Hay, Carol, 'Who Counts as a Woman?', *The New York Times* (1 April 2019).

Held, Virginia, *The Ethics of Care* (Oxford: Oxford University Press, 2005).

Heyes, Cressida J., 'Feminist Solidarity after Queer Theory: The Case of Transgender', *Signs* 28(4) (2003).

Hirschmann, Nancy J., 'Choosing Betrayal', *Perspectives on Politics* 8(1) (2010).

Hirschmann, Nancy J., *Gender, Class, and Freedom in Modern Political Theory* (Princeton, NJ: Princeton University Press, 2008).

Hirschmann, Nancy J., *The Subject of Liberty: Toward a Feminist Theory of Freedom* (Princeton, NJ: Princeton University Press, 2003).

Hobbes, Thomas, *Leviathan*, ed. Edwin Curley (Indianapolis, IN: Hackett 1994 [1651]).

Hochschild, Arlie Russell, The Managed Heart: Commercialization of Human Feeling (Berkeley, CA: University of California Press, 1992).

Hochschild, Arlie Russell and Machung, Anne, *The Second Shift: Working Parents and the Revolution at Home* (London: Piatkus, 1990).

Hoffman, Joanna, 'Athlete Ally: Navratilova's Statements Transphobic and Counter to our Work, Vision and Values', *Athlete Ally* (19 February 2019), https://www.athleteally.org/navratilovas-statements-transphobic-counter-to-our-work-vision/.

hooks, bell, *Ain't I a Woman: Black Women and Feminism* (London: Pluto Press, 1983).

hooks, bell, 'Feminism: A Movement to End Sexist Oppression', in Kemp, Sandra and Squires, Judith (eds), *Feminisms* (Oxford: Oxford University Press, 1997).

Howarth, Calida, Hayes, Jenny, Simonis, Magdalena, and Temple-Smith, Meredith, '"Everything's Neatly Tucked Away": Young Women's Views on Desirable Vulval Anatomy', *Culture, Health & Sexuality* 18(12) (2016).

Huffpost, 'Tom Cruise & Cameron Diaz in London: How Is He So Tall? (PHOTOS)', *HuffPost* (22 July 2010), http://www.huffingtonpost.com/2010/07/22/tom-cruise-cameron-diaz-i_n_656203.html.

Human Rights Commission, 'Circumstances When Being Treated Differently Due to Sex Is Lawful', https://www.equalityhumanrights.com/en/advice-and-guidance/sex-discrimination#lawful.

Ingle, Sean, 'Caster Semenya Case Verdict Postponed Until End of April', *The Guardian* (21 March 2019).

Ingle, Sean, 'Sports Stars Weigh in on Row Over Transgender Athletes', *The Guardian* (3 March 2019).

Intact America, '10 Out of 10 Babies Say NO to Circumcision (n.d.), http://intactamerica.org.

International Olympic Committee, 'IOC Consensus Meeting on Sex Reassignment and Hyperandrogenism November 2015' (November 2015), https://stillmed.olympic.org/Documents/Commissions_PDFfiles/Medical_commission/2015-11_ioc_consensus_meeting_on_sex_reassignment_and_hyperandrogenism-en.pdf.

International Olympic Committee, 'When Did Women First Compete in the Olympic Games?' (n.d.), https://olympics.com/ioc/faq/history-and-origin-of-the-games/when-did-women-first-compete-in-the-olympic-games.
Jaggar, Alison, *Feminist Politics and Human Nature* (Totowa, NJ: Rowman and Allanheld, 1983).
Jaggar, Alison, 'Global Gender Justice Edition', *Philosophical Topics* 37 (2009).
Jeffreys, Sheila, *Beauty and Misogyny: Harmful Cultural Practices in the West* (Hove: Routledge, 2005).
Jeffreys, Sheila, *The Idea of Prostitution* (Melbourne: Spinifex Press, 1997).
Jeffreys, Sheila, *The Industrial Vagina: The Political Economy of the Global Sex Trade* (London: Routledge, 2008).
Jeffreys, Sheila, 'The Need to Abolish Marriage', *Feminism & Psychology* 14(2) (2004).
Jeffreys, Sheila, *Unpacking Queer Politics* (Cambridge: Polity Press, 2003).
Jenkins, Katharine, 'Gender Identity and the Concept of Woman', *Ethics* 126(2) (2016).
Jones, Bethany Alice, Arcelus, Jon, Bouman, Walter Pierre, and Haycraft, Emma, 'Sport and Transgender People: A Systematic Review of the Literature Relating to Sport Participation and Competitive Sport Policies', *Sports Medicine* 47(4) (2016).
Joyce, Helen, *Trans: When Ideology Meets Reality* (London: Oneworld, 2021).
Kelly, B. and Foster, C., 'Should Female Genital Cosmetic Surgery and Genital Piercing Be Regarded Ethically and Legally as Female Genital Mutilation?', *BJOG: An International Journal of Obstetrics and Gynaecology* 119(4) (2012).
Kemp, Sandra and Squires, Judith (eds), *Feminisms* (Oxford: Oxford University Press, 1997).
Khader, Serene, *Decolonizing Universalism: A Transnational Feminist Ethic* (Oxford: Oxford University Press, 2018).
Kingston, Anne, *The Meaning of Wife* (London: Piatkus, 2004).
Kiraly, Miranda and Tyler, Meagan, *Freedom Fallacy: The Limits of Liberal Feminism* (Ballarat, Victoria: Connor Court, 2015).
Kirkpatrick, Jennet, 'Selling Out? Solidarity and Choice in the American Feminist Movement', *Perspectives on Politics* 8(1) (2010).
Kittay, Eva Feder, *Love's Labor: Essays on Women, Equality, and Dependency* (New York, NY: Routledge, 1999).
Kitzinger, Celia and Wilkinson, Sue, 'The Re-Branding of Marriage: Why We Got Married Instead of Registering a Civil Partnership', *Feminism and Psychology* 14(1) (2004).
Knox, Taryn, Anderson, Lynley C., and Heather, Alison, 'Transwomen in Elite Sport: Scientific and Ethical Considerations', *Journal of Medical Ethics* 45(6) (2019).
Kowal, John F., 'Is Marriage Equality Next Target for SCOTUS Conservative Supermajority?', Brennan Center for Justice (14 June 2022), https://www.brennancenter.org/our-work/analysis-opinion/marriage-equality-next-target-scotus-conservative-supermajority.
Kramer, Matthew H., *Liberalism with Excellence* (Oxford; New York, NY: Oxford University Press, 2017).
Kymlicka, Will, *Liberalism, Community and Culture* (Oxford: Clarendon Press, 1989).
Laden, Anthony Simon, 'Radical Liberals, Reasonable Feminists: Reason, Power, and Objectivity in MacKinnon and Rawls', in Abbey, Ruth (ed.), *Feminist Responses to John Rawls* (University Park, PA: The Pennsylvania State University Press, 2013).
Larmore, Charles E., *The Morals of Modernity* (Cambridge: Cambridge University Press, 1995).
Lawford-Smith, Holly, *Gender-Critical Feminism* (Oxford: Oxford University Press, 2022).

Lawford-Smith, Holly and Chappell, Sophie-Grace, 'Transgender: A Dialogue', *Aeon* (15 November 2018), https://aeon.co/essays/transgender-identities-a-conversation-between-two-philosophers.

Lees, Sue, *Carnal Knowledge: Rape on Trial* (London: The Women's Press, 2002).

Leng, Mary, 'Amelioration, Inclusion, and Legal Recognition: On Sex, Gender, and the UK's Gender Recognition Act', *Journal of Political Philosophy* 31 (2023).

Levinson, Meira, *The Demands of Liberal Education* (Oxford: Oxford University Press, 1999).

Levy, Ariel, *Female Chauvinist Pigs: Women and the Rise of Raunch Culture* (New York, NY: Free Press, 2006).

Lewis, Anna, 'I'm a Celeb Campmates Are Divided on Whether Wolf Whistling Is Sexist or Not', *Cosmopolitan* (30 November 2016), http://www.cosmopolitan.co.uk/entertainment/news/a47701/im-a-celeb-campmates-wolf-whistling-sexist/.

Lewis, Jane, *The End of Marriage? Individualism and Intimate Relations* (Cheltenham: Edward Elgar, 2001).

Lewis, Sophie, *Full Surrogacy Now: Feminism Against Family* (London: Verso, 2019).

Liew, Jonathan, 'Why the Arguments Against Trans, Intersex, and DSD Athletes Are Based on Prejudice and Ignorance', *The Independent* (22 February 2019).

Lippert-Rasmussen, Kasper, 'Arneson on Equality of Opportunity for Welfare', *The Journal of Political Philosophy* 7(4) (1999).

Lloyd, S. A., 'Situating a Feminist Criticism of John Rawls's Political Liberalism', *Loyola of Los Angeles Law Review* 28(4) (1995).

Lloyd, S. A., 'Toward a Liberal Theory of Sexual Equality', in Baehr, Amy R. (ed.), *Varieties of Feminist Liberalism* (Oxford: Rowman & Littlefield, 2004).

Locke, John, *Two Treatises of Government*, ed. Peter Laslett (Cambridge: Cambridge University Press, 1994 [1689]).

Lodge, David, *Small World* (London: Penguin, 1985).

Loland, Sigmund, 'Fairness in Sport: An Ideal and its Consequences', in McNamee, Mike(ed.), *The Ethics of Sports: A Reader* (London: Routledge, 2010).

Lorde, Audre, *Your Silence Will Not Protect You* (London: Silver Press, 2017).

McBee, Thomas Page, *Amateur: A Reckoning with Gender, Identity, and Masculinity* (Edinburgh: Canongate Books, 2018).

MacCallum, Fiona and Widdows, Heather, 'Altered Images: Understanding the Influence of Unrealistic Images and Beauty Aspirations', *Health Care Analysis* 26 (2018).

McCartney, Jamie, 'The Great Wall of Vagina', *The Great Wall of Vagina* (2022), http://www.greatwallofvagina.co.uk/home.

MacIntyre, Alasdair, *After Virtue: A Study in Moral Theory* (London: Duckworth, 1996).

Mackay, Finn, *Female Masculinities and the Gender Wars: The Politics of Sex* (London: Bloomsbury, 2021).

MacKinnon, Catharine A., *Are Women Human? And Other International Dialogues* (Cambridge, MA: Harvard University Press, 2006).

MacKinnon, Catharine A., *Feminism Unmodified* (Cambridge, MA: Harvard University Press, 1987).

MacKinnon, Catharine A., *Sexual Harassment of Working Women* (New Haven, CT: Yale University Press, 1979).

MacKinnon, Catharine A., '"The Case" Responds', *American Political Science Review* 95(3) (2001).

MacKinnon, Catharine A., *Toward a Feminist Theory of the State* (Cambridge, MA: Harvard University Press, 1989).

MacKinnon, Catherine A., *Women's Lives, Men's Laws* (Cambridge, MA: Harvard University Press, 2005).
McKinnon, Rachel and Conrad, Aryn, 'Including Trans Athletes in Sport', presented in lecture form (13 January 2018), https://www.youtube.com/watch?v=EImjVGxAlv4.
McNay, Lois, *Foucault and Feminism* (Cambridge: Polity Press, 1992).
Maese, Rick, 'Stripped of Women's Records, Transgender Powerlifter Asks, "Where Do We Draw the Line?"', *The Washington Post* (16 May 2019).
Magowan, Alistair, 'Transgender Women in Sport: Are They Really a "Threat" to Female Sport?', BBC Sport (18 December 2018).
March, Andrew F., 'What Lies Beyond Same-Sex Marriage? Marriage, Reproductive Freedom and Future Persons in Liberal Public Justification', *Journal of Applied Philosophy* 27(1) (2010).
Marx, Karl, *The German Ideology*, in McLellan, David (ed.), *Karl Marx: Selected Writings* (Oxford: Oxford University Press, 1977).
Mason, Andrew, 'Equality of Opportunity, Old and New', *Ethics* 111(4) (2001).
Mason, Andrew, *Levelling the Playing Field: The Idea of Equal Opportunity and Its Place in Egalitarian Thought* (Oxford: Oxford University Press, 2006).
Mayeda, Graham, 'Who Do You Think You Are? When Should the Law Let You Be Who You Want to Be?', in Shrage, Laurie J. (ed.), *"You've Changed": Sex Reassignment and Personal Identity* (Oxford; New York, NY: Oxford University Press, 2009).
Medico Beauty and IVF, 'Labiaplasty', Medico Beauty Clinic (25 October 2017), https://medicobeautyclinic.com/aesthetic-surgery/procedures/labiaplasty-labia-minora-reduction (no longer available online).
Metz, Tamara, *Untying the Knot: Marriage, the State, and the Case for their Divorce* (Princeton, NJ: Princeton University Press, 2010).
Mill, John Stuart, *On Liberty and The Subjection of Women* (Ware: Wordsworth, 1996 [1868]).
Mill, John Stuart, *Utilitarianism, On Liberty, Considerations on Representative Government* (London: Everyman 1993 [1859]).
Miller, David, 'Equality of Opportunity and the Family', in Satz, Debra and Reich, Rob (eds), *Toward a Humanist Justice: The Political Philosophy of Susan Moller Okin* (New York, NY; Oxford: Oxford University Press, 2009).
Miller, David, 'Liberalism, Equal Opportunities and Cultural Commitments', in Kelly, Paul (ed.), *Multiculturalism Reconsidered: Culture and Equality and Its Critics* (Cambridge: Polity Press, 2002).
Miller, David, *Principles of Social Justice* (Harvard, MA: Harvard University Press, 1999).
Miller, Geoffrey, *The Mating Mind: How Sexual Choice Shaped the Evolution of Human Nature* (London: William Heinemann, 2000).
Miller, Michael E., '"A Steep Price to Pay for 20 Minutes of Action": Dad Defends Stanford Sex Offender', *The Washington Post* (6 June 2016), https://www.washingtonpost.com/news/morning-mix/wp/2016/06/06/a-steep-price-to-pay-for-20-minutes-of-action-dad-defends-stanford-sex-offender/.
Mills, Charles, *Black Rights/White Wrongs: The Critique of Racial Liberalism* (Oxford: Oxford University Press, 2017).
Mills & Reeve LLP, 'The Female Genital Mutilation Act and Its Relation to Female Genital Cosmetic Surgery', *Lexology* (16 October 2013), https://www.lexology.com/library/detail.aspx?g=2afbc225-8ba6-4e83-803c-034c070529de.
Ministry of Employment, 'Chronological Overview of LGBT Persons Rights in Sweden', Government Offices of Sweden (12 July 2018), https://www.government.se/articles/2018/07/chronological-overview-of-lgbt-persons-rights-in-sweden/.

Moran, C. and Lee, C., 'What's Normal? Influencing Women's Perceptions of Normal Genitalia: An Experiment Involving Exposure to Modified and Nonmodified Images', *BJOG: An International Journal of Obstetrics & Gynaecology* 121(6) (2014).

MYA Cosmetic Surgery, 'Labiaplasty' (2022), https://www.mya.co.uk/procedures/body-procedures/labiaplasty#dqD4VLXScbtZAKUk.97.

National Collegiate Athletics Association, 'Scholarships' (NCAA, 2022), http://www.ncaa.org/student-athletes/future/scholarships.

National Organization of Circumcision Information Resource Centers, 'Making a Safer World for Children' (n.d.), http://www.nocirc.org.

Nedelsky, Jennifer, *Law's Relations: A Relational Theory of Self, Autonomy, and Law* (Oxford: Oxford University Press, 2012).

Nestle, Joan, Howell, Clare, and Wilchins, Riki Anne (eds), *GenderQueer: Voices from Beyond the Sexual Binary* (Boston, MA: Alyson Books, 2002).

NHS Choices, 'Circumcision in Boys' (27 June 2022), http://www.nhs.uk/conditions/Circumcision-in-children/Pages/Introduction.aspx.

Nozick, Robert, *Anarchy, State and Utopia* (Oxford: Blackwell, 1993).

Nuffield Council on Bioethics, *Cosmetic Procedures: Ethical Issues* (2017), http://nuffieldbioethics.org/project/cosmetic-procedures.

Nuffield Council on Bioethics, *Cosmetic Procedures: Ethical Issues—Online Questionnaire: Summary* (June 2017), https://www.nuffieldbioethics.org/wp-content/uploads/Survey-Monkey-Questionnaire-analysis.pdf.

Nussbaum, Martha C., 'A Plea for Difficulty', in Okin, Susan Moller, Cohen, Joshua, Howard, Matthew, and Nussbaum, Martha C. (eds), *Is Multiculturalism Bad for Women?* (Princeton, NJ: Princeton University Press, 1999).

Nussbaum, Martha C., *Sex and Social Justice* (Oxford: Oxford University Press, 1999).

Nussbaum, Martha C., 'The Future of Feminist Liberalism', in Baehr, Amy R. (ed.), *Varieties of Feminist Liberalism* (Oxford: Rowman & Littlefield, 2004).

Nussbaum, Martha C., 'The Professor of Parody', *The New Republic* 22(2) (1999).

O'Connor, Roisin, 'Designer Vagina Surgery Could Be as Illegal as FGM, Theresa May Warns', *Independent* (10 December 2014), https://www.independent.co.uk/news/uk/politics/designer-vagina-surgery-could-be-as-illegal-as-fgm-theresa-may-warns-9915466.html.

Okin, Susan Moller '"Forty Acres and a Mule" for Women: Rawls and Feminism', *Politics, Philosophy and Economics* 4(2) (2005).

Okin, Susan Moller, 'Is Multiculturalism Bad for Women?', in Okin, Susan Moller, Cohen, Joshua, Howard, Matthew, and Nussbaum, Martha C (eds), *Is Multiculturalism Bad for Women?* (Princeton, NJ: Princeton University Press, 1999).

Okin, Susan Moller, 'Justice and Gender: An Unfinished Debate', *Fordham Law Review* 72(5) (2004).

Okin, Susan Moller, *Justice, Gender, and the Family* (New York, NY: Basic Books, 1989).

Pannick, David, 'When is Sex a Genuine Occupational Qualification?', *Oxford Journal of Legal Studies* 4(2) (1984).

Parsons, Tony, 'Is It Ever OK to Wolf Whistle?', *GQ* (13 October 2015), https://www.gq-magazine.co.uk/article/is-it-ok-to-wolf-whistle.

Pateman, Carole, *The Sexual Contract* (Cambridge: Polity Press, 1988).

Pérez-Samaniego, Víctor, Fuentes-Miguel, Jorge, Pereira-García, Sofía, López-Cañada, Elena, and Devís-Devís, José, 'Experiences of Trans Persons in Physical Activity and Sport: A Qualitative Meta-Synthesis', *Sport Management Review* 22(4) (2019).

Pieper, Lindsay Parks, 'Sex Testing and the Maintenance of Western Femininity in International Sport', *The International Journal of the History of Sport* 31(13) (2014).

Pike, Jon, 'Safety, fairness, and inclusion: transgender athletes and the essence of Rugby' in Journal of the Philosophy of Sport Vol. 48 No. 2 (2021).
Pike, Jon, 'Why "Meaningful Competition" is not fair competition' in Journal of the Philosophy of Sport Vol. 50 No. 1 (2023).
Pinker, Susan, *The Sexual Paradox: Men, Women, and the Real Gender Gap* (New York, NY: Scribner, 2008).
Piper, John, 'Why the Simple Right to Abortion is Unjust', *Desiring God* (15 January 1990), http://www.desiringgod.org/articles/why-the-simple-right-to-abortion-is-unjust.
Pojman, Louis P., 'The Case Against Affirmative Action', *International Journal of Applied Philosophy* 12(1) (1998).
Press Association, 'Caster Semenya Accuses Sebastian Coe of "Opening Old Wounds"', *The Guardian* (27 March 2019).
Quong, Jonathan, 'Public Reason', *Stanford Encyclopedia of Philosophy* (20 May 2013), https://plato.stanford.edu/entries/public-reason/.
R (Steinfeld and Another) v Secretary of State for International Development UKSC 32 (2018), 3 WLR 415, https://www.supremecourt.uk/cases/uksc-2017-0060.html.
Radcliffe Richards, Janet, 'Equality of Opportunity', *Ratio* 10(3) (1997).
Radicalesbians, 'The Woman-Identified Woman', in Phelan, Shane and Blasius, Mark (eds), *We Are Everywhere: A Historical Sourcebook of Gay and Lesbian Politics* (London: Routledge, 1997).
Radnofsky, Louise, 'Should Women-Only Olympics Sports Be Open to Men?', *The Wall Street Journal* (20 August 2016).
Ramazonoğlu, Caroline, *Up Against Foucault: Explorations of Some Tensions Between Foucault and Feminism* (London: Routledge, 1993).
Rassbach, Eric, 'Coming Soon to a Court Near You: Religious Male Circumcision', *University of Illinois Law Review* 4 (2016).
Rawls, John, *A Theory of Justice* (Oxford: Oxford University Press, 1973).
Rawls, John, *Justice as Fairness: A Restatement* (Cambridge, MA: Harvard University Press, 2001).
Rawls, John, *Lectures on the History of Political Philosophy* (Cambridge, MA: Harvard University Press, 2007).
Rawls, John, *Political Liberalism* (New York, NY: Columbia University Press, 1993).
Rawls, John, *The Law of Peoples with "The Idea of Public Reason Revisited"* (Cambridge, MA: Harvard University Press, 1999).
Raz, Joseph, *The Morality of Freedom* (Oxford: Clarendon Press, 1986).
Reeser, J. C., 'Gender Identity and Sport: Is the Playing Field Level?', *British Journal of Sports Medicine* 39(10) (2005).
Reid, Heather L., *Introduction to the Philosophy of Sport*, 2nd edn (New York, NY: Rowman and Littlefield, 2023).
Reilly-Cooper, Rebecca, 'Am I Cisgender?', *More Radical with Age* (2014), https://rebeccarc.com/2014/08/04/am-i-cisgender/ (no longer available online).
Retter, Emily, 'Joanna Lumley Defends Wolf Whistling and Insists People Are Offended by "Everything"', *The Mirror* (4 October 2016), http://www.mirror.co.uk/3am/celebrity-news/joanna-lumley-defends-wolf-whistling-8980221.
Reynolds, Jill and Wetherell, Margaret, 'The Discursive Climate of Singleness: The Consequences for Women's Negotiation of a Single Identity', *Feminism & Psychology* 13(4) (2003).
RFSL, 'Why Do We Need a New Gender Recognition Act?', *RFSL* (20 March 2020), https://www.rfsl.se/en/lgbtq-facts/gender_recognition/.

Richardson, Janice, 'Jean Hampton's Reworking of Rawls: Is "Feminist Contractarianism" Useful for Feminism?', in Abbey, Ruth (ed.), *Feminist Responses to John Rawls* (University Park, PA: The Pennsylvania State University Press, 2013).

Richardson, Sarah S., *Sex Itself: The Search for Male & Female in the Human Genome* (Chicago, IL: University of Chicago Press, 2015).

Rizvi, S. A. H., Naqvi, S. A. A., Hussain, M., and Hasan, A. S., 'Religious Circumcision: A Muslim View', *BJU International* 83(1) (1999).

Robinson, Dana, 'A League of Their Own: Do Women Want Sex-Segregated Sports?', *Journal of Contemporary Legal Issues* 9 (1998).

Rogers, Rebecca G., 'Most Women Who Undergo Labiaplasty Have Normal Anatomy; We Should Not Perform Labiaplasty', *American Journal of Obstetrics and Gynecology* 211(3) (2014).

Ronzoni, Miriam, 'What Makes a Basic Structure Just?', *Res Publica* 14(3) (2008).

Rorty, Richard, *Contingency, Irony, and Solidarity* (Cambridge: Cambridge University Press, 1989).

Rose, Hilary and Rose, Steven P. R., *Alas Poor Darwin: Arguments Against Evolutionary Psychology* (London: Vintage, 2001).

Rosin, Hanna, 'The Case Against Breast-Feeding', *The Atlantic* (April 2009), https://www.theatlantic.com/magazine/archive/2009/04/the-case-against-breast-feeding/307311/.

Ross, Loretta, 'Understanding Reproductive Justice', *Trust Black Women* (n.d.), https://www.trustblackwomen.org/our-work/what-is-reproductive-justice/9-what-is-reproductive-justice (no longer available online).

Rousseau, Jean-Jacques, *The Basic Political Writings*, ed. and trans. Donald A. Cress (Indianapolis, IN: Hackett, 1987 [1762]).

Rowan, Kate, 'Revealed: Two Out of Five British and Irish Girls "Shun Sport During Puberty" – Far More than Rest of the World', *The Telegraph* (26 March 2019).

Royal College of Obstetricians and Gynaecologists Ethics Committee, *Ethical Opinion Paper: Ethical Considerations in Relation to Female Genital Cosmetic Surgery (FGCS)* (2013).

Rumsey, Nichola and Harcourt, Diana (eds), *Oxford Handbook of Psychology of Appearance* (Oxford: Oxford University Press, 2012).

Ryan, Alan, 'Oxford Blues', *The Guardian* (24 May 2000).

Sandberg, Sheryl with Scovell, Nell, *Lean In: Women, Work, and the Will to Lead* (London: W. H. Allen, 2013).

Sandel, Michael J., *Liberalism and the Limits of Justice* (Cambridge: Cambridge University Press, 1982).

Sandfield, Anna and Percy, Carol, 'Accounting for Single Status: Heterosexism and Ageism in Heterosexual Women's Talk about Marriage', *Feminism & Psychology* 13(4) (2003).

Sandland, R., 'Feminism and the Gender Recognition Act 2004', *Feminist Legal Studies* 13 (2005).

Scheffler, Samuel, 'Is the Basic Structure Basic?', in Sypnowich, Christine (ed.), *The Egalitarian Conscience* (Oxford: Oxford University Press, 2006).

Schick, Vanessa R., Rima, Brandi N., and Calabrese, Sarah K., 'Evulvalution: The Portrayal of Women's External Genitalia and Physique across Time and the Current Barbie Doll Ideals', *The Journal of Sex Research* 48(1) (2011).

Schouten, Gina, *Liberalism, Neutrality, and the Gendered Division of Labor* (Oxford: Oxford University Press, 2019).

Schultz, Marjorie, 'Contractual Ordering of Marriage: A New Model for State Policy', *California Law Review* 70(2) (1982).

Schwartz, Pepper, *Love Between Equals: How Peer Marriage Really Works* (New York, NY: The Free Press, 1994).
Serano, Julia, 'Debunking "Trans Women Are Not Women" Arguments', *Medium* (27 June 2017), https://juliaserano.medium.com/debunking-trans-women-are-not-women-arguments-85fd5ab0e19c.
Shachar, Ayelet, *Multicultural Jurisdictions: Cultural Differences and Women's Rights* (Cambridge: Cambridge University Press, 2001).
Shahvisi, Arianne, 'Why UK Doctors Should Be Troubled by Female Genital Mutilation Legislation', *Clinical Ethics* 12(2) (2017).
Shanley, Mary Lyndon and Pateman, Carole, *Feminist Interpretations and Political Theory* (Cambridge: Polity Press, 1991).
Sharp, Gemma, Mattiske, Julie, and Vale, Kirsten I., 'Motivations, Expectations, and Experiences of Labiaplasty: A Qualitative Study', *Aesthetic Surgery Journal* 36(8) (2016).
Sharp, Gemma, Tiggemann, Marika, and Mattiske, Julie, 'Factors That Influence the Decision to Undergo Labiaplasty: Media, Relationships, and Psychological Well-Being', *Aesthetic Surgery Journal* 36(4) (2016).
Sharpe, Andrew N., 'Endless Sex: The Gender Recognition Act 2004 and the Persistence of a Legal Category', *Feminist Legal Studies* 15 (2007).
Shelby, Tommie, 'Race and Social Justice: Rawlsian Considerations', *Fordham Law Review* 72(5) (2004).
Shipman, Tim and Griffiths, Sian, 'A Young Black Man is More Likely to Be in Prison Than at a Top University', *The Times* (31 January 2016), https://www.thetimes.co.uk/article/a-young-black-man-is-more-likely-to-be-in-prison-than-at-a-top-university-mq699s0hdcb.
Slaughter, Anne-Marie, *Unfinished Business* (London: Oneworld, 2015).
Snyder, Claire R., 'What Is Third-Wave Feminism? A New Directions Essay', *Signs* 34(1) (2008).
Snyder-Hall, Claire R., 'Third Wave Feminism and the Defense of "Choice"', *Perspectives on Politics* 8(1) (2010).
Spelman, Elizabeth V., *Inessential Woman: Problems of Exclusion in Feminist Thought* (London: The Women's Press, 1990).
Stetzer, Ed and MacDonald, Andrew, 'Why Evangelicals Voted Trump: Debunking the 81%', *Christianity Today* (18 October 2018), https://www.christianitytoday.com/ct/2018/october/why-evangelicals-trump-vote-81-percent-2016-election.html.
Stock, Kathleen, 'Changing the Concept of "Woman" Will Cause Unintended Harms', *The Economist* (6 July 2018).
Stock, Kathleen, *Material Girls: Why Reality Matters for Feminism* (London: Fleet, 2021).
Stoddard, Thomas B., 'Why Gay People Should Seek the Right to Marry', in Blasius, Mark and Phelan, Shane (eds), *We Are Everywhere: A Historical Sourcebook of Gay and Lesbian Politics* (London: Routledge, 1997).
Stoljar, Natalie, 'Essence, Identity, and the Concept of Woman', *Philosophical Topics* 23(2) (1995).
Stoltenberg, John, *Refusing to be a Man: Essays on Sex and Justice* (Harmondsworth: Penguin, 1990).
Stonewall, 'Response to *Reform of the Gender Recognition Act*' (November 2020), https://committees.parliament.uk/writtenevidence/17743/html/.
Stonewall, 'The Truth About Trans' (2022), https://www.stonewall.org.uk/truth-about-trans.
Stotzer, Rebecca L., 'Violence Against Transgender People: A Review of United States Data', *Aggression and Violent Behavior* 14(3) (2009).

Student Union of SOAS, 'What Is Decolonising SOAS?', SOAS University of London (2018), https://blogs.soas.ac.uk/decolonisingsoas/what-is-decolonising-soas/.

Sunstein, Cass R. and Nussbaum, Martha C. (eds), *Animal Rights: Current Debates and New Directions* (Oxford; New York, NY: Oxford University Press, 2004).

Swift, Adam, *How Not to Be a Hypocrite: School Choice for the Morally Perplexed Parent* (London: Routledge, 2003).

Taylor, Charles, *Sources of the Self: The Making of the Modern Identity* (Cambridge: Cambridge University Press, 1992).

Teetzel, Sarah, 'On Transgendered Athletes, Fairness, and Doping: An International Challenge', *Sport in Society* 9(2) (2006).

Thaler, Richard H. and Sunstein, Cass R., *Nudge: Improving Decisions About Health, Wealth and Happiness* (New Haven, CT: Yale University Press, 2008).

The Canadian Paediatric Society, 'Canadian Paediatricians Revisit Newborn Male Circumcision Recommendations' (8 September 2015), https://cps.ca/en/media/canadian-paediatricians-revisit-newborn-male-circumcision-recommendations.

The Guardian, 'Just Five Days Off' (9 January 2009), http://www.guardian.co.uk/lifeandstyle/2009/jan/09/women-maternitypaternityrights?INTCMP=ILCNETTXT3487.

The Intactivism Pages, 'The Struggle for Genital Autonomy and Againstt Involuntary Genital Modification of Children of Any Sex' (n.d.), http://www.circumstitions.com.

The Law Commission, 'Cohabitation: The Financial Consequences of Relationship Breakdown', *LAW COM No. 307* (2007).

The Surrey Park Clinic, 'Labial Reduction' (25 October 2017), http://www.thesurreyparkclinic.co.uk/treatments/surgical-procedures-in-clinic/labial-reduction/?gclid=CM6_5frxod YCFcsW0wodp-sBhg (no longer available online).

Thornhill, Randy and Palmer, Craig T., *A Natural History of Rape: Biological Bases of Sexual Coercion* (Cambridge, MA: MIT Press, 2000).

Toerien, Merran and Williams, Andrew, 'In Knots: Dilemmas of a Feminist Couple Contemplating Marriage', *Feminism & Psychology* 13(4) (2003).

Travis, Cheryl Brown (ed.), *Evolution, Gender, and Rape* (Cambridge, MA: MIT Press, 2003).

Tronto, Joan C., *Moral Boundaries: A Political Argument for an Ethic of Care* (London: Routledge, 1993).

Truth, Sojourner, *Ain't I a Woman?* (London: Penguin, 2020).

Tuchman, Ayreh, 'Circumcision', in Richard S. Levy (ed.), *Antisemitism: A Historical Encyclopedia of Prejudice and Persecution* (Santa Barbara, CA: ABC-CLIO, 2005).

Tucker, Ross, 'On Transgender Athletes and Performance Advantages', *The Science of Sport* (24 March 2019), https://sportsscientists.com/2019/03/on-transgender-athletes-and-performance-advantages/.

UK Female Genital Mutilation Act 2003, 'Guidance', http://www.legislation.gov.uk/ukpga/2003/31/contents.

University of Cambridge Centre for Gender Studies, 'About the Centre' (n.d.), http://www.gender.cam.ac.uk/about/.

von Hayek, Friedrich, *The Constitution of Liberty* (London: Routledge and Kegan Paul, 1960).

Wahl, Madeline, '12 Iconic Photos from When Same-Sex Marriage Was Legalized', *Reader's Digest* (23 June 2022), https://www.rd.com/list/iconic-photos-when-same-sex-marriage-was-legalized/.

Wakeman, Jessica, 'The Soapbox: On Feminism and Judging Other Women', *The Frisky* (19 June 2012), http://www.thefrisky.com/2012-06-19/the-soapbox-on-feminism-judging-other-women/.

Walker, Rebecca (ed.), *To Be Real: Telling the Truth and Changing the Face of Feminism* (New York, NY: Anchor, 1995).
Wall, Steven, *Liberalism, Perfectionism and Restraint* (Cambridge: Cambridge University Press, 1998).
Walter, Natasha, *Living Dolls: The Return of Sexism* (London: Virago, 2010).
Walter, Natasha, *The New Feminism* (London: Little, Brown and Company, 1998).
Walzer, Michael, *Spheres of Justice: A Defence of Pluralism and Equality* (Oxford: Blackwell, 1985).
Walzer, Michael, *Thick and Thin: Moral Argument at Home and Abroad* (Notre Dame, IN: University of Notre Dame Press, 1994).
Wardere, Hibo, *Cut: One Woman's Fight Against FGM in Britain Today* (London: Simon and Schuster, 2016).
Warren, Steve, '"It's Not Equal": Parents Outraged as Transgender Athletes Continue to Dominate Girls' Sporting Events', CBN News (25 February 2019).
Watson, Lori, 'The Woman Question', *Transgender Studies Quarterly* 3(1–2) (2016).
Watson, Lori and Hartley, Christie, *Equal Citizenship and Public Reason: A Feminist Political Liberalism* (Oxford: Oxford University Press, 2018).
Wayne, Jemma, 'Mother Judgement: How Women are Undermining Modern Feminism', *Huffington Post* (4 April 2013), http://www.huffingtonpost.co.uk/jemma-wayne/women-undermining-modern-feminism_b_3006752.html.
Weitz, Rose (ed.), *The Politics of Women's Bodies: Sexuality, Appearance, and Behavior* (Oxford: Oxford University Press, 2003).
Weitzman, Lenore J., *The Marriage Contract: Spouses, Lovers and the Law* (London: Free Press, 1983).
Whittle, Stephen, 'Where Did We Go Wrong? Feminism and Trans Theory—Two Teams on the Same Side?', in Stryker, Susan and Whittle, Stephen (eds), *The Transgender Studies Reader* (New York, NY: Routledge, 2006).
Widdows, Heather, *Perfect Me: Beauty as an Ethical Ideal* (Princeton, NJ: Princeton University Press, 2018).
Williams, Andrew, 'Incentives, Inequality, and Publicity', *Philosophy and Public Affairs* 27(3) (1998).
Williams, Bernard, 'The Idea of Equality', in Pojman, Louis P. and Westmoreland, Robert (eds), *Equality: Selected Readings* (Oxford: Oxford University Press, 1997).
Williams, Cristan, 'Sex, Gender, and Sexuality: The TransAdvocate Interviews Catharine A. MacKinnon', *TransAdvocate* (2015), https://www.transadvocate.com/sex-gender-and-sexuality-the-transadvocate-interviews-catharine-a-mackinnon_n_15037.htm.
Williams, Joan, *Unbending Gender: Why Family and Work Conflict and What to Do About It* (Oxford: Oxford University Press, 2000).
Williams, Kiara Imani, 'You Know What Is Worse Than Donald Trump? Other Judgmental Women', *Huffington Post* (18 August 2015), http://www.huffingtonpost.com/kiara-imani-williams/you-know-whats-worse-for-_b_8002682.html.
Winter, Bronwyn, Thompson, Denise, and Jeffreys, Sheila, 'The UN Approach to Harmful Traditional Practices', *International Feminist Journal of Politics* 4(1) (2002).
Wittig, Monique, 'One Is Not Born a Woman', in Kemp, Sandra and Squires, Judith (eds), *Feminisms* (Oxford: Oxford University Press, 1997).
Wolf, Naomi, *Fire with Fire: The New Female Power and How It Will Change the 21st Century* (London: Chatto and Windus, 1993).
Wolf, Naomi, *The Beauty Myth* (London: Vintage, 1990).

Wolff, Jonathan and De-Shalit, Avner, *Disadvantage* (Oxford: Oxford University Press, 2007).
Wollstonecraft, Mary, 'A Vindication of the Rights of Woman', in Todd, Janet (ed.), *A Vindication of the Rights of Woman and A Vindication of the Rights of Man* (Oxford: Oxford University Press, 2003 [1792]).
World Netball, 'Olympic Games' (n.d.), https://netball.sport/events-and-results/olympic-games.
Wright, Jennifer, 'Transgender Women are Women. Transgender Men are Men', *Harper's Bazaar* (23 October 2018).
Yale University, 'Women's, Gender, and Sexuality Studies' (n.d.), http://www.yale.edu/wgss/history.html.
Young, Iris Marion, *Inclusion and Democracy* (Oxford: Clarendon Press, 2000).
Young, Iris Marion, *Justice and the Politics of Difference* (Princeton, NJ: Princeton University Press, 1990).
Young, Iris Marion, *On Female Body Experience: "Throwing Like a Girl" and Other Essays* (New York, NY; Oxford: Oxford University Press, 2005).
Young, Toby, 'David Cameron Is Plain Wrong About Oxford and Race. Here's Why', *The Spectator* (31 January 2016), https://www.spectator.co.uk/article/david-cameron-is-plain-wrong-about-oxford-and-race-here-s-why.
Yousafzai, Malala, Interview at Open Forum Davos (2018), https://www.youtube.com/watch?v=wfxLLyM8iGI.
Zerilli, Linda, 'Feminist Theory and the Canon of Political Thought', in Dryzek, John S., Honig, Bonnie, and Phillips, Anne (eds), *The Oxford Handbook of Political Theory* (Oxford: Oxford University Press, 2008).
Zerilli, Linda, 'Toward a Feminist Theory of Judgment', *Signs* 34(2) (2009).

Index

Because the index has been created to work across multiple formats, indexed terms for which a page range is given (e.g., 52–53, 66–70, e.g.) may occasionally appear only on some, but not all, of the pages within the range.

Abbey, Ruth 47
Abortion 12–13, 171–99, 309, 318
Adaptive preferences 120, 189, 304
Adiche, Chimamanda Ngozi 1–2
Affirmative action 247, 251, 253, 309
All Lives Matter 311–12
American Academy of Pediatrics (AAP) 188–9, 195
Anderson, Elizabeth 54
Animals having equal moral status to humans 180–1
Anti-discrimination law 30–1, 39, 63–8, 92–3, 103–4, 113, 128, 152–3, 164–5, 239 See also UK Equality Act 2010
Aristotle 26–7, 48–9
Arneson, Richard 223–5
Ascriptive characteristics
  discrimination and 209
  in sport 237–8
Autonomy
  comprehensive 108
  first-order 3–4, 58
  Marilyn Friedman's concept of 54
  second-order 3–4, 58
  See also Choice, Freedom

Background culture of society 63–4
Background, economic See Class, economic
Baehr, Amy 68, 90–1
Barrett, Michelle 20–1
Barry, Brian 55–6, 185
Basic structure
  concept of 11, 47–8, 65, 75–98, 220–2
  involving an institutional division of labour 87
  coercion and 93–6
  direct versus internal application of principles of justice to 83–6, 92–3
  institutions within versus comprising the 80–3
  whole structure view of 76, 89–93
Bates, Laura 301–2
Battles of the Sexes tennis match 240–1
BDSM 50, 281
Beauty practices 8–9, 24–6, 28–9, 31–2, 50, 55, 267–8, 271, 274, 280–1, 284–6, 288–313
Benhabib, Seyla 55
Bevacqua, Maria 129–30
Bindel, Julie 1
Biology
  differences between sexes 48–9
  inferiority of women 26–7, 29, 44–5, 286
Bodily integrity 186–99, 265–78, See also Autonomy; Choice; Body modification
Body modification See Circumcision; Female cosmetic genital surgery (FGCS); Female genital mutilation (FGM); Breast implants
Bolt, Usain 240
Born in the wrong body 33–4, See also Gender identity; Trans
Bornstein, Kate 39–40
Bourdieu, Pierre 126–7, 303
Brake, Elizabeth 136–7
Breast implants 302–3
Brighouse, Harry 208, 221–2
Brown v. Board of Education 317
Brownmiller, Susan 286–8
Buchy, Tim 310–11
Burdens of judgment See Reasonable disagreement
Butler, Judith 20 n.6, 32, 39–40, 147–8

Capabilities approach to justice 51–2
Capitalism 22–4, 101–2, 116–17, 121, 304

INDEX

Care work 11, 49, 54, 99–123, 126, 135–6, 139
Caregiver Parity, Nancy Fraser's model of 104, 116, 120–1
Catholic Church 58, 63–8, 164
Check your privilege 311–12
Child abuse 40–1
Childcare 102–4, 112, 137, 139
Children
  same-sex marriage and 88
  moral status of 191–6
  See also Family; Care work; Housework; Children's moral status; Childcare
Choice
  as a normative transformer 7–9, 11, 14, 37, 56, 228, 266–8, 280, 318–19
  capacity for as the basis of moral equality 51
  harm and 8–9, 11, 14, 23–6, 55, 117–18, 271–4
  socially constructed 7–9, 14, 23–4, 38–9, 56, 115–16, 268, 271–4, 280, 290–1, 297, 301–19
Church of England 58, 164
Circumcision
  benefits and harms of 187–9
  practice of 12–13, 171–99, 269
Circumstances of justice 315
Citizens holding a sense of justice 83
Civil partnership 123–4, 131–2, 134–6, 139
Civil union *See* Civil partnership
Class, economic 34–5, 41–2, 111–12, 116–17, 210, 213, 218, 289, 291, 304
Clothing 297
Coe, Sebastian 241, 245
Coercion 5, 7–8, 14, 37, 44–5, 47–8, 59, 62–3, 76, 93–6, 100, 107–9, 112, 154–5, 159–60
Cohen, G. A. 1–2, 76, 93–6
  example of sexism in the family being coercive 94, 228–9
Collins, Patricia Hill 101
Commonwealth Games 236, 259
Communitarianism 55
Comprehensive doctrine 61–3, 87, 183, 196 *See also* Liberalism, comprehensive

Conception of the good 12, 46, 60, 62, 68, 87, 110–11, 143, 152, 154–5, 157, 165, 171, 176, 183–4, 226, 234 *See also* Comprehensive doctrine
Consciousness-raising 36, 39, 46, 280, 285–6, 290–1, 296–7, 302, 304–5, 311
Consent *See* Choice; Sexual assault or violence; Social contract theory
Contractarianism *See* Social contract theory
Court, Margaret 240–1
Criado Perez, Caroline 166–7
Critical theory 54, 304, 313 *See also* Queer studies; Trans theory; Race; Feminism, radical
Cudd, Ann 54

Daly, Mary 34–5
Davies, Sharron 245
de Beauvoir, Simone 29–30, 248, 286–8
Deadnaming 169
Democracy, deliberative 55
Department of Women's Studies at University of California Berkeley 21
Difference principle 78, 90–1, 220–1, 226–7
Differences of sexual development (DSD) 167, 242–3, 251 *See also* Intersex
Disability 209, 237–8
Disadvantage factor 115–16, 119, 268, 274–5
Discourse ethics 55
Discrimination 24, 37, 39, 59, 61, 63–9, 76–7, 103–4, 113, 128–30, 152–3, 159–60, 162–5, 167–8, 175, 197–8, 209–13, 220–1, 234–62, 294
  internal to religious membership 66–7
Domestic abuse or violence 114, 125–6, 281, 284, 290
Domestic work *See* Housework; care work
Drag 39–40, 297
Dworkin, Andrea 1–2, 35, 287, 298–9
Dworkin, Ronald 51, 175–6, 228–9

Ecofeminism *See* Feminism
Egalitarian ethos 94
Egalitarianism, liberal *See* Equality, liberalism and
Emotion work 100–1 *See also* Housework, mental load of

Employment 9, 11, 30–1, 37, 39, 65–7, 99–122, 203–33
English, Jane 249–50
Entrenchment of Gender, the 28–36, 39–40
Epistemic humility 310
Epistemology 14–15, 213–15, 306–16
Equal basic liberty 43–4, 75, 85–6, 88–9, 92
Equal Love Campaign 131
Equality of opportunity 13–14, 91–3, 201
 for welfare 223–5
 as careers open to talents 209–13, 218
 as meritocracy 211, 215–17, 227
 as non-discrimination 209–13, 220–1
 bad incentive effects of 215–17
 difficulty of assessing merit when implementing 213–15
 discussion whether employers can ignore 220–2
 example of individuals deliberately handicapping themselves 216–17
 example of university admissions resembling a lottery 214–15
 Fair Equality of Opportunity, John Rawls's principle of 217–22, 230–1
 formal *See* Equality of opportunity, as careers open to talents; Equality of opportunity, as non-discrimination
 gambling counterexample to hybrid strategy 224
 headmaster example showing how it tends to equality of outcome 206
 hybrid strategy 222–7
 Jeremy and Jason example 203–33
 lifelong 217–27
 private schools and 205–7
 proportional attainment model for sports 249–50
 self-respect and 226
 volcano eruption counterexample to hybrid strategy 223–4
Equality of outcome 205–6
Equality
 liberalism and 5, 43–4, 51, 54, 60–1, 108, 119, 206–7, 217–18, 232–3
 moral or basic 51, 61
Eroticisation of male dominance and female submission 50, 283, 295–6
 See also Pornography; BDSM

Essentialism 32–3, 44–5, 289–94, 299
 See also Gender identity; Feminism, gender-critical; Feminism, difference
Estrogen 28–9
Ethics of care 41, 49, 53 *See also* Feminism, difference
Ettelbrick, Paula 130–1
Exemptions to law 59, 63–8, 164, 185, 270
Existence of Patriarchy, the 36–9

Fair Play for Women 144–5
False consciousness 9, 120, 281, 283, 287, 304, 312
False gender neutrality 48–9, 115
Family 11, 53–4, 75–122
Family leave policies 113–14
Female genital cosmetic surgery (FGCS) 197–8, 265–78
 harms and risks of 272
 mental health-based exemption for 270
 policy reform and 275–8
Female genital mutilation (FGM) 197–9, 268–78
Femininity 8–9, 29–30, 44–5, 258–9, 295, 297–8
Feminism
 activist versus academic 20
 as a unifying movement despite women's different experiences 35, 283, 290–2
 See also Essentialism
 as avoiding judging women in order to make people like feminism or feminists 282
 as confronting men and women with the idea they are not in control 24–6
 as identifying as human over a woman 295
 as not writing off victims of patriarchy in judging them 284
 black 100–1, 120
 choice and 3, 10, 14, 23–4, 45–6, 115, 265–78, 280–2
 choice feminism 43, 49–50, 56, 267, 281–2
 concepts of freedom and 6–7, 45, 47–8, 54, 281–2 *See also* Autonomy; Choice
 difference 41, 104 *See also* Ethics of care
 ecofeminism 2–3, 21–2

Feminism (*cont.*)
  gender-critical 21–2, 144–5, 155–7, 160–2, 299–300
  intersectional *See* Intersectionality
  liberal vs. choice feminism 50–6
  liberal variants in popular culture 49–50
  Marxist 2–3, 20-2
  radical 2–3, 22, 32–3, 39–40, 44, 46, 50, 281–2, 295
  socialist 2–3, 22, 39–42
  three theses of 10, 20, 27–42
  transfeminism 33–4
  universalism in 36, 54–5
Ferguson, Michelle 281–2
Fetishism of Choice 23–6, 33–4 *See also* Choice, as a normative transformer
Flax, Jane 38
Foetuses as full moral persons 175–9
Foucault, Michel 38 n.65, 46–7, 303
Fraser, Nancy 39–40, 55, 103
Freedom
  feminism and *See* Feminism
  liberalism and 5, 45, 47–8, 117–18, 143, 153–5, 266–7 *See also* Autonomy; Choice
  of association 66–7
  of conscience 65–6
  Nancy Hirschmann's concept of 54
  negative 45
  See also Autonomy
Freidan, Betty 34–5, 100, 111
Friedman, Marilyn 54

Gender
  and sex, statistical analysis of 148–9, 159–60, 166–7 *See also* Trans
  as a resemblance type 153–4 *See also* Trans
  as an internal map 153–4 *See also* Trans
  as performative 153–4 *See also* Trans
  as having a particular relationship to embodied phenomenology 153–4 *See also* Trans
  binary 12, 33–4, 39–40, 157, 161–2, 261 *See also* Non-binary; Trans; Butler, Judith
  choice and *See* Choice, socially constructed; Trans
  critical feminists *See* Feminism, gender-critical; Trans
  difference, scientific theories of 26–7, 27 n.29 *See also* Biology
  dysphoria 144, 146 n.11, 234–5 *See also* Trans
  egalitarianism, Gina Schouten's concept of 107–10, 112–14, 119
  identity 33–4, 143–70, 234–62, 291, 293–5 *See also* Trans
  inequality, bearing similarity to the logic of racism 35
  norms *See* Norms, social or gender
  pay gap 7, 9, 39, 102–4, 166–7, 267, 319 *See also* Discrimination
  reasonable disagreement over 153–5, 167 *See also* Trans
  reassignment surgery 239, 243–4, 293 *See also* Trans
  Recognition Certificate 144 *See also* UK Gender Recognition Act (GRA) 2004; Trans
  Recognition Reform (Scotland) Bill 144–6, 159 *See also* UK Gender Recognition Act (GRA) 2004; Trans
  self-identification of 33, 144–5, 153–4, 163, 168–9, 255–6, 259, 293–5 *See also* Gender identity; Trans
  six features of state recognition of 149–53 *See also* Trans
  state recognition of 12, 143–70 *See also* Trans
  studies 20–1 *See also* Trans
  transcending 39–40 *See also* Women, as a sex class
Gendered division of labour 11, 53, 55, 71, 76–7, 89, 99–123 *See also* Family; Care work; Housework
Genderqueer 39–40, 150, 155–6, 161–2 *See also* Non-binary; Trans
Genetic talents *See also* Natural endowments
Genital cutting *See also* Female genital mutilation (FGM); Female genital cosmetic surgery (FGCS); Circumcision, practice of
Gidley, Sandra 277
Gleaves, John 258–9
Globalisation 41–2

INDEX 343

Gornick, Janet 126
Greer, Germaine 29–30

Halberstam, Jack 33
Hampton, Jean 52–3
Hartley, Christie 58–72
Haslanger, Sally 14–15, 291–2, 301–19
  concept of epistemic humility 310
  counterexample to womanhood defined as oppressed social category 291–2
Hayek, Friedrich 47–8
Hegel, Georg Wilhelm Friedrich 26–7
Heterosexism 129
Hirschmann, Nancy 54
History of legal rights for women 37, 39
Hobbes, Thomas 47
Hochschild, Arlie 100–1
Holmes, Kelly 239–40, 245
hooks, bell 19–20, 34–5, 100, 111
Hormone therapy 243–4, 257–8
House of Commons Women & Equalities Select Committee 149
Housework 11, 34–5, 37, 99–123, 126
  mental load of 99–101
Hyperandrogenism 242–3

Identity claim in debates over women's sport 255–8 *See also* Women-only sport
Identity, social construction of 44–5, 55, 147–8, 258–9, 301–19 *See also* Choice, socially constructed; Norms, social or gender
Ideological oppression 14–15, 301–19
  agents of change in 316–19
  racial desegregation example 316–17
Ideology critique 14–15, 301–19
  abortion example of who has better access to facts in 310–11
  affirmative action example of who has better access to facts in 310
  beauty norms example of why epistemological critique is insufficient 313
  crop top example of why epistemological critique is insufficient 313
  necessity of normative theory of justice to 312–16, 318–19

  as different to culture 306–8
  Hall's account of 305
  Marxist sense of 19
  normatively charged account 305–12
  normatively neutral account 305
Imani Williams, Kiara 281
Influence factor 115–16, 119, 268, 274–5
  See also Norms, social or gender; Choice, socially constructed
International Association of Athletics Federation (IAAF) 241–3
International Olympic Committee (IOC) 236, 243–4
Intersectionality 35, 252, 291 *See also* hooks, bell; Feminism, radical
Intersex 167, 242
Intimate Care-Giving Union (ICGU) 135–6, 138–9

Jack, Alister 145
Jo, Flo 240
Judgment
  Burdens of *See* Reasonable Disagreement
  By women 282–3, 299–300
  Feminism as anti-judgment 49–50, 281–3, 293
  Of different ways of life 110–13, 136
    See also Reasonable Disagreement; Liberalism, political
  Male method 282–3
  Normative critique and 286, 288, 308–12
  Of men 284
  Of women 282–4, 294, 297, 302
Justice
  as fairness 83
  domestic 95
  global 41–2, 95
  local 95

Kant, Immanuel 44–5
Keidan, Charles 131
Kemp, Sandra 22
Khader, Serene 3
Kiraly, Miranda 50
Kittay, Eva 54
Kitzinger, Celia 131–2
Kramer, Matthew 171–99

Labiaplasty 265–78
Law Commission 137, 149
Lehrbach, Tim 258–9
Leng, Mary 168–9
Leo, Dan 245
Liberalism
  as justice- and rights-based 46, 49, 52
    See also Ethics of care
  as unable to secure full gender
    equality 68–71
  Carole Pateman's critique of 47–8
  Catharine MacKinnon's critique of 44–7
  comprehensive 46, 60–1, 68, 71 *See also*
    Autonomy, first-order
  individualism and 44, 49–52
  political 3–4, 10, 12–13, 46, 53–4, 58–72,
    107–8, 110–12, 143, 153–5, 171–99,
    219–20 *See also* Autonomy,
    second-order
Liew, Jonathan 252–4
Lippert-Rasmussen, Kasper 223–4
Lloyd, S. A. 68
Locke, John 44–5, 47
Loland, Sigmund 238–9
Lorde, Audre 34–5
Loughton, Tim 131
Luck egalitarianism 223–4, 228–9
Lumley, Joanna 301–2

MacKinnon, Catharine 14, 31–2, 36 n.62,
  44–9, 57, 69, 279–300, 303
  analysis of judging women 14,
    279–300
  analysis of women being defined by their
    social treatment 286–300
  argument that female biology is site of
    contestation 288–9, 293–4
  critique of liberalism 44–7
  distinction between essential reality and
    social reality 290
  non-feminist women being target of
    analysis 294
  rejection of female biology as source of
    women's subordination 286–9
  trans people as example of claim that
    women's bodies are site of
    contestation 293–4
Mansplaining 311–12

Marriage
  bundles of rights and duties attached
    to 133–6
  feminist critiques of 125–33
  legal institution of 11–12, 53, 67, 71,
    94–6, 123–40, 143, 149–52, 155, 164–5
  same-sex 88, 123–4, 129–32
  symbolic effects of 126–31
Marx, Karl 116–17
Marxism 304
Masculinity 8–9, 19–21, 29–30, 44–5,
  258–9, 287, 292
Mason, Andrew 228–9
Mayeda, Graham 163
Men's family lives 110
Merkel, Angela 292
Metz, Tamara 135–6
Mill, John Stuart 4, 27, 29–30, 44–8,
  100, 266–7
Miller, David 1–2, 211, 218–19, 227, 230–1
Mills, Charles 3
Minimal marriage, Elizabeth Brake's
  concept of 136–9
Moment of Equal Opportunity (MEO)
  203–33 *See also* Equality of opportunity
Morganroth Gullette, Margaret 129
Motherhood, different perspectives
  on 101
Multiculturalism 3, 35–6, 304
Murray, Andy 240–1

Nagel, Thomas 175–6
National Health Service (NHS) 188, 276
Natural endowments 206–7, 210–13,
  218, 228–9
Natural talents *See* Natural endowments
Navratilova, Martina 245
Nedelsky, Jennifer 54
Need for Change 39–42
Neutralist dilemma 171–99
Neutrality, liberal *See* Political liberalism
Nietzsche, Friedrich 26–7
Non-binary 150, 152, 155–7, 161–2
Norm of parental care 24, 105–6
Norm of the ideal worker 24, 105–6, 119
Norms, social or gender 3, 8–9, 23–6,
  55–6, 68–70, 99–122, 125–6, 147, 153,
  158, 161–2, 168–9, 234–5, 247, 250–1,

254–5, 265–78, 280–1, 301–19 *See also* Choice, socially constructed; Beauty practices
Nosnipia, Matthew Kramer's example of 183–6, 194–5
Nussbaum, Martha 51–2

O'Reilly, Leonora 100
Obergefell v. Hodges 123–4
Objectification, sexual 55 *See also* Pornography
Okin, Susan Moller 11, 36, 48–9, 53–4, 70–1, 75–98, 126–7
Olympic Games 236, 241, 252–3
Online abuse 282–3
Original position 53–4, 76–7 *See also* Rawls, John

Paralympics 237–8
Parental leave 30, 95–6, 103–4, 112–15, 119–20
Parenting or parents *See* Family; Care work; Parental leave
Parks Pieper, Lindsay 241
Pateman, Carole 47–8
Paternalism 267
Patriarchy 10, 19, 22–3, 29, 36–42, 76–7, 100, 103, 131–2, 135, 282–5, 295–6
Personal is political 47–8, 281–2, 293–4 *See also* Public-private distinction; family
Philosophers in the canon holding misogynistic views 26–7, 48–9
Physiological criteria that qualify an athlete as female 242–6, 253, 260–1
Plato 26–7
Political lesbianism 32–3
Politics of recognition 55
Politics of redistribution 55
Polygamy 65
Pornography 40–1, 50, 271–5, 278, 284–5
Power 44–8, 50, 53–5, 284, 291, 294, 297, 299, 305, 313, 315
Precautionary Arguments in abortion debates 181–3, 196–9
Pride events 261–2
Prison of Biology 26–7 *See also* Biological inferiority of women

Privacy 11, 126 n.12, 139, 144–5, 169, 242
Prostitution 40–1, 49–50, 60, 284, 294
Public political culture 63–4
Public–private distinction 44, 47–8, 53, 64, 77, 87 *See also* Family; Basic Structure

Queer theory 20–2, 32–4, 39–40 *See also* Butler, Judith
Quong, Jonathan 175–6, 181–3, 196

Race 35, 92–3, 100, 111–12, 185, 197–8, 209, 237, 276–7, 289, 291, 304, 309, 316–17 *See also* hooks, bell
Racism *See* Race
Radcliffe Richards, Janet 205–6
Radcliffe, Paula 245
Rape *See* Sexual assault or violence
Rapinoe, Megan 248
Ratjen, 'Dora' / Hermann 241
Rawls, John 3–4, 11, 43–4, 51, 53–4, 59–60, 75–98, 107, 154–5, 173, 182, 205–6, 217–22, 315 *See also* Political liberalism; Justice as fairness
Reasonable disagreement
  concept of 12–13, 70–1, 152–3, 171–99
  due to burdens of judgment 154–5, 154 n.30, 171–99
  over gender 153–5
  over sex 167
  with respect to freedom and equality 171–99
Reciprocity 68–9
Reeser, J. C. 241
Reid, Heather 244
Relationship goods of parenting 221–2
Relationship regulation
  contractual model of 123–40
  holistic model of 134–6
  piecemeal model of 134, 136–40
Relationships, Law Commission's example of the dangers of opt-in model of legal protections for 137
Relativism 56, 178–9, 273, 281–2, 304–5, 315–16
Religion, state recognition of 152–3, 163–5
Religious institutions as private associations 65, 68, 77

Religious liberty 7, 58–9, 65–8, 89, 186, 190–6, 226
Rendell, Baroness Ruth 277
Respect
  as argument addressed to others 62–3 *See also* Social contract theory; Hampton, Jean
  for persons as reasoning beings 62–3
  public reason and 60–3 *See also* Liberalism, political
Riggs, Bobby 240–1
Rousseau, Jean-Jacques 26–7, 47
Ryan, Alan 214–15

Sadomasochism *See* BDSM
Sandberg, Sheryl 105
Schouten, Gina 99–122
  example of a couple rationally and autonomously choosing gendered division of labour 108, 112
Self-esteem 266, 273–4, 276, 303
Self-ID *See* Gender, self-identification of
Self-respect 226, 248–50, 255
Semenya, Caster 242–4
Sex
  biological concept of 12–14, 28–32, 44–5, 48–50, 76–7, 92–3, 118–19, 143–70, 209, 234–62, 288–95, 299–300 *See also* Sex/gender distinction; Biology
  fraud in sports 241
  segregation in places of religious worship 58, 67–8
  state recognition of 165–9
  work 40–1, 49–50, 60, 284, 294
Sex/gender distinction 29–31, 44–5, 146–9, 239 *See also* Sex, biological concept of
Sexual
  assault or violence 7, 9, 40–1, 69–70, 166–7, 267, 287, 297, 299–300, 302
  objectification 55, 279–302
Shelby, Tommie 3
Sikhs carrying kirpans 67
Single-sex spaces 144–5, 234–62
Slaughter, Anne-Marie 106–7, 110–11
SlutWalk 297
Social construction *See* Identity, social construction of; Choice, socially constructed

Social contract theory 44, 47, 52–3 *See also* Liberalism, Pateman's critique of
Social endowments 207, 210–13
Socialism 304
Spence, Laura 214
Sport 13–14, 234–62
  basic versus scarce benefits of 249
  symbolic success in 254
Squires, Judith 22
Steinfeld, Rebecca 131
Stoddard, Thomas 129–31
Stonewall 148, 166
Sturgeon, Nicola 145–6
Surgery on children 183–96
Sweden
  snow-clearing as sexist 166–7
  Gender Recognition Act 1972 143, 147, 166
  Swedish Federation for Lesbian, Gay, Bisexual, Transgender, Queer and Intersex Rights (RFSL) 143, 148, 166
Swift, Adam 206–7, 221–2
Symbolic violence 126–7

Testosterone 26–9, 238–9, 242–6, 252–3, 257–8
Three Theses of Feminism 10, 20, 27–42
Toerien, Merran 125
Trans activism or advocacy groups *See* Stonewall; Sweden, Swedish Federation for Lesbian, Gay, Bisexual, Transgender, Queer and Intersex Rights (RFSL)
Trans
  athletes 234–62
  exclusionary radical feminist (TERF) 311–12 *See also* Transphobia
  men 33, 243–4, 252–3, 255, 257
  people and gender reassignment surgery 239, 243–4, 293, 298
  people, recognition of by others 162–5 *See also* Gender identity
  theory or trans studies 20–2, 33–4, 299–300 *See also* Gender identity; Gender studies
  women 13–14, 33, 166, 234–62, 294 *See also* Gender identity
  women are women 255–8, 261

INDEX   347

Transfeminism *See* Feminism
Transphobia 299–300
Truth, Sojourner 100
Turner, Brock 309
Turner, Dan 309
Tyler, Meagan 50

UK
  Equality Act 2010 67–8, 145, 149–50, 164–5, 239
  Female Genital Mutilation Act 2003 268–9, 276
  Gender Recognition Act (GRA) 2004 144–7, 166
Universal Breadwinner, Nancy Fraser's model of 103–4
Universal Caregiving, Nancy Fraser's model of 105, 116, 120–1
University of Cambridge Centre for Gender Studies 21
US Constitution 48–9

Veil of ignorance *See* Original position

Wages for housework 104, 109–10, 120
Wakeman, Jessica 281
Watson, Lori 58–72
Wayne, Jemma 281
Well-ordered society 64, 83
White Supremacy 306–7
Wilkinson, Sue 131–2
Williams, Andrew 125
Williams, Bernard 206
Williams, Joan 105, 119
Williams, Serena 239–41
Wittig, Monique 21–2
Wolf whistling 301–2, 310–11

Wollstonecraft, Mary 46, 100
Woman
  as a sex class 21–2, 50, 146–7, 153–4, 161–2, 291–2
  as being a feminist 295
  concept of 14, 21–2, 28–36, 153–5, 255–60, 286–300
Womanhood *See* Woman, concept of
Women
  as defined by their social treatment 286–300
  as made rather than born, Simone de Beauvoir's concept of 29–30
  choosing care work over corporate jobs 56
  facing conflicts between religious faith, feminist values and personal freedom 58
Women's sport
  access to 235–6
  and chess 250–1
  Anti-sexism argument for 247–57, 259–61
  Fair Competition argument for 238–47, 250–1, 256–62
  Identity argument for 255–60
  Jonathan Liew's example of trans athletes dominating 252–3
Women's studies *See* Gender studies
Work time regulation 114

Yale University Women's Studies Program 21 *See also* Gender studies
Yogyakarta Principles 158–60, 168
Yousafzai, Malala 1–2

Zapp, Morris 204